Memories and Postmemorie Partition of India

This book examines the afterlife of Partition as imprinted on the memories and postmemories of Hindu and Sikh survivors from West Punjab to foreground the intersection between history, memory and narrative. It shows how survivors script their life stories to reinscribe tragic tales of violence and abjection into triumphalist sagas of fortitude, resilience, industry, enterprise and success. At the same time, it reveals the silences, stutters and stammers that interrupt survivors' narrations to bring attention to the untold stories repressed in their consensual narratives.

By drawing upon current research in history, memory, narrative, violence, trauma, affect, home, nation, borders, refugees and citizenship, the book analyzes the traumatizing effects of both the tangible and intangible violence of Partition by tracing the survivors' journey from refugees to citizens as they struggled to make new homes and lives in an unhomely land. Moreover, arguing that the event of Partition radically transformed the notions of home, belonging, self and community, it shows that individuals affected by Partition produce a new ethics and aesthetic of displacement and embody new ways of being in the world.

An important contribution to the field of Partition studies, this book will be of interest to researchers on South Asian history, memory, partition and post-colonial studies.

Anjali Gera Roy is a professor in the Department of Humanities and Social Sciences at the Indian Institute of Technology Kharagpur, India. Grounded in post-colonial literature and theory, her current research spans fiction, film, performance, oral histories, borders, mobilities, refugees and citizenship.

Routledge Studies in South Asian History

Citizenship, Community and Democracy in India
From Bombay to Maharashtra, c. 1930–1960
Oliver Godsmark

India and World War I
A Centennial Assessment
Edited by Roger D. Long and Ian Talbot

Foreign Policy of Colonial India
1900–1947
Sneh Mahajan

Women and Literary Narratives in Colonial India
Her Myriad Gaze on the 'Other'
Sukla Chatterjee

Gender, Nationalism and Genocide in Bangladesh
Naristhan/Ladyland
Azra Rashid

Evolution, Race and Public Spheres in India
Vernacular Concepts and Sciences (1860–1930)
Luzia Savary

Democracy and Unity in India
Understanding the All India Phenomenon, 1940–1960
Emily Rook-Koepsel

Memories and Postmemories of the Partition of India
Anjali Gera Roy

For more information about this series, please visit: www.routledge.com/asianstudies/series/RSSAH

Memories and Postmemories of the Partition of India

Anjali Gera Roy

Routledge
Taylor & Francis Group

LONDON AND NEW YORK

First published 2020
by Routledge
2 Park Square, Milton Park, Abingdon, Oxon OX14 4RN

and by Routledge
52 Vanderbilt Avenue, New York, NY 10017

Routledge is an imprint of the Taylor & Francis Group, an informa business.

First issued in paperback 2021

British Library Cataloguing-in-Publication Data
A catalogue record for this book is available from the British Library

Library of Congress Cataloging-in-Publication Data
Names: Roy, Anjali Gera, author.
Title: Memories and postmemories of the partition of India/Anjali
    Gera Roy.
Description: Abingdon, Oxon; New York, NY: Routledge, 2019. | Series:
    Routledge studies in South Asian history; volume 20 | Includes
    bibliographical references and index.
Identifiers: LCCN 2019005167 | ISBN 9781138580282 (hardback) |
    ISBN 9780429507458 (ebook) | ISBN 9780429017360 (epub) |
    ISBN 9780429017377 (adobe reader) | ISBN 9780429017353
    (mobipocket)
Subjects: LCSH: India – History – Partition, 1947. | South Asia –
    Politics and government. | South Asia – Social conditions. | Collective
    memory – South Asia. | Memory – Social aspects – South Asia. |
    Memory – Political aspects – South Asia. | Politics and culture – South
    Asia.
Classification: LCC DS480.842 .R68 2019 | DDC 954.04/2 – dc23
LC record available at https://lccn.loc.gov/2019005167

ISBN: 978-1-138-58028-2 (hbk)
ISBN: 978-1-03-209106-8 (pbk)
ISBN: 978-0-429-50745-8 (ebk)

Typeset in Times New Roman
by Apex CoVantage LLC

For my parents

Contents

Figures

Interviews

The following are links to my interviews, talks and media reports on Partition:

1. www.kgpchronicle.iitkgp.ac.in/beyond-the-horror-and-heartbreak-of-parti tion/
2. https://timesofindia.indiatimes.com/city/kolkata/iit-kharagpur-records-oral-history-of-partition/articleshow/62878483.cms
3. www.facebook.com/1947PartitionArchive/posts/indian-museum-kolkata-in-association-with-intach-organised-a-special-lecture-on-/1901275583229476/
4. www.navhindtimes.in/a-language-buried-by-partition/

Acknowledgements

How does one thank those who silently bore Partition's scars to protect their successive generations from its pain and suffering? Writing this book is my way of saying thank you.

I would like to thank all Partition survivors interviewed for this book, and earlier, for reposing their faith in me and considering me worthy of sharing their memories. These include members of my own extended family, of neighbours and of friends, whose narratives helped me understand what it meant to have lived through Partition. The warm welcome and generous hospitality I received in homes all across India made me appreciate the true meaning of the phrase *dukh-sukh-de-sanjhi* often repeated among partitioned families. To protect their privacy, I will not be able to thank them individually.

An award of a Major Research Project (2016–18) by the Indian Council of Social Science Research helped me supplement my own interviews with those collected by Oral History Interns in the project "After Partition: Postmemories of the Afterlife of Partition 1947." These young undergraduate interns would not have been able to undertake the challenging task given to them without Robyn Andrews' expert mentorship. When I shared these stories with Nandi Bhatia, friend and collaborator, it was like picking up from the journey we began together a decade ago.

Thanks are due to all old and new friends who created possibilities for person-to-person dialogues through inviting me to present parts of the book at different fora. They include G M Kapur, Intach Kolkata Chapter, at the Indian Museum, Kolkata; Pippa Virdee, Virinder Kalra and Emily Keightley at the University of Warwick; Anuradha Ghosh at Jamia Millia Islamia and Kamayani Bhatnagar at the University of Delhi; V Shantha and Maya Harave at Jyoti Niwas College, Bangalore; B Hariharan at the University of Trivandrum and, finally, Sharada Srinivasan at NIAS, Bangalore.

I am grateful to Jatinderpal Sethi, Sangat Singh and others whose memories of Lyallpur posted on the blog India of the Past maintained by Subodh Mathur jogged family memories of the colonial city, to Pippa Virdee and Virinder Kalra for sketching the city as it looks like now and to Tohid Ahmed Chattha for walking me through the lanes of the remembered neighbourhood of Lyallpurites' memories. To another Lyallpurite Viney Kirpal who taught me what it means to survive against all odds. I owe a big thanks to Satish Kalra and "Migrated Families of Bhakkar" for his grandfather's mental map of Bhakkar and to Nukhbah T Langah for reintroducing me to the lost language Siraiki. Thanks to my nonagenarian school Principal Visharda Hoon, whose published memoirs took me back to the establishment of Model Town and several of Lahore's iconic institutions, to Ishtiaq Ahmed for his glimpses into what Lahore was before the rupture, to Debjani Sengupta and Fakrul Alam for the tour through the Dhanmondi of Ghosh's imagination and to Aruna Madnani for opening the doors to the havelis of Shikarpuri merchants in Sindh. I acknowledge the support of the Institute of Advanced Study, University of Warwick through the award of a visiting fellowship that provided the initial stimulus and the Indian Institute of Technology Kharagpur through the grant of a short sabbatical leave for completing the book.

I am indebted to the anonymous reviewers of Routledge who believed that there was room for another book on Partition. I am also grateful for the help I received from the entire team at Routledge, particularly from Dorothea, Lily and Alexandra, at different stages of writing. I would also like to thank Eswari Maruthu of Apex CoVantage India and her team for assistance with preparing the final manuscript.

Thanking my family for allowing me the time and space to work on the book would be to belittle their role in the making of this book. Thanks to my mother Santosh Gera and father Om Prakash Gera for not forgetting Partition by reminding us of what matters most in life. To Arun and Bharat for following their advice. And Sayan for listening to all our stories.

1 Introduction

Why remember?

Between one and two million people are estimated to have been killed and fifteen million displaced in the Indian Partition of 1947 (Dalrymple 2015),[1] a tragic event that became part of a collective forgetting in official histories of the Indian nation.[2] With "the emergence of memory as a key concern in Western societies" and the acceleration of memory discourses in the West (Klein 2000: 127) energized by the broadening debate on the Holocaust in the 1980s, oral histories of Partition 1947 compiled by feminist scholars (Das 1990; Butalia 1998; Menon and Bhasin 1998) in the 1990s triggered a surfeit of survivor memories spawning an insatiable Partition industry. What Andrea Huyssen calls "a culture of memory as it has become pervasive in North Atlantic societies since the late 1970s" (2000) has become globalized, and memory and forgetting have become dominant concerns across the world (Ricoeur 2006: 90). Despite Huyssen's issuing a strong caveat against "using the Holocaust as a universal trope for historical trauma" in relation to local, contemporary events (2000: 23),[3] a new commemoration industry converging on projects of archiving, musealizing and monumentalizing Partitioned memories, patterned on the Holocaust model, has bourgeoned even as the last generation of Partition survivors is on the brink of disappearing. However, in view of the Partition generation's resolute refusal to break its silence on the *unsayable* violence of Partition for seven decades or its resistance to musealizing (1983) Partition, one needs to ask, along with Huyssen, "whether and how the trope enhances or hinders local memory practices and struggles, or whether and how it may perform both functions simultaneously" (2000: 26).

The conspiracy of silence, or "non-porousness of Partition", as Sukeshi Kamra aptly puts it in her award-winning book *Bearing Witness: Partition, Independence, End of the Raj* (2008: 106), maintained by Partition survivors for several decades, foregrounds the issue of revisionist histories' recourse to local memory practices for documenting historical events. In contrast to Holocaust survivors' obsession with memorializing and musealizing, Partition survivors' suspicion of memorializing appears to emanate from both a desire for forgetting and scepticism about the power of language to be able to capture the experience of Partition. Unlike survivors, historians', including oral historians',[4] attempt to recover, archive and explain Partition appears to break the pact of secrecy that has strictly forbidden survivors from sharing secrets, especially painful ones, other than in the intimate space of the family. In other cases, rules related to sharing individual or family secrets prevent both perpetrators and victims from sharing stories of their traumatic experiences, even with family (LaCapra 1994). Concealing affairs, mistakes, addictions, even crimes, both from the outside world and from other family members, is an established family practice in many cultures, either because of the shame attached to them or rules related to someone else's right to know personal information. While shame, trauma, patriarchy, inarticulateness and protective concern have been recognized as possible explanations for survivors' concealment of Partition traumas (Das 1990; Butalia 1998; Menon and Bhasin 1998; Raj 2000), the difference in remembering, memory and forgetting in archival, oral and survivor accounts of the event has not been engaged with in sufficient depth.[5]

Attributing the excess of memory to a crisis in memory ushered in through the information explosion and to the marketing of memory, Huyssen argues that public and private memorialization constitute the present century's survival strategies for counteracting the "fear and danger of forgetting" arising from the instability of time and space (2000: 28).[6] As Paul Ricoeur shows, recall and forgetting are intimately related and that it is "the effort to recall that offers the major opportunity to remember forgetting" (2006: 30).[7] The 'unforgetting' of Partition through the retrieval of survivor memories appears to have been impelled by "the fear of having forgotten, of continuing to forget, forgetting tomorrow to fulfil some task or the other" (2006: 30) in the generation of descendants whose "duty memory" is obliged "not to forget" (2006: 30) by discharging its responsibility of documenting and preserving stories before they are completely obliterated.[8]

This book focuses on the ethics and aesthetics of remembrance by posing certain fundamental questions. What good is the memory archive in view of memory being fallible, selective, affective, intuitive and corporeal (Butalia 1998: 13)? How can it deliver what history alone no longer seems to offer? In view of doubts raised by the unreliability of memory and factual accuracy of oral storytelling, why are stories being increasingly used to reconstruct histories of Partition? How do we carry the stories of survivors forward without appropriating them? What is at stake in the stories? Why do we need to circulate stories that were intended to be shared in the intimate embodied space of the family?

The book draws on recent debates in history (White 1973, 2014; Ginzburg 1992a; Levi 2001), memory (Nora 1989, 1996; Malkki 1991; Tonkin 1991; Terdiman 1993; Stoller 1995; Werbner 1998; Huyssen 2000; Ricoeur 2006), postmemory (Hirsch 2012) and trauma (Das 1990; Felman and Laub 1992; Caruth 2016) to uncover the afterlife of the Partition of 1947. Through examining the stories of both adult survivors and those who were children at the time of Partition and grew up listening to Partition, it implicates the process of memory and postmemory in the silence and remembering of Partition. In documenting their narratives, it calls attention to the process through which survivors and their children script and emplot their life-stories to rewrite tragic tales of hapless and abjected victims of violence poignantly documented in oral histories of Partition as triumphalist sagas of fortitude, resilience, struggle, industry, enterprise and success. At the same time, it reveals the silences, stutters and stammers that interrupt these heroic sagas to bring to light the untold stories of traumatic experiences repressed in the consensual narratives constructed by survivors and their families. The book deconstructs the narratives of predominantly middle class, upper-caste Hindu and Sikh survivors displaced by the Partition-in-the-west[9] and forced to resettle in different parts of India to trace the traumatizing effects of both the tangible and intangible violence of Partition in their struggle to make new homes and lives in strange, unhomely lands and transform themselves from refugees to citizens.[10]

Unforgetting Partition

The silence of official Indian histories on one of the most violent events in world history foregrounds the elisions, omissions and erasures of what Gyanendra Pandey memorably labelled "historian's histories" (1992: 189). As Partition scholars have convincingly demonstrated (Das 1990; Butalia 1998; Menon and Bhasin 1998; Pandey 1992, 2001), the masternarrative of Indian Independence could have been produced by the Indian state only through the repression of gendered, classed, casteist, sectarian, regionalist stories of Partition that interrupt triumphalist nationalist history through their testifying to its unspeakable violence and suffering. Through recovering the lost stories of ordinary people displaced by the violence of 1947, they have filled up important lacunae in the official histories of Independence and put together an alternate history of the events of 1947.

The "memory turn" in Partition studies foregrounded individual and collective memories of Partition survivors in providing an alternative understanding of Partition 1947. Urvashi Butalia's highly engaged enterprise *The Other Side of Silence* (1998), which signalled this turn through privileging individual or group memory over archival accounts and oral stories of ordinary people over written histories, was undoubtedly inspired by the Holocaust memory project but went beyond it to suggest a different methodology for documenting Partition memories. Similarly, other feminist historians, such as Veena Das (1990), Ritu Menon and Kamla Bhasin (1998), appeared to have followed a global memory trend both in recovering voices of the women affected by Partition and in using oral history methodologies in articulating the memories of women. Even as Jasodhara Bagchi and Subhoranjan Dasgupta (2003), Manas Ray (2008) and others stepped in by supplementing the stories of Partition-in-the-west with stories of Partition-in-the-east,[11] new narratives of displacement from other parts of India began to emerge, refuting the myth of Partition as being confined to Bengal and Punjab.[12] After the initial impulse to expand the range of narratives, anxieties about the disappearance of memories have catalyzed a surfeit of memory in the shape of transnational memory projects that have dedicated themselves to compiling stories from across the world before the generation of survivors disappears altogether.[13]

Scholars in literary, cinema and cultural studies have similarly analyzed the workings of fictionalized memories to make a convincing case for legitimizing fictional representations of Partition as historical documents in several ways.

These scholars have not only called attention to fictional accounts of local events that find no mention in official histories of the nation (Gera Roy & Bhatia 2008) but also established them as forms of *testimonia* with the author serving as a historical witness (Bhalla 1999; Hasan 2002; Kamra 2002). They have also turned to fiction and cinema to recover marginalized voices of Partition differentiated by class, caste (Mooney 2008; Kaur 2008), gender (Didur 2007), ethnicity (Mukherjee-Leonard 2008), language and religion. Positing fictional representations against historical, they have made a convincing case for literary texts as sole contemporary documents through which the unsayable, petrifying violence of Partition 1947 could have been articulated (Bhalla 1999; Datta 2008; Kamra 2008; Sarkar 2009; Menon and Bhasin 1998). In examining Partition novels of memory, they have provided extremely sophisticated analyses of memory in the representation of the traumas of Partition while acknowledging its limitations in representing chronological events (Yusin and Bahri 2008). Equally important is their privileging of literary explanation of the events of Partition as more multi-layered, complex, nuanced than logical explanations of historians. Together, they have succeeded in establishing the status of fictional representations as memory histories of Partition 1947.

Crisis in history and the memory turn in history

These alternative, counter, oral and literary people's history projects have been facilitated by the crisis in history (White 1966) that largely centres on the doubts raised about history's claims to objective truth (White 1984), its shift in scale and practices. In particular, cultural historian Hayden White's concept of history as narrative and the value of narrativity in the representation of reality (1973, 2014), Primo Levi's notion of microhistory based on close observation and its shift to microscopic dimension (2001) and Carlo Ginzburg's microhistory (1992), which hypothesizes the more improbable sort of documentation as being poten-tially richer, have revealed the conspicuous lacunae in dominant archive-based histories.[14] These projects have increasingly begun to address the scientific claims of history to objectivity and truth and examined the relationship between memory and history (Nora 1989, 1996; Ricoeur 2006). They have also interrogated the conventional polarization of memory as subjective, fallible and unreliable and history as objective, factual and scientific by unmasking historical truth (White 1973, 2014) to be a narrative produced by historians through the process of selec-tion, interpretation, emplotment and explanation (Louch 1969: 54; White 1973, 2014), which intersects with the methods of other narrative genres.

In "Microhistory: Two or Three Things That I Know about It", Carlo Ginz-burg traces the genealogy of the term *microhistory* and shows that it developed in response to political histories' macrohistorical focus on dominant groups and events that failed to encompass the local, the subaltern and the apolitical (1993). In his discussion of microhistory, Ricoeur dwells on the difference in the selec-tion of events by official histories and microhistories (2006). In contrast to offi-cial histories that concentrated on political events and dominant historical figures, microhistories signalled the shift from the political to the social, or even the cultural. Ginzburg's *The Cheese and Worms* (1992a), which deals with the life of a miller living through a particular era, inaugurated this shift from the nation to the village, from the elite to the ordinary and to the interrelation between the political and the economic. In his definition of microhistory, Luis Gonzalez equates it with *matria* history, which focuses on the family, the personal and the affective in contrast to *patria* history's focus on the public, intellectual and critical (1968).

The focus of political histories on dominant individuals or groups and macropolitical upheavals in sharp contrast to microhistories' emphasis on ordinary people and regional, local events is visible in the people's history of Partition produced by Partition scholars. The macronarrative of Independence and Partition is interrupted in these histories through their making audible small voices, selection of a set of events different from those in official accounts and regional or local impact on specific individuals and groups differentiated by class, caste, ethnicity, gender, religion and region. In contrast to archival history, which has compiled documentary evidence of political events related to Partition and the role played by key figures, such as Cyril Radcliffe, Louis Mountbatten, Mohandas Karamchand Gandhi, Jawaharlal Nehru, Mohammed Ali Jinnah and others, to reconstruct the history of the Partition of India and Pakistan, memory histories bring a close focus on Partition's impact on the lives of specific individuals in particular localities and neighbourhoods, whose shared experiences either reconstruct collective memories or interrupt one another to put together discordant versions of the same event.

However, while recovering people's stories of Partition and displaying sensitivity to the small voices of women, Partition historians unintentionally created a macrohistory of Partition in which the Punjab experience became a universal trope for theorizing the Partition experience.[15] Although the Punjab model has been modified through the experience in the east, the multiplicity of memories that have emerged in the last three decades impel that memories of Partition need to be differentiated further. The myth of Partition-in-the-west as a one-time exchange of populations has been refuted by the continuing influx of migrants from Sindh[16] and the presence of Hindus and Sikhs in Pakistan and Afghanistan (Stancati and Amiri 2015).[17] Narratives of Kashmir are inflected by the frequent boundary making in border regions.[18] The clubbing of Hindus and Sikhs as victims of Muslim violence in Partition literature needs further unpacking since they emerge from divergent historical pasts and collective interpretations of past.

This book hopes to correct the common understanding of Punjabi refugees[19] receiving a preferential treatment from the post-colonial Indian state through being rehabilitated in Punjab and areas surrounding the capital Delhi by charting the tortuous itineraries of those who were forced to resettle in parts of Himachal Pradesh, Haryana, Uttar Pradesh, Bihar, Jharkhand, Madhya Pradesh and even in the deep south, by drawing on state as well as filial networks.[20] Through reconstructing these microhistories, it hopes to show that Partition-in-the-west, as in the east, was not one uniform experience shared by all those who crossed the border from the west but varied according to gender, class, caste, ethnicity, region, education, profession, mode of transport and place of settlement. By inquiring if insights provided through close-ups of microhistories of Partition can be extended to the macrohistory of Partition, it aims to investigate the relationship between micro- and macrohistories.

Memory, remembering, forgetting

While discussing forgetting in relation to commanded memory or amnesty, Ricoeur mentions a Greek term that simultaneously means "recalling against" and "not recalling evil", which might be productive in understanding the memory industry's recalling of the evil of Partition against Partition survivors' forgetting. The duty to remember victims lost to political violence that has become the imperative of contemporary memory cultures dictates the resurrection of memories that the willingly forgetful generation of survivors put behind them (Butalia 1998: 24). Oral historians' resurrection of forgotten memories thus raises important issues about the relationship between remembering, forgetting and memory (Ricoeur 2006).[21]

Partition survivors' accounts, which vary according to the time, space, context and listener, mirror the selective eliminations, erasures and distortions practiced by the state, albeit for altogether different reasons. The question why survivors choose not to remember has been explained, among other reasons, through the application of trauma theory in oral histories (Butalia 1998),[22] of poststructuralist theories on the unspeakability of the suffering in fictional representations (Das 1990; Kamra 2002) and of nationhood rhetoric in statist discourses (Tai and Kudaisya 2004). Survivors' own explanations of their inability to perform the work of mourning oscillate between the three tropes of *dahshat* [horror], *himmat* [courage] and *mehnat* [hard work]. Whether they were unable to articulate their suffering because of their petrification by the horrifying violence of Partition, repetitive invocations of proverbial resilience or exhortations to the ethic of hard work ascribed to the particular ethnic communities, survivors undoubtedly indulged in both willing forgetfulness and selective remembering.

In ethnographic accounts of Partition, several survivors admit to never having shared their memories except with the interviewer. Dhooleka S. Raj's ethnographic research on three generations of Partition survivors throws important light on first generation's forgetting of Partition, which, according to her, produced ignorance in the second and third generations. Underlining the need to make a distinction between forgetting and ignorance, Raj shows that "refugee families cluster intergenerational understandings of Partition around their perception of loss, the creation of a golden era, their political gains and their material success" (Raj 2000). As Raj effectively demonstrates, the first generation's forgetting of their initial experience of hardship as refugees, of which the second and third generation remained ignorant, enabled its imagining as migration. One could add that their remembering success contributed to the mythicization of success that looks both backwards and forwards through the frequent invocation of the trope of *mehnat*, the ethic of hard work.

The sharing of painful and humiliating experiences with strangers under the cover of anonymity can, as Butalia and others have argued (1998), have a therapeutic effect and heal the wounds of Partition. But the shame, guilt, or trauma that prevented survivors from sharing their memories even in the intimate family space, in which they instead scripted together consensual narratives of struggle and success that erased these unspeakable memories, drastically complicates the process of forgetting and remembering.

In connection with the documentation of the memories of Holocaust survivors, Hirsch asks herself, "Were we making a career out of their suffering?" (2012: 15), a concern that was reiterated and shared by Urvashi Butalia while recounting her experience of interviewing survivors of Partition 1947 (1998: 44). However, the epistemic violence performed by recollection of memories of physically violent acts as well as psychological trauma to those who are remembering, those who are remembered and those who are forgotten has not been adequately addressed in Partition studies. If Hirsch makes a clear distinction between domestic and public scenes of memorial acts (2012), Michael Pickering and Emily Keightley posit the idea of a "vernacular remembering processes" in examining the relationship between memory, loss and mourning, which is currently dominated by research on public forms of remembering (2015: 14). Making public tortured recollections of physically or psychologically violent acts whispered in intimate spaces, even when willing consent is provided, is tantamount to a breach of confidence.[23] Subjecting a victim to the horror of the violence through repetition and watching her tremble, stutter and babble incoherently makes interviewers participate in the vicarious spectacle of suffering and makes them complicit in the guilt of the perpetrator.[24] Breaking the silence on the infractions or humiliations of those who are remembered to outsiders without the provision of a context is tantamount to tarnishing the memory of the departed, which explains the hesitation of survivors to make public family stories (Das 1990). Similarly, the recall of the forgotten might dredge up memories that could revive the victim's suffering (Butalia 1998). As opposed to remembering that is presented as a form of healing through the release of blocked memories or through the unveiling of manipulated memories, remembering memories, which one has been commanded to forget, definitely constitutes an act of epistemic violence. Duty memory, engaging in memorialization through making visible tales of suffering shared only in the private space of the family or giving voice to unarticulated suffering of the forgetful ancestors, must, therefore, confront the tension between remembering, forgetting and ignorance.

Sites of memory

Defining sites of memory as places where memory "crystallizes and secretes itself," Pierre Nora explains that "a lieu de mémoire is any significant entity, whether material or non-material in nature, which by dint of human will or the work of time has become a symbolic element of the memorial heritage of any community" (1996: xvii). Sites of memory, according to Nora, have three aspects – the material, the symbolic and the functional. According to *La Commission Franco-Québécoise sur les Lieux de Mémoire Communs* (French-Québécois Commission for Common Sites of Memory), a *lieu de mémoire* "signifies the cultural landmarks, places, practices and expressions stemming from a shared past, whether material (monuments) or intangible (language and traditions)." Distinguishing real memory from present memory consisting of "sifted and sorted historical traces" (1989: 8), Nora maintains that sites of memory emerge with the disappearance of real environments of memory, such as peasant and primitive cultures.

Defining memory as life, actual, affective and magical, multiple and plural and history as reconstructed, representational, intellectual, analytical and critical, with claims to being universal, Nora shows that memory and history, which formed a minimal pair in the past, have become split. Due to the seizure of memory by history, he adds, memory history has been subverted by critical history. Nora states that memory takes "root in the concrete, in spaces, gestures, images, and objects" (1989: 9) and that true memory takes refuge "in gestures and habits, in skills passed down by unspoken traditions, in the body's inherent self-knowledge, in studied reflexes and ingrained memories" (1989: 13). He opposes it to memory transformed by history, which is "voluntary and deliberate, experienced as a duty" (1989: 13).

Anxieties about this rapidly vanishing heritage through the disappearance of the dwindling generation of survivors have increased the urgency to preserve sites of memory through acts of archiving, musealizing, commemorating and memorializing. However, since communities and families of survivors had reserves of memory but no historical capital and lived in the memory of Partition, memories of Partition were "entwined in the intimacy of a collective heritage" and were transmitted through everyday practices or rituals rather than verbally. Instead of material objects, like photographs, diaries, jewellery and silverware, that serve as sites of memory in the memories of an elite minority (Malhotra 2017), reconstructed spaces, gestures, rituals, skills, habits and everyday practices have constituted the repository of the majority of survivor memories passed down by families.[25] Survivor memories are simultaneously performed in reconstructed homes in refugee colonies and other places that transpose the spatial plan and organization of the remembered home to compensate for the impossibility of reproducing the architectural design and materials of pre-displacement homes. Memory equally takes root in the performance of remembered rites of piety and conviviality; in forgotten festivals and celebrations, language, food, dress, comportment, gestures, movements of the body and even everyday practices; in the private space of the home as well as in the use of public space. In this book, these performative repositories will be considered both as the real environments of memory and sites of memory.

Memory, trace and remembering

Nora views modern memory as "archival," which "relies entirely on the materiality of the trace", and he calls it a secondary prosthesis memory (1989: 14). In distinguishing between three uses of the trace, Ricoeur makes a distinction between the written trace archived by historians, "the impression as an affection resulting from the shock of an event that can be said to be striking, marking" (2006: 14) and "the corporeal, cerebral, cortical imprint" (2006: 15). The question, according to him, raised by the affection-impression is "how is it preserved, how does it persist, whether or not it is recalled" and "what meaningful relation it maintains with the marking event" (2006: 14). This distinction can help to elucidate the difference between the perspectives of the archival history of Partition, survivor accounts and those of trauma theorists.

The trace as an affection-impression produced by the shock of Partition violence, although not willingly preserved, persists in survivors' memories whether it is recalled or not. The affection-impression inscribed on the soul is an imprint of the image of the event that cannot be erased. Ricoeur's borrowing of Aristotle's distinction between *mneme* and *anamnesis* to propose evocation as the opposite of recall can explain the simple presence of affection-impressions in survivors' memories as opposed to the revivification of memories by way of their deliberate search in the stories at the historian's prodding, which is directed against forgetting. Survivors' silence on the traumatic experience has been variously explained as punishment, coping mechanism, shock and its breaking, with the assistance of the ethnographer or therapist, and a form of healing and closure. Unlike the female respondents of Butalia (1998) and Menon and Bhasin's (1998) studies or the mixed groups of Ishtiaq Ahmed (2011) who were willing to share their experiences of the horrifying violence, those who refused to share theirs suggest both an attempt to erase the affection-impression and an inability to articulate it verbally.[26] Secondly, since the memory does not work like normal memory in victims of physical or emotional abuse, the affection-impression might be deliberately blocked but manifest itself in other ways or erupt with the onset of dementia when the victim eventually gives voice to repressed memories.

Although the survivor's memory has a privileged access to the event through its iconic imprint on his or her brain, the presence of the event turns into an absence in the process of narration. This book demonstrates that as the survivor attempts to vocalize the sensory impression of the event imprinted as a visual, auditory, tactile or olfactory image and weaves together disjointed events in a narrative structure that supports a particular explanation, the boundaries between memory and history are dissolved.

Emplotment

The juxtaposition of private survivor memories against public archival histories as more immediate, personal, faithful accounts of events interrogates history's claim to truth, which is predicated on its status as an objective scientific discipline.[27] While revealing history to be constructed through its selection, interpretation, emplotment and explanation of certain events (White 1980; Ricoeur 2006), Ricoeur maintains that the dividing line between memory as spontaneous and unmediated and history as deliberate and crafted gets blurred at the stages of selection, emplotment[28] and explanation.

The variance in the selection of events in both survivors' and historians' accounts of Partition includes omission, privileging and slant.[29] In addition to filling up gaps caused through the erasures of historians, survivors' accounts complement, contradict and complicate the history of Partition through selection, emphasis or slant of events. Their selection and employment of factual events is oriented towards an interpretation and explanation that provide a counternarrative of the official narrative.[30] In the tug-of-war between survivors' privileging of the personal, filial and local and oral historians' of the public and national, the personal or the local is either eliminated or marginalized to its subsumption into macrohistories of the region or the nation. However, it is the local, the incidental, the tangential, the afterword and the aside that can throw important light on the macronarrative of Partition.

Ricoeur considers emplotment by the historian as a crucial stage in which the historian organizes events selected in a certain sequence in order to substantiate a particular explanation and draws parallels between historical and literary narrative (2006: 262).[31] In archival histories that marginalize Partition to Independence, Partition violence is emplotted and interpreted either as a consequence of the lack of clarity and hasty decision-making by well-intentioned nationalist leaders and their inability to foresee the breakdown of law and order or to build teleological theories of civilizational difference (Bhalla 1999; Gilmartin 2015).

The element of emplotment is equally visible in both structured or unstructured interviews conducted by oral historians. The closed and open-ended questions asked by the interviewer tend to emplot the survivor's memory in a structure that corroborates the interviewer's understanding or interpretation. Ethnographic research and oral historiography has increasingly been concerned with the problem of discovering truth posed by the mediation of the ethnographer or oral historian. These concerns have converged on the appropriation of the interviewee's voice by the interviewer and by the process through which the ethnographer or oral historian scripts herself into the narrative through orienting the survivor's memory in a direction that supports the historian's hypothesis (Butalia 1998: 20).[32] Unedited survivor accounts demonstrate several instances of this kind of derailing by the interviewer's question, which sets off the survivor's memory to detour in tangential directions that are dismissed by the ethnographer as rambling and often scrupulously edited from the story to provide structural coherence to the narrative.[33]

Survivor memories equally exhibit the process of retrospective emplotment through inclusion and foregrounding of previously trivial incidents to suggest premonitions of violence. Survivor memories exhibit not a spontaneous recall but an emplotment of a cluster of events in a narrative structure. In a fashion similar to history, the emplotment of events by survivors repositions their accounts as scripted stories akin to narrative that build towards the illustration of a particular theme or trope. This process of scripting is visible in survivors' organization of events to produce a coherent narrative through a cause-and-effect sequence. This scripting of their lives into coherent narratives casts doubt on the elevation of survivor testimonies as pure, real and authentic and places them on the same level as literary and historical texts.

Oral historians have attempted to identify a victimhood plot in narratives of Partition through foregrounding incidents of atrocities and suffering. A fundamental discrepancy lies in the interviewer's questions that are intended to assist the survivor in recalling traumatic events in order to represent the survivor as a victim of Partition violence and survivors' narratives that arrange the same events to produce triumphalist recollections of survival that have an exemplary value for their descendants. The most important difference appears to lie in their glossing over mass violence to emphasize tropes of courage, resourcefulness, fortitude and resilience that enabled their overcoming of personal trauma. Like Raj's middle-class respondents who glossed over their refugee past to narrate mythicized versions of success to their second and third generations (Raj 2000), survivors transformed tales of trauma into those of triumph. Through scripting the stories of Partition as those of triumph, they not only reverse the victimhood plot isolated by oral historians and gain agency to form new subject positions within the subject positions assigned to them by the nation and historians (Das 1990: 205) but also foreground the mirroring processes of emplotment that obfuscate the distinction between pure and mediated memory.

Interpretation and explanation

Interpretation and explanation have been regarded as the subjective aspects of history in which historians' interpretation of given facts and their explanation is concealed from the representation of history as an objective science.[34] Survivors' experience is viewed as entitling them to knowledge and their explanation accorded a higher status. However, an analysis of their refusal to explain or the explanations offered by survivors equally underscores their limited, subjective, local and biased nature.

Explanation in Partition research has been largely centred on the issue of violence (Tai and Kudaisya 2004). Historical accounts have constructed a plausible theory of fratricidal violence in which communities living in harmony for centuries indulged in acts of violence that are dismissed as aberrant (Pandey 2001).[35] These pathological theories of violence have been increasingly questioned in subsequent works that throw new light on the implication of the economic in the unprecedented violence of Partition (Gilmartin 2015).

Survivor accounts that include perpetrator's recollections in which the guilt, the remorse or anger at the recall of violent acts complicates the trope of deviance attached to explanations of violence. Unlike perpetrators who are unable to work through their memories to provide a coherent explanation of their acts, the interviewer or reader is able to glimpse their ambivalent, complex reasoning (Ahmed 2011). Victims' bewilderment fails to cohere into an explanation, and their explanations, when they are pressed to give one, appear to be coloured by historians' explanations of fratricidal violence due to their active forgetting of personal stories to protect their second and third generations from the hardship and suffering they had themselves endured (Raj 2000).

This inexplicability of the unspeakable acts poignantly articulated in literary representations through the oblique language of description, suggestion and metaphor is reproduced in survivor accounts of violence suffered and perpetrated, thus closing the chasm between testimonial and literary representation. This book juxtaposes fictional representations against testimonial accounts and historical documents to foreground the intersections between memory, history and narrative.

After Partition: memories and postmemories

Marianne Hirsch defines postmemory as "the relationship of the second generation to powerful, often traumatic, experiences that preceded their births but that were nevertheless transmitted to them so deeply as to seem to constitute memories in their own right" (2012: 103). Studies of Partition that have appeared in the last three decades have thrown considerable light on the Partition of 1947 through documenting stories of those who directly witnessed its violence. But stories of those who suffered its indirect impact still remain untold. While few adult survivors remain to narrate their stories, the "1.5 generation" (Suleiman 2002), or those who were children or young adults at the time of Partition, can still bring to light new stories of the Partition of 1947. As this generation is now between their late seventies and mid-eighties, there is an imperative need to document its narratives before time runs out.

This book borrows Marianne Hirsch's notion of postmemory (Hirsch 2008) to examine the afterlife of the Partition of 1947 by largely focusing on the stories of those who were children at the time of Partition and grew up listening to Partition stories. It hopes to examine the aftermath of the violence of Partition in the equally traumatic experience of displacement and resettlement shared by different generations of survivors. What were the processes initiated by the state to resettle refugees after the Partition? How did refugees negotiate with the state machinery to wrest rights and privileges? What were the networks they drew on to begin their lives anew? How did they negotiate with their new status in new regions and host communities? How did their assimilation into host cultures dispossess them of language, culture and a sense of belonging? How did they reconstruct old homes in new places? These are some of the questions that the book aims to answer through collecting the narratives of different generations affected by the Partition of 1947.

Building on the privileging of the memory of the witness in trauma studies as an alternative account of events, Hirsch's concept of postmemory extends the witness's authority to those with no direct experience of the traumatizing violence they narrate (2008). An analysis of the postmemories of several witnesses who were children or teenagers at the time of Partition were and could have had only a partial understanding of the significance of the events they witnessed and subsequently pieced them together through information transmitted by adults questions the rationale for this transference of testimonial authority from ancestors to their descendants.

Making themselves anew

Both archival and oral historians have engaged with the traumatic effects of the corporeal violence of Partition on the bodies and psyches of Partition survivors through investigating symptoms of repression, such as silence, repetition and obsession. Although the corporeal violence suffered and witnessed by survivors cannot be equated with the invisible scars of those who emerged apparently unscathed, the abiding effects of the pervading horror of violence and displacement in the production of what may be defined as the Partitioned psyche has not been engaged in literature on Partition in depth.

Violence's transformation of perspectives, priorities and attitudes of Partition survivors articulated through the habits and everyday practices and transmitted over generations requires a detailed examination. Rather than historians, sociologists' (Das 1990; Gupta 1996; Datta 2002) analyses of displaced refugees' accounts display a tension between admiration of refugee industry, resourcefulness and fortitude and denigration of acquisitiveness, competitiveness and ostentation that has percolated to the popular imagination as refugee materialism. These stereotyped representations of the Partitioned psyche are revised through their contextualization in the violence historically experienced by borderland communities intensified through the violence of 1947. Raised on the ideology of *khada pita lahe da, rahnda Ahmed Shahe da* [What we eat and drink is our own; the rest will go to Ahmad Shah] since the invasions of Ahmad Shah Abdali, Punjabi and Sindhi survivors normalized the ethic of conspicuous consumption after undergoing the loss of life, land, home and possessions during the ethnocidal violence of Partition.

The book throws light on the greater trauma of the disconcerting instability of violence that is inscribed in the radical transformation of subjectivity, community and ethics through the complete rupture with prior understandings of self, morality and belonging. The bodies, habits and everyday practices of survivors become the sites of memories of the violence that is transmitted to those of the following generations.

Chapter division

The introductory chapter began by attributing the renewed interest in the memories of survivors of Partition 1947 to "the memory turn" in history. It introduced key debates in history, memory, trauma and narrative and summarized the literature on refugees, home and displacement before outlining the conceptual framework used to examine the memories and postmemories of survivors of Partition 1947 in the book. It also provided an overview of the existing literature on Partition to show how the book both extends and complicates earlier perspectives on Partition before outlining its primary concerns and arguments.

The first chapter of the book, "Memory and History" compares history and memory to argue that the interrogation of traditional archival history in revisionist histories and historiographies has closed the gap between history, memory and narrative. It argues that the memory turn in history has installed memory as a legitimate historical method, particularly for filling up the lacunae in official histories through its focus on the personal, social and affective lives of ordinary people caught in extraordinary events. After discussing how memory has been effectively deployed in the oral histories of Partition 1947 to supplement, complement and interrupt nationalist histories of Independence, it closely examines testimonial narratives of ordinary people from particular villages, towns, neighbourhoods and regions to highlight the uses of memory in recovering the unknown stories of Partition.

In documenting Partition as a traumatic experience, scholars have pointed to the imbrication of the physical, social and psychological forms of trauma, borrowing the tools of trauma theory. Although the physical cannot be isolated from the social and the psychological, the chapter "Intangible Violence" focuses on the direct, structural and cultural violence experienced by survivors and their children in the years that followed the Partition. At a broad level, intangible violence may be defined as the loss of potential realizations, particularly that of "the hinge generation," the knowledge of poisoned relations and loss of intellectual uncertainty. At a specific level, it is translated as the loss not only of privilege and status but also of language and culture through the pressure on survivors to assimilate into host cultures.

The third chapter, "Scripting Their Own Lives," focuses on the work of memory and postmemory in the narrativization of experience through selection, elimination, focalizing of certain details and imposition of a structure that closes the gap between fictionalized and remembered stories. It argues that survivors, in the process of remembering, sharing and retelling their experiences, transmute experience into coherent narratives that become fixed through their retelling over the years. It also demonstrates that postmemory transforms piteous tales of violence and victimhood constructed both by traditional and oral historians into triumphalist sagas of survival in recalling and reconstructing the past. Survivors' reinscription of themselves from victims to agents underlines the process through which they use memory to script their own lives and gain agency.

The fourth chapter, "They Stuttered: Non-Narratives of the Unsayable," borrows Giles Deleuze's notion of language as a stutter and Veena Das's idea of the *unsayable* to foreground the gaps in stories that punctuate the authoritative narratives of Partition scripted by survivors both for private and public circulation and for intergenerational transmission. In narrating stories, memory works by eliding traumatic experiences or transforming them into acts of agency but is betrayed by language that screams, stammers, stutters or comes to a halt. Unlike consensual narratives rehearsed and retold by narrators to each other and others, including to their succeeding generations, these stutters in language, as narrators skip over some parts of the narrative while dwelling in great detail on others, go completely silent or slip into incoherent speech, disrupt survivors' authoritative narratives to call attention to the unsayable, untold and unscripted part of the stories.

The fifth chapter, "Not at Home," explores the notion of *unheimlichkeit* or the uncanny in relation to Partition survivors' experience of displacement and resettlement in regions familiar yet alien at the same time, which produces in them a sense of feeling uncomfortably strange and disoriented. The chapter argues that the unfamiliarity of the language, culture and region they were forced to resettle in produced a sense of "not being at home" in a new land that was supposed to be home. The uncanny affect is produced as much through its first meaning of unfamiliarity and cognitive dissonance as in its second meaning as hidden through the exposure of those aspects of existence that were meant to be hidden.

"Memories of Lost Homes" uses the notion of affective geographies to examine survivors' reconstruction of lost homes. It argues that memory produces the geographies of lost homes through the cognitive mapping of neighbourhoods, streets, places of work, play and worship and affective images of sights, sounds and smells of villages, towns or cities. Secondly, the imaginings of homelands by migrant memories warn against the production of a unified Punjab as memories locate homes in a specific city, village, neighbourhood, region, language or community.

"Resettled Homes" focuses on the process of homemaking in the new land through inhabitation of physical, linguistic, social and cultural spaces. The chapter argues that two contradictory strains are present in the homemaking process. While migrants reconstruct new homes in the image of remembered homes, their dispossession from certain aspects of the lost home and the pressure to assimilate into host cultures make the reconstruction of the physical spatiality of the old home impossible. Home is reconstructed either as language, as culture, as forms of sociality or rituals and as everyday practices.

The chapter, "Moving On," hopes to convey the migrants' reconciliation with loss – material, psychological, cultural – to make their lives anew in their new homes. It demonstrates that the primary concern of the communities in the early stages of resettlement was survival, which led them to postpone the work of mourning. It argues that the struggle for survival partially performed the task of healing through compelling survivors to leave the past behind and get on with the business of living. It shows that the pressure to integrate into local cultures and communities and to pursue success by all means entails a corresponding erosion of language and cultural continuity.

The book concludes by claiming that the event of Partition constructs a particular partitioned subjectivity that subsumes earlier markers of identity, such as language, religion, caste, ethnicity and region to converge on the event of Partition and the struggle to make life anew in the chapter "Partitioned Beings."

Notes

1 The numbers of displaced cannot be authenticated because of a variety of sources and their biases, according to Gyanesh Kudaisya, who is of the view that the number of people displaced would have been more than 18 million (1995). Paul Brass places the number of displaced between 10–12 million and opines that estimates of those who died "range from around 200,000 at the low end to a million and a half at the high end" and that the "sources that are most likely closer to the truth give figures that range between 200,000 and 360,000 dead" (2003: 75).

2 This confirms Ana Maria Alonso's contention that "historical chronologies solder a multiplicity of personal, local, and regional historicities and transform them into a unitary, national time" (1998: 126). It also corroborates Olick and Robins's observation that critical theories of nationalism show "that nation-states not only use history for their purposes, but make historiography into a nationalist enterprise" (1998: 126). Alessandro Portelli's idea of memory as "monument" and "disturbance" is equally relevant to the commemoration of the nationalist movement and the erasure of the disturbing memory of the violence of Partition that disrupts the triumphalist narrative of Indian Independence. Arguing that what is suppressed surfaces again as soon as control is relaxed, Portelli shows that memories of the rebirth of the nation, or risorgimento, return to hurt (2014: 44).

3 He points out that "while Holocaust comparisons may rhetorically energize some discourses of traumatic memory, they may also work as screen memories or simply block insight into specific local histories" (2004: 24). Ananya Jahanara Kabir confesses that she borrowed heavily from the critical language and assumptions of Holocaust literature, most notably the concepts of "unrepresentability" (Haidu) and the consequent fracturing of language (Kabir 2002) but found herself "struggling with what we may term (cautiously) a 'Holocaust-centric' apparatus grounded in a Euro-American experiential space" in her subsequent examinations of Partition's traumatic legacies partially because of this apparatus's very indispensability (2014: 64).

4 Ricoeur speaks of three kinds of abuses of memory, namely *blocked* memory, which takes place at the pathological level; *manipulated* memory, which works at the practical, ideological level, and *duty* memory, which functions at the ethico-political level (2006: 69). Arguing that the imperative mood in duty memory, the obligation to remember, contradicts the essentially spontaneous nature of memory, he believes that the relation of duty of memory to the idea of justice needs to be interrogated (2006: 89) and asserts that the way in which the duty of memory is proclaimed "can take the form of an abuse of memory in the manner of the abuses denounced earlier under the heading of manipulated memory" (2006: 90). Portelli makes the important point that "the agenda of the historian's agenda must meet that of the narrator; what the historian wishes to know might not coincide with what the narrator wishes to tell" (2005: 128).

5 The difference between memory's archivist and history's archivist and the difference in their interest in the past has been effectively brought out by Brien Brothman (2001: 62).

6 Olick and Robins, in "Social Memory Studies: From "Collective Memory" to the Historical Sociology of Mnemonic Practices," trace "the memory turn" to the 1980s (1998). Other scholars have attributed the contemporary memory turn to a host of reasons, such as the rise of multiculturalism, the fall of communism, and a victimization of politics (Kammen 1995); to three related aspects of 1960–70s culture – multiculturalist identification of historiography as a source of domination, postmodernism's critique of the totalizing aspects of historical discourse, truth and identity (Lee 2000: 128) and hegemony theorists' provision of a class-based account of a politics of memory (Schwartz 1996); to the history of mentalities that has dominated French historiography since the 1960s (Hutton 1993). Others have identified trauma and the consequent return of the repressed and the ineffable as well as decolonization as reasons for memory's becoming a key figure since the 1980s. However, the global race to archive Partition memories appears to have been ignited by the fear of the impending disappearance of survivors of Partition 1947.

7 In Portelli's view, contrasting memory with oblivion is meaningless, since oblivion "is a necessary part of memory" and "memory is a permanent search for meaning" in which "forgetting filters out the traces of experiences that no longer have meaning – or mean too much" (2014: 44). Similarly, Middleton holds that "remembering and forgetting emerge as interdependent features of communicative action" (2002: 81) and suggests that to remember and to forget need "not be viewed as antithetical processes" (2002: 81).

8 In interrogating the relationship of duty of memory to the idea of justice, Ricoeur examines three elements by way of response, i) "the duty of memory is the duty to do justice, through memories, to an other than the self," ii) the duty of memory is not merely concerned about "preserving the material trace, whether scriptural or other, of past events, but maintains the feeling of being obligated with respect to these others, of whom we shall later say, not that they are no more, but that they were" and iii) "among those others to whom we are indebted, the moral priority belongs to the victims" (2006: 90).

9 Partition-in-the-west is a phrase coined by historians to refer to the border on the west that led to the division of Punjab and is loosely used to signify refugees from Punjab erasing differences between diverse ethnolinguistic communities that have historically constructed themselves as different from Punjabi. Demystifying the perception of Punjabi refugees as belonging to a homogeneous Punjabi group, Harjap Singh Aujla traces refugee movements from diverse regions in Punjab to Delhi and shows that other than Standard Punjabi spoken by those from a few districts, all other refugees from Multan division spoke Saraiki and Jhangi dialects of Punjabi language while those from the Peshawar, Kohat, Abbotabad, Haripur, Hazara, Swat and Dera Ismail Khan districts of Khyber Pakhtoonkhwa spoke Hindko dialect. According to him, although 60 percent of the total population of 1,400,000 in 1951 spoke Standard (central) Punjabi, Saraiki, Hindko, Jhangi and Potohari dialects of Punjabi, the Standard Punjabi–speaking population of Delhi overpowered the other dialects over the period of the next two decades (2015). The book deconstructs the unified signifier Punjabi to demonstrate that the umbrella term subsumed differences between survivors who identified themselves as speakers of particular languages/dialects, such as Multani, Derawal, Mianwali, Potohari, Kohat, Bannuwal and so on.

10 Approximately 150 interviews were conducted between 2005 and 2018 in eight languages with largely middle-class, upper-caste Hindu and Sikh Punjabi and Sindhi, Hindu Bengali and some Muslim Ladakhi, owners of small businesses and professionals. While the names of those who gave their consent to be quoted have been included in the original, those of others who did not want to be named have been changed to preserve confidentiality. Interviewees either hailed from landowning, trading communities or/and from families of educated professionals, who were forced to migrate from both rural and urban areas in Punjab, Sindh and East Bengal to different parts of India. The age of the interviewees ranged between 63 and 102 with the average age falling between late 70s and mid-80s. Although some of the interviewees admitted to having been reduced to working-class or lower-middle-class existence after Partition, temporarily or permanently, the majority claimed to have been prosperous landowners, traders, or even professionals, in their pre-displacement homes and to have regained, or even improved, their economic position, if not social status, in their new homes. Interviews were supplemented by diaries, autobiographies and narratives available on memory archives, blogs and community- and place-based websites online. As a third-generation descendant of Partition survivors, I also drew on private family archives in reconstructing narratives of members of my own extended family.

11 Partition-in-the-east refers to the drawing of the border on the east of undivided India through the division of east and west Bengal.

12 With the publication of literature that engaged with Bengal, Partition-in-the-west and Partition-in-the-east emerged as intersecting and diverging events nuanced by process, time, displacement and resettlement. Over the last two decades, multiple, specific Partition narratives differentiated by class (Pandey 1997; Kaur 2007), caste (Mooney 2008; Kaur 2008; Basu Raychaudhury 2004), ethnicity (Virdee 2008; Nixon 2008) and region (Sinha-Kerkhoff 2004; Sengupta 2015), in addition to gender, have surfaced to complicate the homogenizing discourse of Partition. Cross-border stories of Partition compiled by scholars of South Asian origin have been particularly effective in

providing a comparative perspective on India and Pakistan (Virdee 2008), on those of perpetrator (Ahmed 2011) and victim as well as neutral witnesses (Nixon 2008). These microhistories of Partition need to be supplemented with a close analysis of other localities and neighbourhoods, communities and classes for debunking the myth of Partition as a unified, homogeneous witnessing of violence and its aftermath.

13 While individual scholars have been collecting oral histories since the 1990s, the "1947 Partition Archive" launched by Guneeta Singh Bhalla, is "a grassroots non-profit organization dedicated to preserving the fast disappearing memory of Partition." It has been crowdsourcing oral histories of the 1947 India-Pakistan Partition since 2010 and has conducted 4,500 interviews by volunteer Citizen Historians from 12 countries, including Bangladesh, Pakistan, India, United States, United Kingdom, Canada, Australia, Spain, Israel, France, Sweden and Hong Kong in 22 languages until 2017.

14 Brothman's distinction between the past of memory and that of history and his urging archivists to reconsider their working concept of memory "to ponder not only how archives keep records of the past but also how, in the their discourse and practices, they help to preserve a certain concept of what "the past" means," and to entertain the possibility "that multiple perspectives are permissible on 'what the past' might mean in the context of archival practice" (2001: 50) opens the possibility of a dialogue between archival and memory histories.

15 Keeping in mind Ricoeur's warning that the *what* of history depends on the *who*, memories of a single event are bound to vary depending on who is doing the remembering. Partition studies' disproportionate focus on middle-class, upper-caste Hindus and Sikhs has provided a partial vision of the violence that occludes the variegated experience of lower castes, whose mixed identities and pragmatic choices complicated the impact of Partition violence (Mayaram 1997; Kaur 2008; Kumar 2011). This book, focusing on the experience of largely middle-class, upper-caste survivors remains limited for the same reason.

16 Interviews conducted by Satyendra Raj with Sindhi migrants in the refugee colonies of Alam Bagh and Adarsh Nagar in Lucknow revealed that Sindhis first migrated there on Prime Minister Indira Gandhi's invitation in 1971, following their persecution during the Bangladesh war. This set off a chain migration of other Hindu and Sikh Sindhis with reported arrivals in 2001, and even later, many of whom refused to go on record (2017).

17 During the reign of President Najibullah, approximately 80,000 Sikhs, largely prosperous traders and entrepreneurs, are believed to have been living in Afghanistan with 30,000 Sikhs estimated to be in Kabul alone. Bobby Singh Bansal's documentary on Sikhs in Kabul poignantly captures the travails of the 300 odd Sikhs, who, unable to migrate to the UK unlike their prosperous Sikh brethren, have been forced to live for several years in a gurdwara (2012). Ironically, it was not the Taliban strike but the sudden American invasion which overthrew the Taliban regime in 2001 that shattered their unique existence (Bansal 2012). Similarly, Amardeep Singh has brought to light the presence of Sikhs in various sites in Pakistan and Afghanistan. The plight of the few remaining Hindus in Pakistan comes into focus time and again following punitive attacks by Muslims triggered by political conflicts (2002).

18 Bashir Ahmed interviewed dwellers of border villages in Kargil, Ladakh, whose families were divided through a continually changing boundary line that fragmented their village, with one part going to Pakistan and the other remaining in India (2017).

19 Since the term *refugees* was initially used by both the state and old residents to refer to those displaced by Partition, I have retained the term but interspersed it with alternative terms, such as *displaced persons* (the legal term that the state subsequently adopted), *cross-border migrants* and *new arrivals* to interrogate the label *refugee* that abjected survivors of Partition.

20 Thirty interviews were conducted with Partition survivors for this book in Delhi, Lucknow, Ambala, Kalka, Kashipur, Jamshedpur and Bangalore between

January 2005–2015. In addition, 130 interviews were conducted by Oral History interns in Kargil, Delhi, Karnal, Lucknow, Ranchi, Jamshedpur, Kharagpur, Mumbai and Kolkata as part of the Major Research Project (2017–2018) titled "After Partition: Postmemories of the Afterlife of Partition 1947," funded by the Indian Council of Social Science Research awarded to Anjali Gera Roy.

21 Stating that *ars memoriae* was inspired by the exorbitant desire "not to forget anything," Ricoeur inquires if "a measured use of memorization also impl[ies] a measured use of forgetting" and if one can speak of "methodical forgetting" following Descartes (2006: 68).

22 Arguing that "limitations in our current toolkit for the analysis of trauma" that arise from "the cultural gaps and geographic disconnect between the contexts in which trauma theory has arisen, and the contexts of specific traumatic events that continue to unfold across the world," Ananya Jahanara Kabir underlines the need to move away from psychoanalytic models derived from Freud and " 'provincializing' the 'Europe' (Chakrabarty) within the heart of trauma theory" by turning to vernacular understandings of trauma (2014: 64).

23 Portelli's view of oral history as a *co-creation* and a listening art based on a set of relationships and his emphasis on the historian's ability to listen and display empathy, respect and willingness to learn from the narrator is useful in the caution the historian needs to exercise in documenting disturbing histories (2005).

24 As Shoshana Felman notes in her analysis of Lanzmann's *Shoah*, the interviewer is "by definition a transgressor, and a breaker, of the silence" (1991: 52). She focuses on "the silence of the witness's death and of the witness's deadness which precisely must be broken, and transgressed" (1991: 53) in her analysis of filmmaker Lanzmann's attempt to persuade the witness Abraham Bomba to bear witness,

> We have to do it. You know it.
> I won't be able to do it.
> You have to do it.
> I know it's very hard. I know, and I apologize.
> Don't make me go on please. Please. We must go on.
>
> (1991: 117)

25 As Hirsch points out, her parents' stories and behaviour followed a set of conventions shaped by the stories, persecution and fear of the Holocaust (2012). Unlike Hirsch, who could draw on family photographs to catalyze postmemories, the relative absence of photographs in family archives of survivors, other than those of a small elite minority, makes survivors rely largely on mental images or widely circulated private and public narratives to reconstruct their own.

26 Shoshana Felman's essay "Emergence of Testimony: Salzmann's Shoah" engages in depth with different forms of silence in Salzmann's film (1991). Her analysis of the silence of a 13-year-old boy singer named Srebnik, who was the sole witness to death camps, as well as that of the Nazi perpetrators and Polish witnesses provides the most sophisticated examination of the burden of witnessing violence. Although the sole boy witness, Srebnik, whose mellifluous voice won him the reprieve of life, is unable to articulate his feelings when he witnessed the orgy of deaths as a teenager, his softly breaking into the songs he sang for the Nazis on revisiting the site serves as a requiem for those he bore silent witness to.

27 Philosophers have challenged not only history's claims to an objective science but also objectivity itself by arguing that historiography constructs as much as uncovers the "truths" it pursues (Novick 1988; Iggers 1997).

28 White defines "plot" as "a structure of relationships by which the events contained in the account are endowed with a meaning by being identified parts of an integrated whole" (1980: 13). He shows that emplotment is at work even in non-narrative forms of history, such as annals in their arrangement of dates on the left side and events on the other.

29 White argues that an element of narrativity is involved even at the minimal level on which the annals unfold since "what gets put into the account is of much greater theoretical importance for the understanding of the nature of narrative than what gets left out" (1980: 14).

30 For example, the mythicization of success by Partition generations co-opts Partition violence in the personal saga of family wealth and success that was interrupted by their forced migration (Raj 2000).

31 In Louch's view, narration involves selection of certain events and their placement with others in such a manner that narration of events by the historian itself becomes an explanation (1969).

32 As Alessandro Portelli points out, the oral source is always "co-created by the historian" (2005). He places emphasis on a dialogic exchange in the interview, which involves an exchange of gazes. His caveat that "the historian's agenda must meet the agenda of the narrator; what the historian wishes to know may not necessarily coincide with what the narrator wishes to tell. As a consequence, the whole agenda of the research may be radically revised" (2005).

33 Portelli considers oral history primarily as "a listening art" (2005). As he shows, "even when the dialogue stays within the original agenda, historians may not always be aware that certain questions need to be asked. Often, indeed, the most important information lies outside what both the historian and the narrator think of as historically relevant" (2005).

34 As Olick and Robins put it, postmodernists (White 1973; Veyne 1984) have "challenged the 'truth claim' of professional historiography by questioning the distinction between knowledge and interpretation and derivatively between history and memory" (Olick & Robins 1998: 98). According to them, ever since "historiography has broadened its focus from the official to the social and cultural, memory has become central evidence" (Olick & Robins 1998: 110).

35 As Gyanendra Pandey pointed out in his essay "In Defence of the Fragment" (1992), focusing on a particular instance of intercommunity violence can answer important questions on the difference between memory and history.

2   History, memory, forgetting

Introduction

History is defined as the discipline "that studies the chronological record of events (as affecting a nation or people), based on a critical examination of source materials and usually presenting an explanation of their causes" (The Editors of *Encyclopædia Britannica*). Originating in the ancient Greek term *historia* meaning "inquiry," "knowledge from inquiry," or "judge," it was borrowed in classical Latin to mean "investigation, inquiry, research, account, description, written account of past events, writing of history, historical narrative, recorded knowledge of past events, story or narrative." It developed into *stær* ("history, narrative, story") in the late Old English period; *istorie, estoire,* and *historie* in old French; and *history* in Middle English. History came to mean "the branch of knowledge that deals with past events" and the formal record or study of past events, esp. human affairs" (*Oxford English Dictionary*) only in the 15th century. Unlike modern German, French, and most Germanic and Romance languages in which the same word is used to connote both history and story, history and story have become bifurcated in modern English. As a written record of past events, history is privileged over memory in modern western cultures as an objective, reliable, critical account.

Memory, history's older twin in traditional cultures, refers to "the encoding, storage, and retrieval in the human mind of past experiences" (Underwood 1969), "the faculty by which the mind stores and remembers information" or "something remembered from the past" (*Oxford English Dictionary*) and "the power or process of reproducing or recalling what has been learned and retained especially through associative mechanisms" (*Miriam-Webster*). The etymological origins of *memory* may be traced to Anglo-French *memorie* (Old French *memoire*, 11c., "mind, memory, remembrance; memorial, record") and directly to Latin *memoria* "memory, remembrance, faculty of remembering," and Old English *gemimor* "known," *murnan* "mourn, remember sorrowfully"; and Dutch *mijmeren* "to ponder").[1] Memory is, therefore, a capacity of the mind to record, process and recall information and events that may be used individually to document individual life or collectively to commemorate significant events in the life of a group, community or nation. Unlike history, memory is rambling, associative, corporeal, affective and intuitive; it includes both evocation and recall and may be declarative and non-declarative.

In traditional cultures, memory was regarded as a legitimate tool for remembering and preserving the past and remained a tool of history until history's aspirations to be an objective science ended its synonymy with memory. With the emergence of memory in historical discourse in the 1980s, the antagonistic relationship between history and memory appears to have ended with the terms *history* and *memory* being used interchangeably.[2] Memory has become a meta-historical category that subsumes collective memory, public memory, popular memory and social memory.

This chapter compares history and memory to argue that the interrogation of traditional archival history in revisionist histories and historiographies has closed the gap between history, memory and narrative. It argues that "the memory turn" in history has installed memory as a legitimate historical method, particularly for filling up the lacunae in official histories through its focusing on the personal, social and affective lives of ordinary people caught in extraordinary events. After discussing how memory has been effectively deployed in the oral histories of Partition 1947 to supplement, complement and interrupt nationalist histories of Independence, it closely examines testimonial narratives of ordinary people from particular villages, towns, neighbourhoods and regions to highlight the uses of memory in recovering the unknown stories of Partition.

The case for memory

In his essay *Present Pasts* (2000), Andreas Huyssen observes "a memory turn" in contemporary western culture that has countered "the spatial turn" in postmodern theory through its privileging of time over space. Tracing this turn to the 1960s, he believes that it was accelerated in the 1980s with the eruption of repressed traumatic memories of the Holocaust and commemoration of several "German anniversaries" and became globalized.[3] Huyssen identifies a direct relationship between present amnesias and disappearance of memory and the memory boom and attributes the rise in "memory discourses" to the fear of forgetting. Addressing the critique of the transformation of memory as spectacle and memory as industry by the media and a memory industry, he argues against making a distinction between imagined memories and real memories, trivial and serious memories since memory culture fulfils an important function in the current transformation of corporeal experience by the media. Drawing on Hermann Lubbe, who demonstrated that musealization has become central to the shifting temporary sensibility of our time (2000: 32), he shows that musealization can be mapped onto the phenomenal rise of memory discourse within the discipline of historiography. Huyssen argues that memory and musealization are enlisted as bulwarks against obsolescence and disappearance in this prominence of academic "mnemo-histories" (2000: 33).

Other scholars who have unravelled the complicated relationship between history, memory and forgetting (Halbwachs 1951; Bartlett 1964 [1932]; Yates 1966;

Nora 1989; Le Goff 1992; Hutton 1993; Matsuda 1994; Ricoeur 2006) support, contradict and complicate Huyssen's thesis on the relation of the resurgence of memory to anxieties about forgetting. They have explained it variously as loss of historical consciousness, return of the repressed, crisis in identity in 19th-century modernism, the valorization of the history of people without history, the impact of decolonizing movements, the rise of identity movements in the 1960s and so on.

The obsession with memory must be attributed both to the fear of forgetting and the desire to remedy the amnesias of history. The memory turn in history has been ascribed to the limitations of traditional histories that are inherent in the nature of historical study. As a discipline, history is handicapped in throwing light on the economic, social or cultural lives of ordinary people, as well as their amnesias, silences and distortions, and in its inability to incorporate the affective, personal and local.[4] When speaking on the uses of memory, memory has paradoxically been resurrected to recover facts that have traditionally been regarded as the province of history because of the doubts cast on memory's precision, objectivity and accuracy in reproducing facts. However, anxieties related to recovering memory directly emerged as a response to history's selective omissions, elisions, repressions and distortions of facts that disrupted the unitary masternarratives of particular events or the ideological agendas of particular groups. Memory's function is therefore to undo history's amnesias, repressions and distortions through the unforgetting of events that have been obliterated from written histories and public memory.

In positing memory as a panacea for forgetting, mnemonic texts are required to negotiate the problem of unintentional as well as intentional forgetting through the mysterious mechanisms of blocked memory, manipulated memory and duty memory (Ricoeur 2006). The abuses of memory, Ricoeur explains, result from "a concerted manipulation of memory and of forgetting by those who hold power" (2006: 80). Asserting that the abuses of memory are also abuses of forgetting, Ricoeur places an emphasis on "the intersection of the problematics of memory and identity, both personal and collective" (2006: 81). Observing that mobilization of memory in the quest for identity lies at the heart of manipulation of memory, he astutely connects the fragility of memory to the fragility of identity and identifies three causes for the fragility of identity, namely "its difficult relation to time" (2006: 81), "confrontation with others" (2006: 81) and "the heritage of founding violence" (2006: 82). He attributes the abuses of power to the intervention of ideology between the demand for identity and public expressions of memory and shows that the abuses of memory occur because of the distortions at the phenomenal level of ideology. Maintaining that memory is incorporated in the formation of identity at that symbolic, narrative level, he speaks of "imposed memory" that is "armed with a history that is itself 'authorized,' the official history, the history publicly learned and celebrated" (2006: 85). He calls this "trained memory" an "instructed memory" or "a forced memorization" that is enlisted "in the service of the remembrance of those events belonging to the common history that are held to be remarkable, even founding, with respect to the common identity" (2006: 86).[5]

In addition to remedying history's forgetting, memory is burdened with the function of supplementing its omissions, elisions and erasures. History's occlusions partially originate in its disciplinary focus on political and military events to the exclusion of social, cultural, political and economic ones and in its normalization of kings, leaders and politicians as the subjects of history. The naturalization of political and military histories of rulers as "history" in the singular has marginalized economic, social and cultural histories. Memory's critique of historical discourse emerges from its occlusion of the socio-cultural and economic lives of people from the purview of history. Since history's preoccupation with political events, such as wars, conquests, treaties and so on effectively marginalizes their socio-economic or cultural effects, one must turn to memory in order to reconstruct the lived experience of people during a particular historical period. Through filling up historical omissions and erasures that are not a consequence of focalization or disciplinary thrust but of intentional amnesia or distortion, cultural memories can play a more critical role in exposing the manipulations of historical discourse. Memory is invoked to serve as a replacement rather than a complement or supplement through its challenging totalizing histories of foundational events appropriated in the construction of a common identity by disruptive alternative events or memories of events. Through complementing and supplementing political and military history with plural histories of the past and recovering repressed pasts, memory steps in to fill in both the limitations of history and to disrupt unitary, authoritative historical masternarratives.

Memory serves as the sole means of remembering and preserving the past in societies without written records, which were banished by the West to prehistory, in which the heritage of particular groups has been preserved for centuries in collective memories and oral mnemonarratives (Klein 2000). The suspicion of writing in traditional societies as a false, secondary, derivative, artificial memory as articulated in *Phaedrus* is complemented with a sanctification of memory as originary, authentic and true (Plato, 360 BC). In the absence of a written archive in the case of repressed facts, any memory of the facts, reliable or fallible, may eventually lead to a rough reconstruction of factual events. Since the absence of documentary proof disqualified an event from being included in history (Brothman 2001 60), events that have not been inscribed can be recovered only through oral testimonies based on memory.[6] Although the sacralization of memory in oral-aural cultures as a document of the past might appear to be a pragmatic contingency in view of the absence of written documentation, it foregrounds the relationship of history with memory that has been overlooked in history's aspirations to become objective. As opposed to modern history in which memory is positioned as an antonym, supplement or complement of memory, traditional histories were essentially memory histories. The continuities of memory and history, which continued to be acknowledged and recognized in medieval histories, were suppressed in modern history in which memory was dismissed as unreliable, inauthentic and partial.

History's claims to an impersonal, objective science proves to be its limitation in documenting the personal, subjective and the affective, thus allowing memory to step in to fill in the personal, sensory, affective memories of both documented and undocumented historical events. Although historical documents have a distinct advantage over memory in providing a logical, objective, chronological account of the past, their limitations in understanding the motivations or impact of political decisions, laws and policies on the psyche of both state functionaries and subjects have cleared a space for the inclusion of memory.[7] History exhibits a paradoxical privileging and dismissal of the individual and the personal through its occlusion of the private and the personal despite its being chronologically ordered by the period of rule of a leader or a political party. Notwithstanding its cursory inclusion of biographical details of makers of history, details of their private lives or personal motivations are appended or appropriated in the interpretative stage of providing explanations of public historical events. Similarly, the personal affective dimensions of historical events on the populace are outside the purview of historians' histories because of their emphasis on objective data. Collective and affective memories can fill in these historical lacunae through providing a glimpse into the socio-cultural effects of political and economic events and policies on historical subjects.

Partition histories and memories

In his book *Remembering Partition* (2001), Gyanendra Pandey raises two important questions with respect to Partition. He inquires how it was possible for official histories of the Indian nation to write the truth of the violence of Partition 1947 and yet deny its eventfulness. The questions have been answered in *The Aftermath of Partition in South Asia* (2004) by Gyanesh Kudaisya and Tan Tai Yong, who provide a comprehensive account of the representation of Partition in historiography and also ponder the silence surrounding the event. Tai and Kudaisya divide this historiography into several phases, beginning with the hagiographic and autobiographical phase of the first two decades. These include the biographies, autobiographies, diaries and memoirs of those who witnessed Partition, both colonial officials (Darling 1948; Tuker 1950; Campbell Johnson 1951; Moon 1961; Menon 1961; Philips 1962) and Indian political leaders (Azad 1959; Khaliqquzaman 1961). The second phase began in the 1960s with professional historians (Philips and Wainwright 1970; Mansergh 1983) putting together 7,500 documents that were supplemented by papers related to Indian leaders. Asserting that early historiography (Inder Singh 1987; Moore 1974; Page 1998) "set up its problematique with regard to Partition as a problem of reconciling the attainment of freedom with national unity" (Tai and Kudaisya 2004: 12), Tai and Kudaisya point out that *haute politic*, or high politics, was the focus of these histories. Dissatisfied with the limitations of the high politics approach, Partition studies went regional with historians (Gilmartin 1988; Talbot 1996; Chatterji 2002) turning to specific regions to assess the impact of Partition in the 1980s. Tai and Kudaisya identify certain common threads running through these Partition histories, such as the end of the empire, the transfer of power and the emergence of Indian and Pakistani nation states, and make the important point that they do not silence but "circumscribe Partition for their own reasons" (2004: 15).[8]

Since high politics is the focus of the vast body of literature on Partition discovered by Tai and Kudaisya, it is silent on the economic, social or cultural repercussions of Partition on ordinary people. People's experience of Partition 1947, one of the most violent, traumatic and cataclysmic events of "unprecedented magnitude and horror" (Khosla 1949) in world history, is either absent or marginalized in social histories of the nation. Nationalist histories that have largely focused on the process of nation formation have either erased the impact of Partition 1947 on ordinary people or relegated them to a footnote in the masternarrative of Indian Independence. In these political histories of the nation, Partition is examined within the framework of nation formation as a constitutional division and a consensual division of property and assets against the backdrop of the conflict between major political figures and parties. The repertoire of 7,500 official documents archived by professional historians undoubtedly helps in throwing light on the political contingencies that necessitated the division, the rationale for the construction of the lines of the new nations, the systematic process of the devolution of power and the motivations and agendas of important political leaders as well as their internal rifts, constitutional matters and so on. Notwithstanding their meticulous attention to the details of the transfer of power and the process of nation formation or objective, official statistics on the number of people killed or displaced by the violence of Partition, traditional histories eschew an engagement with their effects on the human actors unwittingly embroiled in the events.

Historical debates have had to grapple with the horrifying violence that disrupts the unified official narrative of Independence won through the sacrifice of the founding fathers, which was predicated on the myth of a peaceable civilization and the split between public and private memory. In official histories of the nation, underpinned by the ideology of non-violence, the unspeakable violence of Partition either had to be elided, quantified through hard statistical figures or represented as a pathological, aberrant, "sacrificial offering rendered up at the birth of two nations" (Pandey 2001: 15).[9] Unlike the elisions and omissions of earlier narratives of violence in the production of a unified narrative of non-violence, the cataclysmic violence of Partition accompanying the birth of the nation could not be erased through invocations of ideological rhetoric.[10] Apart from the ideological agenda of the repression of narratives of violence disjunctive with the nationalist masternarrative of non-violence,[11] the limitations of archival histories in engaging with the enormity of violence, except at the level of quantitative data, reports and analysis, explains the perfunctory inclusion of a horrifying event of gargantuan proportions. Traditional official histories have therefore confined themselves to factual reportage, sometimes conflicting, and their debates have centred on finding an explanation for the inexplicable violence. Beginning with explanations of violence as pathological, spontaneous and chaotic, as part of human nature, with British historians attributing it to the clash of personality and the nationalist histories of India and Pakistan blaming each other or the British for their divide-and-rule policies, a general theory of Partition began to emerge in the mid-1980s with more complex and localized perspectives on Partition violence.[12] Explanations in these studies range from establishing state complicity in inciting violence, its genocidal nature, its class and gender divisions, the role of political parties and so on that gesture towards a premeditated plan.

Uses of memory in Partition

The memory turn in the 1980s, as Huyssen pointed out, posited memory both as an ally and rival of history in the West. Before their turn to oral histories and people's stories in filling up the gaps in histories of Partition, the limitations of official archival histories in conclusively explaining the unspeakable violence of Partition and its traumatic effects on victims and perpetrators inspired the literary turn in Partition studies. Although literary texts different from stories narrated by ordinary people in being privileged intellectual accounts, they intersect with stories in their being predicated on individual memory and may be regarded as individual testimonies of those who lived through Partition. A number of historians and literary scholars turned to literary and cultural texts to unravel the mystery surrounding the events of Partition, particularly violence. Although literary texts have been long recognized as sources of history, the recognition of literature and cinema as historical archives compelled a rethinking on the nature and genre of the archive in the 1990s. A spate of literature on Partition that engaged with literary representations of Partition emerged to fill up the lacunae in traditional histories by contesting the single, unified version of Partition through revealing the multiplicity, complexity and absence of closure in stories of Partition. Critiquing official accounts as "compelling narratives concerned with metaphysical identities of various communities" or "teleological histories in which the past is given a 'retrospective intelligibility' and rationality" that did not display any interest in "world-making," Alok Bhalla set the agenda for the examination of literature as an archive of Partition by arguing that novelists "make connections with the social and cultural life of a community in its entirety within a certain period" through containing "all that is locally contingent and truthfully remembered, capricious and anecdotal, contradictory and mythically given" (1999: 3120). The fiction of Sa'adat Hasan Manto, Krishna Sobti, Intezar Hussain, Bhisham Sahni and other writers has been examined by a number of scholars who have made a convincing case for literary texts that provide a more complex, plural, nuanced account of the events of Partition 1947 as testimonies of Partition rather than official histories (Bhalla 1999; Kamra 2008; Datta 2008).

Portelli's distinction between history as monument and history as disturbance is crucial in the articulations of hurt in oral histories, which cannot be vociferated in official histories that put disturbing memories away in the closet.[13] The first answers to general questions about the hurts of Independence have emerged from the small places of women interviewed in the intimate spaces of the home. In these mnemo-narratives, the story of Independence is represented as a patriarchal, malecentric narrative in which state and domestic power as well as national shame and honour was inscribed on the abducted, raped, mutilated bodies of women. Feminist historians' unveiling of the silenced voices of women affected by the Partition have largely drawn on trauma theory, the idea of memory work and acts of mourning performed by silent victims of Partition (Das 1990; Butalia 1998; Menon and Bhasin 1998). As they have poignantly revealed, women's stories of the event of Partition, which function as the counter-memory of objective, logical, masculine official histories through their focusing on the feminine, affective, personal, private, domestic dimensions of public events, have accentuated the limitations of patriarchal historical narratives in comprehending the human, gendered, embodied aspects of political events (Butalia 1998: 94). They have effectively demonstrated how women's remembering of Partition enfolded public events of Partition in the domain of the domestic and the private through invoking personal rather than public memories. Through situating the bodies of women as bearers of the violence perpetrated by male actors, they have foregrounded the symbolic inscription of national honour, purity and identity on the female body (Butalia 1998: 143). Their emphasis on the corporeal effects of the traumatic violence on women has set the direction for the formal installation of embodied memories as a historical method for documenting unwritten histories of the traumatic effects of Partition on other marginalized actors. The methodologies of feminist historians can be productively deployed in recovering repressed embodied memories of other victims and perpetrators of Partition violence.

Similarly, the shift in historical focus from political leaders to subaltern groups, including peasants (Pandey 2001), minorities, Dalits and so on ushered in by subaltern historians has thrown light on the impact of Partition on small players in national history. In the absence of written documentation of these narratives, these historians have drawn on collective memories of disadvantaged and marginalized actors to expose national histories to be partial, partisan accounts of dominant class, caste and religious groups. They have also underlined the inadequacy of the generalized lens of high politics in framing the particular issues, struggles and dilemmas faced by these groups. As the generalized historical framework of civilizational difference used to explain the events of 1947 was critiqued for being a product of modernity, historians of the subaltern school attempted "to remake the meanings of Partition with narratives drawn from everyday lives" (Gilmartin 2015). Historians of the subaltern school assumed the responsibility of challenging the dominant nationalist vision of objectified, frozen and enumerated communities used by modernizing states to develop their authority by turning to "the malleable, fuzzy, contextual forms" of lived community that defined the lives of people living under the Partition drama (Gilmartin 2015). Subaltern historians uncovered memories of diverse lived communities that ran counter to the generalized framework of dominant official histories. The civilizational rhetoric of Hindu-Muslim animosity was refuted by evidence of shared, intersecting religious boundaries at the village level in North India (Ali 1989; Oberoi 1993), as well as in the bodies of certain subaltern groups (Mayaram 2004).

Celebration or mourning

As feminist, subaltern, oral historians and scholars in literary, cinema and cultural studies have brilliantly demonstrated, the memory archive of Partition has brought to light stories of Partition repressed, elided or overlooked in official stories.

Memory has been the primary weapon in the recovery of the event of Partition repressed, elided or marginalized in the construction of the triumphalist master narrative of Indian independence. These counter-memories of 1947 may be counterpoised against institutional and ideological forms of knowledge enshrined in official histories for critiquing the totalizing and universalizing accounts of the history of Independence that appeal to transcendent theories of the transfer of power, nation formation and constitutional arrangements. Official histories of Independence, based on media reports, immortalize August 15 as a celebratory moment in evocative metaphors signifying the joyous birth of the nation:

> And as the twelfth chime of midnight died out, a conch shell, traditional herald of the dawn, sounded raucously through the chamber. Members of the Constituent Assembly rose. Together they pledged themselves "at this solemn moment . . . to the service of India and her people. . . ."
>
> (Rothman 2017)

Historian Gyanendra Pandey found an ingenious way of uncovering counter-memories of triumphalist, celebratory public narratives of Independence disseminated through contemporary media through posing a simple question to residents of Delhi: "What were you doing on August 15, 1947?" (1997). Pandey discerned a sharp division in the responses generated by the question with one end represented by Prime Minister Nehru's well-known, highly charged Independence speech – "At the stroke of the midnight hour while the world sleeps, India will awake to life and freedom . . ." – and the other by "the angry rejoinder of a Sikh shopkeeper now living in Bhogal, a small 'mohalla' sandwiched between the refugee colonies of Jangpura and Lajpat Nagar in New Delhi" (1997: 2242). Arguing that the affective meanings of the historical date swung between Independence and Partition depending on the respondent's location, he perceives the responses to be bifurcated between a "ruling (privileged) class" celebrating Independence and a "refugee class" unable to do so (1997: 2242). When asked to share his views on Jawaharlal Nehru's historic speech about India's "Tryst with Destiny," eminent journalist and novelist Khushwant Singh sarcastically commented, "[W]hat tryst with destiny, people didn't know what they were going to eat?" (Quoted in Raj 2000: 31).

Elsewhere, the multiplicity of responses to the question, which varies according to the gender, age, ethnicity, religion and location of the respondent, disrupt the binary of celebration and mourning in Partition studies.

> On 15th August, 1947, there was electricity in the air. We attended a special service at St James (Delhi's oldest church set up in 1836). After a meal at Carlton, we bought a tricolour and proudly displayed it from our window. Rahman Manzil was lit up with hundreds of lamps and people burst crackers and lit sparklers to ring in a pre-Diwali Diwali. We had a party at home. At that time, we didn't have proper record players, so someone began strumming

a guitar. Even as a four-year-old, I knew it was a special day. The image of a tricolour fluttering out of our window has always stayed with me.

(Rebeiro 2013)

An Anglo-Indian (92) schoolteacher employed in the Bengal Nagpur Railway School, Kharagpur confirmed the festive air that engulfed the Anglo-Indian community through her recalling of her spirited participation in the festivities:

I didn't witness any riots my dear. There was a curfew in the city and we were not permitted to leave our hostel. But we celebrated the Independence Day in the South Institute with music and dancing.

(Lennon 2017)

According to Ram Prakash, Muslims, too, enthusiastically joined in the festivities in Meerut:

We went to the heart of Meerut city and observed Muslim shops and mosques well decorated with flowers. The Muslims were distributing sweets and offering sherbet.

(2005)

Satya Pal Khanna recalled that similar festivities were taking place in Lahore, after the announcement that Lahore would go to Pakistan on the radio on the night of August 14:

We watched fireworks . . . from our roof.
    Whenever August 15th arrives, my mind goes back to the memories of Lahore I have – particularly of the few days I was there after Partition.

(Khanna, Interviewed by Ali, Partition 1947 Archive)

Khanna and his father locked everything up the next day and headed for the train station after leaving their cattle with their friends:

A friend forced us off the tonga as soon as he spotted us. He asked us how we hadn't heard about any of the violence at the train station. We went to stay with him that night.

(Khanna, interviewed by Ali, Partition 1947 Archive)

DAV School was turned into a refugee camp:

We slept on the floor of my school on August 16th. There were 13,000 refugees amassed in the area with little access to food or water. The young and able went to the nearby neighbourhoods to retrieve rice, lentils, salt and wood. People ate from the pockets or folds of their clothing since there were no plates to be found.

(Khanna, interviewed by Ali, Partition 1947 Archive)

Their disillusionment with the ideological construction of the nation manifested in their enraged reception of political leaders visiting the DAV college camp in Lahore:

> It was the evening of August 15 or 16, when Jawaharlal Nehru visited the college camp. Thousands of harassed refugees, victims of unprovoked ferocious and barbaric acts of communal vendetta, accosted Nehru. They shouted, "Go back, go back!" Sensing the mood, Nehru and his colleague S Baldev Singh left.
>
> (Malhotra 2013)

Prakash Raj and his family fled violence in Lyallpur and found refuge in the same camp as Satya Pal Khanna in which they continued to stay until September 1947.

In contrast, Manik Ram, a Hindu railway official posted in Quetta, boarded a train to Pakistan on August 14, 2017, to collect his transfer orders after leaving his wife and six children in Patiala in the care of his wife's brother.[14] The memory of the journey in which he barely escaped being killed must be reconstructed through the postmemory of his daughter who was then barely seven but could recall every minute detail that he had shared with the family on his return even after 70 years.

> When he boarded the train, he was not aware that the Partition had been announced. Suddenly, he heard fellow passengers shouting "Pakistan Zindabad" and joined in the sloganeering. That's when he noticed that his tin trunk had his Hindu name inscribed on it. He had the presence of mind to turn the trunk front side back. Since he, like many Hindus of the region, always sported the *kullewali* Peshawari turban, he managed to pass undetected.
>
> (Deshi 2018)

Similarly, Dhani Ram, a partner in Agmark Ghee Company, Lyallpur [Faisalabad],[15] who had travelled to Delhi to attend a meeting of the Agmark Ghee Manufacturers with the Government of India on August 10, 1947, decided to return to Lyallpur on August 12, 2017, his son recalled (Ram Prakash 2005). Prakash also remembered his father's adamantly arguing with his neighbour that Lyallpur and Lahore, as Hindu and Sikh majority districts, would not be given to Pakistan. Dhani Ram truly believed, like several prominent individuals of the town, that Lyallpur would logically form a part of India since the Chenab River had been fixed as the boundary between the two nations.

Bashir Ahmed Wafa, a resident of Baltibazar, Kargil, was not even aware of the day of Independence, although he did have some idea about the resistance against the British and came to know about it only after the opening of the Zolzilla pass in summer.

> In August 1947, we got Independence. From books and people, I got to know about Independence.

People here knew nothing about the movement for Independence. They didn't know that on 15th of August 1947 both India and Pakistan got Independence and got separated as two different nations.

(2017)

Microstoria

Memory's supplementation of official histories of Partition is facilitated by the problems of scale in macrohistories of the nation, whose wide-angle format is ill-equipped to frame micro or local events, a lack that can be filled in through taking close-up shots of specific regions, cities, neighbourhoods and villages. In contrast to official histories, whose scale spans the nation-state and whose preoccupation with events of national significance leads to the excision of local events, microhistories of a single event, community or individual can be reconstructed only through turning to personal or collective memory, particularly in the absence of written documentation. For example, Sikh leader Tara Singh's visit to Lyallpur in April 1947 is deeply engraved on the memory of the 14-year-old Ram Prakash:

> Before Partition, in April 1947, a huge procession was seen moving towards Dushhera Ground, which was near my house. Master Tara Singh, Akali leader – who tore off the Union Jack flag – was at the head of the procession and was shouting slogans against the Muslim League and its demand for Partition for forming Pakistan.[16] He was saying that Pakistan would be created only on his dead body. I saw the procession, which was lightly lathi-charged by the police.
>
> (Ram Prakash 2005)

In addition, the lack of balance in official histories, due to the overrepresentation of certain regions, events and individuals to the erasure or marginalization of others, may be corrected through mnemonic historical modes. As a partisan perspective of dominant groups, regions and individuals, history has traditionally suppressed or marginalized counternarratives of oppositional or non-dominant groups that disrupt the unified masternarrative of nation formation. These little stories of groups, regions and individuals buried under the grand narrative of Independence can be recovered only through the summoning of individual memory. Complementing, supplementing, disrupting or complicating the stories of Independence, these little stories offer a glimpse into alternative, little, regional, local, sectarian, gendered, caste histories of the nation. A microscopic analysis of the experiences of ordinary people undertaken with the objective of subverting a string of hierarchies can indeed be used to ask larger and more general questions about the events of 1947 "in small places."

Memory, as Halbwachs rightly pointed out, is intimately related with place, a particular locale. In remembering the events of 1947, survivors invariably reconstruct the past in relation to a particular place, a neighbourhood, a village, a camp and so on. The spatialization of memory perfectly reconciles the spatial-temporal division in history through particularizing the homogeneous, unified march of historical events through anchoring them in particular locales. This spatial dimension of memory enables it to reconstruct places or sites erased or marginalized in official histories. This function of memory is nowhere as evident as in memories of remembered villages and cities marked by composite, cosmopolitan cultural formations that have been subsequently overwritten by sectarian nationalisms. The remembered Lahore of old Lahorites or Lucknow of old Lucknowites reinscribed by their appropriation in religious nationalisms survives solely in the collective memories of their older residents. The mapping of the events of 1947 on the forgotten cartographies and landmarks of pre-Partitioned cities, towns and villages provides a glimpse into the socio-cultural history of these spaces that are either overlooked or erased in historians' histories.

Mnemonic accounts can be used to complement documented histories through filling in missing details of recorded macrohistorical events. Unlike the widely documented visit of Jawaharlal Nehru to Dera Ismail Khan in April 1947, which sparked the first wave of riots, the visits of Nehru and Jinnah to the border village of Jamalpur in Dera Ghazi Khan district on August 16, 1947, survives in a teenage witness's mnemonic reconstruction. After learning through an Urdu newspaper that the Prime Minister of *Bharat* [India] was going to pay a visit to the village, a grocery store owner in Lucknow, 79, recalled Nehru, dressed in his signature crisp white churidar with a rose stuck in his jacket, accompanied by "Jinnahsaab" [Mohammad Ali Jinnah] asking him if he was aware that Pakistan had been created. He recalls Nehru accosting him with the question "Are you Hindu or Mussalman [Muslim]?" which he followed by another question: "Would you like to become a Mussalman?" He jocularly recalled boldly declaring to Nehru that as a Hindu, why would he ever consider becoming a Mussalman, and being surrounded by "short-statured" Gurkhas and transported to Attari (Arora 2011). His world being circumscribed to the Dera Ismail Khan region, he confessed to having had no knowledge of the idea of the nation or of "Hindustan" as a teenager growing up in this border village. His knowledge of having met the respective heads of the two newly formed nations not only confirms Nehru and Jinnah's personal interventions in refugee transportation from the North Western Frontier Province (NWFP) but also fleshes out the macrohistory of the referendum of 1947. His memories also corroborate the economic domination of Hindu traders, such as his own family, in the Muslim-majority village and the presence of similar trading outposts that catered to the needs of villagers in the border districts.

Similarly, the aftermath of the declaration of the Mountbatten plan for Partition on June 3, 1947, in Lyallpur city may be recovered through the memories of another teenage witness.

On 3rd June 1947,[17] a Sikh was stabbed near the Randi Bazar near Jama Masjid. The news spread all over the city and Hindus and Sikhs started killing Muslims. I was studying then in the 9th class in DAV (Arya) School, which was about three miles away from my house. School buses would normally pick up children from school after 1 p.m.; but on the said day, all the children were driven home at 11 a.m. in different buses.[18] When I alighted about 200 yards away from my house, I heard some shouts and saw a Muslim vegetable vendor [subziwalla] being hit by many. And then a Sikh pushed him in a nallah [drain] and people stoned him to death. The people started attacking another Muslim and I ran into my house. After two hours, police took control and curfew was imposed on the entire city.

(Ram Prakash 2005)

Memory, as warm and subjective, can complement cold, objective history through its capacity to fill in the personal as opposed to cold, objective numbers, dates and places. An examination of survivors' testimonies reveals a sharp difference in the framing of a documented event through the process of personalization. Without referencing the historical archive, individuals and families emphasize their personal experience of witnessing violence, riots or exodus in remembering Partition. Objective figures on the number of people killed, mutilated or displaced are personalized and humanized through recollection of traumatic experiences and mention of details that paint a microscopic picture of the tragedy of death, mutilation or displacement rather than through the panoramic sweep of the historical record, thereby producing a more human and immediate record of the event. In the memories of a survivor who witnessed her pregnant mother being slaughtered and her elder sister blinded by a Muslim mob, the violent attacks in Mianwali in 1947, mentioned as a mere footnote in official histories,[19] are personalized through haunting images imprinted on the then ten-year-old's memories (Veeranwali 2006). Unable to confront these gory images of violence seven decades after Partition, the child mother retreats into recalling the challenge of dripping milk into the newborn orphan's mouth and recycling the bandage of her other four-year-old brother, who was hit on the skull. Another survivor personalizes the trauma of displacement through the recovery of her most prized possession, her personal diary, by the family when it returned to the family home in Model Town to recover possessions (Hoon 2013). A third recalls making the difficult choice of having to leave behind the treasured hand lotion gifted by a brother to underline the importance of the banal and catastrophic in the process of individual recall.

Memory has a distinct advantage over history in its ability to activate the corporeal-affective impressions of events and the images that surround them (Leys 2011). Memory has been explained as an affection-impression on the mind of the subject experiencing an event that is represented through an image. Since affect is "pre-personal," "a nonconscious experience of intensity," it is "a moment of unformed and unstructured potential and can be captured only through memory (Shouse 2005)." Remembering the violence of Partition evokes a shudder of fear, the heat of anger or the melancholy of loss. The very word *Partition*, the name of a city or a date can serve as a cue for the recall of emotional memories. A survivor who was seven years old at the time of Partition trembles at the memory of the train from Pakistan stopping in the middle of nowhere, of strangers banging loudly on the door, of her mother violently shaking from head to toe and of her father being chased by a Muslim mob when the train stopped at Bhatinda station and he ventured out to fill a pot of water (Deshi 2005). A 75-year-old confesses that the memory of those days sends shivers down her spine (Veeranwali 2006). A 79-year-old goes completely silent at the recall of witnessing, as a 14-year-old, his kinsmen's bodies floating in the well (Ram Prakash 2012). The traumatic effect of violence on both perpetrator and victim captured by Sa'adat Hasan Manto in his short stories underlines the corporeal dimensions of memory as the imprint of an event on the perceiver's mind manifests in a physiological recall even though the witness is unable to comprehend the experience in its entirety. Through mapping the corporeal-affective terrain of Partition as well as that of the nation, memory can foreground the relationship between affect and cognition in the interpretation of the events of Partition (Leys 2011).

Memory, at other times, contradicts, replaces or corrects history through its appropriation of an event in a parallel, alternative, disjunctive history of the nation. In Sikh representations of the violence of Partition, it is imagined as Ghallūghārā (the general massacre of Sikhs)[20] through which it is incorporated in a parallel history of violence (Chattha 2013). In being linked to the anti-Sikh violence of 1984, it disrupts the unified history of the Indian nation and reactivates the memories of the three-nation theory repressed in the construction of the binary narrative of Hindu Islamic civilizational difference. Ghallūghārā evokes an alternative memory of the Indian nation through the rememoration of Vaḍḍā Ghallūghārā, also known as the Sikh Holocaust of 1762, and situates it in the Afghan Sikh wars. Similarly, the incident of Thoa Khalsa in which 93 women died by jumping into a well to protect family honour invokes the history of Sikh *shaheedi* [martyrdom] against the backdrop of the centuries-old Sikh resistance to Muslim invaders and emperors rather than that of the Hindu Indian nation.

The Thoa Khalsa massacre also foregrounds the spatial and temporal erasure of microevents in the macronarrative of violence. The amnesia of Indian and Pakistani nationalist histories on the March 1947 riots, the worst carnage and destruction that swept through the villages of Multan, Rawalpindi, Campbellpur, Jhelum and Sargodha (Pandey 2001: 23), contradicts the retaliatory logic proffered of August 1947 violence in West Punjab through their predating the temporal sequence of violence against Hindus and Sikhs.

> I was doing my matriculation in Rawalpindi at that time. I was going to take the exams. We had a two-day holiday for Holi. The riot took place during that time. At the time of the riot, I was sitting in the RSS branch. Our instructor came; he said that a riot had taken place near Raja Bazaar in Singh Sabha and ordered us to go home after giving us tea and breakfast. Our home was barely half a kilometre from there. So, we left for home. It was about half past eleven. When we arrived there at noon, I told my father, a teacher and a widower, that there was a riot in Raja Bazaar. There were almost twenty houses of Sikhs in that colony. We were attacked on the same day at around half past four in the evening. In that attack, one or two of our elders fought against the rioters, in which they got killed. After that – at around half past six – those people went away.
>
> (Baldev Singh 2017)

Other than direct victims and witnesses of violence who broke their silence prompted by Butalia, the violence of March is commemorated through a maintenance of silence by others or mentioned as a footnote in memories of disturbances in urban neighbourhoods. Ram Prakash, 79, recollected accompanying his father and elder brother to visit their mother's village, Leiah, on hearing about the outbreak of riots, peering into a well and letting the silence narrate the story of his maternal clan being butchered. However, his memory does not make a connection between the two events in his recollections of the curfew in Lyallpur when he was packed off from his school and brought home early.

In another border village, Baltibazar, Kargil, Wafa's memory fills in missing gaps in the authoritative account of the permanent closure of the border on the West through recounting the tragic fate of his divided family:

> Till 1965, despite Partition, people used to cross the border illegally. No restrictions were imposed. Total restrictions were imposed between India and Pakistan after the war of 1965. After that, the movement of people across the border was severely restricted.
>
> (Wafa 2017)

His personal narrative of his family that hailed from Paarik (which formed a part of Kharmang now in Pakistan Occupied Kashmir) but had migrated to Baltibazar for work provides an unexpected glimpse into the macronarrative of the closure of an ancient trade route between India and Central Asia, namely the Kargil-Skardoo route,

> We used to go to Pakistan and they used to visit us. Goods were freely exchanged between us. You must have heard about the Kargil-Skardoo route. This was one of the routes to Central Asia, from here to Srinagar, Skardoo, Zanskar, Leh. Business (barter system) was most common during those days along this route.
>
> There was not much development in the region like today and we had to travel from one place to another for work. Those were the days of scarcity. No democratic government existed like today. We were under the rule of kings (the Dogra Rulers); kings were oppressive, due to which, some people fled from the region.
>
> (Wafa 2017)

"At that time Kargil-Skardoo were together. Paarik, the place we belong to, is 80 km from here," he said, explaining how the borders of the new nations overwrote ancient political, ethnolinguistic spatialities (Wafa 2017),

> Kharmang and Kargil are part of the same area. They are not distinct areas. Kharmang comes under the province of Kargil. Till Khardung Paarik, it is Kargil Tehsil [district]. My state is Kargil according to official records (Bashir Ahmad Wafa-Kargil), and Paarik is my village name, though now it is in Pakistan.

Some places from Paarik to Khardung still fall under Tehsil Kargil. Up to 80 kms from here, the area falls under Kargil Tehsil at present. Till today, our language, culture and pronunciation bear some similarity to that of Khardung.

(Wafa 2017)

The unknown stories of border villages like Skadu and Shilikchey caught in the successive attacks by the Pakistani and Indian armies, reconstructed through the postmemory of a seven-year-old schoolgirl, introduce a note of disjuncture in the macronarrative of the Partition-in-the-West dominated by the Punjab model,

I remember only a few things. We were in school. Then all of a sudden, jets began to fly over the sky. Till then we had never seen any airplanes. Now I understand these were fighter jets as they bombarded many places. We were here in this place (Skadu), but then all the people of this place fled to Shilikchey (a village 5 kms far from here). As Shilikchey is closer to the mountains, it had a number of mountain caves. We used to hide in the caves during the day and take shelter in the houses of those villagers at night. We did this to avoid getting bombarded as the jets came into action during the day. I remember cattle and other animals died after being hit by bombs; a madwoman, who was among us, was also killed after getting hit by a bomb.

(Begum 2017)

Despite her sharp recall of her own experience of fleeing military attacks, the child witness's postmemory relies on the accounts of others ("we heard from people") to hazard a political explanation of her harrowing experience.

During this period, one day the Indian forces invaded the town, and the Pakistani forces (Gilgit Forces) withdrew from Kargil. They went to Pakistan through Shilikchey, where we were hiding during the war, and we saw Pakistani forces retreating in lines.

At that time, many Sikh families used to live in Kargil. They were wealthy compared to other Kargilis; they owned all the big shops. When Pakistani forces came to Kargil, all the Sikhs fled as they thought the Pakistanis would kill them. Now only a few Sikh families live here.

(Begum 2017)

On the eastern border, another Muslim League–fuelled massacre in Noakhali in October 1946 went unreported for five days and has gained prominence in histories of Independence as a reminder of Gandhi's preferred site for testing his haloed ethic of non-violence and aesthetic of peace. In order to capture the microdetails of those affected by the riots, memories of refugees fleeing the Noakhali violence serve as a microhistory of the region,

I don't remember the details. All I can recall is that the riots took place a year or two [October 30, 1946] before Gandhi (Mahatma Gandhi) died. Gandhi had visited our place during the riots [October 10 to November 6, 1946]. I must have been 14 or 15 years old when the riots began. During the riots, Muslims would not kill grown up females. They would "take" our girls away with them professing that they would "marry" them and would murder the male members of the family mercilessly. Riots had begun all over the place. My sister was married in the neighbouring Korpara village in the Noakhali district closeby. The riots first took place there and then fanned in all directions. . . . We could see smoke rising in a circle a long way off from our house – meaning they had set the houses on fire. But exactly at 12 noon the Military arrived and seeing the Military, the Muslims fled. In between, they couldn't do anything in the Laxmipur town.

(De & Gera Roy in Driesen et al. 2013)

A similar close focus of violence postdating events of 1947 is visible in Amitav Ghosh's non-fiction and fiction that commemorates the riots of 1965, which are marginalized in official histories of Independence because of his drawing on personal and family memories.

Memory makes a major departure from history in its emphasis on the everyday, the ordinary, the banal, even in the recall of cataclysmic events. Irrespective of whether they witnessed violence directly or not, survivors dwelt on the everyday, the ordinary, such as details of the items carried along and the food given to refugees, even as they continued to narrate the most traumatic events.

My mother was cooking dinner. The sun had almost set when one of my brothers came running to our house. He said that the rioters were heading towards their neighbouring village Hasilpur and advised them to abandon everything immediately. We had to flee the house without taking any of our belongings along. I still remember we didn't even turn down the burning stove.

(Harbans Singh 2017)

Through recalling the social and moral community that existed prior to Partition and the everyday interactions of ordinary people, it deviates from the teleological movement or civilizational difference traced by official histories in documenting the events of 1947. Survivors from Punjab did not recall instances of enmity between Hindus and Muslims at the village or everyday level despite Hindus being a minority. A female survivor from Dera Ismail Khan, then 14 years old, recalled having several Muslim friends whose homes she visited and going to both the mandir [Hindu temple] and the gurdwara [Sikh temple] in the Muslim-dominated village where they lived "liked brothers" even though they were not permitted to eat in Muslim homes and were frequently attacked by wazirs (Shanti 2011). Similarly, the male survivor from Jamalpur corroborated the *aman chain* [peace] that prevailed before the Partition riots during which he witnessed the same Muslims brandishing swords and throwing boiling oil and hot chillies on Hindus and the *maarkaat* [slaughter] that followed. He also recalled visiting the temple in the village (Arora 2011). Veteran socialist, painter-artist and sculptor Rana Muhammad Azhar Khan confirmed Hindu-Muslim amity in the village of Hariana in Hoshiarpur that not only boasted of a Hindu-Muslim school but also the celebration of festivals by all communities, the help rendered by Hindus and Sikhs to Muslims and management of a Sufi shrine by a Sikh after Partition (Ahmed 2011). Not only the growing friction between Hindus and Muslims but also the division of Muslim families through the continually changing boundaries was the price to be paid for Partition,

> My grandparents' business was established here [Baltibazar], so we moved here. My mother was initially married to my uncle. When he died, the goods of the shop were abandoned. So, my father took over the responsibility of running the shop. My mother was widowed at that time. So, my father married her. Now, we are five siblings. We are three brothers and two sisters.
>
> The consequences of Partition were grim. Half of us got separated. My father was left alone here. My father's four brothers and two sisters remained there.
>
> (Wafa 2017)

Conclusion

Memory's function, according to some, is to deflate history's pretensions to be complete through underlining the partial nature of truth. Multiple by nature, memory, as opposed to history, juxtaposes multiple perspectives of a single event to reveal truth to be contingent, partial and subjective. The definitive nationalist narrative of Independence temporally structured to lead towards national formation suppresses multiple memories of the events of 1947. In view of the absence of written documentation of facts, which is seen as equivalent to their absence in modern historiography, memory's challenge lies in establishing the veracity of facts of that have been documented either in memory or orally. Alternatively, the corporeal presence of witnesses or victims of those events itself authenticates the occurrence of the fact irrespective of the accuracy of their memories. As in the case of the victims of the Holocaust, the very presence of survivors is a testimony to the violence of Partition regardless of the reliability of their accounts (Felman and Dori Laub 1991). Finally, the repetition of similar facts or details by different subjects is equally useful in verifying the authenticity of the information.

Notes

1 Noting that memory has become a key word in contemporary discourse, Kervin Lee Klein traces back the history of the term to argue that the use of the term *memory* may be found only between 1624 and 1730 if one leaves out references to its cognates, such as commemoration, memorial and memento. He avers that it was marginalized until Hugo van Hofmannstahl introduced it in 1902 and Maurice Halbwachs defined it in 1925 and that its revival began only in the 1980s (2000). Olick, Vinitizky-Seroussi and

Levy, however, argue that Halbwachs's ideas did not emerge in a vacuum and unfold the ancient history of memory to contend that while " 'memory studies' may be a 'new formation,' 'collective memory' and interest in it is not" (2011: 29).

2 Klein maintains that the conventional positioning of history and memory as antithetical has been altered in contemporary memory discourses as reflected in the pairing of history and memory in current usage and in the employment of the terms collective memory, public memory, or even memory, as synonyms of history "to soften our prose, or to humanize it, and to make it more accessible" (2000: 29). Disputing the posing of history and memory as opposites, he argues that continuity between history and memory has long existed.

3 Other scholars concur with him on the emergence of memory as a key term in the 1980s (Klein 2000; Olick and Robbins 1998).

4 Klein maintains that our use of memory as a "supplement" or "replacement" reflects "both an increasing discontent with historical discourse and a desire to draw upon some of the oldest patterns of linguistic practice" and attributes its return to its figuring as "a therapeutic alternative to historical discourse" (2000: 145).

5 This forced memorization or instructed memory is enlisted in the service of the remembrance of the attainment of Independence, which constitutes the founding event of the Indian nation. The abuse of memory occurs through the nation's forgetting of Partition through its manipulation of memory.

6 Alessandro Portelli's distinction between oral sources and oral history is important in understanding the shift. He points out that oral sources that are often used "as a secondary tool in the historian's panoply" serve in oral history "as the axis of another type of historical work in which questions of memory, narrative, subjectivity, dialogue shape the historian's very agenda" (2005).

7 Brothman "proposes that the construal of records as cognitive memory artifacts, rather than merely as legal, evidence-bearing artifacts, opens up a potentially endless field of possibilities for institutional and professional growth that only a failure of imagination can limit" (2000: 52).

8 More recently, David Gilmartin has updated Partition historiography by arguing that the explanations of Partition have remained a pivotal issue in political conflicts in the present on the Indian subcontinent as well as in the world. He isolates two major strands in Partition historiography, namely the difference between Hinduism and Islam, as a civilizational difference and the making of a modern, secular nation that was predicated on an essentialist construction of religion through colonial forms of knowledge (2015). Gilmartin argues that these two strands in Partition historiography are mirrored in both Hindu rightist movements in India and in the rise of Islamophobia across the world.

9 This view is summed up in H. S. Suhrawardy's contention that "bloodshed and disorder are not necessarily evil in themselves, if resorted to for a noble cause" (Suhrawardy, quoted in Dalrymple 2015). This corresponds with Portelli's view that "each birth of a nation, then, is not only the creation of a new order, but also the trauma of a break and violation of an older one" and that memory sets out to "exorcise the conflict" (2014: 45).

10 Portelli points out "the violence, the war, the contradictions out of which nations are born, are buried in the 'cellar' of oblivion, but return to haunt us as ghosts and nightmares" (2014: 45).

11 Portelli observes that there is a conflict between the pacifying and satisfactory public narrative and suppressed troubling and problematic memories in relation to resistance in Italy, a conflict that hinges on the meaning of the birth and rebirth of the nation (2014: 45).

12 Bates points out that one explanation for "the chaotic manner in which the two independent nations came into being" is "the hurried nature of the British withdrawal"

(2011: npg). He believes that the announcement was made after the Labour Party's victory in the British general election of July 1945 with the realization that the British state, devastated by war, "could not afford to hold on to its over-extended empire" (Bates 2011: npg). Yasmin Khan in "The Great Partition," maintains that Partition "stands testament to the follies of empire, which ruptures community evolution, distorts historical trajectories and forces violent state formation from societies that would otherwise have taken different – and unknowable – paths" (Khan 2007: 210). British historian Patrick French, in "Liberty or Death," attributes the Partition to a clash of personalities among the politicians of the period, particularly between Muhammad Ali Jinnah, the leader of the Muslim League, and Mohandas Gandhi and Jawaharlal Nehru, the two most prominent leaders of the Hindu-dominated Congress Party (French 1997). This view appears to be shared by Ayesha Jalal (1994). Ishtiaq Ahmed argues that the Partition of 1947 epitomizes the politics of identity in its most negative form (2002: 9). In examining the violence of Partition as a form of genocide, Paul Brass argues that although Partition violence was not state directed, it was carefully planned and organized and maintains that since it was mutual, the term "retributive genocide" may be more apt in defining it (2003: 71–72). He makes the important point that "in the last days of the British Raj, it was not only the case that violence occurred as a consequence of Partition, but *violence was a principal mechanism for creating the conditions for Partition*" (2003: 76). According to Ilyas Chattha, "Partition violence had clear class and gender dimensions. Politically astute members of the upper-middle class Hindus and Sikhs had started to migrate months and weeks before the actual Partition took place" (Chattha, quoted in Noorani 2012: npg).

13 Arguing that the meaning of Risorgimento cannot be grasped unless one understands where the revival of its memory hurts, Portelli opines that the hurt is visible in "memory that is passed on in families, in personal and private narrative – in other words, in oral history" (2014: 44). According to him, "in these memories and narratives, the rebirth of our nation sounds much more problematic and less respectable than it appears in official celebrations, and even than what the narrators themselves are aware of" (2014: 44).

14 Government servants were given the option to choose their place of work as part of the rehabilitation programme of the government of India (Rai 1965).

15 Lyallpur was renamed Faisalabad after Partition. But I have retained the pre-Partition name throughout the book because survivors know it only by its old name.

16 According to Pandey, Tara Singh and other Akali leaders had come out in support of Congress's plan to divide Punjab before early April 1947 (2001: 32). Prakash's memory of Tara Singh's visit to Lyallpur in April 1947 and his protest against the plan, followed by the lathi-charge, contradicts the historical account.

17 This was the date on which the Mountbatten plan for Partition was declared.

18 Deshi corroborated Prakash's memories of the curfew through recollecting her parents being beside themselves with anxiety until her five-year-old brother safely returned home, escorted by a Muslim rickshawwalla (2005).

19 Pandey mentions that the Muslim League's renewed demand for Partition engulfed Hindu and Sikh minorities in the wave of the March 1947 violence that swept through the Rawalpindi and Multan divisions (2001: 23).

20 "Ghalughara" refers to: "holocaust, massacre, great destruction, deluge, genocide, slaughter, (historically) the great loss of life suffered by Sikhs at the hands of their rulers, particularly on 1 May 1746 and 5 February 1762" (Singh and Gill 1994: 293).

3   Intangible violence

Despite violence being the object of urgent general concern and the proliferation of literature on different forms of violence that is emerging from multiple disciplines and perspectives, the systematic understanding of violence as a broad genus has gravely suffered because of the disjointed and narrowly focused approach of scholarship. Johan Galtung extends the narrow concept of violence as somatic incapacitation through his maintaining that "violence is present when human beings are being influenced so that their actual somatic and mental realizations are below their potential realizations" (1969: 168). In defining violence, he enumerates six different dimensions of violence, the *physical* and *psychological*, *negative* and *positive* approaches to influence, the presence of an *object that is hurt* and a *subject who acts*, *intended* or *unintended* and *manifest* and *latent* (1969: 169–72).[1] Additionally, Galtung identifies three types of violence – direct, structural and cultural – and argues that direct[2] violence is related to both structural[3] and cultural[4] violence (1990). Nancy Scheper-Hughes and Philippe Bourgois, in their Introduction to *Making Sense of Violence*, concur that "violence can never be understood solely in terms of its physicality – force, assault, or the infliction of pain – alone" (2004: 1). "Violence," according to them, "also includes assaults on the personhood, dignity, sense of worth or value of the victim" (2004: 1). The dichotomy between the physical and psychological, social and material; the weight placed on physical vs verbal and written actions; the role of force vs victim complicity; and the emphasis on interpersonal vs. corporate agents and victims, as Mary Jackman argues, has clouded the analysis of violence (2002: 387). Jackman dispels the notion that all forms of violence are driven by malicious intent and are socially repudiated and that diverse motives drive violent actions. Instead of viewing different forms of violence in isolation, Jackman uses the term "a family of violence" to propose a generic definition of violence, freed of ad hoc restrictions, that encompasses the full population of violent social actions (2002: 387).

The unprecedented ethnic violence witnessed in the aftermath of the Partition of India in 1947 has made Partition synonymous with violence. Oral histories of the violence experienced by victims, witnesses and, in some cases, perpetrators of violence have brought to light the unspeakable nature of the violence repressed or put under erasure for nearly half a century. The larger body of this literature has understandably engaged with the traumatic memories of direct, manifest, tangible physical violence. Even though the imbrication of the physical, material, social and psychological forms of trauma is implicit in the analysis of Partition violence, the "social and cultural dimensions of violence" that give "violence its power and meaning" have not been specifically addressed in academic literature except in a few studies (Das 1990; Talbot 1995; Kakar 1996).

Building on the literature on violence that has revealed that the physical dimensions of violence cannot ever be isolated from the social, structural and psychological, this chapter will isolate the imbrication of direct with structural and cultural forms of violence in the traumatic experience of survivors of Partition to bring to light its intangible violence. Intangible violence in the context of Partition may be defined as the breakdown of the known and the normal that followed from the loss of life, property, relationships and home and displacement. Displacement may be defined as a generalized feeling of unhomeliness caused through being uprooted in an unfamiliar region. At a specific level, it is translated as the loss of privilege and status, language and culture and of a familiar world; relegation to an outsider status; and the pressure to assimilate into the host culture. Through juxtaposing John Galtung's category of structural violence, Giorgio Agamben's notion of the refugee as *homo sacer* (1998) and Marcell Mauss's definition of the gift (1950) against the Hindu idea of *dāna* or religious giving and the demotic Punjabi categories of *biraderi* and *vartan bhanji*, it will explore the discursive, symbolic and structural violence in the inscription of Partition survivors as hapless, abject victims by the Indian state and old residents.

Partition 1947

The larger body of Partition literature has been concerned with personal, visible, physical violence, or any somatic injury, including death, maiming and rape, "which reduces somatic capability (below what is potentially possible)" (Galtung 1969: 169). In contrast to these studies that focus on the violence that works on the body, a considerable amount of Partition literature draws on trauma theory to minutely engage with psychological violence that works on the soul through focusing on the traumatic effects of physical violence on the psyche of victims. Another strand in Partition studies investigates its structural violence in order to explain the direct "pathological" violence of Partition. Few, however, have explored the close interdependence of the direct, structural and cultural dimensions of Partition violence. Galtung distinguishes between direct violence that demonstrates a subject-object relation and that is manifest, observable and can be verbally expressed and structural violence. He also makes a distinction between manifest and latent violence or structural violence, which is not there but can easily come about (Galtung 1969: 172). As opposed to those who were somatically incapacitated by violence, the violence that did not have a direct object or an agent affected even those who were not subjected to direct violence except vicariously as witnesses, through reported violence, or through the threat of physical or mental violence. Similarly, those who were prevented from realizing their potentialities not only because of somatic incapacity by the acts of killing, maiming, rape and imprisonment but also because of the structural violence of the division and displacement could also be considered victims of violence. Those who escaped the material violence of Partition were nonetheless seared by the indirect effects of direct violence that shook the very foundations of the world they had taken for granted. Finally, the cultural violence of being treated as others in their new homes engulfed all displaced persons irrespective of the type of violence they had experienced.

Galtung argues that "violence is present when human beings are being influenced so that their actual somatic and mental realizations are below their potential realizations" (1969: 168). He explains that, in addition to direct violence in situations like war in which "killing or hurting a person" certainly puts the person's " 'actual somatic realization' below his 'potential somatic realization'" (1969: 169), there is also "indirect violence in so far as insight and resources are channelled away from constructive efforts to bring the actual closer to the potential" (1969: 169). In addition to those who were victims of the direct violence of killings, maimings and rape, whose somatic and mental realizations were directly affected, the larger majority of Partition survivors were engulfed by the indirect violence of displacement through their loss of livelihood and employment, wealth and status and the known, familiar world. Since "the insight and resources" of Partition survivors were directed at ensuring bare survival for several years following the Partition, the potential realizations of an entire generation were impeded because of the inability of individuals or families to make constructive efforts to bring the actual closer to the potential. Notwithstanding the elaborate rehabilitation programmes devised by the newly formed Indian state to ameliorate the impact of violence and displacement, the potential realizations of an entire generation were aborted or impeded for various reasons. Since *potential realization* is an amorphous term as one moves away from somatic violence to its mental aspects, the ways in which potential realizations were affected are not directly visible.

Lala Dhani Ram, aged 57 in 1947, a rags-to-riches entrepreneur who had acquired diverse business interests in chemicals, branded clarified butter and food processing in Lyallpur aspired to join the ranks of the handful of lakhpatis [whose assets were worth Rs 100000] in the new colonial city (Ram Prakash 2005).[5] His obdurate belief that Lyallpur would form part of India with the Chenab River serving as the boundary line explained his refusal to transfer his moveable and immoveable assets or leave the city. He was finally forced to do so on September 20, 1947, when the *dahshat mardhar* [mayhem and riots] started as he was half a kilometre away from a Peace Committee Meeting in front of the Clock Tower and the Balouch Regiment brutally killed Hindus camped in tents at Khalsa College and DAV school. Arriving in Meerut on October 17, 1947, on foot, nursing the wounded and the ill along the route through his elementary knowledge of medicine, he joined his wife, four daughters and two sons, whom he had agreed to send away to spend their school vacation with his 26-year-old civil servant son then posted in Meerut. He gratefully accepted his firstborn's shelter and hospitality for a few months until he identified an evacuee property in Sabzi Mandi,[6] Delhi, that the displaced family could move into and begin life again. But life had other plans for him. His depressive wife, still reeling under the trauma of having lost everything, accidentally fell to her death from the rooftop. On losing his wife, in addition to his property and livelihood, a devastated Dhani Ram grudgingly accepted his firstborn's generous offer to let the family move in with the son in his newly allotted government accommodation in Lucknow – where he had recently been transferred – and restart his business. Nearly sixty, Dhani Ram had neither the capital nor the energy to establish his pre-displacement business again. The struggle that he had begun on arriving as a teenager in Lyallpur began once again, permanently scarring his marriageable daughter, two teenage sons and three young daughters (Ram Prakash 2005). Dhani Ram's life story is typical of many established entrepreneurs whose inability to provide more than bare necessities to their families for several years after arrival brought their family members' "actual somatic realization" below their "potential somatic realization."

> In Ranchi when I was very young, there used to be one refugee who used to fill his cane basket with fried *papad* and sell it in the neighbourhood called Hindpiri. We came to know that these were people from well-to-do families. I remember a very tall and well-built man with the proportions of a Greek God, clad in a simple kurta pyjama and sweating profusely, who used to hawk cucumber from door to door. When my mother enquired about his whereabouts, he said that he was from Lyallpur a small village in West Punjab. All that he had was left behind and now he was desperately trying to settle his family. Since he had very little money, he could only sell cucumber.
>
> (Sharma 2017)

Unlike victims of direct violence whose scars were clearly visible, individuals or families who did not suffer personal somatic violence that affected their anatomy[7] or physiology[8] and were not destituted because of receiving filial support, would not have been technically considered victims or refugees. To give the state its due, as the various rehabilitation reports prepared in the years immediately after Partition reveal,[9] various forms of redress beyond bare subsistence were indeed provided to displaced persons so as to enable them to put their lives together. However, the implementation gap between the rehabilitation schemes launched by the newly formed state to compensate refugees for the losses they had incurred and the actual receipt of benefits produced "a lost generation" bereaved of any possibilities for potential somatic realization. The indirect violence faced by this generation is comprehensible only within the intimate brotherhoods of Partitioned families reflected in whispered expressions of remorse and commiseration by family members and close friends. Unlike young, educated adult survivors who were in a position to seek employment opportunities on the basis of their educational degrees or skills, uneducated ones whose skills or entrepreneurial capital equipped them to venture into new enterprises or child survivors who came of age when families had partially succeeded in re-establishing themselves, "the hinge generation" of teenage survivors found their potential realization reduced or aborted because of their families' combined efforts being single-mindedly directed at acquiring bare necessities in the first few years of their arrival.

Several educated adult survivors expressed their relief at being provided the opportunity to complete their education, which was aborted because of the shutting down of educational institutions following the outbreak of violence, through the remedial measures initiated by the state and their partial success in finding employment (Hoon 2013), albeit much below their potential somatic realization.[10] However, the silence of "the in-between lost generation" deprived of opportunities for potential realization has prevented the circulation of their narratives since the object of structural violence, "who perceives the violence, usually, and may complain" may be "persuaded not to perceive this at all" (Galtung 1969: 173) unlike that of personal violence. The structural violence that results in inequalities in potential realizations that are brought through a difference in race, gender, class, ethnicity, profession and caste in times of peace was ushered in through the accident of displacement in the aftermath of Partition. The violence of the denial of opportunities for self-development available to the middle class largely through education to teenage schoolboys from displaced families, who were prematurely thrust into the work force or expected to contribute their labour to family businesses (Ram Prakash 2005; Raj 2011; Rajpal 2006),[11] is not visible outside the sphere of affected families since the objects of this form of violence either did not perceive or did not have the privilege to complain about it.

I am not a refugee

Giorgio Agamben's view of the refugee as homo sacer [sacred person], a figure in ancient Roman law whom anyone could kill without committing murder in the legal sense and (inclusion) exclusion of bare life within the social form of life (bio) has been privileged in the Euro-western discourse on refugees. But it must be applied with qualification in the case of the exchange of populations in the aftermath of Partition since those displaced by Partition were deemed citizens of India, albeit displaced.[12] However, the cross-border migrant, despite being granted legal political citizenship of the new nation, was the victim of the epistemic violence of othering. As a person without a home, metaphorically translated as *bastuhara* [who has lost the foundation of his house] in Bengali or as *khanabadosh* [house on shoulder] in Punjabi, he was viewed with suspicion as the alien self, the kin stranger, the related other whose body, language, attire and ways of living marked him as the other. The intangible violence suffered by Partition survivors lies in the discursive and epistemic violence of the modern term *refugee*, translated as *sharanarthi* in Hindi, loosely used by the state and old residents to describe them.

Agamben shows that ancient Greeks lacked a word that could express what we mean by *life* and that they used two terms, "zoē, which expressed the simple fact of living common to all living beings (animals, men, or gods), and bios, which indicated the form or way of living proper to an individual or a group" (1998: 1). He argues that while simple natural life was excluded from the polis in the strict sense in the classical world societies and remains confined – as merely reproductive life – the entry of zoē in the sphere of the polis or the politicization of the zoē constitutes the decisive event of modernity. Drawing on Foucault's notion of biopolitics, he views the control of natural life as implicit in sovereignty and goes as far as to say that the "production of a biopolitical body is the original activity of sovereign power" (1998: 11). Sovereign power establishes itself through the production of a political system, he argues, based on the exclusion of bare life. This is achieved through the enactment of the state of exception in which law is suspended and denied to the human being. Since "[t]he rule, suspending itself, gives rise to the exception" and "maintaining itself in relation to the exception, first constitutes itself as a rule (1998: 18)," it leads to an (inclusive) exclusion of bare life through which the Western state has been constituted. According to Agamben, the definition of human rights in the Declaration of Human Rights is incompatible with being human, or the merely alive, since the synonymy of the human with the citizen in the nation-state presupposes that rights are contingent on becoming a citizen. The refugee is not an outsider but, like the homo sacer, is both included and excluded from the space of the nation. Banned from the domain of political being, the refugee as homo sacer is reduced by the sovereign to life defined only in terms of zoē (1998: 183) and recognized only as a biological being.

Agamben's view on refugees and politics has been critiqued for its universalizing and generalizing overtones and for its application in different geographical, political and societal contexts. Although the notion of homo sacer may be borrowed to define the experience of some Partition refugees,[13] traditional humanitarian discourses that have been formulated in relation to the experiences of detention camps and asylum seekers in the West might fail to elucidate the specific abjection of the Partition refugee as homo sacer. To begin with, those displaced by Partition were not stateless persons but automatically became citizens of the nation state on crossing the border. The Partition refugee camps did not offer a state of exception nor were refugees exempted from the operation of the sovereign state in zones of exemption. As politicized beings protected and represented by the state, refugees of Partition were not the legal subjects of exclusion and, therefore, do not qualify as homo sacer in its meaning as bare or depoliticized life.[14]

The opposition between the refugee as the detritus and interiorized humanity in Agamben, the detritus who is integral to the sovereign law that encompasses the interiorized humanity, is visible in the Indian state's treatment of Partition refugees as a specific kind of citizen and other citizens. Like the homo sacer who could not live in the city of the citizens in Roman times, the refugee was allotted land in refugee colonies constructed on the outskirts of cities so that these pockmarks on ancient cities' maps were not visible to the sight of the city-dweller. Liisa Malkki points out that "it was toward the end of World War II that the refugee camp became emplaced as a standardized, generalizable technology of power (40) in the management of mass displacement" (1995: 198). Like the camps she speaks about, the refugee camp in which Partition refugees were housed "was a vital device of power" (1995: 198). But the experience of refugees of Partition "complicates post-war conceptions of the 'stateless refugee', 'religious homeland', and the 'right of return'" (Naqvi 2012: 2) since they received fewer apparent legal obstacles to citizenship than their counterparts in Europe. However, Malkki's point about how the spatial concentration of people not only allowed their physical control but also their discursive representation is relevant to the circulation of stereotypes of refugees. Although the cross-border arrival was treated as a living being and provided bare sustenance through relief measures, he or she had far fewer rights than the citizens of the new nation-state that cancelled out the principle of the equality of all human beings as sentient beings.[15]

The refugee was also perceived as a margizen, whose life was qualitatively distinct from that of the citizen as a person who has no access to the collective goods and services of our society (security, work, social interactions and so on). The ambiguity that Agamben sees as being contained in this definition in the status of the refugee explains new arrivals' resistance to the label *refugee*. Although the gradual change of the terminology to "displaced person" and the rehabilitation efforts made by the state to ensure that the new arrival was also entitled to social forms of life beyond bare life completed the journey of the cross-border arrival from refugee to citizen, the social and cultural forms of violence persisted among old residents in their denial of rights beyond bare life to the new arrival as did extension of hostility when he or she attempted potential realizations. Even though the new arrival was not excluded from the space of the nation and was deemed worthy of compassion, it was done in the spirit of charity, and the expectation of anything more than bare life on his or her part was considered impudent.

In his examination of the politics of encampment in relation to the positioning of asylum seekers as a group subjected to the biopolitical logic of "compassionate repression," Jonathan Darling considers the asylum seeker as an exemplar of homo sacer (2009). Darling argues that stripping asylum seekers of the right of all housing, social and financial support "is predicated upon an Agambenian sovereign act of abandonment which places individuals outside the law" (2009: 652). He shows that being placed out of the orbit of law is akin to being in a "position of bare life, of survival alone, with no responsibility or necessary demand being placed upon the sovereign to aid in that survival" (2009: 652). Such asylum seekers are placed, according to him, in a precarious position of "perpetual dependence" (Amnesty International 2006: 23) on friends or well-wishers because of this "deliberate policy of destitution" (2009: 649). Contending that asylum seekers are relegated to a position reliant solely upon the ethical sensibilities of others through such acts of sovereign abandonment, he proceeds to demonstrate how asylum seekers and local campaigners employ this position "to make ethical claims and demands upon the relational nature of the citizen as a figure of potential bare life" (2009: 649).

The positioning of Partition refugees as homo sacer is complicated by the absence of a sovereign act of abandonment, which places individuals outside the law. Rather than a deliberate policy of destitution, the inability of the newly formed nation-state to create an adequate infrastructure to prevent the refugees from falling into a state of destitution, coupled with the lack of humaneness in a depleted and inefficient bureaucracy struggling to distribute aid and relief to the displaced, positioned a large number of refugees in a precarious state of dependency on kin, friends and neighbours. Additionally, instead of providing humanitarian aid to cross-border arrivals who were citizens of the new nation as a right, the representatives of sovereign authority and private donors extended it as charity and a gift. This refuted Wright's observation that "those involved in the mammoth Hindu-Moslem exchange of population though they have suffered greatly [had] from their very beginning the security of citizenship, protection and encouragement of their respective co-national state in which they had found a haven a new life, not on sufferance, but as of right" (1974: 45). The refrain that runs through refugee narratives is the claim to the right to work and be provided suitable employment instead of compassionate repression in the relief camps through endowments of charity and gifts.

Unlike the homo sacer who may be killed but not offered as a sacrifice, the evocation of sacrifice in different and competing senses by both the post-colonial state and citizens-in-the-making in India and Pakistan articulates sacredness to the person of the refugee. Post-colonial histories of Independence invariably justify the violence accompanying Partition as a sacred bloodletting that articulates it to the conceptual and political predicament of modern nationalism, which, in Benedict Anderson's view, was encapsulated in the problem of sacrifice. Survivors, in contrast, invoked the metaphor for consenting to relinquish their self-interest for the greater common good when they staked a collective political claim for belonging and recognition. Joya Chatterjee's study of Bengali refugees' claim for greater rehabilitation on the basis of their sacrifice of their interests in consenting to cede their homelands is a case in point (2001). Challenging the Indian government's offer of meagre rehabilitation measures as a form of charity, they demonstrated that participation and political support for the nationalist project did not guarantee recognition and rights after Independence.

The irony of refuge

The idiom of hospitality and refuge within the discourse of Partition 1947 is underwritten by the rhetoric of compassion, philanthropy and accommodation of victims of violence and displacement. While the survivors' primary concern with life, safety and subsistence on arrival elicited from them ungrudging acknowledgement and gratitude for being provided refuge, complaints, particularly against family members or friends, were either never expressed or mentioned only obliquely. The condition of being beholden to a benefactor – kinsman, friend, local residents or even the state – bred forms of violence that are not visible, cannot be articulated and position individuals and groups in relations of power, domination and oppression. Relations of power, domination and control invariably breed responses of resentment and resistance. The ambivalent emotions – gratitude for refuge mixed with a sense of abjection as recipients of hospitality, obligatory submission to the counsel of the host tainted by resentment for being subjugated, marginalized or reduced to a subordinate position – felt by displaced persons, complicate the discourse of refuge and hospitality. Veena Das's metaphor "poisonous knowledge" succeeds in encapsulating the forms of indirect violence created through the irony of refuge that could not be articulated except in an idiom of gestures (2007: 54).

The irony of refuge has largely been examined, and rightly so, in the context of gendered violence by both strangers and trusted family members and friends on recipients of hospitality. The repression of gendered violence both by perpetrators and victims under the pretext of protecting women restricted its representation to fictional texts until a considerable number of women consented to share their stories with feminist oral historians after a passage of nearly fifty years. Out-numbering those who consented to voice their experience of domestic and public violence at the prompting of empathetic ethnographers, there would have been many whose silence still remains unbroken or is communicated solely through a language of gestures. Gratitude and indebtedness for those whose offer of refuge to them or their families rescued them from starvation and homelessness bound these women in a code of silence in which complaint could not be expressed verbally and, if expressed, would be deemed an act of ingratitude, shame or self-ishness. Similarly, the relation between direct, structural and domestic violence that has been emphasized by researchers was most visible in the family violence perpetrated largely on women by marginalized, excluded, dominated male refu-gees whose inability to vent their aggression against the structural violence of refugeehood manifested it in extreme forms of domestic violence.

Since the condition of refuge is shelter and subsistence, the object of refuge is not the target of direct violence that may be perceived and reported but of intan-gible violence that she or he is unable to perceive at all in view of the impossibil-ity of defining the meaning of shelter and subsistence. The homeless young man permitted to work and sleep outside the owner's (who was often a relative) shop in return for victuals fails to complain because he is unable to perceive its vio-lence until his recognition of the thresholds of bare necessity with return to better times (Bishen Lal 2017). Recipients of family or friends' largesse do not dare to question the hostess's logic in labelling the consumption of more than three *rotis* [bread] as a subhuman form of hunger because the starving can choose only between malnourishment and zero nourishment (Ram Prakash 2005). The victim fails to name the agent of the violence as a culprit because the agent, compelled to share limited resources with extended occupants of a house, was as financially incapacitated by the structural violence of Partition as the victim (Deshi 2005).

More important is the condition of obligation binding recipients of hospitality and refuge that perpetuates relations of power, domination and oppression. The provider of hospitality acquires the explicit right to control the dispensation or withdrawal of material well-being but also the implicit right to make decisions, both personal or professional, for the receiver and his or her family. In the major-ity of families who were provided shelter, even if only in the initial months of their arrival, the burden of obligation reversed roles between elder and younger members in terms of decision making in both domestic and work-related matters. It also imposed a relation of obligation on younger members, whose indebtedness and gratitude to the refuge provider impeded their potential realizations in terms of career or matrimonial choices. This form of violence in which the decisions and actions taken by the host or host families were not motivated by the intention to commit violence but reduced the guest to a position of lifelong servitude and submission could not be vocalized but indirectly conveyed through an idiom of gestures. The relation of obligation that compelled elderly females to offer domestic labour in return for succour provided to their families (Deshi 2005), young females to abandon their career or marital aspirations to serve as unpaid cooks and housekeepers and young males to serve as errand boys or handymen so that the chosen few in the family could single-mindedly devote themselves to their educational or career aspirations could only be articulated in the language of gestures (Deshi 2005). The consent obtained for these forms of domestic violence that were justified in the interest of keeping the family together or the necessary sacrifice to be made by the family as a whole to enable the brilliant, talented few to enable the family to recover its fortunes made the direct expression of complaints impossible (Deshi 2005). But they silently remained as a simmering undercurrent between the perpetrators and victims of indirect violence for generations.

Veena Das's explanation of the Punjabi kinship code that obliges brothers to welcome a married daughter or sister home on her periodic visits has familiarized scholars with the rupture in that norm through Partition violence when straitened family circumstances would often compel families to make a married daughter or sister feel unwelcome directly or indirectly. The notion of "poisonous knowledge" proposed by Veena Das in her analysis of the narrative of a woman named Asha, who attempted to re-create her relationships with her siblings "in the face of the poisonous knowledge that had seeped into these relationships" (2007: 64), serves as the most nuanced starting point for the collapse of normalcy in the wake of Partition that may be described as the intangible violence of Partition. Asha, who, despite having opted to live with her husband's family after being widowed at a very young age instead of returning to her natal home, made the then unthinkable decision of marrying an older family friend after Partition while continuing to retain strong emotional bonds with her late husband's family. Asha's decision to marry a senior family friend despite her not having considered remarriage before Partition was motivated by her desire to preserve this pre-displacement code in the face of altered familial circumstances. Although the narrative of Pujandi, a 34-year-old married woman forced to accept her brother's hospitality for three months after arrival, differs from Asha's in several respects, the poisonous knowledge that seeped into her relationships in the aftermath of Partition led to her sundering all relations with her natal family (Deshi 2005). As the eldest daughter based in an urban centre, Pujandi had hosted all her siblings for extended periods in her home prior to Partition in addition to extending other forms of help to her natal family with her supportive husband's assent. Fortunate to have a brother in government service on the other side of the border, she was left by her husband in the care of her brother when he returned to Quetta where he was last posted to bring back his transfer orders (Deshi 2005). After his initial extension of hospitality to her as a beloved married sister whose hospitality he had enjoyed several times, the code of hospitality was stretched in this case by the uncertainty of her husband's return and additional dependents, which permanently poisoned relations between the siblings.

Dāna, the poison of gift, biraderi and vartan bhanji

The rules of hospitality regulating the relations between the host and the refugee / displaced person / migrant engender a complex oscillation between hospitality and hostility, which are inherent in the discourse of hospitality and refuge within the framework of modern nation-states. Barbara Harrell-Bond, Eftihia Voutira and Mark Leopold use the Maussian notion of the gift to call attention to the difference between the rights and charity discourse in "Counting the Refugees: Gifts, Givers, Patrons and Clients" (1992).

> Although the right to life has been enshrined in the 1984 Universal Declaration of Human Rights, refugees are rarely portrayed as persons with rights. Moreover, rather than being organized as the agency responsible for upholding these rights, the work of humanitarian agencies in raising money for relief and distributing it to refugees is dominated by the norms of charity or gift-giving.
>
> (1992: 205)

Although the assistance of international humanitarian organizations was not sought in the rehabilitation of refugees in the bilateral efforts of India and Pakistan, the norms of charity or gift-giving regulated the provision of relief to persons displaced by Partition (1992). Jonathan Parry's definition of the pure and reciprocal gift in his essay "The Gift, the Indian Gift and the 'Indian Gift'" (1986), in addition to Joya Chatterji's distinction between rights and charity that explained the dichotomy between the state's and refugee's understanding of rehabilitation (2001), may be productively applied in comprehending the perception of relief by survivors of Partition as poison. The mismatch between the religious discourse of charity through which the giver provided relief and the notion of the gift through which the receiver accepted it poisoned the hospitality offered by the state, families, friends and hosts to displaced persons. While acknowledging the existence of the ideology of reciprocity in other forms of gift giving in Indian societies, Parry focuses on dāna to distinguish Indian gift giving from that in tribal societies examined by Malinowski (1920), Mauss (1950) and Levi-Strauss through emphasizing its non-reciprocal character (1969). The Hindu,[16] Buddhist or Jain concept of dāna or religious giving that means charity to an individual in distress or need makes giving a compulsory duty for the householder.[17] Charity, conceived as a non-reciprocal gift in Hinduism without expectation of anything in return from the receiver other than the promise of improving one's future life and afterlife, is generally directed at a person belonging to the priestly class or at a destitute. As Parry points out, the gift embodies the spirit of the donor and absolves the donor from sins by transferring them to the recipient, who serves as the carrier of the sins, which enables the donor to expiate for his sins. The strict stipulations imposed on the gift exchange with respect to the recipient, who should be a Brahmin [Hindu priestly class], a fakir [mendicant] or bhikhari [beggar], ensure that the unsuitability of the recipient can harm both the donor and the recipient and impede the donor's chances of attaining salvation.

The relief operations organized by the state with the assistance of private donors were framed within the Hindu concept of religious giving, or dāna, in which the receiver of charity was viewed as an object of compassion rather than of contempt. The unending flows of relief into refugee camps by Hindu philanthropists and individuals were motivated by the spirit of gift giving as embodied in the ideology of dāna. The term *refugee*, initially employed by the state to describe displaced persons, resonated with the vernacular equivalent *sharanarthi*, who is obliged to perpetually participate in the giver's karmic salvation as the receiver of alms. Additionally, the unequal power relations between the giver and receiver required the receiver to be in a subservient position and any attempt to transgress that order through potential realizations led to the withdrawal of both hospitality and compassion, inviting inexplicable hostility instead.

Rather than the obligations of host nations towards displaced persons or refugees enshrined in Human Rights discourses, the traditional practice of vartan bhanji that traditionally regulated relations between members of a biraderi might provide an insight into the dichotomy between the difference in the perception of the relief offered by the Indian nation-state, philanthropists and individual donors and the new arrivals. *Biraderi*, a term of Persian origin derived from *birader* [brother] that means brotherhood, is the defining institution of the kinship system of not only the Muslims but also the Hindus and Sikhs of West Punjab. As defined by Alavi, biraderi signifies a common descent group in its most basic meaning and is a patrilinear kinship system (1972). Although the descent group, the biraderi, in its general meaning, includes all those between whom links of common descent can be traced in the paternal line, regardless of the number of generations that have elapsed, the boundaries between biraderi are difficult to define on the basis of genealogies (Alavi 1972).

Observing the relationship made by historians between the state and kin or family, David Gilmartin examines the role of the biraderi and the nation-state and maintains that the form and size of the biraderi depends on social and political contexts (1994). In view of the reiteration of the "nation-as-family" metaphor in the definition of the nation as well as in the reception of the newcomers in nationalist rhetoric, the cross-border arrivals understandably assimilated this relation to familiar kinship terms and their conceptual associations. The rhetoric of the Hindi name for the nation, Bharat or Bharatvarsha, defined as the nation of the descendants of the mythical king Bharat, mobilized in the construction of a unified Indian nation was literally translated by them as the biraderi or brotherhood of the descent group that could trace its ancestry to the legendary ancestor. As opposed to the cross border migrant, who expected to be accommodated in the extended family or the national home as a member of the family or citizen of the nation in the spirit of biraderi and acted in tune with the obligations and duties that bind members of a biraderi, the hosts extended support to the new arrivals as enjoined on the householder in the Hindu, Jain and Buddhist religions in the spirit of karuna [religious compassion] and dāna [religious giving] for the destitute, needy, the seeker of alms and spiritual beings. It was enshrined in the intricate ritual gift economy of biraderi regulated by "bhaji" or "vartan bhanji" (Wakil 1970: 700),[18] which dovetailed with the nationalist deployment of the metaphor of the family to represent the nation.

Vartan bhanji is a unique Punjabi rural practice governing social, economic, and even political relations between members of a biraderi that has been carried over in urban intercommunity relations (Eglar 1960: 105). In Alain Lefebvre's Maussian interpretation, vartan bhanji [literally meaning giving sweets] consists of a ritual of prestations and counterprestations that defines the categories of various biraderi relatives and ensures the cohesion of the biraderi. It refers to the reciprocal exchange of gifts at life-cycle ceremonies, such as marriage, childbirth and deaths celebrated by all members of the family and to the reciprocal exchange of a whole range of services, favours and good deeds in everyday life. In the complex vartan bhanji gift system of reciprocal exchange, the recipient accepts help in the form of a gift with the rules underpinning the vartan bhanji system that require the recipient to return a gift of a higher denomination in exchange. The donor uses the ritual system to extend economic support to kin in distress by making a gift that cannot be reciprocated by the recipient in the current situation but may be accepted in the spirit of deferred exchange or immediate return of an obligation through a non-material gift.

Although they were initially reduced to accepting relief, or even charity, because of their destitution, Hindu and Sikh refugees, particularly affluent ones hailing from upper castes, accustomed to being givers of charity to priestly and deprived castes and classes in their pre-displaced homes, either declined it or perceived it as a poisoned gift and insisted on performing a service in return to deflect the effects of ritual giving. Both in private homes of their kin or friends or in shelters provided by the state, the refugees accepted shelter and succour in the spirit of complex vartan bhanji relations that entitled family members to turn to their affluent kin in times of financial distress. They accepted it in the spirit of prestation or a duty to do or not do something in fulfilment of an obligation, or as the performance of such a duty by the older residents towards members of the extended biraderi of the nation.

The notion of vartan bhanji connects recurring tropes in survivor narratives – stories of former wealth and status, refusal to beg, restoration to former social position following temporary hardship through kinship support networks – that have been examined in isolation. In accepting succour or relief from old residents, the newcomer invoked the vartan bhanji gift exchange practices that had regulated relations between landowners, tenants and landless labourers in the Punjabi village and different professional castes in urban centres through literally extending the biraderi included in vartan bhanji relations from kin, village and neighbourhood to the community of the nation. Through asserting their former wealth and status, the newcomers established themselves in a relationship of equality with their donors with the tacit understanding that the obligation would be returned with a gift of higher value upon improvement in their financial circumstances. Alternatively, their inability to return the gift made by the donor immediately made them prefer performance of hard labour to acceptance of the non-reciprocal gift. Finally, generous acknowledgement of financial and other forms of assistance received by affluent kin or friends warranted lifelong obligation for a gift that is beyond compensation.

The contradiction between the traditional practice of vartan bhanji and modern meritocracy and trade practices complicates the ethical question of the role of affective ties and informal social networks in vartan bhanji trade practices followed by biraderi networks in privileging kin, friends or inhabitants of their region in recruitment or business dealings and their perception by older residents and the modern state as unscrupulous and nepotist. Vartan bhanji practices continued well after Partition through the preferential employment of those belonging to the kin, social or professional biraderi in businesses and establishments and the deployment of ingenuous protectionist trade practices, such as purchasing from members of the biraderi to assist them in keeping their businesses afloat in a spirit of obligation to help the community turn financially self-sufficient. However, the arrival of the Hindu, Muslim, Jain or Sikh giver, who generously contributed to the relief efforts of the state in the paternalist spirit of dāna or charity in which the receiver is positioned as an object of pity, viewed him as a rival when the receiver challenged this relation through efforts at self-sufficiency or dared to rise above the pitiable condition.

Symbolic violence

Pierre Bourdieu's notion of symbolic violence is useful in understanding the forms of cultural violence (Galtung 1990: 291) that were used to justify the structural violence of the state. Bourdieu's term for the imposition on subordinated groups by the dominant class of an ideology, which legitimates and naturalizes the status quo, is symbolic violence or "the violence which is exercised upon a social agent with his or her complicity" (Bourdieu and Wacquant 2002: 167, italics in original). Symbolic violence is intimately related to symbolic capital and symbolic power. Symbolic power refers to tacit, almost unconscious modes of social domination that occur within social habits maintained by conscious subjects. Three concepts are crucial to understanding Bourdieu's ideas of distinction, namely capital, habitus and field. Bourdieu coined the notion of symbolic capital in his book *Distinction* (1984) to signify a form of cultural capital – non-financial social assets – that enables those who possess it to be able to determine what constitutes taste within society. He shows how the "social order is progressively inscribed in people's minds" through "cultural products" including systems of education, language, judgements, values, methods of classification and activities of everyday life (1986: 471), which leads to an unconscious acceptance of social differences and hierarchies, to "a sense of one's place" and to behaviours of self-exclusion (1986: 141). Habitus designates "a socially constituted system of dispositions" or "the way society becomes deposited in persons in the form of lasting dispositions, or trained capacities and structured propensities to think, feel and act in determinant ways, which then guide them" (Wacquant 2005: 316, cited in Navarro 2006: 16). Field denotes a network, structure or set of relationships and the various social and institutional arenas in which people express and reproduce their dispositions and where they compete for the distribution of different kinds of capital (Gaventa 2003: 6). Bourdieu delineates a social space that can be termed as a "field of social classes" (Bourdieu 1984: 345, 1991: 41). Since the habitus cannot be directly observed, it must be understood interpretatively through the various preferences and practices clustering in each sector of social space that orient the expenditure of economic and cultural capital in a manner that gives rise to the semantic coherence of a lifestyle. The important point that Bourdieu makes is that lifestyles are caught up in social struggles since lifestyles are not merely distinct from one another but also hierarchically arranged.

In addition to the violence in the demotion of the newcomer to the destitute recipient of dāna, the symbolic violence of the older residents inhered in their invocation of symbolic capital and distinction of taste in stigmatizing the newcomer's taste and lifestyle as those of a peasant, an ascription that was doubly violent in its being exercised by the social agent's gradual complicity with consequent dispossession from pre-displacement language, culture and habitus. The peasantization of the newcomer from across the border, which was mapped on the colonial construction of the Punjabi "villager" (Gilmartin 2004) and the literal translation of the bangal [East Bengali] as peasant, exhibits a collapse of class, caste and region in the deployment of taste as a marker in the construction of a hierarchical difference between the insider and the outsider (Ghosh 2013).[19] Not only does the heterogeneous class and caste composition of refugees from both sides of the border challenge this homogenized ascription but also the reason for their degradation to working class lifestyles due to denial of former livelihoods is ignored in the uniform designation of refugees as bearers of low cultures. Additionally, the pre-Partition competing claims of cities like Lahore and Dhaka to the status of the cultural centres of India were overlooked in the belittling of migrants from these and similar cultural hubs as lacking in symbolic, social and cultural capital. The rusticization of the refugee through the invocation of difference in their language and dialect perpetrated insidious forms of violence far more damaging because of the eventual complicity of the cross-border arrivals in their own inferioritization through acceptance of their allegedly uncouth status. The perception of the newcomer by the host as a poor country cousin, entitled to compassion, shelter and sustenance essential for the maintenance of bare life but to be simultaneously derided as a perennial object of amusement, constituted the intangible form of violence whose intergenerational transmission of trauma ensured the virtual extinction of pre-displacement cultures.

Survivors, particularly those who were children and young adults at the time of Partition, have shared their traumatic experiences of being ridiculed in public spaces for the difference in their speech, mannerisms, attire, food and ways of life and their voluntary assimilation into host cultures through their dissociating themselves with pre-displacement ethnolinguistic or ethnocultural lifestyles. The inferioritization of the refugee was predicated on the view of Punjabi language or Punjabi-laced Urdu as uncouth, rustic and loud by the Hindi Urdu elite of North Indian cities and of *bangal* as a rustic dialect of Bengali, which was internalized by the speakers of these languages. Due to the necessity of language assimilation, the colonial divide of Punjabi as the language of the home and Urdu of the public space in Punjab that continued for a generation tilted in favour of Hindi and English over the span of two generations with the irretrievable loss of Punjabi and its related dialects. More destructive was the assimilation of the stereotyped description of Punjabi by the Hindu Punjabi elite, whose intergenerational transmission of this denigration caused the glottophobia of Punjabi among upper and middle classes. Similarly, the disappearance of *bangal* among middle- and upper-class Bengali elite demonstrates the language loss caused by rusticization of certain languages and dialects that demoted them from the shared pre-displacement linguistic space to that of the rural and working-class non-elite.

The taste hierarchies of the Hindi Urdu elite through which the Punjabi newcomer was excluded from the cultural citizenship of the nation despite being bestowed with legal political citizenship were constructed through an amnesia towards the cultural capital attached to cities like Lahore and Multan dating back to the Mughal period and the predominance of Punjabi musical gharanas in the repertoire of Hindustani classical music. The peasantization of the newcomer was paralleled by the folklorization of Punjabi musical heritage through the symbolic alienation of the "classical" from Punjab's culture in both popular and scholarly discourse, as Radha Kapuria has convincingly demonstrated (2015: 78). Despite the Punjabi origins of renowned classical musicians, Punjab was resignified as the centre of a vibrant folk heritage to construct the myth of its rusticity and the rusticity of its people. Similarly, the position of Lahore as the hub of the theatre, dance, music and film industry, whose talent contributed to the production of post-independence Indian film, music, theatre and dance, was overlooked in the ascription of the Punjabi newcomer and Punjabi culture as rustic (Ahmed 2012). The alleged Punjabification of old cities like Delhi and Lucknow that was perceived as signalling the extinction of their elite Hindi Urdu cultures elided the contribution of the Punjabi Urdu elite to this pre-Partition heritage. The assimilation of the stereotype of Punjabi as an uncouth, peasant culture by the displaced themselves accounts for their distancing themselves from denigrated Punjabi origins to stake their claims to cultural citizenship of the Hindi Urdu elite nation.

With the demotion of Punjab and Punjabi to a low, folk, peasant culture, the definers of taste in North Indian cities could hold Punjabiization of the culture with the influx of Punjabi migrants as a corruption of the Hindi Urdu language and a lowering of the old elite tastes in food, dress and lifestyles. Paul Brass's perceptive connection between language, script and the nation (1974) is visible in the use of language as a tool in the stigmatization of the outsider's language as low, in the articulation of Hindi Urdu to high culture and taste and in the multiple symbols of language, food, dress and lifestyles as reflectors of low taste. The Punjabi elite, particularly Hindu, migrant who had been subjected to both the colonial and Hindu nationalist demotion of Punjabi in the construction of a Hindu Punjabi identity that converged on the Hindi literary and cultural corpus was complicit in the inferioritizing of Punjabi as a low language. The Punjabiization of sartorial tastes has similarly been held responsible for the decline in urban tastes through the Punjabi preference for primary and pastel colours, blended rather than natural fabrics and embroidery and flamboyant patterns even in the new millennium, when Punjabi costume has been universally adopted as national ethnic dress and internationally acclaimed designers of Punjabi origin have permanently redefined Indian festive wear.

As Bourdieu demonstrated, the distance from or proximity to "the legitimate culture" determines the hierarchical status of a lifestyle. The distance of Punjabi lifestyles from the legitimate Hindi Urdu or Bengali elite cultures, recognized or universally recognized as "worthy," "canonical," or in some other way "distinguished" in the production of Indian national culture, leads to its being accorded a lower status in the Indian socio-cultural hierarchy. Over a generation, the internalization of the denigration of Punjabi and Punjabi culture as peasant by the displaced, their need for integration in the local culture through making a claim to cultural citizenship of the nation and aspiration to high Hindi Urdu tastes makes them dissociate with pre-displacement Punjabi cultures resulting in the erosion of homeland language and culture.

In disengaging from origins and roots, the displaced person, hence, becomes complicit in the ascription of the refugee as a person without roots, an abomination in a culture in which identity is deeply anchored in ethnic, linguistic and spatial origins.

Conclusion

Galtung developed a threefold typology of violence to show that a host of factors combine in particular historical moments to define the conditions for the promotion of violence, which he names direct violence, structural violence and cultural violence. In examining the traumatic effects of Partition's violence on survivors, Partition scholars have largely focused on the direct violence of Partition. This chapter brought to light the intangible violence of Partition through foregrounding the merging of direct, structural and cultural violence in the closure of opportunities to Partition survivors, particularly to "the lost generation" of teenage survivors, from bringing "the actual closer to the potential" (1969: 168). It also dwelt on the discursive violence of the label *refugee* initially employed by the state to refer to the displaced, on the mismatch between the language of religious giving or dāna in the state's and old residents' extension of hospitality to survivors and their acceptance of the same in the spirit of vartan bhanji and, finally, on the symbolic violence[20] of the peasantization of Punjabi and East Bengali refugees that signalled the demise of pre-displacement languages, cultures and practices. Although intangible violence might have appeared inconsequential both to survivors and their hosts in comparison to the heartrending direct violence with manifest somatic effects, the effects of invisible violence need to be incorporated in the consideration of the traumatic effects of Partition.

Notes

1 Arguing that an extended concept of violence is indispensable, Galtung makes a distinction between six important dimensions of violence (1969: 168). According to him, the first distinction is "between physical and psychological violence" (1969: 169) and the second "between the negative and positive approach to influence" (1969: 170). The third distinction, he explains, "to be made is on the object side: whether or not there is an object that is hurt" (1969: 170), and the fourth distinction "is on the subject side: whether or not there is a subject (person) who acts" (1969: 170). The fifth distinction to be made is "between violence that is intended or unintended" (1969: 171), and the sixth "is the traditional distinction between two levels of violence, the manifest and the latent" (1969: 172).

2 Direct violence refers to behaviours that serve to threaten and/or diminish one's capacities to meet basic needs.

3 Equating structural violence with social injustice, Galtung defines it as those systematic structures and ways through which certain disadvantaged groups are hindered from equal access to opportunities, goods and services that enable the fulfilment of basic human needs (1969).

4 Galtung defines "cultural violence" as "those aspects of culture, the symbolic sphere of our existence exemplified by religion and ideology, language and art, empirical science and formal science (logic, mathematics) that can be used to justify, legitimize direct or structural violence" (1990: 291).

5 By quoting several stories circulated within families from memory, I wish to bring out the implications of growing up listening to stories of those who were subjected to the direct, structural and cultural violence of Partition, a knowledge of poisoned relations that percolated to descendants of Partition survivors without it ever being verbally expressed. Names of respondents have been changed on requests of anonymity.

6 Later in his diary, Prakash mentions that the evacuee property belonged to a well-known Muslim doctor, Yaqub, who "had shot Hoshi the famous Socialist leader during riots" (2005).

7 Galtung's list includes 1. crushing (fist fight, catapults), 2. tearing (hanging, stretching, cutting), 3. piercing (knives, spears, bullets), 4. burning (arson, flame, throwerbargo), 5. poisoning (in water and food, in gases), 6. evaporation (as in nuclear explosion) (Galtung 1969: 174).

8 The second category of physical violence consists of 1. denial of air (choking, strangulation), 2. denial of water (dehydration), 3. denial of food (starvation due to siege, embargo), 4. denial of movement a. by body constraint (chains, gas), b. by space constraint (prison, detention, exile), c. by brain control (Galtung 1969: 174).

9 According to the Record of the Meeting of the Cabinet Emergency Committee, New Delhi, September 22, 1947, "Lord Mountbatten felt that resettlement should be carried out in three phases: 1. Arrange to receive the refugees on arrival in India and direct them to various destinations. 2. Set up an organization to assist refugees for first six months. 3. Formulate a long-term resettlement plan" (Nehru, "Selected Works," 1972: 96). According to the "Report of Displaced Persons, 1950," the government, faced with the problem of accommodating about two and a half million migrants, launched a massive construction programme. "Up to March 1952, 150,000 houses and tenements were built at a cost of Rs. 38 crores, followed by a plan of constructing another 50,000 houses at a cost of about Rs. 21 crores in the course of the following two years to provide accommodation for about a million displaced persons. In addition, about 1 to 5 million persons had already found accommodation in evacuee houses. The government hoped that the housing problem of the displaced persons from West Pakistan would have been substantially solved by the end of 1953–54" (1950).

10 For example, according to one circular, "the students who put in three months of social service in the relief camps would be exempted from appearing in one subject

in Matriculation, B.A. and B.Sc. examinations in 1947. For the students of the M.A. examination, appearing in 1947 would have no such provision, but those who were to appear in 1948 would be allowed to forego one paper out of six in lieu of three months of social service" ("Rehabilitation of Displaced Persons," 1950: 4). Schools were instructed to automatically promote schoolchildren from displaced families to the following grade because of the rupture in their schooling.

11 Ram Prakash shared his memories of having to support his own education through selling beakers to fellow students in school in his diary (2005). Raj insisted that his family was not affected by Partition due to his father finding employment but summarily conceded his hawking fabric on the footpath to supplement the family income in response to the interviewer's repetition of his question only towards the end of the interview (2018).

12 Tahir Hasnain Naqvi clarifies that "while the term 'refugee' was employed within Indian and Pakistani official discourses, it was not employed to designate an alien or a stateless person so much as a member of a communal minority in need of a majoritarian sanctuary" (2012: 2). Haimanti Roy, in contrast, argues that "minorities, the Hindus in East Pakistan and the Muslims in India did not 'become refugees' by crossing the international border and have 'automatic rights to demand citizenship' but were 'produced categories', debated within the hallowed halls of officialdom in Delhi, Calcutta, and Dacca, and given legal sanction through ordinances and laws debated and passed by parliamentary and state legislations" (2012: 4).

13 Amrita Ghosh's introduction of the caste and class dimension in differentiating the homogeneous figure of the refugee defines the limits of the protection offered by the state. Unlike the upper-caste refugees, who had the security of citizenship and protection of the state, in her opinion, the nimnabarno [lower class] refugee could be killed by the state through exercising the state of exception to the rule that Agamben observes in the camps (2016).

14 It would not, for instance, fit the bhadraloka [gentlemen] East Bengali refugees who invoked the idiom of sacrifice to stake their claims to their entitlements and recognition as citizens. Only the lower caste or nimnabarno [lower caste] East Bengali refugees of Morichjhapi who were killed without impunity by West Bengal as illegal occupants of reserved forest lands of Sunderbans embody the subhuman form of life represented by the *homo sacer*, as Amrita Ghosh has argued (2016).

15 Although refugees were automatically citizens of the new state, refugees in humanitarian aid camps, as Barbara Harrell-Bond shows (1992), lacked ready means for legal recourse and were, therefore, outside the law. Harrell-Bond raises the issue of the difficulty of addressing the humanity of the refugee when that humanity is normally guaranteed by the office of the state.

16 According to Rigveda, "Bounteous is he who gives unto the beggar who comes to him in want of food and feeble. Success attends him in the shout of battle. He makes a friend of him in future troubles" (Griffith X 117). Similarly, *Brihadaranyaka Upanishad* 5.2.3 states, "Then the men said to him: 'Tell us something, Sir.' He told them the same syllable Da. Then he said: 'Did you understand?' They said: 'We did understand. You told us, "Datta," Give.' 'Yes,' he said, 'you have understood'" (1879: 190).

17 While *dāna* is typically given to one person or family, Hinduism also discusses charity or giving aimed at public benefit, sometimes called *utsarga*. This aims at larger projects, such as building a rest house, school, or drinking water or irrigation well; planting trees; and building care facilities, among others.

18 *Vartan bhanji* functions as a bank to which individuals can turn in times of financial distress (Wakil 1970: 704).

19 Ghosh quotes two rhymes among the Ghatis [Bengalis of West Bengal] mentioned by Dey (Dey 1945: 97):

   • Du char lathi parle ghare, tabe
   • Bangal bujhte pare

[Bangals are so dull that even elementary things are beyond their grasp] (Ghosh 2013). Another one goes like this (Dey 1945: 49):

• Dhopa jaane konjon kangal,
• Shekra jaane konjon Bangal

[Just as a washerman can easily identify a pauper by a look at his clothes, a goldsmith knows who is a Bangal among hundreds of his customers, since it is very easy to hoodwink a Bangal] (Ghosh 2013).

20 Galtung pointed out that "symbolic violence built into a structure does not kill or maim like direct violence or the violence built into the structure. However, it is used to legitimize either or both, as for instance in the theory of *Herrenfolk* or a superior race" (1990: 291).

4 Scripting their own lives

Introduction

Memories of victims, perpetrators and witnesses have been strategically summoned, meticulously compiled and widely disseminated by oral historians to supplement, complement and complicate the histories of Partition 1947 (Das 1990; Butalia 1998; Menon and Bhasin 1998; Pandey 1992). These mnemo-narratives have provided a more complex, nuanced, multilayered perspective on the events of Partition through the recollections of ordinary people creating, as it has been argued, a history from below. However, the elevation of memory as a legitimate mode of reconstructing historical events and the sanctification of testimonial mnemo-narratives as more authentic modes of remembering the past in the memory turn of the present often takes place without a rigorous engagement with the process of memory. Memory histories' privileging of witness testimonies and survivor memories as authentic posits an axiomatic relationship between experience and knowledge in which survivors' personal experience is valorized as entitling them to a superior form of knowledge. This synonymy between experience and knowledge underpinning the myth of authenticity surrounding oral memory histories often occurs through a disregard for the fallibility, inaccuracy and the intentional or unintentional manipulation of memory by narrators. In their introduction to oral histories or scholarly essays, oral historians have indeed raised issues of historiography, the trustworthiness of memories and the possibilities of witnesses concealing information or reporting contradictory information in making a case for memory (Portelli 2009; Ricoeur 2006: 163). Overall, they have followed the ethnographic ethic of letting the narratives speak for themselves rather than providing interpretations. Rather than oral historians, scholars in literary, film and performance studies have provided extremely sophisticated analyses of memory work in narrativizing experience through examining fictional texts as testimonies (Bhalla 1999; Didur 2007; Datta 2008; Kamra 2008; Yusin and Bahri 2008).

New historiographies have brilliantly elucidated the relationship between memory and history in proposing memory as a base, ally and alternative to history (White 1980; Funkenstein 1986; Nora 1989; Ricoeur 2006; Hutton 1993; Matsuda 1996). Both the divergences and convergences between the two modes of remembering, archiving, explaining and interpreting the past have engaged the interest of several scholars. In several of these studies, the relationship between history and memory is viewed not as oppositional but supportive (Louch 1969; Lee 2000; Brothman 2001; Burke 1989; Olick and Robbins 1998). Of particular interest are the overlaps and intersections between memory and history excavated by historians through their proposing narrative as the connecting link. Hayden White's notion of history as narrative (1980) and Paul Ricoeur's emphasis on testimony as the basis of history and the commonality of emplotment, interpretation and explanation to both history and memory offer strong conceptual frameworks for an analysis of memory as a historical archive (2006). This chapter focuses on the work of memory and postmemory (Hirsch 2008) in the narrativization of experience through selection, elimination, focalizing of certain details, imposition of a structure and provision of an explanation that closes the gap between historical, fictionalized and remembered stories (White 1984: 21). It argues that survivors, like historians, transmute experience into coherent narratives in the process of remembering, sharing and retelling their experiences that become fixed through their repetition over the years. It also demonstrates that postmemory transforms tragic narratives of abjection and victimhood constructed and disseminated by the media and academia into triumphalist sagas of survival in recalling the past. Survivors' reinscription of themselves from victims to agents underlines the process through which they use memory to script their own lives and gain agency (Das 1990).

Narrative, narrativity, emplotment, representation and explanation

In the "Question of Narrative in Historical Discourse," Hayden White defines narrative as a *form of discourse* that may or may not be used for the representation of historical events (1984).[1] Acknowledging the existence of non-narrative modes of historical representation, he makes a distinction between histories that narrate, that narrativize and that let a story tell itself (1984: 2). He argues that *narrativizing* distinguishes history from annals and chronicles, meaning that history is textually mediated and deploys narrative to represent, order and interpret historical facts. In his view, events, in addition to being registered in the chronological framework of their original occurrence,[2] must be narrated as well, by which he means that they must be "revealed as possessing a structure, an order of meaning, which they do not possess as mere sequence" (1980: 9). White observes a significant shift from the view of narrative as "a form of representation" to "a manner of speaking about events," whether real or imaginary (1990: 2). Its earlier perception as merely a form of historical representation, a medium for the message with no more truth-value or informational content than any other formal structure, mathematical equation or code, has been replaced by the understanding of narrative as a complex set of codes and even a form of explanation.[3]

In the view of narrativists or narrative impositionists, including White, the historian's imposition of a plot or a genre on the chronological order of events injects historical representation with a perspective, subjectivity and political ideology that makes it indistinguishable from other imaginative modes. Roland Barthes challenged the distinction between historical and fictional discourse, basic to historicism in all its forms through showing that narrative history, in its imposition of a narrative structure on the chronological order of real events, displays a convergence with literary genres, such as epic, myth, fiction and film (1981). In deconstructing narrative, Barthes foregrounded the constitutive rather than reflective function of narrative and revealed referential reality to be a product of language critiquing both 19th-century fictional realism and objective historiography for their denial of their invented nature and sustenance of "the referential fallacy" (Riffaterre 1984). Other historians have also noted the similarity between narrative history and fictional genres in their reliance on narrative to communicate meaning (White 1984: 2) and analyzed the communicative, conative and performative aspects of discourse to argue that narrative does not merely inform or explain but is also constitutive of meaning (White 1980). These scholars point out that although the referents of historical narratives might be real as opposed to those of fictional narratives and have a given chronological sequence and ending, historians' inclusion and occlusion of particular facts and choice of a beginning, middle and ending connected through a causal chain along with a scale and moral standpoint closes the chasm between historical and fictional narratives, as Levi-Strauss had demonstrated through his comparison of modern narrative histories and primitive and ancient myths (1966). Thus, the element of narrativity, immanent plot, a centred subject and a moralizing impulse connect history with other forms of narrative. What distinguishes "historical" from "fictional" stories "is first and foremost their contents, rather than their form," as White points out, and "the content of historical stories is real events, events that really happened, rather than imaginary events, events invented by the narrator (1984: 2)." While acknowledging that history belongs to "the discourse of the real" as opposed to "the discourse of desire" or "the discourse of the imaginary," he reveals plot to be immanent in real events (1980: 23) and argues that "insofar as historical stories can be completed, can be given narrative closure, can be shown to have had a plot all along, they give to reality the odor of the ideal" (1980: 24).

White asserts that in histories that purport to tell a story, "the problem of narrativity turns on the issue of whether historical events can be truthfully represented as displaying the structures and processes observable in certain kinds of "imaginative" discourse" (1984: 2). Drawing on the literary distinction between story and plot to distinguish between a chronological sequence of events from the structure that connects them through a causal logic, he coins the term *emplotment* to refer to the process through which the historian selects, orders and interprets real historical events and imposes a certain story type (1984: 20). The plot displays the relationship between the chronological sequence of facts, the actors, the setting and the historian's representation of events. Paul Ricoeur agrees that "emplotment" is not an organizational feature of fictional or mythical stories alone but is equally crucial to the historical representations of events (2006: 250). He separates the episodic dimension, which characterizes the story made out of events, from the configural according to which the plot construes significant wholes out of scattered events. Like White, he emphasizes the role of "plot," in figuring forth the "historicality" of events and reveals the plot like nature of temporality itself. He views narrative not merely as a mode of explanation,[4] as a code, a vehicle for conveying information, but also as a symbol that mediates between different universes of meaning (2006: 243–44).

In addition to emplotment, the distinction between fictional and historical narratives has centred on the issues of interpretation and explanation. In *Metahistory: The Historical Imagination in Nineteenth-Century Europe* (1973), White distinguishes between history and metahistory through showing that the explanatory and interpretative aspects of narrative run together in metahistory as opposed to traditional history. He claims that historical texts are marked by strategies of explanation, which include explanation by argument, explanation by emplotment, and explanation by ideological implication. In "Interpretation" (1973), White, while agreeing with Hegel, Droysen, Nietzsche and Croce that all histories are interpretative, rejects the idea of facts as being apodictically provided rather than constituted, as Levi-Strauss had earlier demonstrated (1966), through showing that the historian's task involves both interpretation and explanation (1973). Interpretation in turn involves both the historian's constitution of a story out of a chronicle of events through the exclusion of events irrelevant to the historian's narrative purpose and the provision of pre-generic-plot structures defined by Northrop Frye to identify the kind of story he or she is telling (1957). Narrative explanation essentially entails the emplotment of a given sequence of events in different ways. In addition to the provision of a plot structure, the historical process often includes an explanation in nomological-deductive terms of why something happened. But Ricoeur regards the notion of narrativity in historiography as conducive to the attainment of an "understanding" of the events of which it speaks rather than an "explanation" (2006).

The commonality of narrative as a mode of discourse in both "historical" and "non-historical" cultures and its existence in both mythic and fictional discourse has led to its being regarded suspiciously when speaking about "real" events that are perceived as being more conducive to the non-narrative manner of speaking common to physical sciences.

Testimony as narrative

The *Oxford English Dictionary* defines *testimony* as "a formal written or spoken statement, especially one given in a court of law or as evidence or proof of something." The etymological origins of *testimony* may be traced back to 1400 – "proof or demonstration of some fact, evidence, piece of evidence"; early 15c., "legal testimony, sworn statement of a witness"; from Old North French *testimonie* (Old French testimoine 11c.), from Latin *testimonium* "evidence, proof, witness, attestation," from *testis* "a witness, one who attests" (Testimony, ndt).

Roland Dulong defines *testimony* as "an autobiographically certified narrative of a past event, whether this narrative be made in informal or formal circumstances" (2002: 43). According to Shoshana Felman, "to testify is always, metaphorically, to take the witness's stand, or to take the position of the witness insofar as the narrative account of the witness is at once engaged in an appeal and bound by an oath" (1991: 39). She clarifies that "to testify is thus not merely to narrate but to commit oneself, and to commit the narrative, to others: to take responsibility – in speech – for history or for the truth of an occurrence, for something which, by definition, goes beyond the personal, in having general (nonpersonal) validity and consequences" (1991: 39–40). In his discussion of testimony in *Elements of Rhetoric* (1846), Richard Whately asserted that testimony was of different kinds and may "possess various degrees of force, not only in reference to its own intrinsic character, but in reference also to the kind of conclusion that it is brought to support" (1846: 58). He examined the distinctions between "matters of fact" and "matters of opinion," noting that there is "often much room for the exercise of judgment, and for difference of opinion, in reference to things which are, themselves, matters of fact" (1846: 59).

According testimony a key role in the historical process, Ricoeur reiterates that everything begins with testimony and that it is through testimony that declarative memory manifests itself (2006: 497). He demonstrates that testimony is required to make a transition from the oral to the written stage with its transcription by the historian before it is placed in the archive and is used as documentary proof (2006: 170). In his discussion of testimony, Ricoeur engages in depth with the primary fiduciary character of testimony and the elevation of testimony as existential since the fact of the eyewitness's presence at the event itself serves as a form of attestation (2006: 278). Responding to doubts about the reliability of testimony, Ricoeur holds that

> the suspicion unfolds itself all along the chain of operations that begin at the level of the perception of an experienced scene, continuing on to that of the retention of its memory, to come to focus in the declarative and narrative phase of the restitution of the features of the event.
>
> (2006: 162)

He makes a distinction between oral, written and unwritten testimony and points out that testimony belongs to declarative memory and that the image of the event is already transformed in the process of its narration (2006: 387). This supports Portelli's definition of oral history as the kind of historical work in which memory, narrative, subjectivity and dialogue shape the historian's very agenda and of oral sources as something that are *co-created* by the historian and the witness rather than found (2005).

Ricoeur's unpacking of the various stages of historical representation from testimony to archive has thrown light on the complex process of remembering that blurs the distinction between testimony and historical representation through his demonstration of the impossibility of articulating the real experience even in individual testimonies. Ricoeur shows that in recalling a real event, particularly a traumatic one, the witness is unable to reproduce the experience unfiltered by memory or language because it is originally imprinted in the witness's consciousness as a sensory image that must find an appropriate linguistic expression in the process of recounting it to an interlocutor. In the process of remembering, Ricoeur argues, the witness essentially represents the event through imposing a narrative framework that blurs the divide between testimony and history (2006). Testimonial accounts, in a fashion similar to historical accounts, employ the fictional strategies of emplotment, interpretation and explanation to narrativize reality, which challenges their elevation as authentic and truthful reproductions of real events.

Oral histories of Partition have privileged eyewitness testimonial accounts or memories as raw, unmediated, authentic representations of the events of the experience. However, testimonies of Partition survivors are underpinned by a strong element of narrativity (Vygotsky 1929), performativity and structuring that exhibits a slippage between fiction, testimony and history in their selection, organization, emplotment and explanation of events. In their staging of particular events in the process of recalling events for the benefit of the ethnographer or oral historian, eyewitnesses' and survivors' accounts often betray both a dramatization and narrativization that enables them to script themselves into the macronarrative of the nation as agents rather than victims. Public sharing of personal narratives of violence and suffering is marked by a conspiracy on what is fit to be exposed and what is to be hidden from the public gaze. Repetitive narrations of events within and outside the intimate space of the family and the community over a period of seven decades since Partition result in the production of a fixed, unified narrative of particular events logically arranged in a particular sequence with a teleological explanation.

Survivor testimonies fit the definition of a narrative in their inclusion of more than one event, characters, interlinking of events and a sequential order interlinked through a causal or teleological logic, and they possess a narrative coherence that is produced through the emplotment of referential facts that is an effect of the temporal distance between the time of the event and its recall. They resemble fictional and historical narratives in their narrativization of reality to tell a story marked by both narrative and cognitive intelligibility. The inclusion, elision, occlusion, repression or privileging of certain events by witnesses resembles the historical or fictional process of narrativization that is equally governed by the impressionist, subjective, slanted and fallible perception of the narrator and the ideological beliefs of the community. Even though their ideological bases, organization and explanation might diverge from those of authoritative historical narratives, these narratives are similarly punctuated with gaps and silences that might be conjunctive or disjunctive with those of histories. Privileged over historical accounts as being personal, private and affectual, the conspiratorial accounts of witnesses converge on public events or generalized descriptions of violence and devastation while gliding over or eliding personal details with the consequence that their script runs parallel to official ones albeit with a difference in focus, perspective and explanation. In the belief that oral sources do not passively record the facts but elaborate on them and create meaning through the labour of memory and filter of language, Portelli prefers to use the terms *narrative* and *narratives*, *story* and *storytellers*, instead of *testimony* and *witness* (2005).

Riots in the princely state of Bahawalpur: official and people's stories

The city of Bahawalpur was founded in 1748 by Bahawal Khan, a descendant of the branch of Abbasi nawabs known as Da'udpotras who initially migrated to Uch. This was followed by the founding of the princely state of Bahawalpur in 1802. The Nawabs were British loyalists who had sought British support in defending the princely state from the raids of Maharaja Ranjit Singh and returned the favour by helping the British quell the rebellion of Mul Raj in Multan. Nawab Sadiq Muhammad Khan was the first ruler to extend support to the British on the outbreak of the Second World War. The Nawabs had an established tradition of appointing a British Agent. Sir (Edward) Penderel Moon (1905–87), who had served in the Indian Civil Service, Punjab, between 1929–43 and had to resign following a correspondence related to Mahatma Gandhi's secretary, was asked to serve as an administrator in the Bahawalpur state in 1943. Despite its being a Muslim-majority state contiguous to Pakistan ruled by a Muslim ruler with a Hindu population of 190,000 and Sikh population of 60,000, Bahawalpur was one of the 15 Muslim-ruled states that declined Mountbatten's June 3, 1947 offer of voluntary accession to either India or Pakistan to princely states. The Nawab announced that Bahawalpur would be an Islamic state protective of the rights of its Hindu minorities, who had traditionally dominated the trade and commerce in this important centre on the trade route between India and Afghanistan. Having appointed Mushtaq Ahmed Gurmani as prime minister and Penderel Moon as revenue minister in December 1946, the Nawab appealed to the Punjab Boundary Commission for the retention of its independent status but was persuaded by Mountbatten to sign a Standstill Agreement with Pakistan on the eve of Independence. At the time of the outbreak of violence on August 15, 1947, the state was comparatively peaceful with few riots, and the Nawab continued to remain in London. His newly appointed ministers were left to manage the explosive situation created by his accommodation of 200,000 Muslim refugees from India as an expression of support to the state of Pakistan. In the months between the declaration of Independence and accession of Bahawalpur to Pakistan on October 2, 1947, the state plunged into uncontrollable violence, compelling its Hindu minorities to flee for their lives.

White makes a distinction between three historical modes, namely annals, chronicles and history on the basis of their possession of a structure or an order of meaning. He shows that unlike annals, which represent historical reality as if real events did not display the form of story, and the chronicle, which represents it as if real events appeared to human consciousness in the form of unfinished stories, history is characterized by an immanent narrativity and a closure that has a moral meaning (1980: 6). In the fashion of annals, a time line of the eruption of violent riots in Bahawalpur after the declaration of Independence and a chronological sequence of factual events may be put together in this manner.

Following Pakistan's Prime Minister Mohammed Ali Jinnah's address on August 24, 1947, and the arrival of trainloads of mutilated Muslim refugees from

India, Muslims in Bahawalpur went on a rampage, killing 409 Hindus in the last week of August alone. On receiving information about riots in Bahawalnagar as he returned from Simla after touring parts of Punjab, Penderel Moon drove down to the riot-affected areas in Bahawalnagar, Hasilpur and Chistian, accompanied by Gurmani and others. The team was required to take a detour to Khairpur Tamewali on receiving reports of riots from Hindus forcibly converted to Islam they stumbled upon en route. After investigating the situation there and instructing the local police forces to ensure that there was no recurrence of violence, they proceeded on their journey to Hasilpur but were again diverted to the village of Qaimpur. Here they found the entire Hindu population of the village herded into the compound of a Muslim holy man named Abdullah Shah by the local thanedar [in charge of a thana or police station] to prevent them from being attacked by marauding Muslim mobs. Shah allegedly agreed to provide them protection on the condition that they would hand over their belongings to him and convert to Islam. Moon warned Shah against forcible conversion and personally supervised the evacuation of Hindus from Khairpur Tamewali, Qaimpur, Chistian, Hasilpur, Bahawalnagar and other riot-affected areas to Hindumalkot by train under police escort (Girdhar 2017).[5] On October 7, 1947, Bahawalpur joined the newly formed Dominion of Pakistan.

A comparison of the emplotment of a particular episode in the transfer of population, of the Bahawalpur riots and the evacuation of Hindu residents by Penderel Moon, the British revenue minister of the princely state of Bahawalpur,[6] in his memoir, *Divide and Quit*, and oral histories of the Hindu victims of the riots in Qaimpur and Khairpur Tamewali documented between August 2016 and April 2017 corroborates the intersection between memory, history and narrative through the commonality of narrativity, narrativization and ideological explanation. White's notion of emplotment and narrativity provides a framework for understanding the colonial officer's and survivors' fashioning of their source material and historical data that comprises the bare chronological sequence of the annals into a coherent narrative that approximates narrative histories. These discordant testimonies of the Bahawalpur riots are characterized by the narrativity that historians have discerned in the writing of narrative histories and illustrate the process of interpretation, emplotment and explanation in the representation of the same event through which they narrativize the history of the riots. Similarly, Ricoeur's distinction between oral and written testimonies and Portelli's between oral and written histories provide a conceptual lens for identifying the divergence between the oral testimonies of survivors and Moon's written testimony. In addition to other reasons, the relationship between the time in which the event takes place and the time of the dialogue, considered important to the set of relationships in oral history by Portelli, helps to elucidate the difference between the memoir and oral histories. Although both constitute first-person testimonies of those who were present at the event, one is a written memoir of a colonial officer published within a decade and a half of Partition and the others are oral histories of those directly affected by the riots recorded and transcribed by interviewers 70 years after the event.

White's inclusion of both the selection of particular events from available data; the choice of a beginning, middle and ending; and a pre-generic-plot-type by the narrator in his definition of interpretation and Claude Levi-Strauss's rejection of the idea of a single scale of ordering of events and assertion that there were as many chronologies as cultural-specific ways of representing the passage of time comes to mind when investigating the variations in the choice and relative significance of certain facts, their chronological arrangement and in the beginnings, middles and endings in the colonial officer's account and survivors' testimonies (1966). The difference between the memoir of the colonial administrator and testimonial accounts of the outbreak of violence in the princely state of Bahawalpur primarily lies in the mode and style of their narration; the focalization of certain events and characters; the beginning, the middle and the ending; the chronological sequencing of events; the causal logic connecting them and explanation. The main difference in their emplotment and interpretation of the source material inheres in the British administrator's choice of the pre-generic-plot-type of adventure tale, travel story and colonial anthropology; ironic mode; and the emplotment type of irony and the survivors' of *qissa* [a romantic tragic genre], *var* [heroic ode], *marsiya* [mourning genre] and reliance on metaphor.

Gyanesh Kudaisya and Tan Tai Yong place *Divide and Quit*, Penderel Moon's account of the events of 1947, in the generic category of memoirs penned by civil and military officials in the aftermath of Partition (2004: 9). The new editions of Moon's memoirs market it as a "classic first-hand account of one of the most cataclysmic events of the century, the Partition of India" (1998). In his examination of Australian fiction, Robert Dixon argues that the adventure tales on which Englishmen were raised for two hundred years after *Robinson Crusoe* were "the energising myth of English imperialism" and that Australia, along with India, Africa and the islands was actively constructed from the 1870s down to 1914 as "a preferred site of adventure, with all the ethical and political ambiguity that the term adventure came, almost immediately, to imply" (1995: 1). He makes the important observation that "the moral ambiguities of the colonial adventure tale coincided with conflicts in the emerging discourse of the nation" and that "the conflict between duty and adventure were bound up with a deeply ambivalent relation to empire and nationhood" (1995: 32). Although it was Moon who, always critical of the British Empire, dared to pose the important question of whether or not the terrible massacres and forced migrations that followed the Partition could have been prevented, his framing narrative, which deploys a mix of colonial anthropological literature, travel story and adventure tale, to recount his experiences obliges him to follow the conventions of imperial adventures, justifying the colonial mission. Despite Moon's self-appointed role as a staunch critic of British rule, the Bahawalpur episode appears like a chapter in the self-congratulatory account of a British administrator in the princely state of Bahawalpur. At the same time, Moon, as a member of the Indian Civil Service posted at Bahawalpur, was in a unique position to offer a first-person witness account of the outbreak of violence and communal frenzy and the breakdown of law and order and his efforts retain sanity amid a civil-war-like condition. The features of the pre-generic-plot-type of the colonial adventure and anthropology in *Divide and Quit* are thus complicated by the genre of the memoir of an imperial officer who bore witness to the violence.

The emplotment of the violent events preceding and following the announcement of Partition by the survivors differs from the colonial travel story through its being structured as a tragic romance replete with terror, action, fortitude, resilience and heroism. The violent riots of August 1947 form the peripeteia in the Hindu tragic saga beginning with the fall from fortune and a stable existence. The events of 1947 that gave rise to an unexpected turn – violence – were sudden, "against expectation" (para doxan), as Aristotle put it, producing both "theatrical effects" (peripeteia) and "violent effects" (path⁻e) (quoted in Ricoeur 2006: 243). The centre that provides narrative coherence to the sequence of events is violence and displacement. The protagonists of the narrative are either the survivors themselves or important figures in their own community, and the events included are those that are significant in the progression of their saga of fortitude and resilience. The sequence, the causal logic used for interlinking events as well as the explanation of events, often differs from that of authoritative historical versions as well as that of the colonial official. Not only is the struggle for survival after 1947 prioritized above violence but acknowledgement of the rehabilitation by the state is marginalized to gratitude for individual and community support and resourcefulness. The ending preferred by all but a few narratives is reclamation of lost economic and social position, converting the tragic saga into romance. Through the agentive role they ascribe themselves, they are redeemed from the abject position to which they are relegated in official narratives.

Testimonio and testimonies: Penderel Moon, the colonial officer, and the son of the village headman

Confirming the notion that the historian's choice of a beginning, middle and end imposes an interpretation on real, chronological facts, Moon's description of the riots in Bahawalpur is inserted as a chapter "Outbreak of Violence in Bahawalpur State" in the middle of *Divide and Quit* to chronicle the illustrious albeit chequered career of an idealistic civil servant, who was gradually disillusioned with imperial policies towards the end of the empire. Viewing Moon's *Strangers in India* (1943) as both a critique of British imperialism and a strong defence of the idea of empire, Benjamin Zachariah argues that colonial officials' stand that the British should quit India was not "incompatible with a belief in the imperial ideal, as against imperial practice, which was more difficult to defend" (2001: 71). In *Divide and Quit*, too, Moon's focalization of his role in handling the riots in the Bahawalpur state suggests that the heroic efforts of a British civil servant alone controlled the prevailing lawlessness, even if partially, and that the departure of the British led to a breakdown of law and order.

The chapter follows Moon's witnessing the outbreak of unparalleled violence after the announcement of Partition on August 16, 1947, as he drives from Lahore to Simla and starts back for Bahawalpur across Ludhiana, Ambala and Amritsar. Even as he is congratulating himself on the comparative peace that prevailed in Bahawalpur except for sporadic incidents of violence, he receives a message from Bahawalpur's prime minister about disturbances in Bahawalnagar on reaching Lahore. The chapter begins in the style of a colonial travel story with Moon introducing the main characters – Mushtaq Ahmed Gurmani, the prime minister of Bahawalpur; Nur Hussain Shah, the police commissioner; and a big, burly Muslim in European clothes who turned out to be an ex-officer of the Bahawalpur State Forces – to set the scene and follows the exotic itinerary of the colonial travelogue in the description of the route to Bahawalnagar along the Bahawalpur Canal on which the party sets out early in the morning. Turning the British traveller's observant gaze on the scene unfolding in front of him, he sketches the landscape with the sharp brushstrokes of the European picturesque landscape painter, noting the treelined stretches that afford shade, the extensive cultivation on both banks and "pleasant fields of ripening millets" up to Lal Suhara (Moon 1961: 124). He comments on the change in landscape thereon with the cultivations becoming confined to the north bank, "a dreary grey desert, blotched with tibbas (sand-hills), and in places mottled with juniper and tamarisk scrub" (1961: 124), the treeless canal and the bad road that meet his gaze in a style reminiscent of other British travel narratives. The journey is framed as a grand colonial expedition on which the white man embarks in the company of his native informants to assess the tragic situation and plays the main role in the rescue mission.

In a manner characteristic of colonial anthropological narratives, Bahawalpur villagers, whom Moon espies "bobbing up and down on a small sand-hill" (1961: 125), are represented as amusing caricatures silhouetted against the uninteresting terrain. However, Moon's wry description of his encounter with these Hindus "who had been compelled to embrace Islam to save their lives" and the zeal of the new converts "who started gabbling away at them bits of the Koran which they had hurriedly learnt up" strikes one as dark humour (1961: 119). After reprimanding the Muslim leading them, the team decides to inspect the situation in Khairpur Tamewali, a small town with 5,000 to 6,000 inhabitants, which included a considerable population of Hindu merchants, bankers and shopkeepers since it had traditionally served as a market centre. Its meeting with the *thanedar*, whose assessment of the local Muslims as protective of their Hindu brethren and their conversion as "one of the protective devices adopted for their benefit and to placate the raiders" from outside (1961: 127), has the makings of a colonial saga where the colonial administrator frequently draws on the native informant's knowledge of strange native customs to understand the colonized psyche.

The choice of the beginning, middle and ending in survivors' stories that varies from Moon's meets White's definition of interpretation that begins with the selection of facts. As White points out, what is left out by the historian is as important as what is included (1980: 14). To reconstruct the sequence of events leading to the conversions that Moon accidentally comes upon, one must return to the post-memories of Nand Kishore Chowdhury, the then ten-year-old boy witness of the riots in Khairpur Tamewali. Like Moon's travelogue, Nand Kishore Chowdhury's memory selects, dates and organizes the sequence in accordance with his preferred pre-generic-plot of the tragic tale of his aristocratic Hindu family's fabulous wealth and high social standing, fall from fortune, banishment from home and exile to displacement, refugeehood and return to former position. As opposed to Moon, who congratulates himself for taking control of the situation in Khairpur Tamewali despite the incompetency of the inefficient, ill-equipped police force, the main plot in the story of Nand Kishore Chowdhury, the ten-year-old scion of the Hindu Chowdhury[7] family forced to migrate to Ranchi, is the paterfamilias role played by the Hindu headman in providing security and sustenance to the entire Hindu community in his walled *dera*[8] for 22 consecutive days after the riots, the strong solidarity among the Hindu community and the initiatives they took to withstand Muslim attacks. His commemoration of Hindu victims' preference of death to dishonour forms a counternarrative to Moon's caricature of the abject posturing of the Hindu converts his entourage encounters on the route to Khairpur Tamewali.

Although the survivor mentions the calendar time of the riots, namely the night of August 14, they are personalized through their having occurred when he "was about to take the final exams of Standard Five" (2017). However, it is Chowdhury's traumatized recall and repetition of the exact number – the 64 Hindus – whose lives the headman was unable to save since they either lived outside the Hindu enclave or had stepped outside the protective circle of the dera, offers a counternarrative of the civil servant's complacent congratulatory note on the relatively small number of riot deaths due to the timely actions of the local police and their British master. Chowdhury's explanation diverges from Moon's not only with respect to the number of Hindus killed but also the reason – the Hindus' stepping out of the protective circle of the dera. Similarly, his account varies from that of Moon in its reference to a certain Hindu who had accidentally come upon Moon's party while going to the railway station on some errand and prevailed upon Moon to come to the Hindus' rescue. Whether the 64 people died after Moon's intervention[9] or due to Moon's failure to provide protection despite his best efforts, as Moon admits in his memoir, or earlier, is not clear. If these preceded Moon's arrival, the thanedar's claim about there being no casualties would be rendered inaccurate.

Chowdhury's account lacks narrative coherence since his narrative sidesteps the structure imposed by the interviewer's questions through his frequently digressing into tales of former wealth and status. In contrast to the narrative coherence of the main plot about the family's fall from fortune, the haphazardly arranged subplot of the riots and threat of Muslim attacks must be put together into a coherent whole through deciphering the silences, gaps, tone, facial expression and gestures in the postmemories of the child witness. While emphasizing the family's role in protecting Hindus, he misses several sequential links. He neither elaborates on the death of 64 Hindu men nor that of the planned women's suicide and his father's instructions about administering poison to his sisters if the Muslims were to break into their walled enclave. The repetitions, gaps and silences that punctuate his narrative, which he strings together as a parable of perennial threats to Hindu authority, fall from privilege and restoration of the Hindu moral order, exhibit the selection, occlusions, narrativity and narrativization that define both fictional and historical narratives.

Unlike Moon, who focuses on providing a British civil servant's expert assessment of the inefficient and ill-equipped police force's inability to handle the situation, Chowdhury's narrative dwells on details of the family's status, wealth, networks and orthodox Hindu practices for the greater part and skims over details of the deaths and destruction as he struggles to find the exact words to describe his horror and pain. The ten-year-old boy witness, dumbfounded by the violence, is neither able to provide any explanation for events nor connect the unexpected violence to the cursory schoolboy knowledge he might have had of the nationalist movement. The bafflement of the survivor at the violence he witnessed is reflective of his inability to provide a plausible explanation for the violence of 1947.

The most important information, the violence perpetrated by men on their own women, lies outside what Chowdhury and the interviewer consider historically important (Portelli 2005). His poignant sharing of his most traumatic memory, of being handed sachets of poison by his father to be emptied into his sisters' mouths in the event of an attack by Muslims, is framed within the mythicized narratives of honour killing by Hindu men with the objective of protecting their women from Muslim predators in which their womenfolk were made complicit. It is through his eyes that a heroic saga of Hindus who preferred death over loss of honour is made to subsume the pragmatic, if cowardly, choice of the converts Moon encounters on his way and regards with utter disdain. In the video testimony, the now octogenarian child witness Chowdhury is seen breaking down when recalling the poison sachets handed to him by his father, an affective sensation that represents the image and emotions associated with the memory, which he quickly overcomes to resume the narrative of the family's affluence and social standing.

Testimonio and testimonies: the colonial official, the Muslim holy man and the villagers

As Dixon points out, "the descriptions of adventure are more exciting than exhortations to duty" in adventure tales (1995: 32). The reader is transported back to the adventure tale when Moon and party decide to inspect the situation of a smaller market town called Qaimpur, located 10 miles away from Khairpur Tamewali, where they come upon 20 to 30 Muslim looters[10] on the bridge on the canal and chase them back into the police station in the townlet. In a tone of great amusement, Moon frames the team's handling of the situation here as a macabre adventure tale or dark comedy, featuring high drama, action and adventure. Moon humorously recalls himself and Police Commissioner Shah running helter-skelter "through the crops, scrambling over low mud walls, jumping watercourses and, I think, thoroughly enjoying ourselves" (1961: 124) to nab the looters accompanied by a futile fusillade by the sepoys. The episode concludes with the Honourable Prime Minister's personal supervision of the traditional punishment of shoe-beating of the looters as his idea of an effective deterrent to crime with the memoir focusing on the humour in the state's highest authorities doling out archaic forms of punishment to petty criminals. They are then briefed by the local thanedar about the attacks on the village early that morning by hordes of Muslims from surrounding villages and the looting that ensued. Then, they are led to "a spacious mud-walled shed standing in an open compound" near the police station in which "practically the whole Hindu population seemed to be crowded in a woeful condition of panic and lamentation" (1961: 123). Moon lauds the thanedar's judicious decision in saving the lives of the Hindus by assembling them "in the large shed near the police station which had been placed at his disposal by its Muslim owner and became known" as the "Compound of Abdullah Shah" (1961: 123). But he corrects the thanedar's belief that only two or three had been killed by providing the exact number as seven. As they leave the village, Moon admits that their mood was that of self-congratulatory complacence, and they believed that they could show the entire Punjab that they were able to manage things (1961: 132).

However, the same story of the outbreak of violence and rescue is recounted by the largely non-literate survivors of Qaimpur in the manner of legend displaying a preference for personal village time to calendar time, discrepancies in the dating of the events, stereotyping and polarization of characters, divine explanation and moral tone.[11] After the initial acknowledgement of the distinction between good local Muslims and bad outsiders, the ruthless attackers, the conscientious doctor and the pious holy man, or Pir, the accounts progress into the demonization of the Muslims, including that of the holy man through their attribution of the evil design of conversion to him and the confirmation of the myth of the white saviour. In the process of their emplotment of a horror tale of Muslim monsters and a white saviour, the role of the Muslim thanedar who claims to have saved their lives with the help of the Maulvi and the Pir, or of Prime Minister Gurmani and Police Commissioner Khan, in punishing wrongdoers, is undermined or elided. Except for Abdullah Shah, who is named by one and all, and Moon, whose name varies in each narration and is confused with that of Mountbatten in one,[12] all other actors in the bizarre drama of the night of terror and rescue are generic – a Muslim doctor, a policeman, a family retainer – reinforcing the mode of legend. Details of destruction and death are often exaggerated in the bardic fashion to hyperbolic proportions to accentuate the enormity of their suffering and the heroism of their saviour.[13]

The divergence in the details in Moon's humorous description of his adventurous actions in Qaimpur and those of the survivors calls attention to the difference in the emplotment of events. The first difference lies in the selection and elision of events by each that depends on their respective choice of the beginning, middle and ending. Since Moon could not possibly have had knowledge of the riots preceding his visit, one has to depend entirely on survivor accounts to fill in the gaps in Moon's narrative of the events that preceded the thanedar's assembling of Hindus in Abdullah Shah's compound. Their narratives invariably begin with a description of the night of the riots,[14] their fleeing to the neighbourhood Gurdwara, the Muslim attack on the Gurdwara, in which two of their elders[15] who had stepped out to confront their attackers lost their lives, before moving on to how they came to be in Abdullah Shah's compound. The oral narratives emplot five events in a chronological sequence that are interlinked with a causal logic – Hindus learn about Muslims approaching; Hindus flee to the Gurdwara; Muslims attack the Gurdwara; transfer to Abdullah Shah's compound and threat of conversion; and rescue by Moon and party. The focus of the survivors' narratives is on their close shave with death, the hidden motive beneath the benevolent gesture made by the Muslim holy man, with no mention whatsoever of the thanedar's intervention.[16] They conclude with the *deus ex machina* of the arrival of the white rescuer, Moon, who helped them escape conversion to Islam to which some of them had reluctantly agreed as a price for survival.

The survivors' assumption about the historian's interest in the documentation of the narrative of violence impels each respondent in Qaimpur to begin his or her narrative with the news of the attack on the village, notwithstanding his or her slippage into quotidian, domestic details. Following the cues provided by the questions put by the interviewer, the plot begins in the middle with the recall of the night of terror, escape and rescue and returns to describe the socio-economic scenario and inter-communal relationship much later, after being prompted by the interviewer. The survivors' staging of the scene of the violence for the consumption of the historian appears to have been motivated by the desire to inform the interviewer about the tragic events that the interviewer expresses interest in. The sequence is largely orchestrated across the lines proposed by the interviewer with occasional or frequent detours into voluntary information not sought by the interviewer. Although the story of the riots and rescue is shared on the prompts provided by the interviewer's questions, the tellings reveal the narrativity that White and Ricoeur consider essential to historical narratives (White 1984; Ricoeur 2006).

Moon's memoirs differ from those of Qaimpur survivors in their elision of certain details that are pivotal to survivors' narratives. In contrast to Moon, who states that he decided to inspect the conditions in Qaimpur on encountering Muslim looters on the bridge on the canal, several survivors make it a point to mention that it was the intervention of a Muslim (who is defined as Hindu in one narration) doctor (Midha, Jairamdas 2017), who lived by the bridge on the canal, that led to Moon's detour.[17] One of them clearly recalled being one of the 15 Qaimpur Hindus who had lain down on the road the entourage would have to pass through in order to draw Moon's attention to the impending conversion of the Hindus in Qaimpur on the point of the sword (Girdhar 2017).[18] Unlike the survivors' accounts that highlight the role of a Muslim doctor or their own in preventing the massacre at Qaimpur through their appealing to the revenue minister to visit Qaimpur before proceeding to his destination, Hasilpur, the doctor or the 15 people who stopped them are completely elided in Moon's narrative of high adventure and comedy in which he arrogates a lead role in investigating the situation in Qaimpur and congratulates himself for preventing the slaughter of Hindus by his timely action. It is surprising that Moon, who spent more than a paragraph expressing the annoyingly ingratiating behaviour of the Hindu converts, who were waving a Pakistani flag on the party's route to Khairpur Tamewali, should have had no memory of 15 grown men lying on the road or of the Muslim doctor.

It is in the recall of events of which the interviewer had no knowledge that survivors acquire greater autonomy in the emplotment of events. The Pir, Abdullah Shah, and "Abdullah Shah's compound," mentioned in Moon's memoir, play a crucial role in the counternarratives of attack (1961: 129), impending conversion and rescue with the difference that when Moon arrives at the scene, all the Hindu residents have already been assembled to safety in the mud compound by the conscientious thanedar and are on the verge of being converted. Unlike Moon, who cannot be expected to have had knowledge of the events that transpired before his arrival in the compound and is relieved to find that further loss of lives was prevented by the thanedar's prudent action, the survivors' narratives minutely dwell on their travails in the compound to foreground the looming threat of conversion as the climactic event in their plot.[19] Moon's admission that he had hoped to convey through punishing wrongdoers to the people that civil administration was in place is seconded by the faith that the survivors put in Moon if not in the police. Unlike Moon, who summarily declares that he had entrusted the responsibility of protecting the Hindus to the police and to Abdullah Shah, survivors recall the exact words of the warning he gave to Abdullah Shah.[20] Each of the survivors confirms the role of Moon, the saviour, in their rescue through his strictly warning Abdullah Shah that not a single Hindu should come to any harm. In the survivors' accounts, even though Moon's name or designation changes in each narration, their deferential attitude towards the white man confirms his self-ascription as the natives' *mai bap* [father and mother].

Not only in the interlinking of events in a causal sequence but also in their explanation, the survivors exceed the interviewers' brief and fulfill the condition of emplotment enjoined by White upon historical narratives and script their stories that vary from the official's script. The British civil servant's informed perspective significantly diverges from that of the victims, particularly at the level of the events' explanation. Unlike the thanedar, who perceives himself to be sincerely discharging his duties by preventing loss of life even at the cost of conversion by escorting them to the safety of Pir Abdullah Shah's compound, which Moon approves as a pragmatic decision, the Pir's actions are imprinted on the survivors' memory as a betrayal and an affront to their religious identity. The survivors from Qaimpur reproduce identical details of the events of the night of the riots in the same order, even though they disagree with the thanedar on the number of people killed and on Pir Abdullah Shah's intentions in offering them protection. While they concur on the respect the Pir commanded in the town and his appeal to Muslim looters not to harm their Hindu brethren in the name of Islam, the majority attribute an evil design on the holy man's part that included extortion, conversion,[21] and even murder, even though one of them concedes that Abdullah Shah could have been under pressure from Muslim outsiders.

Therefore, the difference in the explanation of the transfer of the Hindus to Abdullah Shah's compound provided by the Muslim thanedar as protection and interpreted by the survivors as extortion and conversion, demonstrates the subjective nature of both historical and testimonial explanation.[22] The official compromise, "convert, if unavoidable" as a last resort for saving Hindu lives (1961:

127, 129) and the survivors' defence of the Hindu faith and their choosing death over forcible conversion, through personal and generalized references to information about the secret design of conversion, mass suicides and marriages, provide two competing explanations of the same events. The survivors decide to intercept Moon's entourage to appeal to him to save them from the impending threat of conversion and the death of those who refused to. The survivors' heroic explanation – defence of Hindu pride and honour – collapses in the face of contingencies, the providential passing of Moon's entourage and their admission to having agreed to convert were they given no choice.

In the largely malecentric narratives, Hindu honour is primarily inscribed on female bodies and defended through mass suicides of women or killings by their own men. While generalized narratives of mass suicides and killings of women are shared openly as evidence of the upholding of Hindu honour, those directly affected by these acts of honour, such as the two child survivors pulled out of the water even as one's mother was left to drown and the other's sister-in-law was killed, either go silent or gloss over these traumatic memories in the process of narrating the male party's triumphal escape from conversion (Vij 2017). Other than extralinguistic cues that suggest recall of traumatic images, the survivors' struggle to bring the event into the realm of the declarative requires a transition to the verbal and borrowing of the formulaic prose, of clichéd metaphors and the structure of other consensual Partition narratives. The interpretation of events recalled 70 years later or immediately after the event is bound to be post facto, for the survivors are expected to have had only partial knowledge of the explanation of the events – such as the motives of their Muslim benefactors, of the government officials or even of their own elders – at the time of their occurrence.

Moon's description of the arrangements he made for the evacuation of Hindus through special trains once it became clear that the Hindus were not willing to stay back foregrounds his heroic role in providing protection to Hindus until they had safely crossed the border. The chapter in his book on the arrangements made for the trains engages with the logistics of the transportation of the refugees. It also dwells on Moon's problems in convincing the railway drivers and the crew to drive across to the Indian side, which they agreed to do only after his assurance of providing security and personally accompanying the train (1961: 160). It is believed that Moon's heroic personal supervision of the evacuation of refugees through special trains did minimize loss of lives, despite the incident of attacks on the Qaimpur Khairpur route and the butchering and looting of passengers.[23] A planned attack on the trains by the Muslim and Pathan mob was effectively warded off by his giving strict instructions to the drivers to speed up the train in the face of such threats.

The survivors express their appreciation of Moon's personal intervention in ensuring that they were able to cross the border to Hindumalkot and escape from attacks of marauders through the arrangements made by him for their safe travels. It is obvious that the survivors, although confronted with the threat of death during the journey, made their way to Hindumalkot with the help of the administration and were not on the trains that were butchered. Their memories, therefore, are of those of fear, hunger, cold and hardship during the journey and other losses of a personal nature.

Survivors, as well as Moon, narrate stories to make sense of the events they witnessed (Portelli 2009: 69). Narrative and narrativity are not merely forms of representing facts but part of the meaning-making process based on memory, which, as Portelli explained, is "a permanent search for meaning, in which forgetting filters out the traces of experiences that no longer have meaning – or that mean too much" (2014: 44). The inexplicable violence of Partition, which turned communities against each other overnight, according to historians, becomes comprehensible to the teller via a retrospective construction of meaning through their interlinking discrete events and assigning them a form of causal logic. The estrangement of neighbours and friends can make sense only through the attribution of a teleological link and interpretation not available to the witness at the time of the occurrence of the event. Hence, prevailing official explanations, varying from the minority status of the Hindus; their control of trade and ownership of land and property, which invited the jealousy of their Muslim neighbours; refugee Muslim outsiders' desire for revenge in return for mass killings of Muslims crossing the border; and greed and the scheming nature of those who masqueraded as friends are proffered as possible reasons for the unexpected violence.

A memoir and oral histories

Both Moon's memoir and survivors' stories fulfill the six defining features of testimony unpacked by Ricoeur. The first feature, "the assertion of the factual reality of the reported event" and "the certification or authentication of the declaration "and establishment of the narrator's "presumed trustworthiness" is present in both the oral and written testimonies (Ricoeur 2006: 163). The second feature, that is, "self-designation of the testifying subject" and the exchange between the writer and reader or the interviewee and the interviewer, where the witness asks to be believed, connects the memoir with oral histories (Ricoeur 2006: 163). The third comprising the opening up of "a space of controversy within which several testimonies and several witnesses find themselves confronted with one another" (Ricoeur 2006: 164) pertains to the juxtaposition of survivors' testimonies not only against Moon's but also against one another's. With the availability of the Partition witnesses to "repeat their testimony" as opposed to the absent colonial administrator, a supplementary dimension gets grafted to the moral order meant to reinforce the credibility and trustworthiness of testimony and this "willingness to testify makes testimony a security factor in the set of relations constitutive of the social bond" (Ricoeur 2006: 164–165).

The intentionality of the narrator rather than of the recorder being paramount in the written autobiography or memoir is crucial to the difference between Moon's memoir and the oral histories of survivors. The emplotment of survivors' narratives is predetermined to a certain extent by the intentionality and the structured questions posed by the interviewer as opposed to Moon's emplotment of the memoir to foreground his distinguished career. Their mnemo-narratives exhibit a proclivity to furnish information that the survivors believe is important to the interviewer, and they provide the answers that the interviewer wants to hear. The sequence of the plot is structured according to the sequence of questions posed by the interviewer with some digressions into apparently irrelevant details, unlike the account of Moon, whose chronological arrangement follows his professional and personal itinerary. As Portelli warned, oral history being a *listening* art (2005), the interviewers may not always be aware that certain questions need to be asked even when the dialogue remains within the original agenda and that often the most important information lies beyond what both the interviewer or survivors think is important (2005). As Portelli pointed out, oral history is an art based on a set of relationships, the first of which is the relationship between the interviewer and interviewee, and the dialogue may be based both on their similarity and difference (2005). The difference in the age of the interviewees (between mid-70s to 95) and that of the interviewers (ranging between 20 and 25) facilitated a form of disclosure largely due to the empathy and the deferential but affectionate tone used by the young interviewees along with their feeling that they had something to learn by listening to the stories of grandparent-like survivors. The relationship between the private and public was equally significant in survivors' choice of information that they considered relevant. The majority focused on the public discourse of riotous mobs, threats of conversion and rehabilitation and recovery while carefully guarding intimate details either because they failed to realize their historical importance or because they perceived the personal to be outside the historical. The issue of unreliability of oral histories due to their being based on memory and subjectivity that are essentially distorting could be resolved through cross-checking the narrative by comparing one narrative with the other as well as with Moon's account. Finally, Portelli's warning that remembering and retellings are not only shaped by the historical context and social frameworks of memory but are also filtered by individual responsibility was visible in the survivors' attribution of explanations of events that had percolated to them by the media and community leaders and dominant political groups (2005). The relationship between the orality of the stories and the writing of the memoir is complicated by the fact that the oral history document is one of performance and dialogue, whereas writing, testimonial or historical, is a monologue. Since the tone and accent of the speakers carries information about their history and identity and transmits meanings beyond what the speaker conveys, the interviewers were specially asked to add affective markers in their written transcriptions to incorporate the unsaid, gestural, corporeal, non-linguistic component of the testimony that the memoir is ill-equipped to convey. Moon's account seeks to legitimize the state by narrating its role in the transformation of helpless refugees into productive citizens. First-hand accounts of the survivors, in contrast, write the state out of the rehabilitation if not the transfer process.

Conclusion

Although oral testimony is the oldest form of evidence, it was regarded with suspicion in traditional histories for being based on memory, oral, subjective and biased and therefore untrustworthy as testimony. However, it has lately been at the centre of historical study as historical evidence, as an act of memory, as an alternative account of events particularly since the period of the "explosion of testimony," the 1980s. Testimonial narratives have even been elevated as an authentic, unmediated representation of events by witnesses whose presence at the scene of events certifies the authenticity of their declaration.

The oral testimonies of survivors and the written testimonial account of Penderel Moon were juxtaposed to investigate the riots in the princely state of Bahawalpur to examine the truth claims attached to testimonial narratives and the recognition of written accounts of elite official eyewitnesses as documentary proof. Both oral and written testimonies of the same historical event were revealed to be structured by narrativity, emplotment, interpretation and explanation to foreground the constituted nature of testimony. The privileging of testimonial narratives as possessing a strong link to truth-claims due to their being eyewitness accounts is, thus, interrogated through the revelation of the narrativity through which events are structured into coherent narratives by the tellers, interpreted and explained.

Notes

1 White states that this depends on whether the purpose is to *describe* a situation, *analyze* a historical process or *tell* a story and that the amount of narrative in a given history will vary and its function will change according to the purpose (White 1984: 2).
2 Claude Levi-Strauss asserted that representation of events in a chronological order of occurrence is common to all fields of scientific study prior to the application of a structure (1968).
3 The analytical philosophers, in sharp contrast to the criticism of narrative from the Annales school and structuralists and poststructuralists, defended narrative both as a mode of representation and as a mode of explanation (Ricoeur 2006: 181).
4 Critical of narrativists' emphasis on emplotment as a mode of explanation, Ricoeur problematizes how the "configuring act of emplotment gets articulated through the modes of explanation/understanding placed in service of the representation of the past" (2006: 186). He stresses the need to distinguish between "narrative intelligibility" and "explanatory intelligibility" and between "narrative coherence" and "causal and teleogical connection (connectedness) arising from explanation/understanding" (2006: 243).
5 "British troops sat on top of our train to ensure that it reached its destination safely, since there was news of trains being stopped and people in the trains being killed. Even on our way to India, we were attacked by the Muslims but by God's grace we managed to escape and finally reach India" (Sidana 2017). "Mount [Moon] Saheb gave us protection till we had reached Hindustan. Many times on the way the train was attacked by Muslims. But Mount Saheb helped clear the situation and brought us to Hindustan" (Midha, Balakram 2017).
6 Moon was recalled by the British government to help with the transition of power in 1946–47 and in Bahawalpur in 1947–48 and helped Pt. Jawaharlal Nehru frame his policies in independent India in 1948–61.
7 The term *Chowdhury*, holder of four measures of land, denotes the head of a community or caste.
8 *Dera* means camp, mound or settlement in Bahawalpuri language.
9 According to Moon, he learnt about the riots in Khairpur Tamewali on August 28–29, 1947, when they were driving back from Chistian and that only 25 people had died following which 80 miscreants were taken prisoner by the thanadar (1961: 173).

10 Govardhandas Makkad confirms that these Muslims were waiting to attack any Hindu who passed by (2017).

11 In addition to Nand Kishore Chowdhury, 15 witnesses from Qaimpur were interviewed by Oral History interns Ankita Halder and Ekata Biswas between August 12, 2017, and January 12, 2018.

12 Meherchand Arora names a certain Mr. Rip, who rescued them when they were hiding in a corn field to escape Muslim attacks. It is not quite clear whether Arora was part of the same group Moon encountered in Abdullah Shah's Compound or if he is talking about a different set of riots. "The year was 1947 as we all know. August was a dreadful experience. One night in the month of August, the Muslims gangs attacked us. They had come in with a lot of weapons and guns. We somehow escaped and hid in a corn field. But couldn't hide there for long. So an Englishman named Mr. Rip came along and saved us from there [becomes teary-eyed and pauses]. Kabaili Pathans were waiting to kill us but Mr. Rip saved our lives. But they still attacked us at the end of the month of August" (Arora 2017).

13 "20–25 miles away from our village, there was another village named Hasilpur where similar attacks had taken place. Most of the population of that village was killed. The women and children who were still alive, jumped into wells to commit suicide; some died while the others who survived were abducted by the Muslims" (Nagpal 2017).

14 The exact date of the attack and exodus to the Gurdwara provided by survivors ranges between August 15 to 26–27, 1947. Most narratives begin with the formulaic opening "On one night," transforming the historical event to a mythical narrative.

15 The Muslim mob have been described by some as the refugees arriving from Patiala and Amritsar, whose number rises to 1,000 in Qaimpur resident Rishi Kesh Girdhar's account. One of them, who went out to reason with the Muslim attackers in the hope that they might include some familiar faces from their village and could be appealed to (Nagpal 2017) and was killed, has been named by Girdhar as his cousin brother-in-law Bal Kishan. Papneja's theory that the attacks occurred due to the slight suffered by a rival Muslim leader, Mohammed Gor, when they sought Abdullah Shah's help instead of his is not mentioned by anyone else (2017).

16 Balakram Midha and Jairamdas Midha recall that it was their schoolmaster Maulvi Mohammed Arif who promised to help them and led them to Abdullah Shah (2017). This supports, rather than contradicts, the thanedar's contention that he had tried to save the Hindus' lives with the help of some Muslims.

17 "Getting to hear this news [of the Hasilpur riots], the Home Minister was travelling in a jeep to that village along with the Gorkha Regiment. He was passing through the road near the bank of the river that used to flow through that village. On the way, a man stopped him and inquired, 'Why are you driving that way? The attackers are approaching our village after killing the people of Hasilpur.' Hence, our Home Minister diverted his route to our village instead of proceeding to Hasilpur" (Nagpal 2017).

18 "The Revenue Minister helped us a lot. 10 to 15 of us went to the road from where the Revenue Minister would be passing in order to make him listen to what we had to say about our situation. I was among those 15 people who had decided to go and lie down on the road in order to stop the revenue minister's car and talk to him. Had we not done this he would have crossed over without paying heed to us. However, the Revenue Minister asked us what the problem was and listened to what we had to say. The elders of our group, in their wisdom, sketched the entire scenario for his benefit. They told him that we were staying in Pir Abdullah Shah's place and were continuously being threatened with death if we did not agree to convert to Islam. When we told the Revenue Minister that all the Hindus were going to be killed within a few hours, he took pity on us and sent a few military men with rifles along with us for our safety and sent strict orders that we were not to be harmed in any manner" (Girdhar 2017).

19 Nagpal recalls that he "even got married at that time since we were all being asked to convert to Islam" and the pragmatic decision of the community was to get their daughters, "who were merely 13 to 14 years old, married to each other's sons" to prevent females from being converted. His mention of 100 marriages, including his own at the tender age of 14, taking place in the Gurdwara within a day confirms the seriousness of the threat of conversion (2017). Brij Mohan was also married in haste when they left on August 11, 1947 (2017).

20 "Mr. Batten [Moon] came to our village along with the police and counted all the Hindu heads present. He made a list of kids, women, and men separately and announced that if anyone were to be found missing until he returned, he would punish the entire Muslim community. He left us in police protection and asked us to stay back in safety until he returned. He gave this assurance in the presence of all the big politicians and leaders of Muslim community so that no one could retract" (Midha, Jairamdas 2017).

21 "Abdullah Shah had a mighty compound. It had a large verandah in which we were kept. They brought four of us together. The underlying plan was to bring a few people at a time from the Gurdwara and kill them" (Midha, Jairamdas 2017). According to Girdhar, the condition of conversion was imposed by Muslim attackers on the Pir for sparing their lives, and they had indeed agreed to convert (2017). Govardhan Das Makkad confirms that the Pir "wanted to kill us secretly" since he knew that "he'd not be able to kill us when we were together" (2017). This view of the Pir's intentions is echoed by several others (Midha, Balakram 2017; Nagpal 2017; Girdhar 2017).

22 The woeful conditions mentioned by Moon are corroborated by a survivor who recalled the panic and suffocation he experienced at being crowded and by others who mentioned that they were made to buy and cook food they had themselves produced and that they were subjected to other forms of extortion by both the Pir and the police officer in charge. Several mention Abdullah Shah's asking them to deposit all their valuables with him for safekeeping, which were never returned to them (Nagpal 2017). One complains about the officers in the Post Office demanding a share for agreeing to transfer their money.

23 "It took us three days to reach here. We started off on a train journey from Bahawalpur. We were re-attacked upon by the Muslims in Bahawalnagar. They killed a lot of people and looted us as much as they could" (Arora 2017).

5   They stuttered

Non-narratives of the unsayable

Introduction

Ram Prakash loved narrating his Partition stories to family, friends, visitors and anyone who cared to listen. With his remarkable memory, incredible eye for detail and penchant for telling stories, he could reconstruct events with precise recall of specific names, dates and places, varying his narrative as well as details in tune with the occasion and the audience. But each time he was probed on personal losses, such as the massacre of his wealthy landowning maternal clan in the border village of Leiah in the North Western Frontier Province, he would dismiss the question with a sombre assent, "Yes, they murdered my uncles!" before quickly returning to make fresh disclosures on untold public events. When forced to recount the memory of the murders in his final interview a month before his demise, he reluctantly admitted to accompanying his father and elder brother to Leiah and peering into a well before going completely silent (2012). What did he see in the well that he could not find the words to describe when recalling it 65 years later?

In sharp contrast, Veeranwali reconstructed a gruesome scene of violence, from which she still bore ugly scars, in graphic detail as though she were narrating the sequence of events in a horror film ghost-written by someone else in a language and a dispassionate tone that had lost touch with life.[1] She summoned each searing image – of a Muslim mob breaking open the door and bursting into the family's temporary shelter; of her pregnant mother being brutally vivisected and her newborn emerging from her womb; of her 12-year-old sister racing up the stairs leading to the rooftop and returning holding an eye; of being brutally hit with an axe and finding herself in an army camp – that, she admitted, sent a shudder down her spine to this day. But her everyday Punjabi language failed her as she repeated these traumatic details, making her retreat into the familiarity of a forgotten dialect spoken in the Mianwali district of West Punjab, which grew increasingly foreign as she rehearsed the sequence of the events of 1947 (2006).

In his essay, "He Stuttered" (1998), Deleuze speaks of three ways of representing the stutter in literary works, by *doing it*, by *saying it* and by *saying and doing* it. Deleuze maintains that novelists have three ways of indicating the difference in voice intonation. According to Deleuze, bad novelists vary "he said" with different dialogic markers, such as "he murmured," "he stammered," "he sobbed," "he giggled," "he stuttered," to indicate different voice intonations (1998: 107). In indicating these voice intonations, the writer, Deleuze argues, has two choices, which is *to do it* or *say it without doing it* but adds a third possibility, when *saying is doing*. In this case, "it is no longer the character who stutters in speech; it is the writer who becomes a *stutterer in language*" (1998: 107). In this case, he makes "the language as such stutter, an affective and intensive language, and no longer the affectation of the one who speaks" (1998: 107).

In her ethnographic research on the violence of Partition 1947, Veena Das corrects the widely held view that survivors suppressed Partition trauma by explaining that it remained at the surface but with fences built around it (2007). Distinguishing between speech and voice, she observes that although survivors did not narrate their experience of Partition, it remained on the edge of all conversations. Borrowing Wittgenstein's notion of the voice and Cavell's notion of the everyday, she proposes that the survivors of Partition 1947 engaged with the experience of violence not through dramatic gestures of mourning but through their inhabitation of the everyday, thereby turning the everyday into a site of the ordinary in which the violence of the Partition had seeped in. Arguing that Partition signalled a collapse of forms of life and disruption of given kinship relations, she deconstructs conversations with female survivors to show that the memory of the event of Partition is enfolded in the everyday and that the manner in which the violence of Partition was folded "was *shown* (sometimes with words) rather than *narrated*" (2007: 10).

This chapter borrows Deleuze's notion of language as a stutter and Das's of non-narrative (2007: 90) and inner language to foreground the gaps that punctuate the major stories of Partition scripted by survivors for both private and public circulation. While narrating their stories, survivors' memory works by eliding traumatic experiences or transforming them into acts of agency but is betrayed by language that screams, stammers, stutters or comes to a halt. Unlike scripted narratives rehearsed and retold by narrators to each other and others, these stutters and non-narrations in language, as narrators skip over some parts of the story while dwelling in detail on others, go completely silent or slip into incoherent speech,[2] disrupt their master plots to call attention to the unsayable, the untold and the unscripted part of the stories.

He stuttered and non-narrative

Das's analysis of the articulation of the unsayable in fictional representations overlaps with her ethnographic work on the women affected by the violence of 1947 in which she commented on the silence of survivors on what happened to them and what they did in the context of the Partition. She discovered that "when asking women to narrate their experiences of the Partition," she "found a zone of silence around the event" (2007: 84). While they recounted the violence in general using metaphoric or hyperbolic language, specific experiences of abduction and violation remained unnarrated. Das uses the term *non-narration* or *non-narrative* to describe the narratives of women abducted during the violence of Partition. Although they eschewed any explicit mention of the violence done to them personally, their narratives of suffering were framed within the field of force of the widely circulated stories of abducted and raped women. Borrowing Wittgenstein's notion of forms of life, she argues that the non-narratives of these women belong to the unsayable in the forms of life and that language deserted women in describing their personal experience. Instead, they resorted to the realm of the sayable in Punjabi kinship networks and language of performative gestures to express their pain on which the original emotion of the violence was mapped.

The stutter, non-narrative and fiction

Partition literature offers numerous examples of both *doing, saying* and *saying is doing* in indicating the differences in voice intonations. In particular, Sa'adat Hasan Manto's stories offer the classic example of the writer alternating between these choices to problematize the failure of language in representing the unspeakable violence of 1947. Partition scholarship has largely converged on Manto's short fiction to focus on the failure of everyday language in articulating its unspeakable violence and the struggle of the writer to evolve an appropriate idiom to convey the fracture of language. Das's observation that Manto's "mutilation of language testifies to an essential truth about the annihilating violence and terror" of the Partition era is reiterated by a number of scholars (1995: 184). Das argues that language is struck dumb as human understanding gives way, and since violence annihilates language, the terror cannot be part of the utterable. Sukeshi Kamra agrees that Manto's challenge as a writer lay in the impossible condition of bringing within language an experience that is not within the purview of language (2008). Problematizing the transparency of language associated with literary texts, Jill Didur argues that the silence imposed on abducted women by their families is not given voice in literary fiction (2007). She maintains that literary texts which, like testimonies, remain silent on the details of the experience, foreground the limits of language in articulating the women's pain. Jennifer Yusin and Deepika Bahri, thinking through Partition together with trauma theory, maintain that to do so is also to engage the status of Partition as a historical trauma within the problem of language (2008: 85). Yusin and Bahri argue that in so far as a traumatic event remains within a past unable to be accessed as an experienced present through memory, language fails to account for the traumatic event in the present (2008: 85). They concur with Didur that fiction fails to account for or refer to trauma but that it enacts the impossibility of representing trauma and makes witness possible in its inherent failure.

The classic example of Deleuze's *doing it* is the untranslatable incoherent babbling of a mentally challenged character named Bishan Singh in his much-anthologized story "Toba Tek Singh" (1994). When the news of Partition and the exchange of the mentally ill reaches the asylum located in a village that lies on the newly drawn border between India and Pakistan, Bishan Singh breaks into incoherent nonsense, "Opad di gud di moong di dal di laltain di Hindustan te Pakistan di dur fitey munh" (Manto 1994). This corresponds to Das's idea of the boundaries between the eventful and the ordinary as a failure of the grammar of the everyday (2007: 7) by which she means *what is put into question* is how we ever learned what kind of object something like grief, or love, is (2007: 8). Returning to the preceding oft-quoted passage from "Toba Tek Singh," Kamra contends that the issue of language is raised not only in the rupturing of language through the device of nonsense syllables with words separated out from meaning in a classic illustration of nonsense verse but is raised more pointedly "as an issue of trust in language's capacity to engage in any meaningful way with the historical world" (2008: 102). Kamra echoes Das's argument about the striking dumb of language as both sign and part of the terror that signals not only a loss of sociality but also ensures that brutality and torture remain outside the purview of narrative. She regards the nonsense words used by Bishan Singh as "the use of a language that messes with the usual distinction between the irrational and rational use of language" (2008: 104) and argues that the effect of the catastrophic experience is visible in the traces, which, in this case, are somatic and psychological shifts (2008: 104).

In her analysis of Manto's "Siyah Hashiye," or "Black Borders," Kamra maintains that the Partition is measured here in painful detail after painful detail that describes "a completely shaken voice" and that shock and disbelief in its happening "informs the entirely descriptive and deliberately intransitive writing" (2008: 99). Here, like a good novelist, Manto refrains from commenting on the tone of the narrator, leaving it to Kamra to detect the undertone in the voice "shaken in its faith in a vision of progressive history" that had been synonymous with the Indian struggle to end colonial rule (2008: 100):

> Rioters brought the running train to a halt. People belonging to the other community were pulled out and slaughtered with swords and bullets.
>
> (Manto, "Siyah Hashiye" 1994)

She points out that the non-communally inflected term "rioters" is meant to stand in a disjunctive relationship with a violence that is genocidal and that the collective and active subject of the first sentence is replaced by a generalized and indefinite sense of victimhood as an example of a language that refuses a will to meaning. Commenting on the journalistic sparseness of the preceding sample, Kamra points out that "language itself is recognized here as a casualty of this encounter with the unthinkable" (2008: 100) and explains that Manto "speaks" not in the words but in turning the catachrestic phrasing into a literary text of the impossible condition facing him as a writer – to memorialize the messy experience of Partition within existing frameworks that are incommensurate with the experience itself.

However, the language in "Khol Do" (1994), as Das demonstrates in her brilliant analysis of his story, is not the affectation of a mentally disturbed character but an instance in which the language itself begins to stutter. The story recounts the experience of an elderly Muslim named Sirajjudin whose attempt to recover his abducted daughter results in a shocking betrayal and violation by young members of his own community. The high point of the story is the recovery of the missing daughter, albeit unconscious, whose display of signs of life at the mention of the attending doctor's functional command "khol do [open it]" to the father to open the window makes him leap with joy and the doctor break into cold sweat (Das 2007: 46).

> They handed the girl over to the hospital. Sirajuddin stood leaning against a pole outside the hospital for some time. Then he slowly walked into the hospital.
>
> There was no one in the room. Only the body of a girl lay on the stretcher.
> He walked up closer to the girl.
> Someone suddenly switched on the lights.
> He saw a big mole on the girl's face and screamed, "Sakina!"
> The doctor, who had switched on the lights, asked, "What's the matter?"
> He could barely whisper, "I am . . . I am her father."
> The doctor turned towards the girl and took her pulse. Then he said, "Open the window."
> The girl on the stretcher stirred a little.
> She moved her hand painfully towards the cord holding up her salwar.
> Slowly, she pulled her salwar down.
> Her old father shouted with joy, "She is alive. My daughter is alive."
> The doctor broke into a cold sweat.
>
> (Manto, "Khol Do" 1994)

Not the characters, but the writer Manto becomes a *stutterer in language* as he attempts to convey the enormity of the violation. The unsayable violence of the rescuers-turned-perpetrators puts the articulate writer Manto at a loss for words. The mutilation of language is articulated through the fracture of everyday speech by way of the simple command acquiring a chilling signification as the hands of the lifeless violated woman clumsily fumble to loosen the drawstrings of her trousers. Through describing the effect on the doctor, who is drenched in sweat, Manto opts for the third possibility *saying is doing* through using an affective and intensive language to transmit the unsettling horror of Partition violence.

Manto's "Thanda Gost" illustrates Deleuze's *doing it, saying it without doing it* and *saying is doing*. Manto indulges in the habit of bad novelists through using several variations of "he stuttered" to describe different voice modulations to depict the effect of violence on a male perpetrator. Manto's reversal of the gendered code of silence through silencing the voice of Eesher Singh displaces the effect of violence usually mapped on the victim to the perpetrator. The story begins with Eesher Singh returning home to his wife, Kalwant, well past midnight after an eight-day-long absence.

Manto informs the reader that a strange and mysterious quietness appeared to have gripped the city on the night on which Eesher Singh returned, and a few minutes passed in complete silence between the couple. He uses different phrases – "shrieked," "asked angrily," "asked lovingly," "asked affectionately," "started yelling," "holding her lips tight and emphasizing each word," "steaming" – to indicate changes in Kalwant's voice modulation as she patiently tries to extract an answer from her husband, who had disappeared after covering her from head to toe in jewelry he had looted during the riots.

- Kalwant Kaur finally broke the silence, but the only words she could utter were "Eesher darling."
- "Eesher darling," Kalwant Kaur *shrieked* but immediately controlled her tone, "where were you all these days?"
- "What kind of answer is that?" asked Kalwant Kaur *angrily*.
- "What's the matter with you, darling?" Covering Eesher Singh's forehead with her palm Kalwant Kaur asked *lovingly*.
- Kalwant Kaur ran her fingers through his hair and asked *affectionately*, "Eesher darling, where were you all these days?"
- Kalwant Kaur was quiet for a minute, then she suddenly *started yelling*, "But I don't understand what happened to you that night."
- Kalwant Kaur was now even more suspicious. *Holding her lips tight and emphasizing each word*, she said, "What's the matter with you, Eesher darling? You are not the same person you were eight days ago."
- Kalwant Kaur was *steaming*. "I asked who's that whore (Manto, "Thanda Gosht")?"

Eesher Singh's stolid silence in the face of the barrage of questions is betrayed by the author's description of the somatic affect that betrays the secret of his nocturnal absence.

His hand that held the dagger *was trembling*.

Eesher Singh *turned pale*. Despite her persistent cajoling and threats, Eesher Singh refuses to break his silence, but his crime and remorse is evident in Manto's use of various sonic and somatic descriptions to indicate voice modulations:

- "I don't know." Eesher Singh moved his tongue over his *dry lips*.
- Eesher Singh, who was staring at the ceiling, looked at Kalwant Kaur and gently stroked her familiar face. "Kalwant."
- His voice had *deep pain*.
- "No one, Kalwant, no one." Eesher Singh *sounded very tired*.
- "I swear there's nothing wrong." There was *no life in Eesher Singh's voice*.
- "Let go, Kalwant, let go," Eesher Singh said with *his voice weakening*. He had *deep sadness in his voice*.
- "I threw the trump card . . . but . . . but . . .," Eesher Singh's voice was *now a mere whisper* (italics mine) (Manto, "Thanda Gosht").

Manto's intermixing of the linguistic with the somatic in Eesher Singh's dying confession of his violation of the body of a dead woman, as he urges his wife to feel his hands, which turn into ice, makes language itself tremble from head to foot in an example of a brilliant use of language to express the unsayable.

- Blood was now reaching Eesher Singh's mouth. He tasted it and his whole body shivered.
- His hand was colder than ice (Manto, "Thanda Gosht").

Additionally, Manto's graphic description of the amorous foreplay between the conjugal couple in a language of circumlocution that bristles with aggressive sexual energy and culminates in Eesher Singh's impotency makes the language itself stutter, get charged, tremble and rise to a frenzy as Kalwant, suspecting him of being with another woman, stabs him. Here, stuttering no longer affects the words but itself introduces the words it effects, which cannot exist independently of the stutter.

Deleuze explains that unless *the form of expression* is supported with *the form of content* – an atmospheric quality, a milieu that acts as the conductor of words (1998: 108), the efficacy of the external marker will be lost. Manto's story is replete with the form of content that brings together the shriek, the yell, the whisper and the emphasis and makes the indicated affect reverberate through words. The stutter in Eesher Singh's speech is positioned within an atmospheric quality, the sexually charged movements of the couple that produce the intended desire in the woman but have a benumbing effect on the man despite his desperate attempts, which weaves together markers indicating his internal suffering and remorse. To demonstrate that if language can stutter without being confused with speech, Deleuze unmasks the process of the transfer from the form of expression to the form of content through the author's inserting himself in the middle of a sentence to make the language itself stutter through various means.

The stutter, non-narrative and testimonies

Cathy Caruth argues that "not knowing and knowing in trauma connects literary to psychoanalysis" (2016). Turning to "the central problem of listening, of knowing, of representing" a crisis (Caruth 2016: 5), Caruth raises the important question about the transmission of a crisis that is "marked not by a simple knowledge, but by the way it simultaneously defies and demands our witness" (2016: 5). In her insisting that it "must, indeed, also be spoken in a language that is always literary: a language that defies, even as it claims, our understanding" (2016: 5), Caruth confirms the intersection of the literary and testimonial in their forging of a complex idiom to articulate the incomprehensibility and reality of the violence, "the unbearable nature of the event and the unbearable nature of its survival" (2016: 8). An analysis of the testimonial accounts of both female and male survivors of Partition reveals that the incomprehensibility of the violence witnessed by them could be articulated only through the stutter or non-narrative. An application of

Deleuze's notion of the stutter to testimonial narratives demonstrates that *doing,* *saying* and *saying is doing* in indicating the differences in voice intonations have equally been observed in survivors' reconstructions of their narratives of Partition.

Ethnographers transcribing the recollections of Partition survivors invariably fall back on the technique of bad novelists by using variations of "he said" and by using dialogic markers like "he went silent [veh chup ho gaye]," "he broke down [phir veh rone lage]," "he sobbed [veh phut phut kar ro pade]," "he whispered [veh dhire se bole]" and "he stammered [veh haklane lage]" in indicating the change in voice intonation. In the narration of irreplaceable loss, either the survivor's voice acquired a frozen, slide-like quality or manifested in other traumatic symptoms.

> The train to India blew its whistle to indicate that it was leaving the station and here was my wife going into labour. She gave birth to my son. The station was not too far from the place. After her delivery, I helped my wife get into the train and sit down with the newborn on her lap. I sat with my three brothers with all of us holding each other's hands. We reached India.
>
> My new-born son – once we reached the station – we swaddled him in a white cloth – since we had not brought anything else while fleeing from Pakistan – and tucked the baby under my wife's dupatta – and sat in that manner the entire night in the tent in the camp put up by the Birlas.
>
> In the morning, Hindus [Hindustanis] came, made us have our meals in the *langar* [community kitchen] and asked us to leave the place since there were more people arriving from Pakistan. People went away to different places – like Dhanbad and other places – in order to settle down there.
>
> Meanwhile, we found our new-born, as my wife took him out from under her dupatta, dead. Within a day of his birth, he was dead. [Tears ran down Mr. Papneja's cheeks and his voice started breaking].
>
> (Papneja 2017)

In response to the interviewer's question whether anyone in his family had got separated from them during the exodus, a 97-year-old interviewee from Bangla Rugera Tehsil in Multan admitted in a "deeply anguished tone,"

> All of us got separated from one another. My uncle remained in Pakistan and was killed.
>
> The kids in my family [my siblings and cousins] were so young that we had to leave them behind [in a sad tone]. My brother was only two and a half years old and we left him behind.
>
> (Nagpal, Lal Singh 2017)

Dialogic markers used by ethnographers indicate the change in the voice intonation of the interviewees.

> They looted us of course, what else did they do [in an angry tone]! We had locked our houses and left everything for them to take away. They took

everything away from us. My family had everything; we even owned a horse and they robbed us.

(Nagpal, Lal Singh 2017)

A survivor from Jamshedpur narrated his family's escape with the help of some Muslims from his village, Karoli, located in district Dadan Khan, in a truck; he talked about the truck getting stuck on the way and about refugees being forced to disperse to different parts of India in a calm, level tone. After he had perfunctorily acknowledged that some lives were indeed lost during the passage, his gaze suddenly turned downwards, his eyes began to glisten with tears and his mouth went dry as "he thickly repeated" his personal experience:

[T]here we all began to feel very thirsty – feel very thirsty – there was no arrangement for water – there was no arrangement for water, there was a spring close by that had salty water – we drank that water.

(Chawla 2015)

The pauses, sighs, choking and incoherence that punctuated another witness's recall of the Great Calcutta Killings of 1946 accentuate the stuttering effect of violence on witnesses irrespective of whether they were part of the exodus or not.

Yes, I remember the riots. 1946? It was called the Great . . . The Great Calcutta Killings. I was in Kolkata at that time. The house in which I used to live – I stayed on the second, no, the third floor – there was a shop on the ground floor. In that shop, there was a boy. The fighting had already started by then. At that time, the Hindus, they chased and beat him. He was a Muslim. What could he do? He was looking for shelter. The shop was open; so, he entered the shop [long pause]. Then [pause], the Hindus who were chasing him pulled him outside and beat him badly. It was a painful sight [sighs]. I remember this incident.
Bullets were fired [incoherent answer].
It was very painful [voice chokes]. Humans killing humans. It hurts your humanity a lot.

(Roy, Haripada 2017)

Grown-up men break down while narrating their experience of both the tangible and intangible violence of Partition. When asked about the kind of employment he found on arriving in India, embarrassment and anger turned Lal Singh Nagpal's tone harsh:

What kind of work do you think we did? We performed daily labour in various places. We used to labour at the rate of Rs. two per day.

(Nagpal, Lal Singh 2017)

Recalling the days when they had to go hungry or had to work as errand boys in shops, a well-to-do entrepreneur broke down completely and was able to recover only after a five-minute gap to be able to resume his narrative:

> We went hungry for three days. . . . We worked at a salary of Rs 200 [on arrival in 1971] a month in a shop. I, my father, my brother [breaks down].
>
> (Bishen Lal 2017)

Non-narrative

As Das points out, women remembered Partition through repeating hyperbolic metaphors and spoke in general terms about their shared experience but invariably refrained from providing specific details of their personal experience. According to Das,

> this code of silence protected women who had been brought back to their families or who had been married by stretching norms of kinship and affinity since the violation of their bodies was never made public.[3] Rather than bearing witness to the disorder that they had been subjected to, the metaphor that they used was of a woman drinking the poison and keeping it within her.
>
> (2007: 84, 85)

Like the shame and loss of honour through abduction and rape during the riots that have been documented, the shame of the auto-violation of the female body through compromises women were forced to make can be shared in the public space only in general terms,

> When most people hear of the Partition, they think about the violence and the honour killings, they don't think of the women who suffered silently, day in and day out, who were forced to scrape together a little money for their family. So many became a part of the darkness in innumerable dance bars and brothels knowing that at the end of the day, money is money.
>
> (Manorama 2017)

In their inability to articulate their experience linguistically, these women were, however, denied the healing offered through the expression of pain in language (Das 2007).

Speaking about how she and her siblings were sent away from Lahore by their father to the safety of Amritsar, Krishna, aged 78, reasoned, "In those days if a train came butchered from that side, it would have to be returned butchered from this side as well. They were in competition with one another" (2008). However, when asked if she had witnessed any trains herself, she turned to her husband, whose sister and sister's husband were indeed killed during such a journey even though their mother and children survived. While her husband quietly nodded in agreement, she recalled that they would find many corpses floating in the stream near Phagwara when the floods began. It was only when she agreed to recall her own family's resettlement in an evacuee Mohalla or neighbourhood of Muslim butchers in Kalka that the memory of her horror at being accommodated in the evacuee property of butchers, with butcher's hooks still intact, made her voice quiver and turn shrill.

In recalling her memories of the riots of 1950 in Ganderia that finally compelled the family to leave, Sova Mukherjee dwelt on minute details of the time, the menu of the food she served on the particular day, the exact route by which they left and the names of shops, schools and clinics. But her description of the heartwrenching sight of a mother holding a bleeding, wailing impaled child, with a knife still stuck in his back, is almost lost in quotidian domestic details.

> Yes, during the riot of 1950 we could not stay in Ganderia. We could not submit my fees on Thursday after I gave my examination on Wednesday. The HDO, who was our neighbour, told us that we had to leave immediately because right opposite our house – with only a four-foot wall separating us – were West Pakistani Muslims who posed a threat to our lives. Then, one morning, at 10 a.m., just after I had served food to my five brothers – boiled potatoes, lentils and rice, we were told that we had to leave the place immediately under police protection. We had to cross a school called Rajinikanth School and head towards Sadhana Medical. Then, we saw a group of women from the village area of Genderia running towards us and one of them was carrying a child in her arms with a knife stuck in his back; blood flowed from the wounds and he was wailing in agony. They all went to the Sadhana Oushodhalaya's [Clinic] camp, which wasn't a medical centre anymore. There were already around 5000 people in the camp. We had to stay on the first floor where medicine bottles were kept. Every night, we were mortified by the dreaded cries of "Allah-u-Akbar" between 2 and 2.30 a.m. in the middle of the night. At that time, the police really helped us and the camp was not attacked.
>
> (Mukherjee, Sova 2017)

Mira Paul narrated the attack on her house, the largest one in which the entire village had taken shelter, in Sondhar Diya in Dhaka district, during the April 1948 riots in a coherent fashion. But her voice rose, and she paused to take a deep breath as she recalled her traumatic experience of having escaped illegally on a steamer concealed from the police.

> Then, we went to Narayanganj from where the steamers would leave. We stayed on the jetty an entire night. That was one experience I can't really describe. At night, the police came to our jetty. It was the month of April, and it was really windy at the time. The breeze from the river was chilly. We were all sleeping with blankets wrapped around us. You wanted to hear it all, so I will tell you everything. The police came on the boat and poked us with their

sticks and said "Why are these sacks here? Remove them." The police even tried to kick us out. No one moved an inch because they were scared that they would be thrown into the river.

(2017)

After she had shared banal details about the food they ate, the slur in her speech became more pronounced as she recalled their miraculous escape from a marauding mob.

At night, we had to cross a stop called Chapakhola. It was a halt for the streamer. We saw that it was raining torrentially and there was a storm. Water seeped into the cabin from the deck. We were in the cabin. But the Captain, an elderly Muslim man, did not allow us to move. Then we noticed that there were hundreds of people standing on the Chapakhola station waiting for us with raised swords – back then they didn't have pistols like now. We were all terrified. All of them were Muslims. They didn't want to let us pass. The day before that, a lot of people had been killed on the streamer. There were still blood stains on the streamer. Our Captain then told us not to be afraid, he wouldn't stop the boat at Chapakhola. He asked us not to move, he said he couldn't bear sacrificing so many lives, just for the sake of his own. The people on the shore tried to swim to the streamer but they did not succeed.

(Paul 2017)

Although her ethnographic work focused on women, Das acknowledges that the poisonous knowledge of the violence, betrayal and accusations equally seeped into the lives of male survivors as they engaged with Partition not through dramatic gestures but through inhabitation of the everyday. Partition remains at the edge of conversations not only in the memories of women but also of men. In their narration, the alacrity with which male survivors related general information about major events was matched with their inability to provide specific details of particularized instances of violence they had personally encountered. In describing their personal experience of violence, they resorted to a language so general and metaphoric that evaded the specific to capture the particularity of their experience or by dwelling at length on the surrounding events but skimming over their own witnessing of violence.

Repeatedly asked about the effect of the Noakhali riots, Jogesh Chandra Majumder, born in 1935 Rafiqpur in Noakhali, reiterated established historical and media perspectives on the political involvement of the Muslim League but carefully evaded the direct question about his own experience.

The riots were Hindu-Muslim riots instigated and created by politicians. Suhrawardy and others made people suffer. Hindus and women, too, were tortured. The memories of the riots during my childhood are forever enmeshed in my mind. I try to forget them but alas. . .

(Majumder 2017)

However, his acknowledgement of the deep imprint of his childhood memories of the riots and his inability to erase them confirms their traumatic effect. In the uncompleted sentence ending with the phrase "but alas . . .", the unsaid expresses the unspeakable horror of the riots.

> We devised different ways to hide from the rioters as we were further warned by our elders. We would hide in small water bodies with only our noses above water level. Our women had to hide too in order to preserve their family's honour. As we grew older, riots continued for some time and eventually I was sent to my maternal aunt's house.
>
> (Majumder 2017.

Rather than the 1946 riots, Majumder recalled the riots of 1971 when the personal threat faced by the family motivated its decision to send him away.

> Hindu houses were being burnt down and people were being murdered. The village consisted of both Hindus and Muslims and we were a well-to-do fam-ily in a developing village. My father and his brothers hired 10 to 12 local Mus-lims to stay in the outer space of the house (office space) so that they could protect us. They were paid a hefty sum of 10–11 rupees. We didn't have elec-tricity and when my uncle got a torch from a nearby village, we were all very excited. Under such circumstances, my father decided not to let me stay there.
>
> (Majumder 2017)

After recalling specific details about the exact amount paid as protection money by the family to the Muslim goons and his grandfather's smart tactic of chasing the rioters, he abruptly detoured, as he did at several other points, to indulge in nostalgic recollections of his childhood pursuits.

> I have very good memories from my childhood in East Bengal – running around in fields, swimming in rivers. I used to work in the shop we had in the village. At that time, we never thought of Hindus and Muslims as being any different from one another.
>
> (Majumder 2017)

Another witness, who was eight, recalled a personal experience of looting in Barisal in which his father narrowly escaped being killed by not naming the Mus-lim attacker whose name he had over heard when he was being held captive.

> They began torturing us in our everyday lives and in many other ways. They said, "You all are staying in our country. India is your country. Go to India." They began riots, looting, burglary, took away all our possessions, especially from the Hindu households. After Independence, there was a huge burglary at our house in Bangladesh. They could not kill my father but hit him hard

on his forehead with a sickle, whose scars remained for the rest of his life. And we felt as if we were enslaved even after having attained Independence from the British.

While leaving our house, one of the burglars called out the name of his fellow mate. My father was acquainted with the name. He recognized him. They realized that my father might have heard the name and recognized him. So, they returned and interrogated my father by demanding to know if he had heard anything thing. My father told a lie to save his life. He said "How would I hear anything? You have hit me so hard on my temple with the sickle that I am in acute pain. I did not hear anything." He knew that if he had admitted that he had heard the name of his attacker, they would surely have killed him and gone away. So, they went away taking all the valuable assets they could find. It was an unfortunate event. And they were so many in number that they blocked even the doorways so that we could not call out for help.

I never went back. There was nothing for the Hindus out there. They were dark times indeed. People, who had given us so much love, began behaving in a different manner.

(Chakravorty, Noni Gopal 2017)

However, while recalling stabbings of Muslims, the memory of a then 12-year-old Hindu witness of Bagbazar riots reconstructed graphic details of the Great Calcutta Killings, albeit through implicating a Sikh driver.

I have very vivid memories of my childhood. How my brother got injured, how we used to store acid in anticipation of attacks. We had taken a training in case we were faced with any danger and were required to defend ourselves. Then, when the riot got out of control, I saw the stabbings with my own eyes. There was a huge bus stand at Bagbazar. All the buses for Basirhat, Barasat and Barrackpore used to leave from there. The driver of the bus was a Sikh, and the Sikhs were actively involved in the riots. One day, I saw a man holding the hands of a person and another his legs. A Sikh, brandishing a sword, slit that person into half and, then, they all threw him away in the nearby swamp.

(Chakraborty, Samir Kumar 2017)

His memory supplements horrifying images of violence through sounds.

Then when the riots escalated, the stabbings began to increase in number. When I was returning from school, I saw stabbings at the Bagbazar junction.

The man who was stabbed at Bagbazar, I saw his intestines coming out and then he fell down on the ground with a thud. There used to be secret stabbings. In Park Circus, the Hindus were stabbed and then the Hindus began to stab the Muslims in other places. These were rampant. Hindus avoided Muslim localities and vice versa a few months before Partition.

(Chakraborty, Samir Kumar 2017)

Recalling the outbreak of violence in Qaimpur following the declaration of Partition, Inderlal Vij, then eight years old, remained completely calm and composed as he traced the exact sequence of events – the mayhem that prevailed when he returned home from school, his family and neighbours hiding in the sugarcane fields, Muslims of a neighbouring village providing them refuge and the second attack that followed the day after – to his young interlocutor. Although his facial expression remained deadpan and his tone carefully measured throughout the narration, he was betrayed by the language of gestures, particularly a hand to throat gesture, as he recounted the most painful detail, of his mother, aunt and other women in the family jumping into the river fearing the fate that awaited them if they were to fall into the approaching Muslim mob's hands.

> The next morning, we saw crowds of Muslim people advancing towards us. They came and brought with them sticks and weapons.
>
> They all were ferocious and their intentions were evil. So, the women in our families – my mother, my aunts and others – resolved that they would end their lives. There was a river near our house. All the women jumped into it and ended their lives. The river was deep and the current was strong. So, every woman committed suicide. The stray woman who managed to survive was killed by the men – my uncle and others.
>
> (Vij 2017)[4]

His face remained impassive as he launched into a long description of the generalized violence of Partition in the metaphoric language routinely used by Partition survivors.

> There were a lot a killings. Entire trains were butchered. It would be like this. A train would be sent from this side with everyone butchered and the other would return from the other side in the same condition until the cycle ended.
>
> (Vij 2017)

When gently probed on the fate of their young children as the womenfolk jumped into the river, his squirming and readjusting himself in his chair and repeated hand-to-head gestures betrayed his discomfiture puncturing his placid façade.

> Many children were drowned in the river. The wife of one of my brothers had jumped into the river with two of her children. Her children drowned in the river but she survived. My brother then slaughtered her.
>
> (Vij 2017)

In response to the interlocutor's inquiry about his own mother's suicide, he could not reconstruct the exact sequence of events.[5] He explained that his mother had gone ahead along with four other women in the family and several others, leaving the men and children behind, and had jumped into the river. When repeatedly asked if he was with his mother when she jumped to her death, he denied any knowledge but looked distinctly uncomfortable. When pushed further, he finally admitted that they all had indeed been together but got separated in the chaos and muttered that someone had picked him up as well and thrown him into the canal. "But my brother had not moved too far; he somehow dragged me out of the canal," he muttered incoherently (2017).

In sharp contrast to Vij, who maintained a stoic demeanour throughout the interview, Nand Kishore Chowdhury broke down several times while narrating his experience to his young interviewee.

> On 14th August 1947, Pakistan was formed and, on 15th August, India. But in the midst of all these events, we could never guess the intensity of Partition. We never thought that Partition would make us *refugees* [stops and takes a breath or two] and force us to leave our homes, [takes a long pause and a few seconds to control his tears, with an anguished facial expression] homeland and run for our lives! . . . No. I don't feel bad [pauses again to search for the right words]. But when I recall the entire episode, fear grips my mind and I get goose bumps [voice turns hoarse and he wipes away his tears].
>
> (Vij 2017)

Chowdhury's tortured recall of violent events conveyed his inability to overcome the trauma of the deaths he had witnessed as a ten-year-old in Khairpur Tamewali.

> 1947 made us witness intense and unpredictable chaos and destruction. After India and Pakistan got divided, we began to face a huge upheaval [swallows, pauses and steadies his voice]. The terrorism of the people was insanely spreading everywhere. And 64 people from our village were tortured to death because of the outbreak of inter-communal violence [voice breaks, gaze grows distant and he takes a long pause].
>
> (Vij 2017)

Unlike Vij, whose apparently unmoving countenance ironically betrayed the traumatic return of his repressed memories, Chowdhury was unable to repress his guilt and remorse while recounting the memory of a similar incident of proposed honour killing involving his family.[6]

> Young women were at risk. Their dignity and honour were in danger since the Muslims were trying to assault them. I had two sisters. One of them was 14 years and the other 16 [breaks into a long pause and his face reddens]. My father had no option but to pack deadly poison in tiny sachets [in a quivering voice] and give it to us. He asked us to break open the poison packets in their mouths if we smelt danger, that is, if Muslims tried to abduct any woman of our community. Strict commands were given, which enjoined us to sprinkle kerosene oil if the situation went out of control and set fire to everything including to our house. We were raised not to sacrifice our honour.

[bursts out crying]. This was the command given to all the people above 10 years of age. Two newly-wed brothers of mine, too, had wives around 16–18 years old – marriages took place at an early age those days – women were usually married at around the age of 12 to 14 years. We were resolute about protecting our honour. By the grace of God, none of us got harmed and we had enough surplus. Our food stock was so huge that we could serve six thousand people for another month or more without any difficulty. This was because most of the property and business was with the Hindus. And since we were Chowdhurys, we had a vast business. When the situation worsened, no one was discriminated against on the basis of their financial status [in a thick voice].

(Vij 2017)

Brij Mohan Vohra from Bannu, who was 12 at the time of Partition and was rescued by his Pathan family retainer from a Muslim mob during an earlier riot waxed eloquent about his Pathan saviour.

During the riots, when they were taking me away to the station, the Pathan, who noticed Muslims carrying me away, rescued me. I was very young and did not even understand what was happening.

(Vohra 2017)

But his admission that his uncle's entire family was murdered remains cursory:

Our aunts. Aunt was killed. Her whole family was killed.

(Vohra 2017)

In contrast to his summary description of the scene of the riot and his failure to recall the details of his harrowing experience, he recalled precise details of his house in Bannu as well other properties owned by his family and affirmed the family's amicable relationship with their Pathan retainers and landworkers. However, on being asked whether he would like to return to Bannu, he vehemently declined:

No, never again. There is nothing there for me now, why would I want to go there?

(Vohra 2017)

Kishenlal Chugh, from Hyderabad in Dera Ismail Khan, then 12 years old, recalled the riots of April 1947 when he was taken from his Church Mission School to the safety of his uncle's house by good Muslims.

1947, on Tuesday, our schools started. I was admitted in High School on that day. After passing the 9th standard, it was my first day in High School. Barely half an hour after we had sat down, RSS youth came running and informed us that Muslims are here, go home, get out of here. Our school was located on the outskirts, which had a large Muslim population. Muslims came and started shouting "Ya-ilahi-illah-Pakistan ke mane kya." They were coming to kill us. Our Principal took us all out of the class and took us into the town.

(Chugh 2017)

He narrated his family's close shave with death on August 14, 1947, in another firing by Muslims in which four of them lost their lives.

Then the Indian army arrived to take us away. On the way, before we could reach Lahore, we had to take rest in an open ground as evening had set in. This happened after 15th August. You could say, it was already September. In this open ground, Muslim villagers, who were hiding in the adjacent fields, started firing. We were lying down. As we put our heads down in the open ground – our luggage beside us, bullets started flying past [tilts his head backwards to demonstrate how they bent backwards to dodge the bullets]. In that firing, four of our people were killed. A couple of people who had come from India to take their children back were also killed on the spot. Then, the day broke [gestures].

(Chugh 2017)

Melaram, 97, hailing from a landowning zamindar family from the village Thatha Chawan in Gujranwala district narrated the tragic tale of the murder of two of his second cousins, one of whom was killed by Muslims a few months before Partition as they were escorting their married sister to her husband's house. Although he was not personally affected by the attacks that followed, he mentioned that one of their relatives was indeed murdered during the Partition riots but that the joint family did not deem it appropriate to return to claim his body, as the attacks had begun in right earnest and their village had been set on fire. He mentioned how Hindus were attacked even in the camp at Kale ke Mandi, where they had sought shelter, and recalled people firing with rifles to ward off attacks on the camp. However, his summary narration of the violence of 1947, which borrowed the general language of attacks [*hamle*], arson [*aag*] and devastation, without any affective display, took up barely ten minutes of the hour-long interview. Considering that all the 25 houses in the village belonged to a single clan, his mention of the first eruption of violence, as two of his cousins escorted their married sister to her *saure* [marital home] and the family's dereliction of its filial duty to their murdered kin, gestures to the disruption of the forms of life. The alacrity with which he dwelt on his readjustment to a life of hard labour stood in sharp contrast to his glossing over of details of the violent incidents that forced them to flee.[7]

In a manner similar to that of Melaram, Ram Prakash's narration of the family's move to an evacuee property in Delhi reflects the family's inhabitation of the everyday with the poisonous knowledge of the violence literally invading their personal space through the presence of the bodies of the previous occupants.

My father moved to Delhi and occupied a demolished house in Subzi Mandi, Basti Panjabian. I, along with my sisters and mother, also moved to Delhi and

[we] started living in two rooms which we got repaired somehow just to be able to live. *Two bodies were found in the debris, even in the month of Dec* (italics mine). I was not able to get admission in any school of Delhi. A new section was opened in Birla School and I got admitted in 9th class which was only for Arts students. I, who had ambitions of becoming a doctor, had to be reconciling to completing the 9th grade in April 1948 with Arts.

(2005)

The cursory reference to the presence of the corpses of the slain occupants as the narrator dwells on the family's personal travails in detail stands out as the permanent trace of the violence of 1947 that insinuated itself in the family's struggle to inhabit the everyday. Instead of narrating the unsayable violence, the narrator verbalizes the affective memories of the violence of 1947 through allusions to generalized narratives of economic privation and loss of career opportunities shared by the hinge generation of teenage survivors that were sayable in the context of Punjabi kinship and Indian friendship networks.[8]

Das's point about words working like gestures to show this violence – drawing boundaries between what could be proclaimed as betrayal and what could only be moulded into a silence – is pertinent to the non-narration of traumatic memories by survivors. The survivor's inexplicable omission of an irreplacable personal loss, the accidental demise of his mother, which triggered the family's move to resettle in Lucknow, illustrates the non-narration of the direct violence and of the traumatic events whose emotions are mapped on the sayable, which Das observes in the women's narratives.

Through piecing together the fragments of his detailed description of the family's wealth and social standing with fragments of rare confidences he subsequently shared with his spouse, the non-narration of the poisonous knowledge of violence, betrayal and accusation that altered relations between kin may be reconstructed through their particular ways of inhabiting the loss in a gesture of mourning. The first fragment is inserted in the context of his wife's astonishment at his abstaining from mourning the loss of his mother, whom he was reportedly extremely close to, while recalling events of that difficult period.[9] The demise of the mother, allegedly through an accidental fall from the terrace of the same house, must be indirectly reconstructed through his confiding in his spouse at a certain point.

He found his father sitting quietly in a dark room after the death of his mother and his telling his children that they must regard their elder brother's wife as their mother from then onwards.

(Ram Prakash 2005)

The narration skips to Lucknow, the scene of the next paragraph, where the family comes under the care of the eldest son and an elaborate language of spoken and unspoken gestures is employed to allude to the unsaid obligations and accusations governing Punjabi kinship relations. This language explains the destitute paterfamilias's hesitation to accept anything in excess of shelter and subsistence from his firstborn.

> My brother was transferred to Lucknow from Madras and I moved to Lucknow to seek admission in the XI class, Science group. As my father was not able to spare even Rs 10/- for paying my monthly school fees, I started selling test tubes, platinum wire, beakers etc. to fellow Science students of Birla School to pay my fees to be able to continue my studies.
>
> (Ram Prakash 2005)

The second fragment, another confidence shared with his wife, "He murmured that his father refused to give him Rs. 10/- for his fees" sounds like a silent accusation even though he never explicitly expressed any grievances against his father in his entire life. As in Das's narrative, the survivor's use of words, which worked like gestures that drew boundaries between what could be proclaimed as betrayal and what could only be moulded into silence, is visible in the narrator's omission of any direct reference to the family's near destitution or the mother's untimely demise in his passing mention of the father's inability to spare the paltry sum of Rs. 10/- for his school fees.

The third fragment of confidence, "When his brother's wife noticed him shedding silent tears, she offered to pay his school fees" that explains the lifelong bonding he shared with his surrogate mother, is undercut by the accusatory suggestion of his having to work part-time to be able to raise his school fees. This veiled accusation recurs several times in the narrative in his allusion to his career goals aborted by the need to augment the family income. His permanent state of emotional blunting while inhabiting the everyday in a gesture of mourning illustrates the failure of the grammar of the ordinary by which Das means *what is put in question is* how we ever learnt what kind of object love or grief is (2007: 7–8).

In recalling the experience of violence, survivor memories raise the pertinent question of the *thing* that is remembered or the object-oriented understanding of memory. If the event as an absent memory image is imprinted on the survivors' memories as an affection-impression and spontaneously appears as a sensation, the active recall of the absent image through language at the interviewer's prompting transports it to the realm of declarative memory. Husserl's distinction between primary remembrance and secondary remembrance can help to explain the difference between survivors' primary remembrance or retention of the events of Partition and their secondary remembrance or recall (quoted in Ricoeur 2006). Husserl explains the process of primary remembrance in terms of duration and shows that perception is not instantaneous and retention involves a modification in terms of perception. Retention begins with experience, which is related to an "object in its way of appearing" standing before us, its impression and its modification (quoted in Ricoeur 2006: 33). Secondary remembrance or recollection is a reproduction of the primordial "not-now" temporal object in the present that is always a re-presentation and belongs to the realm of the imagination. To this effect, the retention of the temporal object of violence occurs through the perception of a collage of fragmented visual or auditory images. The laborious recall of this experience for the benefit of the interviewer, which involves a reproduction, a re-presentation that is removed from perception and the recollection that posits that it is reproduced, places it in a relation between the actual present and the original temporal field to which the recollection belongs.

Conclusion

Speculations about silences that surrounded the Partition of 1947 and incidents of violence prior to and after 1947 have largely centred on *manipulated memories* of the nation in which memories contradicting the masternarrative of non-violent nationalist ideologies had to be effectively silenced for the imposition of a unified, triumphalist narrative of Independence and nation formation. The survivors' silence has been similarly explained through the lens of trauma theories as pragmatic protective decisions taken by families or the state to facilitate the rehabilitation of victims. This chapter demonstrated that the silence of survivors is an effect not only of *blocked memories* but of the gap between the affection-impression of the unsayable violence, its eidetic image and its representation through a language. Deleuze's idea of the stutter and Das's concept of non-narrative defines the survivors' traumatic recall of both the corporeal and non-corporeal, the tangible and intangible violence of Partition. Rather than a unified narrative of the way they remembered traumatic incidents, diverse non-narratives, ranging between complete silence and incoherent stuttering to glossing or skimming and gestures, from oblique language to hyperamnesia, define the recall of traumatic experiences of Partition by survivors. Like Deleuze's novelists, the variations used by the ethnographer to describe differences in voice modulations of survivors enable them to say, show and say and show the violence of Partition. Similarly, the narration of the unsayable with the sayable within their own communities illustrates Das's idea of non-narrative.

Notes

1 This confirms Das's view that it is not that people did not want to talk about Partition but that words had a frozen slide quality to them, which showed their burnt and numbed relation to life (2007: 12). Das's point that "the very language that bore these memories had a foreign tinge to it as if the Punjabi or Hindi in which it was spoken was some kind of translation from some other unknown language" (2007: 11) is illustrated by the survivor's unintentional slippage from Hindi and Punjabi into Mianwali as she re-enacted the horror of the violence. Das's suggestion that "inner language" might be used to describe this language may enable an understanding of the foreignness of the language used to describe violence.

2 In her analysis of Salzmann's *Shoah*, Felman argues that the film is able "to make the silence speak from within and from around the false witness: the silence within each of the testimonies; the silence between various silences and various testimonies; the irremediable silence of the dead; the irremediable silence of the natural landscapes; the silence of the church procession; the silence of the ready-made cultural discourses pretending to account for the Holocaust; and above all, in the center of the film, Srebnik's

silence in front of the church, in the middle of the talkative, delirious, self-complacent Polish crowd" (Felman and Laub 1991: 67).

3 Although the violation of their bodies was not made public, it was common knowledge in their neighbourhood. Deshi recalls that even as a seven-year-old child, she was aware of two young female neighbours traumatized in different ways, one named *bhape di voti* [Brother's wife] by all, hastily married to an abusive man more than twice her age to cover up her pregnancy and the second ostracized for her alleged deviant sexuality (2005). The example of the second young woman who, silenced by her male siblings in whom she had confided, turned to child companions to share lurid details of her sexual experiences in which she apparently took delight and possibly turned to lesbian relationships disrupts the classic narrative of rape survivors.

4 Vij's narration may be compared with Bir Bahadur Singh's account of the martyrdom of Sikh women in Butalia's book (1998: 226).

5 Significantly, Bir Bahadur Singh did not mention his mother, Basant Kaur, when he narrated the heroic tales of the women he spoke about with a sense of pride, grief and loss (Butalia 1998: 213).

6 Unlike the incident of Thoa Khalsa framed within the Sikh narrative of martyrdom recalled by Bir Bahadur Singh (Butalia 1998: 212), Chowdhury did not portray the men who killed their women as victims even though he justified it in the name of Hindu honour.

7 Despite being repeatedly asked about how he felt about his straitened circumstances in view of his family's former wealth, he explained that since it was a fate shared by a large number, he did not feel any remorse or self-pity.

8 Raj's narrative of Partition mirrors that of Ram Prakash's in its dwelling at length on his inability to pursue career choices while skimming over the miraculous escape first to Lahore and then to Amritsar and of the humiliation of hawking goods on the pavement.

9 Das explains that the language of lamentation through which the body combined with acoustic and linguistic codes to perform the work of mourning in normal times in the Punjabi sociocultural context was displaced by silence in mourning the loss of life during the violence of Partition (2007).

6   Not at home[1]

Homelessness and displacement have largely been examined in relation to exiles, diasporas, asylum seekers and refugees who are forced to cross the borders of nation-states. Although the plight of internally displaced people has now begun to receive international attention, the displacement of nearly 15 million people during the Partition of the Indian subcontinent in 1947 has receded too far in public memory to figure in contemporary debates on forced migration. However, Partition, in addition to violence, is deeply etched as *deshnikala*, or exile, in the memories of survivors. In remembering Partition as exile or banishment, the survivors of Partition contest the nationalist representation of the exchange of populations in 1947 as a return to domicile of Hindus and Sikhs to India and Muslims to Pakistan. Narratives of domicile in Partition memories and stories present a peculiar example of "being at home" and, at the same time, "not being at home." After being uprooted from places they called home, Partition survivors were sheltered in new locations where they did not feel "at home."[2] This feeling of *unheimlichkeit*, of unhomeliness, had as much to do with the unfamiliar physical and cultural geography of the places of resettlement as local communities' ambivalent reception of refugees. For this reason, the literal and metaphorical loss of home, the materiality of home and its psychological aspects are conspicuous in Partition survivors' struggle to make homes in new lands.

Since the boundaries of home were defined and circumscribed in pre-Partition cartographies by the village, neighbourhood, town, city or region, Hindustan, still a fuzzy formation, was imagined by those crossing the border from the West as an unfamiliar terrain inhabited by "Hindustanis," which denoted to them speakers of Hindi language. Pujandi, originally from Bhakkar in the vicinity of the Thal Desert, continued to use the term "Hindustani" to refer to the residents of Uttar Pradesh, a Hindi-speaking region she and her family were forced to settle in, even half a century after Partition (Pujandi quoted in Deshi 1993). Although she had travelled several times as far as to Kolkata in the east and Bombay in the west with her railway official husband after their migration to Lucknow, her sense of place was firmly rooted in her birthplace, Bhakkar, and its *Thalochi* dialect, whose imaginary boundaries ended in Ambarsar [Amritsar] with all areas lying outside the Majha region of Punjab conceived as a foreign land (Pujandi quoted in Deshi 1993). Urdu writer Joginder Paul reiterated a similar sentiment in his admission "I felt I had suddenly turned grey while taking charge of our dire circumstances beyond the borders in distant Bharat, with which we were familiar only through the slogans and speeches of political bigwigs" (2007: 146). The complete disorientation of people's sense of place with the formation of post-colonial nations and subjectivities through their having to make a transition overnight from strong identifications with ancestral birthplaces, dialect groups, sects and subsects to new allegiances to a newly created nation resonates with the idea of the uncanny, or the psychological experience of something as strangely familiar, an encounter with incidents "where an everyday object or event is encountered in an unsettling, eerie, or taboo context" (Royle 2003: 1). Intellectual uncertainty, meaning that "the uncanny would always, as it were, be something one does not know one's way about in" (Jentsch 1906: 7), sums up the feeling of survivors of Partition 1947 forced to migrate from their old homes and become refugees in new lands.

The ambivalent reception of Hindu and Sikh refugees by their hosts, which swung between hospitality and hostility and simultaneously recognized and othered them, heightened their sense of not feeling at home. While their shared religious sameness with the older residents of India entitled them to be part of the Hindu/Indian self and the ritually and legally entitled recipients of hospitality, their ethnocultural and ethnolinguistic difference marked them as foreigners inviting their hosts' suspicion and hostility. This chapter explores the notion of *unheimlichkeit* or uncanny in relation to Partition survivors' experience of resettlement in regions familiar yet alien at the same time, which produced a sense of their feeling uncomfortably strange. The chapter argues that the unfamiliarity of the language, culture and region they were forced to resettle in produced a sense of not being home in the new land that was supposed to be home. The uncanny effect was produced as much through its first meaning of unfamiliarity as in its second meaning as the exposure of those aspects of existence that were meant to be hidden, as that which is "concealed, kept from sight, so that others do not get to know about it, withheld from others" (1919: 3). In addition to the uncanny, the chapter draws on Derrida's views on hospitality, Simmel and Baumann's idea of the stranger, Kristeva's notion of abjection and Tyler's idea of social abjection to examine the ambivalent reception of displaced persons that made them foreigners in their purportedly new homes.

The uncanny, das heimlich and unheimlich

Horace Alexander, explaining that his use of the word *refugee* to describe people who were forced to flee violence was technically accurate, warned that it did not quite fit survivors of Partition since the state specifically instructed its officials that they were not to be treated as foreigners. The refugees' appeal to the filial sentiments of their hosts, "We are flesh of your flesh; we are blood of your blood. Please do not treat us aliens and foreigners" (Alexander 1951: 5–6) was underpinned by a similar sense of entitlement. Ritu Menon gives credit to the state for its "enlightened attitude" towards Punjabi refugees (2003: 156), which was engendered by the feeling that these refugees were never "aliens" but part of the nation-building process.

However, as Derrida points out, "the guest, even when he is well received, is first of all a foreigner, he must remain a foreigner" (2000: 73). The Kantian host treats the one who is staying with him "as a human being, but he sets up his relationship to the one who is in his house as a matter of the law" (2000: 71). Although the refugee was warmly welcomed, provided asylum and had the right to hospitality, he had to "ask for hospitality in a language which by definition is not his own, the one imposed on him by the master of the house, the host, the king, the lord, the authorities, the nation, the State, the father, etc." (2000: 15). The nation, the state and its old residents imposed on the newcomer the condition of "translation into their own language" in return for hospitality, which, according to Derrida, constitutes "the first act of violence" (2000: 15). The act of hospitality began with the implicit demand that refugees understand the language of their hosts, speak their language, in all the senses of this term, in all its possible extensions, before they were able to welcome them into their country. Derrida explains that when the home is violated, one can see a privatized and familialist reaction directed against the technological power that threatens the home, the traditional notions of hospitality. Anyone who encroaches on the home of the host is perceived as an undesirable foreigner and a hostile subject.

Georg Simmel's notion of the stranger is equally pertinent to the perception and representation of the displaced person in the native's imaginary. As Simmel pointed out, the stranger, despite being a member of the group in which he lives, remains distant from native members of the group. The difference of the stranger inherently lies in his origins and his being perceived as extraneous to the group with his "distance" emphasized more than his "nearness" (1971). Zygmunt Bauman, in "The Making and Unmaking of Strangers," provides the most convincing explanation of the integration of migrants and settlers in recent times (1995). Bauman argues that host populations' hostility towards new migrants is based on first arrival rather than indigenous rights. After a period of estrangement, migrants are gradually integrated into host societies and hostility shifted to new arrivals.

Simply translated, *heimlich* means "friendly, intimate, homelike; the enjoyment of quiet content, etc., arousing a sense of peaceful pleasure and security as in one within the four walls of his house" (Freud 1919: 3). Jentsch asserts that "uncanny" happens when one is "not 'at home' or 'at ease' in the situation concerned, that the thing is or at least seems to be foreign to him" and that the word suggests "a lack of orientation that is bound up with the impression of the uncanniness of a thing or incident" (1906: 8). Jentsch repeats the truism that "the traditional, the usual and the hereditary is dear and familiar to most people, and that they incorporate the new and the unusual with mistrust, unease and even hostility (misoneism)" to propose his notion of intellectual certainty (1906: 3). He defines the uncanny as "the sensations of uncertainty" and "lack of orientation" produced by the "new/foreign/hostile" that takes on "the shading of the uncanny" (1906: 4–5). The uncanny may be explored in survivor testimonies with reference to the Jentschian meaning of being not "at home" or "at ease" and "a lack of orientation," which shows that "what is 'uncanny' is frightening precisely because it is not known and familiar" (Freud 1919: 3) but also because it is "concealed, kept from sight" (1919: 3).

Sigmund Freud modified Ernst Jentsch's definition of the uncanny through tracing its etymology to the German adjective *unheimlich* with its base word *heimlich* ("concealed, hidden, in secret") to propose that that social taboo yields an aura not only of pious reverence but also of horror and even disgust. The term *uncanny*, according to Freud, is a vaguely defined term that "belongs to all that is terrible – to all that arouses dread and creeping horror" (1919: 1) and traces its origins to the unheimlich, the opposite of heimisch, as "familiar," "native," "belonging to the home" (1919: 2). Disagreeing with Jentsch on the equation of unheimlich with unfamiliar and the idea that "uncanny" is frightening precisely because "it is not known and familiar," he argues that although "what is novel can easily become frightening and uncanny," something has to be added to what is novel and unfamiliar to make it uncanny. This something is to be found in the second meaning of the unheimlisch, "concealed, kept from sight, so that others do not get to know about it, withheld from others" (1919: 3).

The Hindi-Urdu elite and the uncanny city

Accounts of the alleged "refugee invasion" of Kolkata, Delhi, Lucknow and other cities of India have concentrated on the uncanny feeling produced in their older residents through the defamiliarization of their beloved cities with the mushrooming of unsightly camps, colonies and slums for sheltering hordes of refugees but have made no mention of their own othering of the refugees (Gupta 1981; Pandey 1997; Datta 2002; Dalrymple 2006; Ali 2015). As Bauman points out, the arrival of migrants in new places involves mutual distrust and lack of acceptance. The twin terms "refugee" and "displaced," used interchangeably by official agencies to describe migrants to India after Partition, provide a clue.[5] The word *refugee* is multiple, heterogeneous and segmented, not only in its meanings as asylum, shelter and/or hospitality but also with respect to the kind of refugee who is welcome (or not welcome) and in which part of the home. Though their political status entitles refugees to asylum and official aid, local populations often exclude them from the social and cultural life of the city, accentuating their displacement. While they were given refuge, in the limited sense of protection and shelter, they were still regarded as cultural aliens. As the nation's "own" (being Hindus/Sikhs), but outsiders in Delhi, Lucknow and other parts of India, Punjabi refugees were made to occupy the space reserved for strangers. Nikos Papastergiadis examined the image of the refugee as defined by the fear of the other in proposing his notion of the invasion complex to explain the psychic forces that differentiate the self. His view that "psychoanalytic theories of projection and anxiety can help unfurl the fears that have been directed against the refugee" is applicable to the othering of the refugees of Partition (2006: 431). Similarly, Kristeva's comments on the hijab controversy in France, which posit "the stranger" as a body that is constituted as foreign (and abject) by the bodies of citizens who comprise the normative body politic of the French nation, may be successfully transposed to explain the constitution of the Punjabi body as foreign by the normative body of elite Hindi-Urdu citizens.

One must remember that rather than the monolithic institution of the state, local host populations determine the extent of hospitality and control the socialization process through which the stranger is made into one's own. Diaries and memoirs of national leaders, social workers and intellectuals echo local hosts' attitudes towards refugees, which oscillate between altruism, compassion and philanthropy and repulsion, disgust and horror. Notwithstanding their ungrudging provision of asylum to displaced victims of violence,[3] the residents firmly believed that the celebrated Hindi Urdu high culture of precolonial Delhi and Lucknow encapsulated in the Urdu term *tehzeeb* was contaminated by the invasion of Punjabi language, refugee aggressiveness and commercial enterprise. Although "the Peshawari salwar kameez and the uniquely Afghan male headgear with its golden peak" sported by refugees from across the western border was "not an uncommon sight in the streets of Delhi till the mid-1960s" (Hashmi 2017), or even in the 1970s, it unambiguously marked the Punjabi, Sindhi, Bahawalpuri, Derawal or Multani refugee strolling on its streets as an alien.

"The city that was once a Mughal city, then a British city, had by the 1950s emphatically become a Punjabi city," according to historian V. N. Datta, causing great concern to its cultural custodians (2002). Similarly, Delhi Congressman Brij Kishan Chandiwala's complaint, in his 1950s correspondence with Pt Jawaharlal Nehru, was representative of the prevailing sentiments of the city's older residents:

> The people of Delhi are living a life of helplessness. . . . They have on their own wiped out their exclusive identity forever. None remains, neither their language nor their attire and tradition. The Delhi residents have become strangers in their own house.
>
> (Quoted in Kaur 2008)

Similarly, the alleged Punjabi invasion of Delhi was perceived as ushering in a linguistic and cultural vacuum. "All that made Delhi special has been uprooted and dispersed. Now the language has shrunk. So many words are lost," Imtiaz Ali, the author of *Twilight in Delhi*, dolefully declared to William Dalrymple in 2015 (Ali quoted in Dalrymple 2015). Historian Narayani Gupta's description of contemporary Delhi in *Delhi Between the Two* "as a place where 'Tilak Nagars and Nehru Roads proliferate, and hardly anyone knows of the poetry of Mir and Zauq, the humour of Ghalib, the quality of life that Chandni Chowk once symbolised'" sums up the attitude of Delhi's intelligentsia towards Delhi's alleged Punjabiization several decades later, even though the term *refugee* is not specifically mentioned (1981).

Lucknowites in the 1950s who had never seen a Sikh in person or heard Punjabi language, shared the sentiments of native Hazratganz Sikh kebabseller Gianbhai mentioned by writer and old Lucknowite Ved Mehta: "Saale Sardaron ne Lucknow ko tabaah kar diya (the damn Sikhs have destroyed Lucknow)" (Mehta

2007). Historian William Dalrymple, too, sides with his Muslim native informant, Lucknow poet and writer Mushtaq Naqvi, in viewing the refugee arrival as Lucknow's Punjabi invasion.

> It was Partition in 1947 that finally tore the city apart, its composite Hindu-Muslim culture irretrievably shattered in the unparalleled orgy of bloodletting that everywhere marked the division of India and Pakistan. By the end of the year, the city's cultured Muslim aristocracy had emigrated en masse to Pakistan and the city found itself swamped instead with non Muslim refugees from the Punjab.
>
> (Dalrymple 2006)

Dalrymple is invited to look at Lucknow through the Mughal lens and guided through its historical Mughal landmarks.

> "Come," said Mushtaq. "Let us go to the Chowk: there I will tell you about this city, and what it once was.
>
> "When I was a boy, before Partition, I came here with my brother," said Mushtaq [to Dalrymple]. "In those days the Chowk was still full of perfume from the scent shops."
>
> (Dalrymple 2006)

In the cities of Delhi or Lucknow, known for their linguistic chauvinism, not only the Thalochi or Punjabi, but also the Urdu that cross-border migrants spoke accentuated the foreignness of refugees "who insist on speaking their Urdu in Punjabi!" as Urdu writer Joginder Paul puts it (2007: 144). Mushtaq had complained to Dalrymple,

> But now the language has changed. Compared to Urdu, Punjabi is a very coarse language: when you listen to two Punjabis talking it sounds as if they are fighting. But because of the number of Punjabis who have come to live here, the old refined Urdu of Lucknow is now hardly spoken. Few are left who can understand it – fewer still who speak it.
>
> (Dalrymple 2006)

Sharing the colonial view of Punjabi as "an uncouth dialect not fit to be a permanent language," it took their elite residents several decades before their "ears got accustomed to the sound of Punjabi language" (Ali, quoted in Dalrymple 2015). Refuting Sehba Ali's optimistic narrative of transformation in Lucknowite attitudes over the generations and its young people "finding Punjabi a warm and friendly language," some of whose expressions they assimilated into their own speech (2015), Naintara Maya Oberoi in "What Does It Mean to Be a Punjabi" recalls that "Punjabiyat seemed something to be embarrassed about" even for someone like her growing up in Delhi in the 1990s (2015).

The exile and the uncanny

Locating its history in banishment, Edward Said defines exile as "the unhealable rift forced between a human being and a native place, between the self and its true home: its essential sadness can never be surmounted" (Said 2001: 173). He maintains that exile, once "the exquisite and sometimes exclusive, punishment of special individuals," has been transformed in the 20th century "into a cruel punishment of whole communities and peoples, often the result of impersonal forces such as war, famine, and disease" (Said 1994: 47). Interestingly, Said includes, along with Armenians, Palestinians and Jews, those displaced by Partition in his category of the exile. He uses exile as a broad category to include "anyone prevented from returning home" but distinguishes between exiles and refugees. "The word 'refugee' has become a political one, suggesting large herds of innocent and bewildered people requiring urgent international assistance, whereas 'exile' carries with it, I think, a touch of solitude and spirituality" (Said 2001: 181). Though he admits that exile is no longer the exclusive privilege of special individuals but the suffering of entire peoples, Said tends to theorize broadly in relation to these individuals, particularly intellectuals, rather than to large hordes. He is also inclined to privilege the exile's double vision as a privileged insider/outsider experience, which is further romanticized by Salman Rushdie. Yet Said's views on the condition of exile can be useful in elucidating the experience of ordinary Punjabis displaced by Partition.

The nostalgia of Zahir Al-Din Muhammad Babur, who invaded India in the 16th century to found the Mughal Dynasty, for his native Samarqand, explains the sense of the uncanny that the conqueror encountered on arriving in the new land:

> Hindustan is a country of few charms. Its people have no good looks; of social intercourse, paying and receiving visits there is none; of genius and capacity none; of manners none; in handicraft and work, there is no form or symmetry, method or quality. There are no good horses, no good dogs, no grapes, musk melons or first-rate fruits, no ice or cold water, nor bread or cooked food in bazaars; no hamams, no colleges, no torches or candlesticks.
>
> (Babur 1922)

Although the refugee and the displaced share a lack of orientation and the uncanniness produced by the unfamiliarity of the language, culture, climate and region with the exile, the explorer and the conqueror, the Partition refugee's experience differed from theirs in her not being "at home" in what was promised by the state as home. The uncanny encounter of the conqueror with the unfamiliar territory he subjugated and brought under his control is reproduced in that of the refugee Pujandi on first encountering the gnawing poverty of the unknown terrain she had imagined as "Hindustan" – its pests and termites, its strange flora and fauna, its "dark-skinned" inhabitants, its women "who wore no underwear" – when she arrived in Lucknow, the utopian city of Deewane Maulvi Sahib's demented imagination in Paul's *Sleepwalkers* (Pujandi, quoted in Deshi 1993).

Paul's *Sleepwalkers* (2007), in which Urdu-speaking mohajirs from Lucknow sleepwalk through a reconstructed Lucknow, complete with its iconic chowks and bazaars, in Karachi, offers a poignant translation of the sense of dislocation that fits the definition of the uncanny.

Echoing Deewane Maulvi Sahib's yearning for Malihabadi mangoes, Allahbadi guavas and the lanes of Aminabad that his traumatized mind had transposed to Karachi, the 34-year-old Pujandi bundled along memories of Bhakkar in the *phulkari*[4] quilt she had lovingly embroidered for her trousseau and improvised the cuisine of Cholistan's medieval city, known for its saints and forts, confirming that the refugee, whether stigmatized as the *sharanarthi* in Lucknow or as the *mohajir* in Karachi, interminably dwells in the realm of the uncanny (Pujandi, quoted in Deshi 1993).

The new / foreign / not hostile is experienced first of all as a foreignness of language/dialect that creates a sense of disorientation. Miscommunications resulting from Punjabi refugees' inability to use the appropriate Hindustani[5] term, idiom or tone, ranging from the jocular to the traumatic, foreground the foreignness of languages and dialects. One of the commonly shared jokes post-Partition was about a Punjabi woman producing inadvertent laughter in her desperate attempt to translate the Punjabi phrase *tid vich peed* [stomach ache] into Hindi by lengthening the Punjabi vowel sounds in the Punjabi word for stomach [*tid*] to *teed* instead of using the Hindi equivalent *pet mein dard* [stomach ache], based on the erroneous assumption that mastering Hindi was merely an issue of lengthening Punjabi vowels, to the consternation and amusement of the helpless doctor (Deshi 2005). Another survivor, then barely seven, recalled being heartbroken when his promise about performing well in studies if given an opportunity to join a Delhi school in the idiomatic Punjabi phrase *tusi vekh lena* [you will see] to the Hindi-speaking headmaster was misconstrued as a threat (Rajpal 2006). Unlike the seven-year-old who succeeded in overcoming his ethno-linguistic handicap to ascend to one of the topmost positions in the Indian judiciary, 34-year-old Pujandi's unsuccessful trek from the Thalochi dialect of the Thal Desert to unfamiliar Hindustani to stake her claims to citizenship of the new nation called Bharat marked her as a foreigner till the end of her life, as Gera Roy points out:

> But Pujandi, now Satya Kumari, valiantly fights her way through the maze of Hindi to get across basics, no matter if her strange accent causes much merriment, from both the dialect and the vernacular tongue; the family's increasing fluency in the national language is an indicator of the success of the rehabilitation scheme.

> (Gera Roy 2004)

The inferioritization of Punjabi as a crude, uncouth language was assimilated by refugees themselves, corroborating Fanon's view of the colonized's interiorization of the colonizer's view of the colonized and Imogen Tyler's idea of abjection as including those who are abjected. Captain Harbhajan Singh, who migrated from Pakistan, admits that "Punjabis and Sindhis were outspoken and their language was rash" (Quoted in Srivastava 2006). Sikh Punjabis, like Harjap Singh Aujla, chide "the communally divided Punjabis of Delhi," who "by acts of omission and commission, did not assert enough to preserve their language and culture" even though Delhi was "a de-facto Punjabi speaking region" from 1947 to 1967 (2015). However, their abandoning their language could instead be viewed as Hindu, and subsequently Sikh, refugees' response to their abjection and the inferioritization of Punjabi as a loud, uncivilized language by their hosts, underlining their otherness and the sense of the uncanny.

Sartorial difference has been described as a key marker of cultural difference and can be translated into corporeal difference. If the unisex salwar kameez sported by Punjabis was the most visible sartorial signifier of difference in the settler imagination, the cotton *dhotis* and *saris* draped by dusky Hindustani males and females respectively, along with their trademark vermillion mark on the forehead, symbolized the foreignness of purity and pollution taboos in the Punjabi Hindu or Sikh imaginary. "Hindustanans [women of Uttar Pradesh] change their saris before entering the kitchen but only rinse them with water, hai, how would they ever become clean?" (Pujandi, quoted in Deshi 1993). Pujandi would wrinkle her nose at the yellowing whites drying in the dhobi ghat [washermen's quarters] and proudly hang out snowy white linen, salwars and pyajamas she had scrupulously boiled in tins of carbolic soap and beaten with a wooden stick on the line in the open space outside the military barracks where they were accommodated for eight long years until allotted compensatory plots in refugee colonies. "Hau hai [Shame on them], even old women with grey hair put *sindoor*[6] in their partings and sport a vermillion bindi. And, hai rabba [oh my God], the primary colours they wear, red, yellow, green!" (Pujandi, quoted in Deshi 1993), she would click her tongue disapprovingly strictly forbidding her pre-pubertal daughters to perform shringar [make-up] that was best left to kanjris [courtesans] in her opinion. Female children, as young as 10, were demurely covered from head to toe with strict instructions never to let the chunni [a long scarf] slide below their bosoms and pubertal young women made to cover their heads, contradicting Harbhajan Singh's contention that Punjabi "women were never in 'purdah'" (Quoted in Srivastava 2006).

Historians, sociologists and culinary experts have lamented or celebrated the deterioration of the food cultures of cities like Delhi, Mumbai and Lucknow with the arrival of Punjabi refugees through the introduction of Punjabi street foods like *kulche chhole, dahi bhalle, daal makhani* and butter chicken. The cultural shock of the refugees' encounter with unfamiliar flora and fauna and cuisine, however, has been restricted to family anecdotes circulated by Partition survivors. The climactic difference between refugee homelands and places of migration accounted for divergences in agricultural produce, dietary conventions and culinary practices.

If the coarse peasant diet of Punjabi refugees appeared uncouth to the old residents of Delhi and Lucknow habituated to an elaborate cuisine and culinary rituals, the refugee was equally perplexed by the prospect of finely ground flours and spices, the size of the rotis [bread] and the thinness of *daals* [cooked lentils]. Unlike Delhi, which had a flour mill dating back to 1917, Punjabi refugees were still accustomed to hand ground or coarsely ground flour obtained from the neighbourhood grinding mill. Wheat being the most important ingredient in the Punjabi diet, Pujandi and her neighbours bought only Punjab wheat and washed and dried it on the rooftop before getting it ground to the right degree of coarseness in the neighbourhood *atta chakki* [flour grinding mill]. Fine thin rotis were perceived as a sign of miserliness of housewives among Punjabis under their erroneous assumption that hussifs reduced the size and thickness of the rotis to put away some pin money for personal needs.

Thus, the shock produced through the elite encounter of the open, transparent, collective culture and communal living of West Punjab with the private, opaque, individualist nature of the Hindi-Urdu high culture could be considered mutual, signifying the alienness of each to the other.

Uncanny as intellectual uncertainty

Peter Somerville, in "Homelessness and the Meaning of Home: Rooflessness or Rootlessness?", warns against confusing homelessness with merely the fact of rooflessness, derived from the meanings of home as shelter and abode. Arguing that the meanings of both home and homelessness are complex and multidimensional, he considers both home and homelessness as ideological constructs, involving compounds of cognitive and emotional meanings (1992: 537). The meaning of uncanny as intellectual uncertainty, as "something one does not know one's way about in" (Jentsch 1906) needs to be unpacked at an existential plane. The loss of intellectual mastery in an unfamiliar world whose rules are unknown produces a sense of disorientation and the irruption of the uncanny. Unlike the old, familiar world in which the intellectual mastery of the environment produced a reassuring sense of stability, the breakdown of all established norms and verities following the outbreak of the violence produces cognitive dissonance and the uncanny.

The feeling of not being at home emerges from indeterminacy, uncertainty about all givens that refugees had taken for granted and a lack of knowledge about the rules of the new order in which they were propelled coupled with a sense of the loss of their place in a particular order. Punjabi poet Amrita Pritam summed this up in her conversation with Nonica Dutta:

> Voh to hai na jade hil jaati hain. Kimate hil jaati hain. Jitne vishvas bane hote hain voh hil jate hain, zameen hil jaati hain (Do you know those roots? They are shaken. Values are shaken. Trust is shaken. The ground is shaken.)
>
> (2017)

The refugees' inability to establish conceptual connections with the previous ideational sphere of the individual or intellectual mastery of the new, foreign or unfamiliar produces a sense of mistrust, unease, even hostility. The sense of disorientation experienced by refugees emerged from their cognitive dissonance in comprehending the ways of the new world through the previous ideational sphere of the self.

Sommerville's point about home and homelessness being an experiential and intellectualized reality as well as an imagined reality is pertinent in examining the feeling of unheimlichkeit in Partition refugees. The embeddedness of home and homelessness in systems of social relations that Somerville elucidates helps in understanding the alteration of class relations and organization in the new social order, particularly through the legal designation of survivors as refugees or displaced persons. The conceptual difference between the old and the new inhered as much in the exceptional circumstances of displacement as in the distinctness of socio-cultural structures of Punjab from other regions in Hindustan.

Refugees shared with their hosts a notion, a form of subjectivity defined in relation to the sociocultural hierarchies of the ancestral place and one's traditionally assigned place within that structure. Hence, their experienced reality of being without or with barely functional shelters was paralleled with the ideological loss of home through their being reduced to the status of the homeless underclass and of the uprooted. The figure of the refugee signifies a primordial homelessness without any anterior antecedents, connoted by the Punjabi term *jida agga pichcha nahin* [one whose future or past is not known], which, in turn, causes a deep intellectual uncertainty. Although they were provided hospitality, and even charity, refugees were excluded from the space of the host as foreigners merely because of their ways of doing things being different from those of older inhabitants. As persons whose antecedents were unknown, they were initially viewed with a mix of compassion and suspicion and with downright hostility when they began to compete for resources. Their failure to establish a conceptual connection of the new, unfamiliar world with the ideational sphere of the home left behind emerges from the absence of a predesignated space for the refugee in the old established order.

Since the sense of place means both one's position in society and spatial location, the refugee is doubly disoriented through geographical displacement as well as displacement from his position in society. If, as Marjorie Grene suggests, "the primary meaning of 'place' is one's position in society rather than the more abstract understanding of location in space" (1968: 173) and spatial location derives from one's position in society rather than vice versa (Sorokin 1964), the refugee's unheimlichkeit ensues from loss of social position rather than spatial dislocation alone. The loss of position is connoted through the designation of the survivor as refugee, as an abject being who does not belong but is dependent on the kindness of the host for survival. The cultural difference that repels the hosts is partially the product of the difference in lifestyle due to the demotion of all survivors to the homogeneous category of the refugee.

As Yi-Fu Tuan points out, people are defined by their positions in society and their lifestyles, what they wear, the foods they eat, the places where they work and live, the practices they follow (1979). The subtle class, caste, rural, urban and regional differences signified through the upper and lower garment, headgear, even facial hair, tone, speech and mannerisms in traditional Punjabi society connoted Punjabi foreignness to their hosts. Their hosts' ignorance of the linguistic, sartorial or behavioural codes of Punjabi social hierarchy, the relative positioning of castes, professions and skills coupled with their subsumption under the generalized category of the refugee or displaced person denoted a loss of social position in relation to which place is defined.

In registering the cultural shock of the difference in attire, speech, behaviour, food and ways of living and working that announced the refugees' foreignness to the old residents, the connotations of these visible signifiers in marking social hierarchies through which refugees made feeble attempts to retain social positions have been completely overlooked. Ironically, the more the refugees attempted to reassert their preordained social position through visible symbols, the more alien they appeared to their hosts.

> Before Partition when I came to Kaithal to see my mama (uncle), everything was so beautiful. I used to wear a long-tailored coat on a sari. My uncle remarked that the people in town were asking after me and found me fashionable. I was a Pindi [Rawalpindi] girl. But when I came to Panipat [after Partition], no one asked after me. No one . . . Nobody bothered to even look at me. I felt poor and rejected. And I took to wearing salwar kameez.
>
> (Vash, quoted in Datta 2017)

Refugees from Punjabi villages and upstart towns, Mushtaq alleges, have "brought with them their own very different, aggressively commercial culture" and "what was left of the old Lucknow, with its courtly graces and refinement, quickly went into headlong decline" (quoted in Dalrymple 2006). The perceived affront to local Brahmin, bania and Hindi-Urdu elite sensibilities through the blatantly commercial culture transported by Punjabi and Sindhi refugees to old colonial and Mughal cities like Kolkata, Delhi and Lucknow that recurs in accounts of refugee reception conveniently ignores the historical fact of the strategic social engineering of Punjabi Hindus as *lalas* [traders and shopkeepers] and Sikhs as *jats* [villagers] by the British. Narratives of the phoenix-like rise of Punjabi and Sindhi trading castes from rags to riches within a span of a few years after Partition abound in Partition oral histories. The rapid emergence of Punjabi entrepreneurs as contenders to local businesses and industry was also noted by the contemporary and present media. However, the mercurial rise of Punjabi and Sindhi trading communities and entrepreneurs in India's ancient and new cities and towns has been severely decried in local accounts. These accounts primarily focus on the newcomers' competitive temperament, unscrupulous trading practices and materialistic outlook with only a grudging acknowledgement of the industry, resourcefulness and resilience that the newcomers brought with them.[7] The cognitive dissonance between Hindu trading castes' self-ascription as the one fuelling the economy of West Punjab and their ascription by the Hindi-Urdu elite as reviled traders or shopkeepers reflects the induction of refugees from an old established order to a new one that denigrated their business acumen and entrepreneurial competencies and rendered them as strangers in their own land.

A contest between two conflictual codes of propriety appears to be in evidence in the difference between residents' and refugees' organization and inhabitation of the neighbourhood. For the "aggressively commercial culture" held culpable for the demise of feudal Lucknow or Delhi is deeply rooted in the biraderi network, a long-established business practice based on social kinship bonds, through which refugee hawkers of Aminabad or Chandni Chowk, located in the heart of Lucknow or Delhi, are reported to have monopolized Lucknow's or the Indian capital's retail business. It is this mapping of peasant or shopkeeper civilitas on the courtly architecture of Lucknow and Delhi that is interpreted by its decadent aristocracy as a radical desecration of the city's revered monuments.

Partition scholars have criticized refugees' nostalgic dwelling on their former status and wealth as fabricated narratives of fabulous wealth. The refugees' detailed descriptions of the size of their dwellings, property and businesses and their family standing are often dismissed as attempts to ameliorate present suffering or penury. Since the significations of particular markers of language, dress and behaviour are lost in the new land, refugees often indulged in lengthy explanations to orient themselves by defining their place in the social order. Dwelling on these details is refugees' way of negotiating the loss of a sense of social position through providing equivalents of the new, unfamiliar social order in order to stake their claims into the new, unfamiliar social hierarchies.

For Partition and nation-making also heralded the emergence of new signs of power and status attached to modernity in which old markers of landownership, property and family pedigree were displaced by education and skill-based status definers.

Uncanny as hidden from the public eye

> From the hospital, one had a vantage view of the entire camp. As far as the eye could see, tents and tin-roofed shelters were crowded together. In their midst was a ceaseless traffic of naked children, dishevelled women, bareheaded girls and men burning in defiance and humiliation.
>
> (Kidwai 2011: npg)[2]

The image of "naked children, dishevelled women and bareheaded girls" aptly captures the second meaning of unheimlich, which includes all "that ought to have remained secret and hidden but has come to light" (Freud 1919: 224).

Unheimlich, in its related meaning as what "ought to have remained secret and hidden but has come to light" (Freud 1919: 224), has primarily been interpreted as "the return of the repressed" in the analyses of the behaviour of direct victims of violence and rape. Memory narratives of shame and humiliation have largely focused on "the return of the repressed" in survivors of rape and perpetrators of violence that were manifested in repetitive behaviour until they found a cathartic release through their sharing of their narratives with the oral historian. However, the exposure of the hidden and intimate spaces of the self to the public gaze in the open camps that simultaneously aroused emotions of disgust and fascination in local residents was misinterpreted by these hosts as an essentializing difference between the self and the stranger rather than one forced by economic contingencies.[8] The horror of residents at the sight of exposed bodies in the camps was mirrored in the humiliation experienced by refugees at the bodily exposure, particularly that of the female body.[9] Considering that the metaphor of the veiled woman has conventionally functioned as a signifier of male honour in patriarchal North Indian cultures, the abjected image of bareheaded girls encapsulates the humiliation faced by families through the exposure of sexualized female and destitute male bodies, signifying violation and privation, which should have remained hidden from the outsider's gaze.

The notion of the uncanny has often been read together with the notion of abjection. Abjection, meaning "the state of being cast off," has been explored as that which disturbs conventional identity and cultural concepts (Kristeva 1982: 92). Abjection refers to the process by which one separates one's sense of self from what disturbs one's sense of life. In particular, Julia Kristeva's idea of the abject as "the jettisoned object" that is "radically excluded" and rejected by/disturbs social reason that underpins a social order has been extensively used in genocide studies (1982: 3). According to Kristeva, xenophobia is a form of abjection which constitutes the foreigner as a "border abject" which the citizen-subject – and the community or state – can manage (through hate) (Kristeva 1991: 103). Imogen Tyler revises Kristeva's notion of abjection as that which disturbs identity, system, and order to propose her notion of social abjection in relation to abjected groups like minorities, women and asylum seekers. Tyler includes in her idea of social abjection both those who abject and those who are subjected to abjection by deconstructing the dictionary meaning of abjection to argue that abjection "not only describes the action of casting out or down, but the condition of one cast down, that is the condition of being abject" (2013). The representation of the spaces of abjection – the squalor, disease and open living of refugee camps or the crass, aggressive commercial ethos by the powerful hosts as repulsive or disgusting is complemented by the resistance of the oppressed who find themselves abjected. Tyler's notion of social objection and how it operates in relation to different forms of governmentality and impacts particular groups is particularly instructive in explaining the abjection that accompanied the uncanny in the Partition experience.

Tyler draws on George Bataille's idea of abjection as violent exclusionary forces of sovereign power that strip people of their dignity and reproduce them as dehumanized waste to develop her notion of social abjection. Bataille foregrounded the inclusion/exclusion of "the waste populations created by sovereign power," which, he held, "at the same time intrude at the centre of public life as objects of disgust – the 'national abjects'" (Tyler 2013). As Martha Nussbaum and Ngai have argued, disgust has been used throughout history "as a powerful weapon in social efforts to exclude certain groups and persons" (Nussbaum 2004: 107) or "as a means of reinforcing the boundaries between the self and 'contaminating'

others" (Ngai 2005: 338–39). The refugees of Partition 1947, who, as citizen subjects of the newly formed nation hailing from various classes, were neither the
social underclass nor moral outcasts, were still produced by residents as objects
of disgust through their disgust consensus. Since refugees were part of the same
and their citizenship offered them a framework for belonging to the state, it did
not "address or resolve the deep-seated, 'prickly passions aroused by the intrusion
of the "other" in the homogeneity of . . . a group'" (Kristeva 1991: 41).

In explaining the politics of disgust, Tyler points out that although disgust is a
guttural aversive emotion, it is saturated with socially stigmatizing meanings and
sustains the low ranking of things and people. Notwithstanding her compassion
for the refugees to whose rehabilitation she dedicated herself after the brutal murder of her husband in the Partition riots, Begum Anis Kidwai's horrified reaction
to refugees living in the camps, representative of the Indian urban elite, is underpinned by the politics of disgust that accentuated the relationship of residents with
refugees. Cohen explains that people are denounced as filthy because either the
physical aspects of their bodies or perceived attributes repel the onlooker. He adds
that "actions, behaviours, and ideas are filthy when they partake of the immoral,
the inappropriate, the obscene, or the unaccountable" (Cohen 2005: x), which are
invariably used to make a distinction between the same and the other. However,
Mary Douglas denies the concept of "natural dirt" by arguing that dirt is constituted by prevailing beliefs of what is clean and what is not (1966).

Aurel Kolnai's phenomenology of disgust, which intertwines physiological,
emotional and moral aspects of disgust, description of disgust as a spatially aversive emotion that creates boundaries and introduction of moral disgust through
the transference between physically and morally repulsive reactions, elucidates
the sliding of the physical experience of disgust of residents confronted with the
filth in rehabilitation camps and other spaces of abjection occupied by refugees
into contempt and judgements of value. In Mushtaq Naqvi's denunciation of the
degradation of the aristocratic Nawabi culture of Lucknow through the alleged
refugee invasion, the physiological repulsion for the Punjabi refugee is transferred
to the moral in the contempt he displays for the Punjabi businessman.

> I'll tell you one incident that will bring tears to your eyes. A young girl
> I know – 18 years old, from one of the royal families – was forced to take up
> this work. A rickshaw driver took her in chador to Clarkes Hotel for a rich
> Punjabi businessman to enjoy for 500 rupees. This man had been drinking
> whisky but when the girl unveiled herself, he was so struck by her beauty that
> he could not touch her. He paid her the money and told her to go.
>
> (Dalrymple 2006)

Although disgust is offset by compassion in the memoirs of state officials, social
workers and cultural custodians, it is framed within the logic of hygienic governmentality that requires "that an abject population threatens the common good and
must be rigorously governed and monitored by all sectors of society" (Berlant
1997: 175). Finally, the notion of abject normativity works through a particular

form of abjection, which is "dependent upon the ways in which a norm is culti-
vated, incited, repeated, practiced, mediated and performed" (Tyler 2013). Tyler
emphasizes the need to examine "the mechanisms through which norms of abjection are fabricated, operationalized and internalised" and argues that "it is only
by critically engaging with abjection as contingent expressions of normativity"
that we might be able to disarticulate the effects of abjection as lived (2013).
The cultivation and reiteration of the aristocratic Muslim or Hindu *bania* [trading
caste] norm in Lucknow and Delhi respectively produces the different, aggressively commercial culture that refugees brought as abject normativity, which must
conform to be the universalized normativity of a refined but indolent aristocratic
Muslim or Hindu bania culture.

As Michelle Meagher argues, "disgust is not a condition of an object but an
effect of a beholder's intentional relationship with an object" and "objects are rendered disgusting or dirty through implicit social agreements" (Meagher 2003: 32),
which may be defined as disgust consensus. Viewing disgust consensus as deeply
political, Tyler asserts that disgust consensus is produced through repeated cita-
tion and enters the perceptual field. The repeated disparagement of the mercantile
culture of Punjabi and Sindhi traders and merchant castes to which they added
quintessential refugee aggressiveness as crass and commercial by the old aristocratic and trading elite threatened by industrious, highly competitive newcomers
produced a disgust consensus and the myth of Punjabi materialism that persists in
the Indian imaginary. When the abjected refuses to remain in its abjected space of
charity provided by the host and begins to compete with the host, the host's physiological response to the filth of refugee camps slides into judgements of value and
twice abjects the refugee as a moral outcast.

Fanon's account of epidermalism shows how abject identifications and inter-
pellations of the colonized by the colonizer were internalized by the colonized
themselves. His work offers a glimpse not only into what it means to be made
abject but also how subjugated populations revolt against their abjectification.
The repression of the abjection to which refugees were subjected returns as refugees articulate it seven decades later after having concealed it even from their own
families. It is these memories of abjection, of prosperous traders and merchants
having to perform manual labour, having to sleep on the pavement or hawk goods
in public spaces on their arrival that are now shared with both pride and pain with
complete strangers.[10]

The invisible refugee city

Lucknow has a particular emotional resonance in mohajir (immigrant) narratives as the symbol of a glorious Muslim past. For example, mohajirs in Karachi Joginder Paul's *The Sleepwalkers* nostalgically reconstruct the Lucknow of
nawabs and taluqdars (large landowners) marvellously documented in Attia Hosain's *Sunlight on a Broken Column* (1961) and Qurratulain Haider's "Chandani
Begum" (1999). The city and its landmarks also figure prominently in Raj narratives as well as in Allan Sealy's ode to Lucknow, *The Trotternama* (1988). But no

historical or literary account of Lucknow has deigned to look at its considerable immigrant Punjabi population except William Dalrymple's travelogue in which, however, all its evils are attributed to Lucknow's Punjabi invasion (2006). I will follow urban planner Kevin Lynch's method to contrast alternative maps of the Lucknow city: the decadent Muslim of Dalrymple's travelogue and the refugee Punjabi of my respondents. As Lynch found out, the space of the city as understood by Lucknow's different ethnic populations varies in its memorable features (Hayden 1997: 27). The "communocentric map" of Lucknow that follows, marks an overlap between the city as *civitas* – the space of a community, and as *urbs* – 'mapped or architecturally conceived concept of the city' – in the territorial struggle between the two groups over the spaces of the city (Barbara Mundey, quoted in Giard 2000: 56).

Had Dalrymple stepped out of the crumbling palaces, *havelis* (mansions) and the decaying Clarke Hotel to listen to the stories of elderly men and women reclining on the charpoys in the Chowk's cramped refugee quarter of Lajpat Nagar, he would have come to hear a different version. We shall revisit the Chowk and now look at the city as it appears to the refugees living and working there.[11]

Among the figures flitting on the resettlement rooftops in the Chowk is Prem, a pleasantly plump "after Partition born" Punjabi girl who has never been to Punjab. The Chowk, the most disreputable residential address in Lucknow today, is the only place she can call home. A youth from Lucknow's refugee camps and colonies – let us call him Ram Lal – would, unlike Mushtaq, have been strictly forbidden to stray into the lanes of the Chowk laden with the cloistering smell of cheap perfume, precisely because of its role in the history of the decadent seductions of the old city symbolized by courtesans.

In the narrow lanes of the Chowk, the beautiful poetry and songs of the famous courtesan of Lucknow, Umrao Jan Ada, would have been drowned in the wailings of refugee mothers and children. One of these mothers (call her *Beeji, Bebe, Jhai* or any other Punjabi name for mother), cooking in the open, could be heard muttering at the beggars who have descended like flies in her native Mianwali or Bannuwali *boli* [speech], "*Pehlan hi asi lutte putte aye aan, phir wi sanoon naheen chodde!*" [We have already been looted! Are we not to be left alone?]. But the recent memory of unaccustomed starvation would have made her add more ghee-dripping *paronthas* to the heap allocated for those the householder must feed, including the birds, the animals and the Brahmin. One wonders if she ever got to feed Mushtaq's "tonga drivers and the tradesmen in the bazaars" with "exquisite manners" and was thanked by them in "the most chaste Urdu" (Quoted in Dalrymple 2006). It would hardly have mattered because their chaste Lucknowi Urdu would have been Greek to her.

The language that summons Prem to the kitchen sounds close to Punjabi, but it doesn't sound like fighting as alleged by Mushtaq (Dalrymple 2006), rather like a singsong voice. Dari,[12] the language in which she communicates with her parents, is a Punjabi dialect spoken in the Mianwali district, then part of North West Frontier Provinces (NWFP), whose grammar, intonation and vocabulary differ from the Punjabi spoken in Lahore or Amritsar. It is different from the Punjabi spoken in most other homes in Lucknow as well, because the Chowk has the largest concentration of refugees from the Mianwali district in West Punjab who are not fluent even in standard Punjabi, leave alone chaste Urdu. Prem's parents, despite not being from West Punjab, are members of the Mianwali *biraderi*, which helped them set up a grocery shop.

Dalrymple, standing on the roof of Mushtaq's school in Aminabad, saw only "the oldest quarter of the city and the heart of old Lucknow."[13] His Orientalist prose filters through Lucknow's great Mughal past that includes "the great swelling, gilded domes of the city's remaining mosques and imambaras." The "flight of pigeons" that Dalrymple describes may certainly have "wheeled over the domes and [come] to rest in a grove of tamarind trees to one side." But it could have been Ram Lal's little boy, whom he saw flying "a kite from the top of a small domed Mughal pavilion." Dalrymple's exoticizing gaze is fixed on "the spectacular panorama, still one of the greatest skylines in all Islam." From his vantage point, the signs of decay were clearly visible but not the life beginning anew just across the mosques and minarets in Aminabad's bustling lanes.

Refugee Lucknow, like refugee Delhi, arose out of disintegrating palaces and mansions. On arrival, the hypothetical Ram Lal and his family would forcibly have occupied one of these crumbling havelis, an uneasy compromise at best for those having fled Muslim persecution very recently.[14] Ram Lal's relative, the owner of a garment workshop in the Chowk, might have sub-contracted chikanwork to a former *begum* (lady of a large house) for a measly sum.[15] Even Mushtaq is forced to acknowledge that the owners of *havelis* might have been reduced to penury because "they were never brought up to work – they simply don't know how to do it" (Quoted in Dalrymple 2006).

Aminabad's new landmarks bear the inscription of its refugee history, most notable in Mohan Market, earlier called Refugee Market.

> Earlier known as Refugee Market, there are about 250 shops, 80 in the two rows of each lane, most of them selling cloth and readymade garments, ladies' footwear etc. The market forms a major shopping area for a big population of the city.
>
> (TNN 2004)

A walk to the Aminabad main crossing from any of the four approach routes gives one a different vantage point but all lead eventually to the old Maidan, the present-day Mohan Market (see Figure 6.1). If one were to enter from the direction of Gola Gunj, one would come face to face with the giant hoarding of Prakash's *kulfi* (local ice cream) *falooda* shop. Alongside and in the parallel rows, there are 250 shops selling Lucknowi embroidered garments, Benarasi tissue and footwear in various shapes and sizes. The Punjabi ownership of the shops is announced by the Punjabi-tinged Urdu of the majority of the shop owners. While among the Punjabi Hindus, the Khatris and Aroras were traditional trading castes who owned shops in Lyallpur and Lahore, Partition appears to have brought other castes too into this fold.

Figure 6.1 Mohan Market, Aminabad, on the Muslim Festival of Chand Raat

Figure 6.2 Members of Purusharthi Merchant Association, Mohan Market, holding a protest march for allotment of shops

The Aminabad bazaar testifies to the refugees' ability to negotiate with host cultures for economic concessions. Most of these shopkeepers began by selling their wares in the Aminabad Maidan. Refugee hawkers plying their trade from the pavements in the Maidan gave local shopkeepers tough competition by selling at extremely low margins and eventually drove them out of business.[16] Initially allotted space in the Maidan, they were provided wooden shacks after some time. The pucca shops are reported to have been allotted after several years through the refugees' negotiation with local authorities to win a place in the Lucknowi spaces of production (see Figure 6.2).[17]

Conclusion

Nostalgic reconstructions of old cities reflect the disgust and revulsion produced in old residents through the defamiliarization of their beloved cities by the refugee influx following the Partition of 1947. The uncanny city has rarely been examined from the perspective of the refugee other than in Joginder Paul's *Sleepwalkers*. Although the state and old residents extended hospitality to displaced persons, their cultural difference from host communities led to their being perceived as strangers. The strangeness and unfamiliarity of the language, culture and lifestyles of the places they were forced to migrate to in addition to the cognitive dissonance and abjection of life in the open produced in the displaced a sense of the uncanny in both its meanings.

The sense of the uncanny produced in their secure hosts at the sight of the familiar city transformed by the refugee influx was mirrored by the terror produced by the unfamiliar city and its dwellers in the refugees. The lived experience of terror, *dahshat*, of those who have been caught in mob violence that defined an entire generation and the unhomeliness experienced through the home, a place of security, turning into a space of terror have not received adequate attention in the literature on Partition. The permanent rupture of the loss of the sense of security associated with the home and the homeland is articulated by refugees not verbally but through their affective responses to the overwhelming sense of uncertainty, indeterminacy and contingency. Paul's sense of terror in the aftermath of Partition violence captures the sense of the uncanny experienced by other victims and witnesses of violence.

> When the front door of our house would be locked, I would jump from one roof to another, jump into the inner courtyard of our house and go to sleep; even with my mother away and the door locked from outside.
>
> (Paul, in Gulzar 2017)

Premonitions and anxieties related to stepping out of the house, the neighbourhood, the mohalla and to be surrounded by religious, linguistic and cultural others explain survivors' reluctance to step out of refugee enclaves. Their commute outside the little Punjabs, Derawals and Multans of cities like Delhi, Lucknow[18] and so on into the unfamiliar terrain of Hindustani and Urdu produced in cross-border refugees a sense of dread, the uncanny even as the homogenized figure of the refugee as Punjabi signified "the other" to the hosts (Gupta quoted in WSJ Staff 2011). Like Paul's sleepwalkers, who believe themselves to be living in Lucknow and make a daily commute to Karachi through parts of the city they name Pakistan, a name that produces in them a strong feeling of dread, inhabitants of refugee colonies in Alam Bagh and Adarsh Nagar reconstructed a "little Punjab" in Lucknow from which they commuted daily to "Hindustan" with its distinctive Lakhnavi "pehle aap"[19] syndrome.

In the little Punjabs of Adarsh Nagar and Alam Bagh in Lucknow, refugees bridged the gap between Thalochi, Punjabi and Urdu by crossing the *tehdi pulia* [crooked bridge], which they continued to pronounce without the aspirated /dʰ/ sound for half a century and three generations, into the Islamicate and colonial precincts of Char Bagh, Aminabad and Hazrat Ganj before they could get the pure Hindi-Urdu pronunciation of "the crooked bridge" right. In sharp contrast, Punjabi refugees in Delhi, required to traverse the apparently unbridgeable chasm between Punjabi and Hindi/English to be able to master the Standard Hindi pronunciation of the refugee colonies named after Indian national leaders, domesticated the resettled homes through their Punjabiized pronunciation. As Naintara Maya Oberoi puts it, "Rajinder [*Hindi* Rajendra] Nagar was, without doubt, a Punjabi c'lony [colony]" (2015). The reconstruction of the mohalla strengthened the biraderi networks and enabled their inhabitants to overcome the unheimlichkeit they experienced when out of its bounds.

The feeling of "being" and "not being" at home, therefore, is a product of refugees' acceptance of new lands as home and of their hosts' acceptance of them as their own. It is obvious that their economic contribution to old Indian cities and towns, which probably arrested their disintegration, has yet to earn Punjabis recognition or participation in the city's public culture. The new city that arose from the decaying minarets and mansions of old cities and towns, home to Punjabi enterprise, demonstrates Punjabi commerce rubbing shoulders with Mughal or Hindu bania grandeur in the mix of castes, classes, languages and cultures through refugee settlements in old cities.

Notes

1 Excerpts from my essay "Adarsh Nagar diyaan Gallan: At Home in a Resettlement Colony". *Interpreting Homes: South Asian Literature* (ed) Malashri Lal and Sukrita P. Kumar, (Delhi: Pearson Education) 2006, pp 16–33 have been included in this chapter.

2 With a notice of five weeks, close to 17 million people were forced to bundle up their childhoods, belongings and future and head towards an unknown land that was now to be their "home." And the land which actually was known to be our "home" now had a new name called Pakistan (Harbans Singh 2017).

3 "Most of the locals were shocked by our tone, but did not reject us. Rather, we were welcomed with open arms," Harbhajan Singh acknowledged the extension of hospitality by Lucknowites (Harbhajan Singh, quoted in Srivastava 2006).

4 Phulkari [floral embroidery], an embroidery particular to Punjab done on female garments, such as chunni, salwar kameez, saris and wall hangings, originated in the

phulkari [quilt] that young women were required to embroider as part of their dowry to exhibit their skills to prospective in-laws.

5 Hindustani with a lower case "h" is used here to refer to the mix of Hindi and Urdu spoken in Hindustan [the Punjabi term for the land of the speakers of Hindi] as well as the inhabitants of the linguistic state of Uttar Pradesh. It might be noted that the Greek view of the stranger as barbarian was based on the stranger's inability to pronounce Greek words that appeared like "blah blah" to native Greek speakers.

6 The practice of wearing sindoor, a vermillion powder, by married women in the parting of their hair to signify their marital status was limited to newlywed women in the region of Punjab before Partition. Both unmarried, middle-aged and elderly Punjabi women refrained from wearing bright primary colours and makeup.

7 The role of biraderi support networks and the practices of vartan bhanji that enabled new arrivals in the resumption of their former trades and vocations after the initial phase of hard labour and homelessness in some cases has largely remained unacknowledged except in personal testimonies.

8 Arguing that "the image of the refugee has been defined through the fear of the other," Nikos Papastergiadis proposes his notion of the invasion complex, which he defines as "a new conceptual hybrid that draws upon elements of psychoanalytic theory and complex systems theory, and Giorgio Agamben's analysis of sovereignty" (2006: 429).

9 Gyanendra Pandey provides an extremely nuanced analysis of the horror of Delhi's elite Muslims at the transformation of Delhi, a city of Muslims with a predominantly Muslim culture, following the influx of refugees. "Shahid Ahmad Dehlavi notes in his detailed memoir of Delhi in 1947 that, for 700 years before that time, the people of Delhi (Hindus and Muslims) had never had to experience the vulgarity that was now everywhere. 'Behayai aam hai.' Meat was now sold out in the open, women bathed in the streets, even the Hindu women had altogether stopped going out into the markets. 'Dilli ab bhi baqi hai, aur vahan Musalman bhi baste hain, lekin ab vah Dilli kahan?' (Delhi still exists, and Muslims live there too, but where is that Delhi of yore?)" (1997: 2267).

10 Statements such as "We pawned the last silver pot so that we could eat" (Mangal Singh 2011), "I carried gara [concrete] on my shoulders when I arrived in Lucknow. I have built Halwasia Market brick by brick" (Arora 2011), "My father's back was lacerated by having to unload heavy sacks of vegetables in the wholesale vegetable market" (Kathuria 2006), "I sold fabric on the footpath," "I would help my father sell fabric in the park. I can still tear fabric with my fingers" (Rajpal 2006), "I slept outside the shop" (Bishen Lal 2017) accompanied by a wry laugh or a break in the voice articulate the experience of abjection that appears to be as lacerating as the wounds of physical violence.

11 The biggest Punjabi concentration in Chowk is of non-literate or semi-literate frontier-people from regions neighbouring Dera Ismail Khan and Dera Ghazi Khan. I have personal knowledge of a number of families migrating from Bhakkar in Mianwali district who were allotted quarters in this resettlement colony.

12 Dari is used here as a short form for Derawal language and must not be confused with the language Dari spoken in Afghanistan.

13 As a child, I lived in one of the houses in the "oldest quarter of the city," the sole Hindu dwelling in a Muslim compound. From the balcony, I could see pigeons wheeling over the domes and minarets and hear the call for prayer from the mosques.

14 I have in mind, 36, Jagatnarayan Road, the house located on the main Gola Gunj *chauraha* [square], I lived in as a child. I learnt later that the original house had an ornate style, which was knocked down to make "modern" rooms for the family. Across the crossing, I could see Dalrymple's minarets and latticework balconies.

15 The chikan industry still functions with burqa-clad Muslim women coming to the middlemen's homes to be allotted piecework by middlemen's wives or female relatives. Muzzaffar Ali's *Anjuman* (1986), which movingly brought out the plight of Lucknow's

purdahnasheen chikan workers, did not interview Chowk's refugee wholesalers who work on abysmally low margins to survive in the cut-throat chikan work industry. My understanding of the readymade chikan garments business is based on the experiences of a close relative who is a wholesaler operating from the Chowk area.

16 A highly successful member of my family recalls hawking fabric along with his father, a trader, in a similar Maidan in Delhi as a child on arrival from Pakistan (Rajpal 2006).

17 Until January 2019, the shopowners were not given ownership of the shops and held a protest march demanding that they be allotted the shops. Harish Chandra Midha narrated a similar journey of the Shastri Market in Ranchi: "Back then there were no shops constructed; there were only wooden tables kind of set up at the Shastri market area where we sold our goods. There was a small kiosk where they gave us all the fabric from where all the arrangements were made and fabric was divided among sellers. . . . The ground, the boundary wall was built first and then all those 43 shops of 8 by 8 feet were then made and allotted to the immigrants" (2017).

18 Lucknow received 5 percent of Punjabi refugees migrating to Uttar Pradesh. Other towns in Uttar Pradesh that received Punjabi refugees include Kanpur, Dehradun, Meerut and Saharanpur. Strangely, the Bollywood blockbuster *Bunty aur Babli* (2005) acknowledges UP's refugee population by locating one of the two protagonists as a Sikh Punjabi.

19 *Pehle aap* [After you] is a phrase that is used to refer to the hyper-refined cultural sensibilities of the original residents of Lucknow, particularly of the aristocratic Hindi Urdu elite. A story about two Muslim aristocrats waiting at the railway platform, who kept urging the other to board the train stating *pehle aap* [after you] in tune with established etiquette and ended up missing the train, is ironically repeated to illustrate the impeccable etiquette [tehzeeb] of Lucknowites.

7   Memories of lost homes

With the turn to affect, atmosphere and emotion in geography, modern geographical surveys and cartographies of material spaces and places have been supplemented or displaced by affective and emotional geographies that privilege the emotions and affects evoked by particular places over their geographical entities. In particular, Brian Massumi's theory of affect (1995); Ruth Leys's turn to affect (2011); Nigel Thrift's non-representational, affective geographies and cities (2004, 2007); Amanda Kearney's emotional geographies (2009); and Ben Anderson's affective atmospheres (2009) have interrogated the Cartesian notion of abstract space and geographical coordinates through their rethinking of materiality, embodiment and representational spaces. Additionally, the contributions of geography in foregrounding the relationship between culture and space, the production of space and the idea of mental maps of inhabitants and walkers have revealed space and place to be imagined, subjective, social, cultural, and embodied. If homelands are produced through the emotions that material landscape evokes in its inhabitants, cities are reconstructed through effects and affects. In these subjective and collective imaginings of places, the role of memory, such as the relationship between space and memory in Halbwachs's collective memory (1950) or the symbolic significance of space in Nora's sites of memory (1989) and Bachelard's analysis of the space of the home (1994), has been accorded a key role that often produces images of homelands or cities that might not correspond with their material, geographical coordinates. These new understandings of space, place, homeland and cities have been dexterously applied in throwing light on the representation of villages, cities and regions in individual and collective imaginaries.

Partition literature abounds in survivors' nostalgic reconstructions of remembered homelands, villages, towns, cities and neighbourhoods in which emotions, affect and atmosphere displace the material, real, cartographic spaces with emotional and affective geographies. These affective and emotional geographies produced by survivors' memories are viewed as complementing, supplementing and disrupting the cartographic contours of real cities, villages and regions. Both fictional (Rushdie 1982; Das 1990; Paul 2007) and testimonial narratives (Chakrabarty 1995; Hoon 2013) succumb to a desire for the pre-displacement homeland, home, community, friends, culture and practices disrupted by Partition. The thrust of these memoirs is to foreground the affiliations and affective geographies of lost homelands as opposed to real inhabited spaces in identity formation that produce a dual attachment.

In documenting emotional geographies of home and homelands that draw on humanistic geographies concerned with emotional qualities of place and human life and feminist geographies dwelling on the feeling women experienced in particular places, the larger body of literature privileges people's expressed emotional responses failing to provide a political antidote to the manipulation of precognitive/non-cognitive emotional life. The significance of that which cannot be brought into representation, non-representational geographies that deal with inexpressible affects, has been relatively neglected. However, the range of emotions that intervene between homeland nostalgia and desire for return complicates the role of emotional and affective geographies in the production of remembered spaces that are privileged over geographical cartographic maps. Despite the expressed emotions of love, care, security, stability, privilege and well-being attached to the homeland, the desire to revisit or return to the place is not shared by all survivors. In psychological geography, this is often interpreted as the need to protect the memory of a place unaltered by the ravages of traumatic experience, time and development, which might not correspond to the contemporary material coordinates of the real spaces. Steve Pile, in his essay "Emotions and Affect in Recent Geography" (2010), points out that although emotional and affective geographies intersect in their being mobile, in being marked by intimacy, proximity and reliance on ethnography and in sharing the unconscious and the space in between, they need to be distinguished through demonstrating a conceptual break between emotions and affect. Pile's distinction between emotional and affective geographies is useful in differentiating the expression of emotions and the affect involuntarily produced by the evocation of the homeland in survivor memories (2010). Additionally, Anderson's notion of atmosphere can complicate the intensities of emotions and affect (2009). This chapter draws on theories of emotional geographies and affective cities to examine the homelands produced by survivors' memories to isolate the complex interplay between emotion, affect and atmosphere in their convergence on remembered places.

Imaginative geographies

The most celebrated site for debating the material reality of imaginative geographies produced by nostalgic desire was the India imagined by Salman Rushdie in his novel *Midnight's Children* (1982). Critiqued by his detractors for portraying a tourism image of India, Rushdie famously defended his portrayal of Indian cities and neighbourhoods as "imaginary homelands" reconstructed by the nostalgic memories of a pre-teen resident of particular neighbourhoods in Delhi, Meerut and Bombay that were partial, incomplete and inaccurate but not entirely a fiction because they were based on the mental map of the neighbourhoods Rushdie had actually lived in before being sent to school in the UK (1991). Rushdie's mental map of elite South Bombay neighbourhoods in Bombay was not entirely a fiction since it was grounded in the concreteness, substance and reality of buildings of

Warden Road, Peddar Road, Kemps' Corner, Walkeshwar, Marine Drive or Cuff Parade. Unlike the maps of other urban neighbourhoods of cities devastated by Partition, the elite neighbourhoods in South Bombay that Rushdie inhabited had remained comparatively unaltered until the 1980s when he published his novel. However, Rushdie made a strong case for the imaginative geographies of places that are never the product of purely cognitive operations but, as Edward Said brilliantly explained, are animated by fantasy and the play of desire (2000, 2005). Rushdie's acknowledgement that his India would always be an India of the mind and a particular version of India that is in the past reaffirms the imaginative geographies of survivors whose imagined homelands are not entirely fictions even though they are made up because they did have a concreteness, substance and reality in the past that has all but disappeared. Although Rushdie's representation of other places, peoples or landscapes of India has been criticized for the ways in which these images reflect the desire, fantasies and preconceptions of their expatriate author and the grids of power between the elite tourist and his subjects, imaginative geographies can sustain the image of imaginary homes as well as of what is far away (Said 2005: 55).

Nostalgic homelands

The memory turn in humanities and social sciences has engendered a renewed interest in the phenomenon of nostalgia among geographers, historians and sociologists. Originating in the Greek term *nostos* [longing] and *algia* [home], nostalgia is roughly translated as a longing to return home and has been deconstructed through a variety of disciplinary lenses. Nostalgia has been defined as a narrative or act of loss, an articulation of homelessness, a declaration of distance from one's object of desire. Fritzsche called nostalgia "a moment of alienation, a familiar symptom of unease" (2001: 62). Susan Stewart's definition of nostalgia as a sadness for an absent object, which existed only as a narrative and is experienced as a haunting lack attached to a dwelling (1984), explains the impossibly idyllic flavor of Utopian origins attached to the lost home because nostalgia, as Lowenthal maintains, is "memory with the pain taken out" (1985: 8). The desire that the nostalgic Partition survivor seeks is "the absence" or "a desire for desire" (Stewart 1984: 23) and the home that memory constructs might not be real. Yet, as Davis points out, nostalgia is not an isolated mindtrick or solipstic narcissism but is rooted in experience (1979). In addition to Davis, Svetalana Boym's "reconstructive nostalgia" (2001) and Alison Blunt's "productive nostalgia" (2003) have disengaged nostalgia from an absent past to its efficacy in negotiating the present. Nostalgic reconstructions have been critiqued for their romanticization of the past, their disconnect with real spaces and their desire for a unified centre. As Elizabeth Wilson has argued, nostalgia is marked with ambivalence (1997). She shows that while nostalgia conjures memories, feelings and evocations that are socially and discursively constructed, they are lived in the present as sensations and pleasures and are yet bound to loss and discomfort with a familiar world removed and reimagined. She makes the important point that the romance of nostalgia is bound both to a place that is lost and the present and that we appropriate it for the present through viewing it from the distant perspective of the present. However, imaginary homelands enjoy a centrality in theories of nostalgia, irrespective of whether they view nostalgia as positive or negative or are past-oriented or future-oriented.

Edward Said's seminal insights into the functioning of memory, desire and the unconscious in the production of the imaginary geographies of both home and the other provide a framework for the complex work of desire and memory through which the homeland is imagined by survivors of Partition 1947 (2000, 2005). Imaginings of homelands – a village, a city, a town or a neighbourhood – are invariably products of nostalgic recollection. They follow the logic of memory in the selection of the convivial and erasure of the traumatic experiences, exhibit an exilic yearning for a lost home and are coloured with emotions of love, care, attachment, friendship, happiness and comfort for spaces, objects, practices and people. Nostalgic homelands map an emotional geography of spaces and places whose spatial coordinates are produced through the relations between human beings and their environment and social, economic and cultural activities and relations between groups. The overwhelming emotion in imagining is attachment to the birth/ancestral place and a sense of belonging through shared speech, culture, food, rituals and practices; architectural objects and spaces; institutions and so on. The emotional affiliation and affective belonging to the homeland imbues it with a sense of enchantment that produces affective magical cities of memory. The Bombay of Sa'adat Hasan Manto and Salman Rushdie, the Lahore of Manju Kapoor and Bapsi Sidhwa, the Lucknow of Joginder Paul and the Lyallpur of Gurcharan Das construct a fictional city, an "imaginary homeland" lost in the past that is a "different country" produced through the desire of the city (Rushdie 1982). These fictional representations of the city are replicated in the testimonial accounts and memoirs of Partition survivors whose nostalgic recollections construct them as the comforting space of home.

In his exploration of the connections between memory, place and immigration, Alastair Bonnett has addressed issues of memory and myths of place in those who have left the city and used mental mapping techniques to investigate how memory and nostalgia shape representations of the city (2015). Bonnett uses the term *mobile nostalgia* to refer to the complex relationship of those who left the city and shows that the two aspects of nostalgia – historical and spatial – can be connected. Engagements with nostalgia have focused on the temporal rather than spatial dimensions of nostalgia that characterize the attachments of survivors who have left the city. The survivors' desire for the lost home replicates the polarization of *yahaan* [here] and the *wahaan* [there] that structures orientalist representations of the other in Said's schema. Wahaan is the exoticized other, the place of beauty, plenitude and wholeness that is experienced as a lack in the squalid, impoverished, indeterminate yahaan, the romanticized home that is contrasted with the unhomely dwelling. Pran Neville says though he left Lahore fifty-five years ago, that's where his heart has always remained:

> In a way, you can say, I never left Lahore because it is always with me. I have carried it with me wherever I have gone, and when I look back and there is no

place on earth I haven't been and all through those years, Lahore has stayed with me. I am an unreconstructed Lahoria, you can say, who never thought he would ever live elsewhere.

(Quoted in Hasan 2003)

With the psychographic turn in geography, the re-enchantment and re-mythicization of ordinary places through the nostalgia and memory of residents has been examined in considerable detail. The dissonance between the imagining of an idyllic home in metaphors of the *desh* [village, country], *pind* [village], *mulk* [domain], *vatan* [nation, homeland], *ilaka* [area] and *mohalla* [neighbourhood] and belonging to the nation has been examined in detail in Partition literature to emphasize either the pull of the originary homeland, the arbitrariness of political boundaries or new forms of belonging and citizenship. In the nostalgia industry, which has mushroomed in the last few decades, nostalgic recalls of beloved villages, cities and neighbourhoods are summoned to reiterate cultural continuity across artificial national divisions, syncretic communities and humane person-to-person encounters.

Ironically, the nostalgia for the originary home is shared by both those who draw on its restorative potential to cope with their present dilemmas and those who have successfully overcome the dislocating experience of Partition. Anasua Basu Raychaudhury analysis of the memories of desh in East Bengali refugee memory subscribes to Boym's idea of restorative nostalgia in her emphasis on the ameliorative role of homeland nostalgia in refugees' struggle with the experience of displacement (2004). Dipesh Chakrabarty, in "The Remembered Village," offers a more sophisticated interpretation of the nostalgia for the desh in *bhadraloka* memories (1995). Similarly, Dhooleka S. Raj's nuanced interpretation of the intergenerational difference in the knowledge of Partition through the selective transmission of the first generation of narratives of wealth to the second and third generation throws important light on nostalgic recall. But the most incisive understandings of the meanings and functions of nostalgic homelands emerge in the fictional elevation of the memories of desh in interrogating the nation in Amitav Ghosh's fiction (Roy 2000), the traumatic experience of displacement in *The Sleepwalkers* (2007) or the restorative nostalgia or imagined wealth in Jhumpa Lahiri's story "A Real Durwan" in *The Interpreter of Maladies* (1999).

Shahr ashob

The nostalgia of those who were forced to leave their beloved cities finds expression in hyperbolic and exaggerated terms that are used as a standard practice in a Persian, Arabic and Urdu poetic genre known as *shahr ashob*.[1] *Shahr ashob* [the disturber of cities], a Persian term originally used as an appellation for a beautiful beloved, could also be a short lyric addressed to a young boy who coquettishly offers his wares to the love-struck poet. In Masud Sad Salman's poems (Sharma 2000), the description of the Utopian metropolis included beloveds who were distinguished not only by their craft and trade but also by religion. The catalogue of trades provided a sense of the dynamic and complex structure of the city in which everyone had an assigned place. Zuhuri and Abu Kashani, in describing Ahmednagar or Akbarabad respectively, include Hindu and Rajput young men and professionals, such *bazzaz* [grocer or textile merchant], *attar* [druggist], *jawaharfurush* [jeweller] and *sarraf* [money changer] in their catalogue as an indicator of the flourishing economies of the cities. In Urdu shahr ashob poetry, the topos became a lamentation for a ruined city and a reflection on a political, social or economic crisis. A. Hameed's lamentation for the fabled cosmopolitanism of pre-Partition Lahore resonates with Zuhuri's descriptions of the taverns and kehvanas of Ahmednagar:

> Then there was the Nagina Bakery which was the hangout of Lahore's intellectual heavyweights such as Maulana Salahuddin Ahmed, Dr Syed Abdullah, Dr Ashiq Hussain Batalvi, Bari Alig and Abdullah Qureshi. It did not survive for long after Partition. The famous Lahore restaurant Lorang's on the Mall was a cool and sophisticated place. It served the best tea in town and was one of Hamid Nizami's favourite haunts. Its closure was a sad day for the city. Shezan was an aristocratic place and so was its clientele. The Pak Tea House crowd stayed away from these places. Anwar Jalal Shamza lived right behind Shezan and he it was who had designed the Shezan lettering that is still in use. The S was identical to the S with which he signed his paintings. There was also Stiffles, which was a popular bar before Partition. It is the same site that made way for Casino and Lord's in the 1950s and 1960s. In the Regal Chowk, there stood the famous Standard, owned by a Hindu gentleman everyone called Paul. Across the road was another popular restaurant of the 1960s: Gardenia. Where Wapda House now stands, once stood Metro, where there was ballroom dancing on weekends. The famous cabaret dancer, the lovely Angela, used to perform there. To beat the prohibition, beer was served in teapots. None of the restaurants that I have written about are any longer in existence. Today there is not even one decent tea place in Lahore, which says something about the city and how it has changed. Who would say it has changed for the better?

> (Hamid 2006)

Although shahr ashob poetry has been mined as a historical source on cities, Sunil Sharma warns that the poet's manipulation of his sources in creating a kaleidoscopic image of a social landscape combined the historical and the metaphorical equally (2004). Partition poems and fiction have been analyzed in terms of the Indo-Persian definition of the shahr ashob as a lament of the poet for a city devastated by the violence of Partition. But Partition narratives could also be seen as exhibiting an influence of both the Persian and Indo-Persian meanings of shahr ashob.

The writer's mythopoeic imagination transforms remembered cities into utopian spaces inscribed through hyperbolic descriptions, such as "*jis Lahore nahin vekhya oh jamya naheen* [one who has not seen Lahore is not born]" or "the Paris of India,"

"*Lailpur shair bada gulzar* [The city of Lyallpur is very beautiful]," "*Lakhnavi nazakat* [fine sensibility] and *adaab* [etiquette]," "*yeh hai Bombay meri jaan* [This is Bombay, my love]," that romanticize Lahore's and Bombay's legendary cosmo-politanism, Lucknow's aristocratic heritage and Delhi's and Calcutta's precolonial and colonial history. In these literary or cinematic representations, the privileging of proverbial descriptions of particular spaces map new mythical places on their physical coordinates through their tracing of complex networks of emotion and affect. It is these mythical places that are reproduced in the testimonies of survivors that dwell on relations between spaces and various bodies to produce nostalgic spaces of affection and comfort. Both fictional and testimonial accounts converge on material spaces to trace affective itineraries of real spaces marked with convivi-ality, harmony, comfort and wealth to produce the myth of a rural or urban idyll. Nostalgic memories linger on selective details and collate them into an overpow-ering, singular, indelible affective image of the place that reiterates its proverbial historical stereotype. The reiteration of identical iconic spaces in diverse testimo-nial accounts reinforces the collective memories of convivial spaces that have been transmitted over generations and immortalized in local legends. Young residents of Lyallpur, for instance, spontaneously break into a doggerel about Lyallpur that echoes, almost verbatim, Indo-Persian poet Nuruddin Muhammed Zuhuri's shahr ashob of the new bazaar on the outskirts of Ahmednagar.

> Lailpur shahr bada gulzar
> Ghantaghar hai vichkar
> Ode wich ath bazaar
> The city of Lyallpur is like a garden
> The Clock Tower at the centre
> And eight bazaars in that (Popular Lyallpur doggerel)
> What can I say of the bazaars?
> They are not bazaars, but fresh rose gardens.
> Or "the city is bejewelled with skilled ones."
>
> (Zuhuri quoted in Sharma 2004: 75)

Although former Lyallpurite Jatinder Pal Sethi's mental map that he shares with those of the educated elite begins by emphasizing the city's colonial modernity through the reference to the Union Jack, his descriptions unwittingly slip into the idiom of shahr ashob:

> I am not quite certain where Aminpur and Bhawana Bazaars led to.
>   Aminpur Bazaar was the place where most of the stationary and bookshops were located. . . . We always went to the same shop. It used to be on the corner of a lane, the right hand side of the road from Ghanta Ghar.
>   Bhawana bazaar was full of shops selling baans (bamboo) and other such material. If I remember correctly, it also led to the festival grounds where the annual Dassera festival used to take place.
>
> (Sethi 2012)

Sangat Singh's memory map of Lyallpur includes an elaborate catalogue of the diverse traders and professionals inhabiting their respective neighbourhoods.

> My father had a shop at the corner of Gole Bazar just next to Dr. Chaman Lal's dispensary and next to Bhagat Ram Sawhney's office and home. His son Ravi was my friend. . . . Our shop was just in Cooperative Bank building next to the vegetable stall, and also a *Mochi* (cobbler) used to sit.
>
> (Sangat Singh 2016)

Sethi and Sangat Singh's desire of Lyallpur converges on the humble figure of the cobbler who made their shoes:

> Lal Photo, next to Aleem Painter, was opposite our house in Gole Bazaar now that you mention I remember the Vegetable walla and the Mochi. In fact, our father used to get our shoes made from a Mochi who had a shop on the left hand the moment you entered Kachery Bazaar from the court side.
>
> (Sethi 2012)

Paromita Vohra's father's recall of the boy called Akhtar in his shahr ashob of his home in Anarkali Bazaar helped her locate his house when she visited Lahore.

> We would go to Mochi Gate to buy kites – Lahori kites are special – *patangs* and *guddis*. On summer evenings, we would be taken to play in Lawrence Gardens. To go home, we would go down the Mall, which was lined with white British buildings. On this side (he would indicate left with his hand), there was Faletti's Hotel. And then you would turn right and pass the Neela Gumbad. Then go around and you were in Anarkali Bazaar, where our house was.
>
> There was a boy called Akhtar, whose family owned a trunk shop below their house.
>
> (2016)

The hyperbolic descriptions of the amorous city as a desirable beloved in the style of shahr ashob poetry are most pronounced in the prose of Pran Neville, one of Lahore's most articulate former residents. The pull of the pleasures of Lahore in Nasir Kazmi's lines "*Shehr-e-Lahore, teri raunaqain dayam aabad, Teri galyon ki hawa khainch ke layee mujh ko*" [Oh, City of Lahore! Your magnificence and bustle, the air of your streets have drawn me here] proves irresistible for Neville (quoted in Hasan 2003).

> Lahore was always very prosperous; it was the hub of North India right up to Peshawar. Everything about Lahore was special. If you wanted to see the best-dressed young men in India, they were to be found in Lahore. The best food in India was to be found in Lahore. It was a city of gourmets and it had romance.
>
> (Neville, quoted in Hasan 2003)

Neville recalls a popular film song to reaffirm the legendary beauty of the women of Lahore and to imagine the city as an object of desire through the male lover's gaze:

> A popular film song of those days went: *Ik shehr ki laundia, nainoon ke teer chala gayee* [The wenches of a city, who slayed with the arrows of their eyes]. And this doggerel that we all knew and I to this day remember: *Tibbi mein phir ke jalwa-e-Parwardigar dekh: Hai dekhney ki cheez issay baar dekh* [Walk around Tibbi, oh Lord, and take a look, it is something worth looking at, don't take your eyes off]. The great stars, the great movers and shakers of the Bombay movie world were all from Lahore.
>
> (Quoted in Hasan 2003, translation mine)

In addition to celebrating young men plying particular trades and crafts, the shahr ashob genre also describes the beauty of the city's people as in the description of its men by Ajit Kaur, an 85-year-old former resident of Dumaili:

> "The men from Dumaili are handsome, tall, fair, always wanting to go on an adventure, even if it is to a desert." She laughed throwing her head back. She was in the mood this frail old lass from Chamberlain Road.
>
> (Sheikh 2014)

Desire for the city can converge equally on objects and activities, such as mango-filled afternoons as in the memories of Narendra Luther.

> About 200 metres from our house flowed a small feeder canal. We learnt swimming there and even dared diving from the culvert wall. Some evenings, we took a basket of mangoes along. The basket was lowered into the water to cool the mangoes. Thereafter, one of the seniors would start throwing mangoes in the air. The fruit was to be caught before it fell into the water. By way of equity, no one was allowed to catch more than one mango. On holidays, both banks of the canal were dotted with picnicking families.
>
> However, the greatest joy of the family was to sit under the mango trees, eating mangoes in the summer and sugar cane in the winter, sitting on jute charpoys in a circle, or enjoying the performances of snake charmers and the monkey wallas.
>
> (2017)

Bonnett has pointed to the multifaceted and mobile nature of nostalgia and identified the complex relationship of his respondents to the past, which refuted the representation of nostalgia in terms of a past yearned for and in some ways wanted back (2013: 398). He notes the situationist nostalgia of groups who, despite expressing a desire for older forms of solidarity, subverted their restorative nostalgia by a futuristic vision of the city (2013: 394).

Stewart's notion of nostalgia as a sadness for an object that does not exist partially explains the mythicized homeland produced by refugee nostalgia, which is experienced as a lack attached to a dwelling, a desire for desire. The choice of places and objects – a street, a terrace, a fruit, a snack, a sport or a melody – that evoke sentiments of longing in Partition refugees is inexplicable to those who have not partaken in the cultural memories of those shared pleasures. The Malihabadi mangoes of Deewane Maulvi Saheb in *The Sleepwalkers*, the *hilishmach*[2] of East Bengali refugees, the *falsa* or *pindiwale chole* of West Punjabi ones, the crossing of the Indus or the Padma, the ancient bazaars of Lucknow and modern ones of Lyallpur, the Dusshera Ground or Davis Road, the *gali* [street] or the *mohalla*, the *haveli* [mansion] on the Chowk or the *kothi* [bungalow] on Davis Road possess an affective intensity that flows from the objects or places to the bodies of the dwellers. The inexplicable yearning for the elusive ordinary objects and places that remains unfulfilled is the sadness that corresponds to Bryan Turner's second level of nostalgia as a loss of personal wholeness and moral certainty (1987). The nostalgic recall of a *kachcha* [mud] house in a narrow street, a grocery store in a remote village, a shophouse in a trading post, a walled mohalla in a small town, a routine drill in a school, a play in an elite college even when one is seated in a luxurious mansion is a desire for those emotions of nurture, belonging, a sense of being, status or position that Halbwachs regards as the reason for remembering places and objects (1950). No amount of achievement, success and prosperity in the new land can compensate for that displacement from the stable, known, whole world induced by Partition, leaving the nostalgic refugee to desire something that does not exist and must be experienced as a permanent lack.

Sunil Sharma argues that shahr ashob poetry provides an important historical document on the transmission of knowledge about the social and political modes of interactions between the people of a city (2004). The imaginary, or social imaginary, is defined as "the set of values, institutions, laws, and symbols common to a particular social group and the corresponding society through which people imagine their social whole ('Imaginary')." The social imaginary of the residents of pre-Partition cities included the religious other even though their interactions were regulated by strict codes related to interdining and intermarrying in the deeply segregated spaces of the village or the city.

Elizabeth Wilson, in highlighting the ambivalence of nostalgia, mentions the presence of the Other who is the object of both desire and terror (1997). In memories of Partition survivors, the presence of the Muslim Other with whom interactions are differentially regulated in the public and private space contributes to the sense of place. Even though the violence witnessed by them turned the Other into an object of terror, the ejection of the Other through ethnic violence ironically contributes to the unhomeliness and disorientation in the new place. Like the shahr ashobs of the Indo-Persian poets, Hindu shahr ashobs include the Muslim Other even though his presence now evokes an ambivalent desire and dread.[3]

> Before Partition, the city had a healthy mix of Sikh Jats, Muslim Sheikhs, Hindu businessmen and a very limited Anglo Indian community. Jats held the agrarian side, Sheikhs and the Hindus did the industry and Anglo-Indian community was busy in keeping the stiff upper lip traditions of Raj through

clubs, schools and offices. While Ganesh Mill and Khushi Ram Behari Lal Mill (now known as Lal Mill) provided a lifestyle to the city and kept the city on toes during day, evenings would see Ganda Singh, a local landlord, ride his famous Tonga majestically.

(Miraj 2013)

Delhi offers a mirror age of Lyallpur or Lahore in the domination of the bazaars of Chandni Chowk by Muslim shopkeepers whose presence produced a sense of the neighbourhood.

On our gali and the surrounding galis there were many shops owned by Muslims. They were small merchants, whom we always called *Miyan ji*, or *Miyan Sahib* (terms of respect). They were usually bearded, sold kites, knickknacks, candy, and small toys. We had high regard for these *Miyan Sahibs* who were very friendly and always extended credit to us kids. While no Muslim families lived on our street, nearby there was *Ahmad ka Mohalla* a U-shaped street, now called Krishana *gali*. It was inhabited solely by Muslims, and gossip had it that they were all rich.

(Rohtagi)

In view of the fact that the social whole is imagined through the preassigned role of each group in the village's or city's social, political or economic order, the eviction of the Other produces a lack manifested in the desire for the Other in Partitioned selves. Partition survivors display a desire and dread of the space of the Other as they traverse the spaces of the Other in new lands.

The killings of Partition live within me. It will only go away when I myself am cremated. But I miss Lahore and dream of returning to our house on Chamberlain Road, and visiting my village in the Potohar. I am from Dumaili and my father had a huge business in Lahore and I went to Kinnaird College when 1947 came upon us.

(Ajit Kaur, quoted in Sheikh 2014)

Mental maps

The concept of the mental map, which originated in cognitive psychology, particularly in Edward Tolman's idea of the cognitive map (1948), has increasingly been borrowed in the disciplines of geography, cultural anthropology, history and urban planning. The notion of mental map or cognitive map, a component of behavioural geography, is increasingly being used by social scientists, urban designers, geographers and historians. Defined as "a model of the environment which is built up over time in the individual's brain" (Sarre, in Graham 1976: 259)[4] or a person's perceptual mapping of their area of interaction, a mental map often combines factual information with judgments or subjective interpretations, and possibly distortions, as they "reflect the world *as some person believes it to be*"

(Downs/Stea 1977: 6). Although the terms *cognitive*[5] and *mental map*[6] are used interchangeably, mental maps have become common in geography and standard practice in historical research on understanding collective concepts of geographical and historical macroregions.[7] Arguing that the term *mental maps* implies a distinction between fictitious mental maps and their real counterparts, Götz and Holmén prefer to make a more formal distinction between charted maps (endowed with varied claims of objectivity) and latent mental maps (with correlations to the physical world) (2018).

Mental maps have been decoded to reconstruct spaces that have disappeared, to trace alternative cartographies through exploring ways in "which collectives and individuals orient themselves in their environment,"[8] "to reveal biases of objectified cartographic knowledge such as socio-spatial hierarchies that structure the world" (Götz and Holmén 2018) or resist the structured spaces by urban planners and geographers since the 1960s when urban planner Kevin Lynch demonstrated that when people interact with their surroundings, they interpret and encode them into mental maps (1960). The most important development in mental map research is not to compare personal concepts of space against an objective reality but to treat them as a historical reality in their own right and not to compare these concepts of space against an "objective reality."

The consensus that all maps are representations and subjective in the two streams in cartography, on the relationship between map and territory and maps as self-referential systems has led to the interrogation of the planimetric accuracy of measured maps. Imperial cartographies have been viewed as being complicit in overwriting the spaces of the colonized through reinscribing the sacred riparian cartography of Punjab's rivers with European cartography through the systematic survey, measurement and division of land (Talbot 2007). Imperial maps, masquerading as objective representations of the territorial boundaries of Punjab, have been revealed to be masks of the civilizational agenda favouring British imperial power in which Punjab, imagined as *terra incognito* or *terra nullius*, was transformed through modernist land reforms (Talbot 2007). If maps essentially bear evidence of cognitive systems of human spatial thought and communication, the difference in the cognitive maps of survivors located both in early maps of Punjab and new imperial maps would indicate the difference in the world views of the colonizers and the colonized. More important is the new understandings of maps as expressions of political and economic power in different ideological contexts. Brian Harley's project of searching the social forces that have structured cartography "to locate the source of power – and its effects – in all map knowledge" (1989) can provide an insight into the unruly geographies produced through cognitive maps of survivors that interrogate nationalistic cartographies.

Mental mapping researchers (Götz and Holmén 2018) have dwelt on the hand-drawn sketches that people draw on paper to represent their mental maps of places, which reveal their embodied, lived, experienced knowledge of their region and include places that are either absent on charted official maps or display a strong difference in orientation. Mental maps of geographical spaces constructed by Partition survivors bring into being villages, towns, cities and neighbourhoods that have either disappeared or have been reinscribed, whose coordinates do not match the present geographical coordinates of those spaces and display a strong difference in orientation. The roughly drawn maps by survivors, rather than sketching the geographical map of undivided India or Punjab, converge in deriving their sense of orientation from the metaphysical geography of the region. This ethno-regional memory is mapped on the geography of the six eponymous rivers from which Punjab acquires it names rather than on the macronational geography of national Hindu rivers like the Ganges.[9] Homelands are located in a particular direction along or across one of the six rivers or between two rivers or in the doabs of Punjab's rivers. Bakhtin's notion of chronotopes or prototypical cultural formations of time-space found in specific narrative genres, such as the myth, folktale or so on, can elucidate the time-space of the qissa – of Heer Ranjha, Sohni Mahiwal, Mirzan Sahiban – in which the rivers of Punjab, unlike the sacred Hindu national rivers Ganga and Yamuna, resonate with romance instead of piety (1981).[10] Punjabi popular memory displays an amnesia to the sacred Hindu myths surrounding the rivers, such as the myth of Shiva's wife, Gauri, in *Rajatarangini* (Kalhana), through privileging the river Jhelum's local name over the Sanskrit Vitasta and celebrating the Chenab as the moon river (*Chan* moon and *Aab* river) or the river of romance rather than the Sanskrit Askini or Chandrabhaga. In Punjabi popular memory, the local myths of the five rivers dominate those related to their Sanskritic origins.[11] The five rivers are tributaries of the river Indus, the Sindhu of the Sanskrit saptasindhu that engendered the term *Hindu* but was marginalized to the Ganges in later Hinduism. Unlike the feminized Ganges and Yamuna associated with Hindu goddesses, the sacred mythology of the Indus that portrays the Sindhu as Shah Darya, or the King of Rivers, is dissonant with the goddess cults of mainstream Hinduism. Unlike the Ganges and Yamuna, Shah Darya Sindh is the progenitor of several cultures.[12] Like all maps, which are symbolic representations of spatial features that involve choices of inclusion and modes of depiction, spaces are segregated by gender, class, caste, profession and religion in hand-drawn sketches or descriptions of mental maps of spaces.

Like Lars-Erik Edlund's grandfather's mental map of his village in Sweden (2018), the inner, mental map of survivors indicates what is important to them and reveals their knowledge of the specific spaces inhabited by them. They also illustrate how personal conceptions of space are shaped by world views passed on culturally and how shared cultural representations of spatial landscapes are crucial in group identity formation. A comparison of three mental maps, one by a Hindu trader in Bhakkar, another by an educated Hindu from a family of lawyers in Lyallpur and a third by a Sikh shopowner's son in the same city throws light on these dominant Hindu or Sikh spaces in both Muslim-majority and Hindu-majority spaces. Rather than their Islamic or colonial landmarks, they exhibit a deep knowledge of the street, shops and places of worship that formed the lived space of the Hindus. Mythicized homelands in the Hindu imaginary across the border are essentially mapped on the Hindu spaces of the temple and the Gurdwara, the Arya School or Khalsa College, the Dusshera Ground or the Hindu mohalla that marks them as enclaves of the dominant Hindu trading, landowning or educated elite from where the Muslim majority, other than the odd neighbour, friend, retainer, serviceman or trader, is elided.

In juxtaposing older metaphysical maps of roughly the same territory or cognitive self-referential maps, it must be kept in mind that the cognitive maps of survivors are also representations and "constructed according to culturally defined semiotic code, the knowledge is constructed using various intellectual and instrumental technologies; the knowledge and its representation are both constructed by individuals who work for and within social institutions" (Edney 1997: 338). The reconstruction of a primarily Hindu or Sikh space even in Muslim-dominated villages and cities by Hindu or Sikh survivors replicate such socio-spatial hierarchies.

> Our house actually was in a Muslim area though quite a few Hindus and Sikhs were also there. Our main door in the back *galli* was right opposite the Jama Masjid, next to the house of Hakim Sahib.
>
> These two lanes – ours, on the left hand side of Katchery Bazaar (if you were coming from Ghanta Ghar) in the Jama Masjid lane, and the opposite Gurdwara lane of Verma brothers – got divided as Muslim and Hindu zones.
> (Sethi 2012)

The mental maps of Hindus and Sikhs reflect the socio-economic dominance of the Hindu and Sikh landowning, trading and educated elite, who controlled a proportion of property and wealth incommensurate with their numbers. Their mental maps foreground these socio-spatial hierarchies of spaces in West Punjab and a longing for positions of privilege and power that Khatri, Arora Hindus and Jat Sikhs enjoyed despite their insignificant numbers. In the mental maps of Hindu and Sikh survivors, the Muslim majority is either elided, marginalized as service providers (Chela Ram, in Kalra 2015; Chowdhury 2017) or criminalized (Sethi 2012). As a consequence, these mental maps are framed through a Hindu or Sikh geography of the city converging on the public space of worship (gurdwara, mandir), school, workplace and street and the private space of the home or kitchen.

Chela Ram's mental map of the microspace of the shops and homes in the Main Bazaar in Bhakkar owned by his immediate and extended family in which the iconic Jinnah Gate and the Gurdwara form the points of orientation, drawn by his grandson (see Figure 7.1), is a telling sketch of the domination of the Hindu trader in the Muslim-dominated Bhakkar city (in Kalra 2015). All the seven shops, including grocery, textiles and luggage, drawn on the basis of the mental map, with the exception of a Muslim *teli* [oilmill press], belong to Hindus, predominantly from a single family, thus mapping the Hindus' domination of the city's trade as well as the trading community's location on the map of the city. Chela Ram's memory map elicits an economic geography of the city and nostalgia for the space of trade constructed through kinship networks.

Nandkishore Chowdhury's (2017) mental map of the enclosed Hindu dera in the Hindu-dominated town of Khairpur Tamewali that dwells on the gigantic size of the house and the spaces within the house that could house the entire Hindu population during the riots again foregrounds the Hindu landowning family's

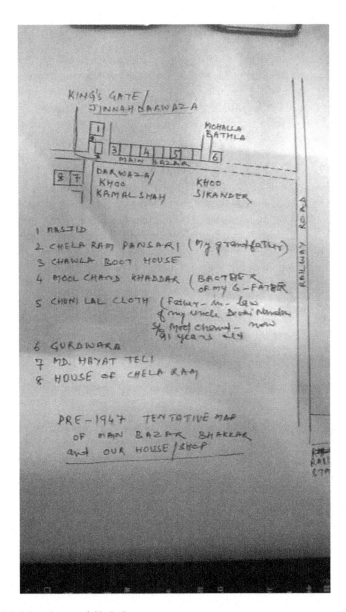

Figure 7.1 Mental map of Chela Ram
Source: Satish Kalra

pre-eminence within the precincts of the town as well as their links with Hindu pilgrimage places in the rest of India.

The map of Jatinder Sethi, hailing from an educated family of lawyers who had migrated from Jhang to Lyallpur, offers a charted map of the architectural plan of the Lyallpur city and its famous eight bazaars, which was a replica of the Union Jack, as a tribute to the Queen of England.

> A rectangle containing a Cross and two Diagonals. All the eight bazaars started from the Ghanta Ghar (clock tower), which was the focal point of the town. Four of the eight bazaars were perpendicular, and you could see the full face of the Ghanta Ghar. The other four bazaars were diagonal to the Ghanta Ghar; from these bazaars, you could only see the diagonal face of the tower.
>
> (Sethi 2012)[13]

However, his point-of-view perception of the bazaars – "you could tell which bazaar you were in by looking at the angle of the tower" – etches the mental map of one of the dwellers and walkers of the bazaar rather than of the architect.

Unlike that of Sethi, who visited the bazaars, the mental map of Ram Prakash, who hailed from a trading family that owned several businesses in those bazaars, walks one through the bazaars from the perspective of the owners of small businesses rather than of walkers.

> Our chemist shop was in Rail bazaar, near Gopinath Mandir, opposite Bhagat Ram Lohewala. Just [a] year before Partition, our shop moved to outside Bhowana Bazaar. Our Agmark grading Company, Chanab Pure ghee Ltd (UTTAM Ghee) was opposite Jamma Masjid.
>
> (2006)

Although Prakash, Sethi or Sangat Singh might never have met, the mental maps of the three teenage Partition survivors of Lyallpur intersect with respect to their shared spaces, family trade (shopwowner), residential space (Douglaspura),[14] place of worship (Arya Samaj) and school (DAV school).

> The Primary Arya School was also located around there. Was it Douglaspura?[15] I think so. Because that's where we used to go after having finished Kutchi (lower) class nursery school, and before going to the High School at Mai-Di-Jhuggi.
>
> (Sethi 2012)[16]

> If you wish to know, MB School shares a wall with Khalsa High School, and next to it is DAV School. Across the road is Ismalia [Islamia] School. At 2 O' clock, there is a Police Station. At 3 O' Clock is the Telephone School. Also in front of your house must be a big Nala.
>
> (Sangat Singh 2016)

The shared cultural representation of the spatial landscape of the DAV school and the Dushhera Ground sketched by the Hindu teenage residents, Sethi and Prakash, affirm a Hindu Arya Samaji identity. Although Sangat Singh and Sethi are able to

Figure 7.2 Clock Tower Lyallpur 2004
Source: Pippa Virdee

trace common friends, vendors and food joints, their maps diverge due to Sethi's Arya Samaj upbringing, which forbids him to enjoy the pleasures of the cinema halls that the Sikh Sangat Singh has fond memories of.

> I am still in Ketchery Bazar and standing near the right entrance of Gole Bazar. Now you cannot forget what I was seeing. You would remember of the three cinema halls.
>
> (Sangat Singh 2016)

> I continued following him [his brother]. Instead of turning on the road to Gurdwara before Grand Hotel, he walked straight past the Ghanta Ghar to Minerva cinema.
>
> (Sangat Singh 2016)

Feminist geographers have thrown important light on the gendered constructions of space in foregrounding the inner, private, secluded spaces of women and the role of gender in circumscribing the space of women to that of the kitchen, the home and the street. The mental maps of female survivors of Partition understandably differ from those of the males. The mental map of a child survivor of the cities of Bhakkar and Lyallpur foregrounds this difference. Although she was too young at the age of seven to recall her postal address,[17] to trace the roadmap to her school or the three cinema halls, Deshi recalled walking past Mai-di-Jhuggi to her school, Kanya Vidyalaya, across from which was the dispensary where her mother worked,[18] riding pillion on her father's cycle and being taken to one of the cinema halls across the canal.

Considering that these spaces that are engraved in the memories of the dwellers do not figure in the town planners' map and reconstruct a space that has no material existence because of the processes of decolonization, Islamization and modernization, these memory maps reconstruct a geography that has been erased from the map of Pakistan. For instance, both Sethi and Deshi trace the route to particular schools, MB School and Kanya Vidyalaya, in or after the landmark of Mai di Jhuggi. But the present residents who know Mai di Jhuggi as a suburb several kilometres away are unable to locate buildings along this pre-Partition landmark. Instead of comparing these mental maps to the objective reality of Faisalabad, they may be used to reconstruct a planned pre-Partition city with its segregated spaces.

In the memory maps of Lyallpur's former residents, the city of Lyallpur, with its clock tower and the eight bazaars, signifies the space of the modernity of a colonial city named after its British founder. Unlike other narratives of ancestral homelands recalled in Partitioned memories of desh, Lyallpur is remembered as a city of migrants who left their secure ancestral spaces to seek opportunities in the newly established planned city. Nostalgia for Lyallpur or for the canal colonies is a desire for an immediate colonial rather than a precolonial ancestral past. For instance, Sethi contrasts his parents' Lyallpur cosmopolitanism to the provincialism of their Jhang siblings. Prakash, similarly, distances himself from his landowning maternal clan in Leiah and Piplan through identifying with Lyallpur as home.

Viewing the map not as a planimetrically accurate representation but more as a socially constructed one and enlarging the scope of maps to include non-metric worlds can close the gap between the planimetric accuracy of official imperial or national maps and the culturally constructed maps of the survivors and foreground the dual function of maps as measured and symbolic.

Sensuous geographies

Humanist geographers have interrogated the idea of space as an abstract entity through proposing the idea of experienced space. The work on emotional geographies (Thrift 2004; Davidson, Bondi, and Smith 2005; Kearney 2009) has demonstrated that the human world is constructed and lived through emotions, has privileged the body as the site of emotions that govern human relations and held that this geographical knowledge can help one understand how people perceive the world. Yi-Fu Tuan's revelation of spaces that are sense bound, that respond to existential cues and urgencies of day-to-day life, and his emphasis on visual perception, touch, movement and thought has opened the way for a sensuous geography of places (1979). Tuan considers space to be implicated in the body and the body as defining space and regards the sense of place as produced by the feel of a place (1979). Paul Rodoway defines sensuous geography as a geographical understanding that arises out of the stimulation of, or apprehension by, the senses (1994). Sensuous or affective geographies are particularly illuminating in understanding the sense of place produced through visual, haptic, olfactory, auditory and gustatory memories of places. In emphasizing the role of emotions and affect in the perception of space and place, geographers have engaged with not only iconic public spaces but also the everyday space of the street, the home and the workplace. In view of the heavy emotional investment of survivors in the grief, loss and suffering accompanying their experiences, a sensuous geography of remembered homes becomes particularly important in understanding both the emotions attached to places and the social relations between groups.

The affective accounts of a city provide a reflexive, habitual relationship between it and its inhabitants. Affective responses to the sensescapes of a place are at the heart of the Partition survivors' subjectivity, such as in their self-identifications as Lahoria, Lyallpuri, Ambarsaria or Ludhianvi. The affective ties between former inhabitants of Partitioned cities possess an affective charge that subverts the division of nations as in the case of four friends, Amar Kapoor, Asaf Khwaja, Agha Raza and Nishat Haider, hailing from elite Lahore families who "had lived within a three-mile radius, visited each other's homes, shared street snacks on the way home from convent school" (Thapliyal 2017) through their convergence on shared memories.

> "We have common memories and common experiences that bind us so closely together that no adventitious circumstances can wrench us apart," he wrote in one of his letters.
>
> (Quoted in Thapliyal 2017)

Kaifiyat, an untranslatable Urdu term, loosely translated as state or condition, a pleasurable, ineffable one that is near mystical, has been used to describe the feelings produced by the memory of the exchange of energies palpable in the bazaars of old cities, particularly Hira Mandi, the bazaar-e-husn [bazaar of beauty].

> Come evening and they would be out in their balconies in the finest of silks and jewels. Their eyes would be lined with kohl and their lips red with dandasa, bark of the walnut tree and the most fragrant of eastern perfumes or itars would fill the air. They were known as diamonds and such was their glitter that the whole street would seem studded with stars. These were the courtesans of Heera Mandi of Lahore in the years before Partition in 1947.
>
> (Dutt 2009)

Shunali Khullar Shroff's visit to the same Heera Mandi neighbourhood fore-grounds the uncanniness of the imaginary city overwritten by new meanings.

> Walking down these forbidden parts of the city, you get the feeling that noth-ing here has changed from how it was a century ago, and yet everything has changed. Rows of Peshawari sandal booths, dairy and mithai shops in hues of blue and green sit cheek by jowl with houses that go by names like Hari Niwas and Ram Niwas, houses of rusty doors and steep steps that lead to balconies where sometimes the *tawaifs* could be spotted running ivory combs through their hair. Some of these shopkeepers are looking at me with curious interest.
>
> (2017)

The olfactory geography (Rodoway 1994) of beloved villages and cities decades after they left them overwhelms survivors as they provide smellscapes (Porteous 1985, 1990), which may be spatially ordered and place related (1985: 369), affirm-ing Lefebvre's idea that when an intimacy exists between a subject and object, it must be the world of smell where they reside (1991: 197). Partition literature has examined the smellscape of memories both in their positive meaning as aroma and negative as smell or odour. The most celebrated geography of the nose is traced by Salman Rushdie in Saleem Sinai's extraordinary gift of smell in *Midnight's Chil-dren* that enables his protagonist to sniff his way through cities. But narratives of both educated journalists and ordinary people reverberate with olfactory experi-ences of places that produce both longing and dread. Siloo Mehta, who would visit Anarkali between 1945 and 1947, recalls the quaint charm of the bazaar:

> My memories of the Bazaar are of a long narrow meandering street crowded with camel carts loaded with baggage and people. Sitting at a shop window among jute bags of walnuts, almonds, dried apricots and pistachios, it felt weird to be stared at by a camel at eye level ambling past. Horsemen clattering by, tongas and people everywhere. Beautiful men and women in colourful costumes bargaining, eating in coloured glass decorated, brightly lit eateries. Delicious smells of food and attar. Shops and shops on either side with exquisite handicrafts at unbeliev-ably low prices. I wonder what Anarkali Bazaar looks like today.
>
> (Mehta 2010)

Nothing evokes nostalgia more strongly than the smells of food that appear to have travelled across the border with restaurants on either side capitalizing on migrants' olfactory links with the cities on either side.

> It's where my family is from. I am from Karachi, I was born here but cultur-ally I am also a Delhi Wallah. There should be better relations with India, they are our neighbours, we have much in common," he said.
>
> (Yusuf, in Saifi 2017)

The food culture of Delhi has been permanently transformed through the intro-duction of Partition refugees who introduced street food like *dahi bhalley, moth kachori, papri chat, daal makhani* and the famous butter chicken of *Moti Mahal* and *Kake di Hatti*.[19] These warm, pleasurable memories of the mouthwatering aromas of favourite foods must be placed against the terrifying stench of burning and decomposing flesh indelibly settled on the olfactory memories of witnesses,

> As soon as the fires subsided in Shah Alami Gate area, I revisited the locality escorted by police but was not able to reach our house due to the simmering fire and was not sure whether it was still intact. I could see, from a distance, some dead bodies burning and the smell of their flesh created terror in me. The death toll in Shah Alami fire was not terribly high as many residents had already moved apprehending trouble. The victims were those who were too old to move, or too attached to their property or had nowhere else to go. Those who surrendered to security forces were escorted to the Refugee Camps near the City.
>
> (Seth 2010)

> It was a horrific sight. My ailing mother fainted but getting a glass of water was impossible. The stink of the dead bodies coming from outside the compartment and the appalling smell inside it made the situation worse. I must admit that even after all these years I have not forgotten the sight and the stink. The scenes and the smells are still fresh in my memory.
>
> (Chopra, August 2017)

Sonic geographies of spaces and places have largely addressed musical traditions and genres in defining the sense of place. While the predominant musicality of a space is crucial to its sonic map, the everyday sounds of places and spaces have an equally important role in producing the rhythm of cities and towns. Partitioned memories converge on the recall of songs and musical traditions across the border, such as popular film or folk songs and the legendary status of popular, classical and folk singers shared on both sides. In tracing the recall of these sonicscapes, scholars have identified the presence of a shared cultural and social imaginary that can be redemptive (Kapuria 2017; Ahmed 2006; Kabir 2013). Less attention has been devoted to the particular rhythms of pre-Partition cities produced by everyday sounds of people going about their everyday activities that create the sensuous geographies of places. In contrast to Partition desire that is articulated to the folk, classical and popular musical heritage and to particular melodies, songs or ditties, the sounds of tongas, rickshaws, cycles, hawkers and crowds that survivors recall brings alive the sensuous geography of the spaces. As they proceed to narrate the atmosphere prevailing before the onset of Partition, familiar comforting sounds are displaced by the nightmarish sounds of a fearful city reverberating with chants of religious groups. The days before the Partition are filled with the sound of gunfire, which plays a major role in producing the fearful city of Partition survivors.

> In a village just west of Lahore, Kanwal was working away in the fields, when he heard a commotion in the distance. Temperatures soared well above

120 degrees and he worked in his undergarments. The sounds seemed to come from his village and grew louder as he stopped to listen: the swishing of swords, screams . . . then gunshots.

(Bhalla 2014)

"Outside my uncle's house, I saw seven bodies, covered in blood," he says. "Their blood was flowing into the street, and I stepped over it to get into the house. I still remember that blood today. The blood touched my feet and, as I was walking down the street, a man said to me: 'Is this the freedom that you wanted?'"

(Khanna, in Asad 2017)

The emotions that overwhelm Sarab Kaur Zavaleta, the daughter of the station-master of Lahore at the time of Partition, who waved refugee trains off, including the one carrying his own family, on her visit to her former home are evidence of geographical investment in the intergenerational affects of home.

Then I also visited the Station Master's home near the railway station, and again it was so surprising to see that the large home built in the British Colonial style was still there, unchanged, but somewhat old and dilapidated. The banyan tree that an older sister had told me about, was still there in the backyard. As I walked through the empty house, I imagined the voices, footprints and fingerprints of my parents echoing through my body. I could picture my mother in the front garden, giving instructions to the gardeners what flowers, vegetables and fruit trees they were to plant. The smell of jasmine flowers made her presence so strong in my mind. It was so emotional that I shed some tears, thinking of what my parents must have suffered through the Partition, having to leave everything behind and starting a completely new life with none of their possessions.

(Zavaleta 2017)

The lack of correspondence between spaces and places constructed by survivors' memories and the cartographic geographies and physical coordinates of real places is due to the disappearance or absence of these affective geographies in real spaces through the process of renaming reconstructed neighbourhoods and altered relations. These nostalgic homelands of memory are produced through an assembly of the affects of these places that are reflected in their spatial divisions and arrangements. The spaces and objects on which refugee nostalgia converges are the spaces of Hindu privilege, in which the Hindu minority controlled the economy and community (Chowdhury 2017; Kalra 2015; Sethi 2012; Sangat Singh 2016).

Affect

Despite the nostalgic emotions expressed by survivors for lost homes, the reluctance of many to revisit or return has been ascribed to the psychogeography of fear traced in victims and witnesses of violence. Several survivors who waxed eloquent and sank into a reverie or daydreaming when asked to describe their homes, villages and cities would turn evasive and tight-lipped or go completely silent when asked if they would like to revisit or return to their old homes. Unlike the few who admitted to being haunted by the violence they had witnessed, the majority cited altered political conditions and improved economic status to posit the impossibility of return. The deep discord between expressed emotions of love and longing and unexpressed fear or reluctance to return can be elucidated through Pile's emphasis on the need to make a distinction between emotion and affect. Pile complicates the commonly understood division between emotion as expressed, cognitive and reflexive and affect as pre/non-cognitive, reflexive, conscious and non-representational by arguing that affects emerge through encounters between bodies and are registered by the changes in the capacity to affect and being affected and/or changes in intensity. Unlike emotional geography in which the body is a site of feeling and experience, in affective geography, the body is not seen as personal but transpersonal and enables the researcher to reveal the transhuman, the non-cognitive, the inexpressible. Unlike emotional geographies, which ensure that there is no split between thought and affect, affective geographies split thought from affect. Unlike carefully expressed emotions of love, longing, romance and nostalgia for home, the affect produced in the bodies of the survivor that is transmitted to that of the interviewer at the mention of an event, a city or a person through corporeal changes such as silence, dry mouth, slurred or quivering speech, pitch change, averted or moist eyes, tears or shaking or clenched hands visible to an attentive interviewer can explain the reluctance to return.

Notes

1 Kumkum Sangari's tracing of the revival poetic genre of viraha [a song of separation consisting of a lamentation for a lost beloved] in the songs in the Hindi films throughout the 1950s through which makers and consumers responded to the trauma of Partition offers a comparative use of traditional genres for the expression of nostalgia (2011).

2 Hilishmach or Hilsa fish is considered a delicacy in Bengali cuisine. Chickpeas cooked in a particular style known as Pindiwale [from Rawalpindi] chole is a favourite Punjabi street food. Falsa is an orange-coloured sweet-and-sour fruit that grows in West Punjab.

3 Rehana Bano Bokhari recalls being the only Muslim child in the Hindu colony of Model Town and swearing by kali mata [the Hindu Goddess Kali] when playing with her Hindu friends. She has no regrets for her house being burnt down by Hindus as retaliation for the burning of a Hindu house in Anarkali (As told to Ahmed 2007).

4 Phillip Sarre, in his discussion of perception, provides us with a definition which is very close to the idea of a mental map, namely, "a model of the environment which is built up over time in the individual's brain" (1973: 16).

5 Downs & Stea define mental maps as those "that enable us to collect, organize, store, recall, and manipulate information about the spatial environment" and maintain that "these maps can be described as subjective understandings of spatial reality which are determined by the individual's position, perspective, and range of movement" (Downs/Stea 1977: 6).

6 Gould and White argue that "our images" as "the maps and models of the world we carry around with us" provide "for the orientation, comfort and movement of man

within his environment" (Gould and White 1974: 197). Elspeth Graham, in "What is a Mental Map?" points to the lack of coherence in the central concept by arguing that if the mental map is supposed to be in a person's brain, any attempt to represent it in spatial terms would be elusive (1976).

7 While the focus in cognitive maps is to identify the difference in an individual's spatial orientation, the thrust of the mental map is to show how personal concepts of space are shaped by the (world) views passed on culturally and how shared collective representations of a spatial landscape are instrumental in cultural group and identity formation.

8 A cognitive map helps the human to get his bearings in his spatial environment.

9 Despite the primacy accorded to the six rivers, the Ganges continues to dominate ritual performances to suggest an accretive regionalism.

10 Sangari's examination of the qissa of Laila Majnoon as a trope for longing for the lost home is pertinent here (2011).

11 Sutlej River is called Zaradros in Ancient Greek and Shutudri or Shatadru in Sanskrit, whereas Beas is called Vipasha.

12 Although Jhelum and Chenab were lost to East Punjab, the five rivers constitute a part of the Punjabi collective memory. The Chenab serves as the most important metaphor of love and longing but also of pain in the works of writers and painters of Punjabi origin. For instance, Amrita Pritam used the image of Chenab flowing with blood when she called out to Waris Shah to witness the suffering of the daughters of Punjab.

13 The eight bazaars of Lyallpur included Katchery Bazaar, Rail Bazaar, Bhawana Bazaar, Jhang Bazaar, Aminpur Bazaar, Karkhana Bazaar, Gol Bazaar, Chiniot Bazaar and Montgomery Bazaar (also known as Sutar Mandi).

14 Prakash's family lived on the street of Manaktala Building opposite the Dushhera ground. Sangat Singh lived "in *Wakila da mohalla* next to *Zail Ghar* and shared a common wall with Pandi Wakil (lawyer) whose house was opposite the small *Kasi* and a small bridge" (2016).

15 According to Alimuddin, Hasan and Sadiq, Douglaspura was "the main residential area" of Lyallpur (1920).

16 Ram Prakash went to the same school as Sethi, the DAV School (Arya School), which was about three miles from his house.

17 She recalled a *band gali* [closed street] in Douglaspura which had only two houses. It was the last street at the end of Douglaspura that led to Mai di Jhuggi (Deshi 2012). Taken on a virtual tour of Lyallpur in 2018 by a young historian from Lyallpur, she led him through the labyrinthian lanes of Douglaspura guided by her mental map to the red parapet and the gate to her house that had just been demolished (Deshi 2018).

18 "They would cross Mai di Jhuggi, a long road, and a canal to reach their school Arya Kanya Vidayalaya, opposite which was the hospital/clinic where her mother worked as a compounder under Dr. Chhabil Das" (Deshi 2012). The same doctor's dispensary figures in Sangat Singh's map (2016).

19 Reena Nanda mentions her family recall these street foods of Lahore, including *chole bhature*, *golgappe*, *buddi mai de bal* in her biography (2018).

8 Resettled homes[1]

Resettlement and rehabilitation of refugees in the aftermath of Partition has been represented in official histories of Partition as an infrastructural, housing and administrative problem encountered by the newly formed Indian state that it masterfully resolved through launching resettlement schemes and colonies ("Report on the Working of the Relief and Rehabilitation Committee" 1949). The large body of this literature engages the political or economic aspects of displacement, focusing on the causes of displacement or protection of refugees through summoning impressive policy statements, statistical data and descriptive reports listing details of resettlement camps and colonies (Randhawa 1954; Rai 1965; Chatterji 2002; Tai and Kudaisya 2004; Talbot 2006; Ghosh 2016).[2] The debates on resettlement and rehabilitation have largely converged on the preferential treatment of Punjabi refugees as opposed to East Bengali and the ecological and cultural dissonance between the resettlement regions to which Bengali refugees were dispersed and their physical, mental and occupational competencies (Zinkin 1957; Luthra 1971; Kudaisya 1998). The psychological and cultural experience of displacement and resettlement has been largely neglected or partially addressed in fictional and testimonial literature. Unlike the large body of fictional representations that has poignantly captured the trauma of Partition violence, few have turned to dwell on the travails of displacement and resettlement.

Michael Peter Smith, in *Explorations in Urban Theory*, argues that "perhaps the most familiar response to deterritorialization, particularly among exiles and refugees, is the desire to reterritorialize" (1994: 19, 2016). Sandra Dudley, in *Materializing Exile*, addresses "the material, visual, spatial and embodied aspects of the fundamentally cultural processes through which refugees make meaning out of the social and physical rupture of forced migration" (2010: 1). She investigates the connection of bodily senses with memories and imaginations of the past home and its influence on the ways refugees create a sense of home and place in the new location. Rob Sullivan, in *Geography Speaks*, views the creation of place as a process that is deeply implicated in speech acts and performativity, which focus on stunning performing acts that can transform unbounded space into demarcated place (2016). The distinction made between the house and home – home as affect, emotion and identity – and practices in theories of home is crucial in comprehending "the sense of place" produced in refugees of Partition in the squalid tenements allotted to them in resettlement colonies.

This chapter focuses on the process of homemaking by Partition refugees in the new land through material, visual, spatial, embodied and performative acts by which they inhabit physical, linguistic, social and cultural spaces. It shows that refugees construct a new "sense of place" anchored in the geographical space of the resettlement colony that evokes memories of the event of Partition and displacement. The chapter argues that two contradictory strains are present in the homemaking process. While migrants reconstruct new homes in the image of remembered homes, their dispossession from certain aspects of the lost home and the pressure to assimilate in host cultures makes the reconstruction of the physical spatiality of the old home impossible; it is reconstructed either as language, as culture, as forms of sociality or as rituals and everyday practices.

Ideologies of the home

In his examination of Euroamerican notions of home, Witold Rybczynski's book, *Home: A Short History of an Idea* (1986), maintains that "seventeenth century ideas about privacy, domesticity, intimacy and comfort emerged as organizing principles for the design and use of domestic spaces among the bourgeoisie, particularly in the Netherlands" (Mallett 2004: 66), and were extended to other parts of Europe. Hepworth argues that the design and organization of Victorian homes valorized notions of security, privacy and respectability, as demonstrated by an emphasis on rooms and external surrounds bounded by walls, doors, locks and keys. The home was conceived as a fortress from the potentially deviant realms of the outside world. As Ginsberg points out, we make our homes not necessarily by constructing them but by the organization and furnishing of the space in which we live (1999). Other researchers have emphasized the ways design, spatial organization and furnishings of domestic dwelling influence and shape concepts and ideologies of the home.

In the *Poetics of Space*, Bachelard explores the affective meanings of everyday spaces, such as the attic, the cellar, closets, drawers and so on, in producing a sense of home (1994). Even though Bachelard's phenomenal ontology of space, dwelling and place has illuminated the meanings of emotions attached to home, his spatial poetics of the attic and the cellar, hearth and kitchen table are not universally applicable. Since the ordinary spaces of the European home have no counterpart in vernacular Indian architecture, the affective and relational meanings of vernacular spaces of the traditional residential unit of Punjab [vasughar], the reception room [deodi], which guarded the courtyard entry, the courtyard [verah], the male sleeping and social room [baithak] and the rooftop [kotha] in rural homes in Punjab must be foregrounded in the performance of home and place in resettlement colonies.

According to Mehar Singh, a farmer's house was entered through an elongated room, known as deodi, beyond which lay the verah, enclosed by high walls on two sides. Deodi constituted a social space behind which lay the private space. The deodi had two doors, one opening into the street and the other into the inner part of the house, but positioned in a way that nothing was visible from the outer door so as to provide privacy [purdah] to the private space (2004). In tracing the evolution of the traditional Punjabi house from the rural vasughar, Mehar Singh shows that carving a straight wide corridor out of the deodi robbed it of its importance in blocking access to the inner part of the house and that this truncated deodi was used for other purposes and eventually turned into a baithak but without any door or window opening towards the inner side of the house. It had an additional door opening into the corridor, which was used only for serving tea or food to guests (2004).

Van der Horst and Messing assert that the spatial organization of domestic dwellings both influences and reflects forms of sociality associated with and/or peculiar to any given cultural and historical context (2006). In Punjab, the outer space of the street played a pivotal role in performing forms of sociality.

> In the evening, a table, few chairs and a charpoy (cot) was placed on the roadside, after the mashqui (person with a mashaq – a leather container for water) had watered the ground to cool the ground. This was the time for meeting the friends for a chat.
>
> (Sethi 2012)

The vasughar pattern, including the barn, was carried over to urban houses of middle-class educated professionals as in the description of this house from Lyallpur.

> After entering the house from the main gate on the galli-side, the left side took you to the main living quarters. There was huge open courtyard, with a big long marble platform along the wall facing the Jama Masjid lane. On the extreme left corner, there was a tandoor for making tandoori-rotis. On the right hand corner of the slab was a Hamam (with a bucket underneath) for washing hands with Lifebuoy soap.
>
> Next to the tandoor, there was a large arch type opening, without any gate, that took you down two steps to a very big barn, which held our three buffalos, and a cow with a newly born calf.
>
> (Sethi 2012)

The baithak in a traditional Punjabi house was essentially a male reception and sleeping space furnished with a palang [an ornate wooden bed][3] and a few chairs for receiving male visitors.

> You had to climb three steep steps to enter the house, a two-story building. The house had a veranda that was about 20 feet long. The veranda had three doors. The door on the extreme left side opened into a drawing room, (the main entrance was from inside the hall) meant only for the family and friends. The other two doors opened up the big long room, which was my father's office.
>
> (Sethi 2012)

The building in Punjab is designed around the vehra and chulha chauka closely corresponding to the emotions of familiarity and reassurance attached to the hearth and the kitchen table in Bachelard's spatial schema (1994). In the Punjabi court-yard house, the vehra [courtyard], a square or rectangular space, must be viewed as an architectural design that embodies a certain way of living.[4] The verah, which occupied between 1/3 to 2/3 of the total area of the house, constituted the most essential part of the traditional house and was the centre of all family activities with women performing their daily chores and the family sleeping in it for most of the year. The private space of the verah miraculously transformed into a social space with most of the rituals being performed there. In the changing plan of the houses, the verah no longer formed the centre of the house but was separated from the street only by a wall.

> We spent most of the day in our open courtyard where most of the business of the house was transacted. In the summers, we moved from the courtyard to the covered veranda before the sun rose too high. By midday, it was very hot and we went deeper into the cooler rooms inside. The bamboo shades came down after lunch as the house prepared for sleep. We returned to the courtyard in the early evening after the mashkiya had sprinkled cool water on it from his bag of goatskin. We even slept in the courtyard on hot summer nights and watched the brilliant stars high above. In the winters, this process was reversed. We slept inside and came out gradually with the morning sun. We spent most of the day in its luxurious warmth, shifting our chairs and charpais according to the sun's path, and only returned inside at sunset.
>
> (Das 2010)

A characteristic feature of Punjab was the absence of a covered cooking area. Instead, an uncovered cooking space with a long, raised platform called *chauka*, located in the open courtyard with a low wall erected to demarcate it, served as a kitchen.

> Next to it was my mother's kitchen, about 15 feet by 15 feet. There was no door to it. The double chulha (cookstove) was very common in those days – there were no electric or gas cooking ranges. The fuel was dried-up cow dung and wood, which was plentiful.
>
> (Sethi 2012)

The visual image of a mother figure rolling and puffing *phulkas* [unleavened bread] on an open wood fire in a corner with the family seated in a semi-circle in the chauka evokes the warm circle of domesticity and family that the kitchen table does in the West.

Like the predominantly female space of the verah, the chauka is also marked as a gendered space whose rules are set by the women in the family. It is an exclusive space from which certain people (untouchables, Muslims, menstruating females), food items (meat, fish, eggs) and footwear may be excluded and prohibitions related to handling its contents strictly enforced.

The dalan [store] was a multipurpose space used for the storage of grains and large wooden boxes and used as a sleeping space by the women in the house (Singh 2004).

The rooftop, or kotha, is another multifunctional open space that defines modern Punjabi house design and was actively used seasonally and during various times of the day. As an extension of the vehra, it was used during the summer for early morning chores and for recreational purposes in the evening. In the winters, it was a space where the family spent most of their days drying food and clothes, women knitting sweaters and children flying kites. In the patriarchal space of the Punjabi home in which women were concealed from the public gaze, it served as women's window to the world from where they could observe the world pass by without being observed. Forbidden from participating in the public space of the street, women would sprint up to the kotha to observe public and family events in the neighbourhood, concealed from the male gaze. In view of the strictures attached to females stepping out of the gates of the house, the kotha, connected to other kothas by a low wall, permitted young females the freedom to visit their female neighbours by jumping over the low walls. Although imagined as a private space, it simultaneously offered opportunities to young women to reveal themselves to the public gaze on the pretext of drying their long tresses or hanging out clothes.[5] The uses of the kotha in courtship rituals is captured in innumerable folk songs, where young lovers could catch a glimpse of their beloveds on the kotha or exchange glances unobserved by other family members. The kotha was sprinkled with water in the summer evenings to make it cooler and manjaa [string cots][6] placed here in groups (separate male and female areas) for sleeping (Khan 2009). Most important, the terrace was the sole private space into which young members could retreat to study, ruminate or vent their emotions.

Reterritorialization and placemaking

"Reterritorialization as an analytical concept, thus represents the 'spatial process' and spatial strategies that refugees and displaced people develop, in the contradictory experience of being physically present in one location, but at the same time living with a feeling of belonging somewhere else" (Brun 2001: 23). Karin Aguilar-San Juan opines that reterritorialization need not necessarily involve reproducing material places in new lands but can involve "a meso-level transformation of existing places in order to construct and produce new places that strengthen and proliferate certain aspects of community" (Aguilar-San Juan 2013: 380). In his seminal essay, Yi-Fu Tuan identifies two aspects that are inherent in a sense of place, namely public symbols and the fields of care that evoke affection. Unlike public symbols (sacred places, monuments, monumental architecture, public squares) that are visible, he avers, fields of care (neighbourhoods, street corners, homes, taverns, marketplaces) lack visuality (1979: 412) and can be known in essence only from within (1979: 416). With Tuan, one may ask, "How does mere location become place?" (1979: 389).

Unlike nostalgic reconstructions of lost homes by dominant affluent groups that replicate public symbols, such as monuments, architectural styles, buildings, street plans or house designs reminiscent of old homes and homelands, to produce a sense of place in new lands, refugees' inability to reconstruct the material spatiality of the homes left behind in the newly built functional spaces allocated to them is compensated through incorporation of fields of care.

Naming places

Underlining the relationship between place names and emotional geographies, Amanda Kearney and John J. Bradley reflect on the inexplicable power of a place name through showing that the Yanyuwa homeland, Manankurra's, knowledge and memory were never lost, nor disembodied from the emotional experience of homeland despite colonial actions enforcing a physical alienation from this place because of triggers in individual and group remembering (2009).[7] This power of place name is equally visible in the memories of Partition survivors, whose knowledge and memories of remembered homes were passed down generations because of triggers in individual and group remembering. However, unlike the Yanyuwa homeland, Manankurra, which was named by "Yanyuwa Ancestral beings a long time ago" (Kearney, 2009: 81), Partitioned memories converge on both primordial and colonial names to call into being the places that define their identities. Names are embedded and implicated in the way that Partition survivors engage their homelands and transmit narratives to succeeding generations. Dispossessed of their material homes and homelands, names, both indigenous and "whitefella," become the sole repositories of remembered homes, which are embodied in place, body and mind. In the era when birthplace is a mere detail to be entered in birth certificates, passports and other official forms, the emotional geographies of naming birthplaces or ancestral places in a lost land by refugees of Partition through the act of transmission to succeeding generations acquires a totemic significance similar to the name of Manankurra for the Yanyuwa people.

An autorickshaw driver in Delhi, in response to Urvashi Butalia's question about where he hailed from sought a clarification, "Pichche se?" [You mean originally from?], which sums up the origins of generations of Partition survivors (1998: 17). The Punjabi term *pichche se* invariably features in self-introductions to recall originary places whose memories have turned hazy through the passage of time, transformed into alien lands, or have never been visited by successive generations of Partition survivors and their descendants. Naming of the originary home, pichche se, is a declaration of ownership expressing the inalienable right to know and call into being a Partitioned identity. The act of naming is a powerful act that may be used to stake one's claims to a place that one no longer inhabits or has inhabited and "place names can be considered to be one of the material and symbolic artefacts of culture" (2002: 283–84).

Examining the cultural politics of place naming, Kearns and Berg (2002: 286) aver that resistance to naming can occur on at least two levels: the creation and deployment of alternative names (Myers 1996) and the use of alternative pronunciations for established names. They extend these cultural politics to aural aspects maintaining that "*by the way the name is pronounced reflects, and contributes to, the constitution of imagined communities*" (2002: 284). Their view that "the act of pronouncing names also involves strategy: the conscious choice of how a name is pronounced" is confirmed by the appropriation of place names through their (mis) pronunciation that involves a "proclamation of cultural politics" (2002: 283, 284). The use of corrupted pronunciations of established names, such as those of cities like Lailpur for Lyallpur, named after colonial administrators, such as Sir James Lyall, became an act of ownership of colonized spaces through its resignification as the town of the eponymous heroine of the Perso-Arabic epic *Laila Majnoon*. Following its alternative naming by the Islamic state of Pakistan as Faisalabad, Lyallpur, erased from the cartographic geography of Pakistan, survives as an imagined city in its Punjabiized pronunciation only in the memories of its former residents and the signboards of forced migrants from the canal colony town.

Pippa Virdee's ethnographic study that traces the return migration of Sikhs from districts of Lyallpur where they had been settled during the establishment of canal colonies to Ludhiana after being driven out by Partition violence shows that memories of their five-decade sojourn were immortalized through the act of naming (2008, 2018). Lyallpur Khalsa College, which was first established in 1908 in Lyallpur, Pakistan, and moved to Jalandhar City after Partition with two other colleges, one in Kapurthala and the other in Ludhiana, kept alive the memory of the historical institution from which a number of celebrities had graduated. However, the ubiquitous place name Lyallpur figures in the signs of numerous shops and establishments in Ludhiana owned by former residents of Lyallpur who transpose Lyallpur to Ludhiana in a manner similar to the Lucknow reconstructed by mohajirs in Karachi. The most celebrated of these is Lyallpurian di Hatti [the shop of Lyallpurites], a grocery store established in Karkhana Bazaar, Lyallpur by Hans Raj Kharbanda in 1925, which became fabled for its *gachak*, *revadi* and biscuits over the decades. After Partition, the senior Kharbanda used the same name to establish a shop on Gokul Road, Ludhiana, in 1949, whose client base, dispersed across the world, has encouraged the owners to expand overseas under the label "Lyallpur Overseas."

Other Partition scholars have noted the use of place names in retaining memories of old homes in the names of new neighbourhoods and cities after migration. In addition to refugee colonies, such as Multan Nagar, Derawal Nagar and Potohar Nagar, that use the names of places in Pakistan to recall and commemorate originary places, shops, schools and colleges use place names to reinforce their origins. Although his grandsons claim that the name was never a problem, the centrality of place names in the proclamation of cultural politics is reflected in the controversy surrounding the name of the Karachi Bakery, founded in Hyderabad, India, in 1953 by a Sindhi migrant Khanchand Ramnani, who sought refuge in Hyderabad, with the rightist Hindu party Shiv Sena asking for a boycott of its products in October 2015. This was in opposition to the nationalist intentions of the owner in naming the bakery after a city in the mistaken belief that Karachi was a part of India even after Partition and to instill the idea of undivided India through naming the brand (Harish Ramnani, quoted in Nayak 2017). Unlike Karachi Bakery, owners of sweetmeat shops in Mulund, Bombay, insert the place name in the names of their shops, such as "Karachi Sweets," "Shree Mohan's Karachi Sweet Marts" or "Shree Karachi Mithai House" as the sole trace of a city lost forever. They use it to establish the authenticity of their products by claiming their lineage to the Sindhi city's legendary mithaiwalas and to accentuate the Sindhiness of their products, a name whose brand equity equalled that of other pre-Partition Indian brands like Polson Butter, Waman Hari Pethe and Finlays (Punwani 2009). Karachi Sweet Mart was set up by Tarachand Athwani, who was forced to leave behind his flourishing business in Karachi to take shelter in a refugee camp in Pimpri and then moved to Pune in 1948 (Naithani 2011). Karachi is immortalized in the name of a sweetmeat called Karachi Halwa, patented by Chandu Halwai, the owner of a sweet shop established in 1896 in Karachi,[8] who relinquished his shop to a Delhi migrant but not the recipe for the halwa when he was forced to migrate to Bombay in 1947. Similarly, the other Bombay landmark sweetshop, Ghasitaram, a branch of "Ghasitaram Halwai" founded by Ghasitaramdas Bajaj in Karachi, Pakistan, in 1916, was established by his son Shri Goverdhandas Bajaj after his migration to Bombay after Partition, naturalizing the taste of Karachi's iconic sweetshops in Bombay.

The nostalgia for a forgotten city is mirrored in the use of old place names in names of shops in Karachi established by refugees who fled the violence of 1947 with nothing but memories of cities and recipes but who continue to define themselves as Delhi wallah[9] and claim to be purveyors of taste that Delhi itself has lost. According to the owners of the shops on Burns Road, such as "Delhi Rabri," "Dehli Nihari House" and "Delhi Dahi Badas," these names were incorporated by them since the name Delhi was synonymous with all that was good in Karachi in the 1960s (Saifi 2017). In addition to Delhi, many Bombays are found in Karachi, the Indian financial capital's twin city in Pakistan, not only in businesses that insert place names in names of shops, such as Bombay Garments, Bombay Fruit Vendors and Bombay Coconut Vendors, but also in the name of a Bombay Bazaar that helps to preserve the flavour of the cosmopolitan city (Balouch 2014).

Place names of homeland regions used to name refugee colonies in Indian cities, such as Derawal Nagar, Gujranwala Town, Kohat Enclave and Multani Dhanda, may also be viewed as attempts by Partition survivors to orient themselves in an alien environment by locating their origins in specific ethnospatial or ethnolinguistic regions characterized by particularized speech patterns, cuisine, attire, rituals and everyday practices. Observers have been simultaneously fascinated and repelled by the ghetto-like ambience of these refugee enclaves inhabited by groups whose identification with the cultures of small places in Punjab spawns distinctive cultures that refute the myth of a unified Punjabi refugee culture as posited in refugee studies. Through the performance of the collective memories of these small places, Partition survivors attempt to resettle in an unfamiliar home.

Harmeet Shah Singh is of the view that "in west, north and parts of south and south-west Delhi, remnants of little, united Punjabs still exist" with his immediate neighbours being Multanis and a brotherhood that proudly calls itself Attock Biradri located in front of his house (2017).

Shilpi Gulati's oral interviews with members of the Derawal community in Delhi brings to light the feeble attempt of a community hailing from the Derajat region, comprising Dera Ismail Khan and Dera Ghazi Khan to resist being engulfed by the dominant Punjabi refugee narrative of Delhi. It does so through the retention of Siraiki language, inferiorritized as a rustic dialect of Punjabi by the British, Derawal biradris and celebrations of small functions on the festival days of Basant Panchami and Baisakhi by Bohrianwalla Thalla and Dera Ismail Khan Seva Samiti. Migrants from Mianwali congregated to form the Mianwali Nagar.

> Till date my grandfather and grandmother tell us stories of pre independence India, they just can't stop talking about Mianwali and consider Shah Alam (Bakkhar) as their homeland. I believe there was something special in that land, some sort of connect is there which I can also feel and may be that is the source of strength they had shown during their tough times.
>
> (Gera 2017)

Multani Dhanda is home to those who fled Multan during the exodus of Partition and have attempted not only to create the tastes of home, like *moth kachori*, *Multani chhole chawal*, *soya chaap*, *malpua* and *geela kulcha* and Multani Masala in new kitchens like Moth Bhandar but also to retain the trade and ethics of the old city (Suri 2016).[10] However, as Shah Singh puts it, "no one officially commemorates the tragic histories linked to these replicas of what the Partition generation left behind after Independence" (2017).

Space acts

In her examination of placemaking by Vietnamese refugees in the US, Aguilar-San Juan explains that placemaking, in this case, is an extremely complex process that "requires taking apart and reformulating location, material form or representation in order to modify, destroy or rebuild place" (2013: 380).

Unlike refugee colonies named after place names, which evoked memories of old homes allotted to refugees from a particular region facilitating the performance of homeland memories, those named after national leaders, such as Lajpat Nagar, Rajendra Nagar and Patel Nagar, or those reflective of national aspirations, such as Model Town and Adarsh Nagar exhibited a more heterogeneous composition. In these colonies, rather than memories of a particular home, the shared experience of being a refugee produced ways of living, practices and sensibilities that enabled refugees to reinhabit newly constructed spaces. Unlike Delhi's planned middle-class neighbourhoods that were modelled after, and one even named after, Lahore's Model Town, refugee colonies, many of which were euphemistically named Adarsh Nagar [Model Town], were barely functional spaces with two rooms and an open verandah on either side constructed on 107- to 120-yard plots.[11] Allocated to displaced persons from different ethnic, class and caste backgrounds from different regions on the western border,[12] these refugee colonies in Delhi, Lucknow, Jaipur, Kalka and many other towns demonstrate the process through which refugees transformed monotonous, empty space into place and made regulation housing bustle with the spirit of new refugee mohallas. While memories of specific regional homes continued to be performed in the inner spaces of the house, they were rein-scribed with the rhythms of a remembered Punjabi mohalla in the outer space of the street and the neighbourhood, albeit underwritten by the tragic memories of Partition.

The resettlement colony, obeying no architectural style, apart from economy and functionality, literalizes the meaning of home as shelter. Like the houses of the lower castes in Indian villages, the refugees' relocation on the city's outer pre-cincts constructs refugees as the new pariahs of the nation-village. Against archi-tectural historian Dell Upton's view that large urban ethnic groups build little that is distinctive (1986), Hayden holds that ethnicity can be seen as a shaping force of (American) urban places, provided that one looks at the production of social space carefully (Hayden 1997: 34). The production of refugee space in resettle-ment colonies shows that distinctive spaces can be created not only through fine architectural monuments but also through functional ethnic building types or even the way outdoor or indoor spaces, such as streets, yards, gardens and rooftops, are used. Punjabi refugees remapped on city planners' ungenerous lanes and dwell-ings memories of homes left behind in Punjab through what Michel de Certeau (1998) calls "space acts" (Conley 2000: 57), or the inhabitation and organization of space.

Punjabi transparency was married to refugee open living in the cultural prac-tices of Punjabi refugee neighbourhoods. Displaced Punjabis reinhabited reset-tlement places by inscribing the transparency of rustic Punjabi existence on the abjection of refugee open living, and through the everyday act of dividing and utilizing space. By marking the functional space with traditional Punjabi practices governing the distribution of domestic activities in closed and open spaces, they converted rehabilitation camps and colonies into homes. Old Punjabi gendering of space, hinting at past affluence, was retained despite space constraints. The inner courtyard, vehra, which was the female domain, converted routine domestic duties into communal acts. The outer courtyard, deodi, normally a male preserve, turned into a site for female socialization in the afternoons. The open roof in Punjabi homes was another unique space for snatching moments of privacy in a crowded household or for shared family activities as well as for sleeping on summer nights. Thus, the distribution and utilization of space in refugee Punjabi dwellings, encouraging communal rather than individual activity and the conduct of routine activities in open spaces, re-enacted the transparency of rustic Punjabi living and transformed the spaces of resettlement.

Much has been said about the violation of old Mughal and colonial cities' decorum by Punjabi refugees. It could be argued that the perceived desecration occurs as much through the conflict of Punjabi notions of neighbourhood propriety with elite Hindu and Muslim codes of behaviour and propriety as through the exigencies of refugee existence. Similar to Van der Horst and Messing's research on Dutch people's perceptions of immigrants and their "closed curtains" (2006), the disconnect between Punjabi open culture and Lucknowite, Delhi host cultures happened when expressions of aesthetics spilled over into the public areas of the street.

The new mohallas created by refugee colonies were affectionate albeit claustrophobic enclaves where transparent living was the norm and anybody's business was everybody's business. The culture of open living continued to flourish in the refugee colonies of Delhi, Lucknow, Faridabad and elsewhere where the public space of the street and the open courtyard turned into the convivial Punjabi space of *Trinjhan*

> where old, young and middle aged used to come together to perform works like weaving, sewing and perform other household works. During the course of their stay, the aged women used to share their experiences with the younger ones and in this way correct and guide them (2009).[13]

The mushrooming of tandoors [open ovens] at every street corner and push-carts hawking street food may be framed within the Punjabi concept of the *sanjha chulha* firmly entrenched in the Sikh institution of a casteless society. The sight of these open kitchens that defamiliarized their cities to old residents of Delhi, Lucknow and so on produced a comforting sense of the security of homes in refugee existence.

> Punjabi villages and towns had always had common tandoors for baking bread; women would prepare the dough at home and then take it to the communal oven to cook. So tandoors sprang up in Rajinder Nagar too. In the afternoons or early evenings, my grandmother would make atta at home and take it to the tandoorwala who sat down the street, relying on the households of the neighbouring lanes for business. He had no counter, no tables and chairs, no awning – just five bricks and a clay oven.
>
> (Oberoi 2015)

To the notion of a casteless, a classless community partaking in victuals symbolized by the sanjha chulha was articulated the concept of *dukh-sukh de saanjhi* [shared grief and happiness] that extended beyond the idea of the ethnolinguistic, ethnoreligious or ethno-regional community to dispersed populations connected by the trauma of Partition.

Figure 8.1 Reinscribing British Lucknow:Weekly Mangal Bazaar [Tuesday Market at the Entrance to the Alam Bagh Fort 150 years later (Source Rajiv Sachdeva).

At home in a resettlement colony

The refugees migrating to Lucknow, according to Lucknow microhistorian Yogesh Praveen,

> first settled near the station and later in Naka and Pandariba. The government created Chandar Nagar, Singar Nagar, Adarsh Nagar, Alambagh and Lajpat Nagar colonies for the refugees. The migrants turned Alambagh into a Punjabi locality and locals nicknamed Alambagh Lahore of Lucknow.
>
> (Quoted in Srivastava 2006)

A revisiting of Lucknow's colonial history, which runs parallel to that of the nawabs, by crossing the Charbagh station and entering Alam Bagh, establishes the significance of Alam Bagh in the Mutiny or First War of Independence in 1857. The 1911 (online) edition of the *Encyclopaedia Britannica* carries the following entry on Alam Bagh:

> ALAMBAGH, or ALUMBAGH, the name of a large park or walled enclosure, containing a palace, a mosque and other buildings, as well as a beautiful garden, situated about 4m from Lucknow, near the Cawnpore road, in the United Provinces of India. It was converted into a fort by the mutineers in 1857, and after its capture by the British was of importance in connection with the military operations around Lucknow.[14]

Alam Bagh has a historic significance in the war of 1857 as the stronghold of 12,000 rebels and is documented as a memorial to the British army's glory in British histories of the storming of Lucknow (see Engels 1858). But there is no memorial to Partition survivors who have inscribed the history of Partition on the ruins of Alam Bagh.

A hundred and fifty years after the 1857 revolt, the historic gate of the Alam Bagh fort leads to the refugee colony within it. The pavements along the gate that must be crossed to reach any part of Alam Bagh host a bustling daily market where Punjabi matrons can be seen bargaining with fruit vendors and roadside food stalls running a flourishing business in local delicacies. On the streets of Lucknow's "Little Punjab," Alam Bagh and Adarsh Nagar, Punjabi serves as the lingua franca interrupted by the Hindi of the vegetable vendors, rickshawallahs and domestic helps. All shops and small businesses in the neighbourhood appear to be Punjabi owned, as announced by the distinctive features of the shop owners and the Punjabi music played on their cassette players. The owners not only know the colonies' residents by name but can reel off their entire family tree. This refugee colony is no different from those adjoining Adarsh Nagar, a resettlement colony adjoining the fort.

When one is not going down the memory lanes and reliving Lucknow's regal past, the lanes of Lucknow, like those of any old Indian city, present images of dirt, squalor and overcrowding. Adarsh Nagar's lanes are no different. Nor are they sanctified by the memory of courtesans and perfume sellers as those of the Chowk. If the gleaming glass fronts of Punjabi-owned shops appear out of place amidst Lucknow's fabled mosques and minarets, the rows of square houses in Adarsh Nagar carry no trace of the glorious bastion of nationalist resistance to imperial domination. Nor does the colony resemble any other city or village left behind in the past in another country.

Adarsh Nagar is a colony in Alam Bagh, Lucknow constructed in 1954 on an orchard owned by an Englishman (see Figure 8.1). Though its name, Adarsh Nagar, the "ideal city," signifies the hopes of the new nation, this is definitely not the chapter of Lucknow's history Uttar Pradesh Tourism Department is keen to unveil to visitors. All the roads leading from the Charbagh Railway Station to the tourist "must-sees" – Residency, Bada Imambara, Chowk, Kaiserbagh – have been widened. But the approach road from Charbagh to Adarsh Nagar is still the busy Lucknow-Kanpur highway, and one still enters it through tehdi pulia, or the "awry bridge." The few bungalows in the front row eventually turn right to the tree-lined mansions of commissioned officers in the Sadar [Cantonment] area. But if one cares to venture into the houses behind the bungalows, one encounters "unhomely" homes in a location that is far from ideal.[15]

Each row of houses in the colonies had 27 houses with a front and back street and provision for shops, parks and schools. Adarsh Nagar's peripheral location and spatial dimensions are a reflection of the limits of the hospitality extended by host societies to refugees through the subsidized housing they were allotted by the government of India in 1956. A two-room tenement with a covered verandah and a courtyard on either side, constructed on plot sizes of 125 yards each, a pattern repeated in refugee colonies in other northern cities, was allotted to persons displaced by the Partition of 1947 for Rs. 2500/- each on a preferential basis.

Figure 8.2 Adarsh Nagar 2018

Figure 8.3 Renovated 26 A B with the original red stone pillars

Comparatively affluent refugee families bought two adjoining quarters and made additions and modifications within their built constraints.[16] As the back or front verandahs were covered to add more rooms, the middle rooms in each house have no windows opening out, contributing to their claustrophobic air.

The reconstruction of the aesthetics of home left behind by displaced persons demonstrates the process through which the displaced overcame impediments posed by the spatial boundaries and plans of allotted housing. Although the functional spatial plan of the house did not leave much room for alteration, allottees made minor modifications to personalize these basic shelters into homes to produce a sense of privacy, intimacy, security and limited individuality. The kachcha [unpaved] inner courtyard was cemented and turned into the hub of all domestic chores, including cooking, washing and hanging out clothes. The outer courtyard was paved, leaving out rows for planting flowers and fruit trees, and a high wall and a gigantic iron gate were installed to provide a sense of security. Houses that reshaped square spaces into round verandahs with red stone pillars and floors stood out from others.

Prominently embossed names of owners in recesses on outer walls along with house signs proudly claimed house ownership. Despite the occupants' efforts to individualize their homes through a few personal touches, like a red-tiled verandah or a paved courtyard, the monotony of regulation housing is conspicuous. Yet the first

Figure 8.4 Original Name Plate with the Name of the New Owner.

owners of the houses, who moved in after an eight-year wait, have constructed new meanings of home in the cramped space.[17]

Although the state-constructed houses were not constructed according to any vernacular plan, the allottees modified the plan to make it correspond as closely as possible to the traditional Punjab courtyard house structure through the organization and use of spaces. The strictly gendered space of traditional Punjabi homes attaches prohibitions to the crossing of the deodi [deodi langhna], particularly by male visitors and guests, since deodi served as a veil [ghungat] for the house. In the absence of the deodi, which separated the male from the female spaces of the home in the refugee colony plan, male guests or visitors were either received in the front courtyard or in the verandah and females forbidden from straying into those spaces when they were being used by males.

The spatial constraint in the colonies necessitated the conversion of the first room on the front as a baithak, where the patriarch of the house would work, rest and receive visitors even though the palang was replaced by wooden sofa sets in the homes of comparatively affluent refugees. Notwithstanding the fact the presence of a senior male member reclining or snoozing on the sofa set offended the sensibilities of the new generation influenced by the modern Western architectural concept of the drawing room, the traditional organization of space continued to be carried over by refugees even after they moved to more modern housing up to the 1970s.

Figure 8.5 Bronzeware from Bhakkar.

In resettlement colonies, the verah offered the entrance to the house when entered from the back street,[18] which was used by family members and close friends with only formal visitors being received at the front gate.

Verah continued to serve as the hub of all activities until the new millennium with household chores, like scouring dishes, washing and drying clothes, cooking and serving meals, and entertaining relatives and close friends being performed in the open space of the verah.

Although *chulha chauka* is used as a synonym for domesticity or domestic responsibilities in all of North India, the chauka, as an uncovered cooking space, was literally visible in the resettled urban colony, as was the common tandoor shared by several families. Despite the addition of covered kitchens, food continued to be cooked in the open on a coal or wood fire until the 1970s, approximating the idea of the uncovered chauka of traditional Punjab with the covered space used only for storing dishes, pots and pans and groceries. The preference for using wood or coal fire by women on the grounds that modern stoves were unconducive to the preparation of traditional cuisine or the inclusion of an earthern oven called tandoor in the vehras of some houses ensured that the concept of the chauka remained prevalent in resettlement colonies.

Adarsh Nagar lives in the memory of a past, when a self-owned house was a step out of homelessness and in a present, in which to be confined to a home in Adarsh Nagar signifies failure. It is now a crumbling refugee quarter, its hopes for a better future disintegrating with the last of the Partition survivors. Its residents fall into two categories: remaining Partition survivors and their children clinging to memories of what was once home and the grandchildren who have no hopes of finding a better home. Those with a future have moved out to better homes in Lucknow's newly developing colonies, to the Chattarpur farmhouse in Delhi or to the Pali Hill penthouse in Mumbai.[19]

Aesthetics of displacement

While examining the notion of aesthetics in displacement, Tasoulla Hadjiyanni, in "Aesthetics in displacement – Hmong, Somali and Mexican home-making practices in Minnesota," uncovers "the material and immaterial forms that aesthetic constructions can take: from decorative objects to colours, textures, materials, light levels, furniture placement and type as well as sound and smell" (2009: 541).

As Hadjiyanni points out, understanding the home-making process of aesthetic construction under conditions of displacement has engaged little attention. Hadjiyanni inquires "what the notion of aesthetics entail in displacement, if immigrant groups construct a sense of difference in the home, and if so, how" (2009: 542). Arguing that aesthetic constructions can take material and immaterial forms from "decorative objects to colours, textures, materials, light levels, furniture placement and type as well as sound and smell," she notes the impediments "endured in constructing an aesthetic" that the displaced resonated with (2009: 541).

The recent turn to material culture for retrieving memories of pre-displacement has thrown new light on the event and pre-Partition history through focusing on material objects, many of which have been housed in the newly established

Partition Museum in Amritsar. While material objects brought over by elite refugees, such as family heirlooms, photographs and diaries, can help in the reconstruction of the social, economic, material and political history of Partition, materializing of the experience of the majority of refugees who were forced to flee with nothing other than the set of clothes they wore requires identification of more humble objects, such as the ubiquitous sandook [tin trunk] in which the more fortunate among them were able to bring across a few sets of clothes and linen. Unlike the displaced communities interviewed by Hadjiyanni, the closure of the possibility of bringing back decorative objects to be able to construct an aesthetic of pre-displacement Punjab for displaced persons made colours, textures and furniture placement crucial to the production of home aesthetics. Connerton's notion of performative memory, a means through which "societies remember" was translated in the aesthetics of displacement and the objects made by the displaced (1989).

Possessing and making objects, in Sandra Dudley's view, enables refugees' appropriation of alien space to feel at home (2010). Refugees, forced to flee violence, converged on functional objects to produce a sense of home. As opposed to the closet in Western homes, the *sandook* [tin trunk], in addition to serving as storage space, enclosed the secrets of the household in rural Punjab. Unlike refugees fleeing on foot, who bundled their belongings in a piece of cloth, those who travelled by truck or train packed the most essential items, such as clothes, linen and pots and pans in tin trunks, including a giant size tin trunk specific to Punjab, known as vadda trunk [big trunk], in which winter quilts and additional items were stored. This trunk became the most visible signifier of forced migration, displacement and homelessness in a refugee home. Spatial constraints compelled the stacking of tin trunks in living rooms or bedrooms on the vadda trunk instead of the dalan or store room of the traditional Punjabi home.

In examining the aesthetics of displacement among Karenni refugees, Dudley has observed the importance of weaving by Karenni women in the construction of the pre-displacement home (2010). Bereft of material artefacts that could recall memories of home, refugee women's decoration of functional spaces of the allotted homes with exquisite hand embroidery constructed a refugee aesthetic that is visible across refugee colonies in Delhi, Lucknow, Rudrapur, Kalka, Ambala and so on. In view of the rationing of cloth following the Second World War and resource crunch, women personalized the sturdy tin trunks by covering them with inexpensive, thick, durable fabric adorned with pre-displacement embroidery styles. Labour-intensive phulkari embroidery that young women, guided by mothers and grandmothers, would have done as part of their trousseau before Partition virtually ceased because trade routes carrying raw materials for the craft had been completely disrupted. Instead, multi-coloured Sindhi embroidery on white matte done by female members when they were free of household chores synthesized the displaced aesthetic of the refugee home. In view of the small size of the houses and limited resources, linen, tablecloths and fabric covers, finely hand-embroidered by the women in the family, concealed minimal, functional furniture, such as wooden cots, tables and storage racks to construct a unique aesthetic of embroidery through which alien spaces were transformed into familiar homes.

Figure 8.6 Aesthetics of embroidery

Textures, in addition to colour, played a significant role in constituting the aesthetic of the displaced home. In addition to white dusuti for cross-stitch embroidery, casement for satin stitch and matte for Sindhi embroidery preferred by women in displaced families for tablecloths and trunk and shelf covers, the texture of thick woven linen in bright colours formed the aesthetics of a displaced Punjabi home. Along with the phulkari that had formed a young woman's trousseau, the *khes*,[20] a floor spread and bed covering unique to Punjab that is traditionally made of cotton, formed an essential part of the household linen. Although the khes could no longer be woven at home by women,[21] manufactured khes and durree, largely unknown to the world, constituted an indispensable component of the linen that softened the hardness of the manjaa or string cot.

Instead of bedsheets, a preference for thick, woven, non-crushable bedcovers in bright shades suitable for a lifestyle in which the palang or manjaa functioned as multi-purpose furniture, on which families slept but also lounged, ate, played cards, and even entertained relatives and close friends during the day, was visible in refugee homes.

Rich, ornate, heavy furnishing and curtains in thick, silken fabric that have been cited by host communities to stigmatize Punjabi décor as loud or flamboyant was used by the displaced to reproduce an aesthetics of opulence to compensate for the loss of family heirlooms. Vibrant colours, such as dark brown, burgundy, maroon, navy blue and bottle green, used in furnishings interspersed with covers in light-coloured fabrics produced the distinctive ambience of the displaced Punjabi home.

Unlike other parts of India in which traditional weaves in natural fibres, such as cotton, tussar or silk, were used for apparel, the trade routes in which Punjab formed an important node have long enabled flows of fabrics and fabric designs from across the world to Punjab, which was strengthened by British period imports. Middle- and upper-class families' traditional association of soft, flowing, silky fabrics like taffeta, shantung, satin, chenille, bosky, voile and lawn with a Chinese, Persian or French origin with better living explained the continuity of these defining clothing styles in displaced homes. Similarly, a preference for primary colours for the young, pastel for the middle aged and muted for the elderly females in floral prints or embroidered in Punjabi embroidery styles rather than the earthy hues with vibrant block prints popular in other parts of India constructed a sartorial aesthetic of displacement that made the displaced feel at home.

Performing place

According to Yi-Fu Tuan, "a place is the compelling focus of a field: it is a small world, the node at which activities converge" (Tuan 1974: 236). Michael Jackson's notion of home in "At Home in the World" as less being grounded in a place than in the activity that occurs in that place and the idea that home is not a person, thing or place but an activity performed by, with or in a person's things and place, is particularly useful in understanding the sense of home performed by refugees in the resettlement colonies (1995). Although refugees were unable to reconstruct remembered physical homes in the Little Punjabs, Multans, Derajats or Sindhs in the resettlement colonies, they reterritorialized lost homes through speech acts and performativity.

The Punjabis also devised a language of small, semi-private and semi-public territories between the dwelling and the street that supported certain kinds of public behaviour. The intrusion of privacy was countered by the aesthetic of gestures similar to those used by individuals when they are squeezed into cramped spaces. The lack of distance or overlap between the male and female spaces was compensated by a delicate code regulating male and female behaviour. Both males and females resisted the forced intrusion of private space by norms governing eye behaviour, posture, facial expression, conversation and even laughter. The much-reviled veil worn by female members was also used as a gesture of marking private space. Similar norms regulated socialization. Female visitors were discreetly escorted to female quarters while male socialization was restricted to open areas like the front gate or the outer courtyard. An elaborate code of modesty dictating male and female behaviour was the displaced person's feeble attempt at maintaining pre-displacement codes of propriety in view of the forced emergence of refugee females in the public space. Spatial organization and norms of behaviour and socialization, the experience of violence and memories of the old place constituted a new "enacted environment" and social space in the resettlement colony.

Pierre Bourdieu's concept of the habitus can elucidate the role of the body in the Partitioned subject's self-constitution. He distinguishes between "the history objectified in things, in the form of institutions" and "the history incarnated in bodies, in the form of that system of enduring dispositions," which he calls the habitus (Bourdieu 1990: 190). He shows how the "body is in the social world and the social world is in the body" and expresses itself in "standing, speaking and thereby of feeling and thinking" (190). "Dress, bearing, physical and verbal manners" are the sites for the core values of the society. The body becomes the memory, acting as a repository of the principles embodied within it. The habitus offers a means of conceptually conditioning and conditioned freedom. Undivided Punjab's memory is inscribed on the refugee's body on which the history of the Partition is inscribed. The refugee's conflicting loyalties are betrayed by the confusion of the "social game" found in biological individuals. Despite the refugee's will to the new national game, his or her physical leaning towards the old social world is betrayed in particular ways of "standing, speaking and thereby of feeling and thinking" (ibid: 190). Since the core values of any society are believed to be inscribed on dress, bearing, physical and verbal manners, any transgression of the code is perceived as a shock to the society's self-definition. The body, its coverings and its demeanour, metaphors of the social, incarnates both the history of Partition and the story of struggle constructing a particular aesthetic that redefines the refugee self and sociality. The refugee's body was a body in various postures of humiliation and shame. The formulaic rags-to-riches saga of the refugee was literalized in the set of clothes in which she or he escaped.[22] Shame and humiliation continued to be signified through a corporeal vocabulary of concealing and exposing even in the "obscene" performance of intimate bodily functions in open living. In fact, open living necessitated a strict legislation of propriety and control of sexuality enforced through the rules governing the draped or undraped female body, in which the chunni [veil] acquired metonymic significance. These positions are articulated in traditional Punjabi iconography through the body's exposure, particularly exposure of the head, represented by the female chunni and the male pagdi [turban].

In Partition narratives, the removal of the chunni or pagdi serve as powerful symbols of the exposed body, connoting the loss of Punjabi honour and pride. Bodily exposure is a matter of cultural legislation. It might be difficult to connect the shame of a lost headdress with the relative lack of inhibition that has been observed in Punjabi males.[23] Similarly, the modesty of the head covered with a chunni appears incongruous with the transgressive presence of females in the public space after Partition. The chunni, which covers the torso and the head, has always been a marker of the metaphorical boundary against the other in old Punjabi patriarchy. It conceals the female body, both virginal and maternal, from the stranger's profane gaze. The protection or exposure of the female body has been central to the encoding of the community's honour and shame. The female body, abducted or raped, represents one aspect of the Partition violence and became the site for the construction of nationalist patriarchy. The code of propriety in the resettlement colony constructed itself in relation to a rigid female dress code as a feeble attempt to retain a semblance of honour and dignity even in the resettlement camp's indecent exposure. The legislation of female modesty occurred in spite of, and against, the jettisoning of females in the male public domain.

If the female body was the site for encoding community honour and values, the male body was converted into a family asset. The new corporeal aesthetic, in which the body's health and labour translated into economic capital, demanded a redefinition of the old warrior and peasant ethic of industry and physical strength. The refugee Punjabi body was the old hard-worked body, put to the test by the privation and stress of settlement. It served as the basis of the displaced Punjabi morality, defined in relation to labour, industry and struggle. With no assets or capital other than the corporeal body, the refugee etched the memory of struggle on the body. The signification of the male body as a family investment was expressed in an unvoiced code that demanded the bigger allocation of the nutritious portions of the family meal for earning males. Though the female body was also enlisted in domestic labour, it did not merit extra nurturing as its labour did not contribute directly to the family income.

Michel de Certeau includes bread and wine among the permanent items on a French table, and names these as part of everyday practice through which French subjectivity is constructed. He views bread "as the symbol of the hardships of life and work, it is the memory of a better standard of living acquired the hard way over the course of previous generations" (de Certeau 1998: 86). Locating bread in the "gastronomy of poverty," he shows how it is transformed from a basic food to "a cultural symbol," arousing the most archaic respect. Bread, according to de Certeau, stands as a monument to averting suffering and hunger. Roti, or Indian bread, performed similar semiotics in the aesthetic of the refugee body. An indispensable item in the Punjabi meal, the roti came to connote the essential ingredient for the body's nourishment. The body in struggle was conceived as hard-worked, its labouring capacity linked to the quality of the diet. Refugees recount with pride their sustaining themselves even in their worst crisis without having to beg for a meal. Roti became a metaphor for two square meals that the refugee procured through labour. But it was also the canvas on which old-place ontologies were inscribed. It bore the inscription of the core value of sharing. None who turned to the relatively affluent for shelter was denied roti even if it entailed cutting down on non-essentials. The need to nourish the body in conformity with valourized labour makes food a key signifier in Punjabi refugee identities.

Levi-Strauss's point about cuisine forming "a language in which each society codes messages which allow it to signify a part of what it is" or "a language through which that society unconsciously reveals its structure" is also relevant here (quoted in de Certeau 1998: 180). Food is the item of everyday life that remains the longest as "a reference to the culture of origin . . . it becomes a veritable discourse of the past and a nostalgic narrative about the country, the region, the city, or the village where one was born" (Certeau 1998: 84).

One aspect of food is nostalgia, the contrast between the rich past and the destitute present. The refugee diet was a "lean, mean" diet, a watered-down version of the proverbial rich Punjabi diet. Every social group consumes different products and prepares and ingests them in different ways, which are defined in order to respond to local agricultural production and necessity. The refugee suffers a double displacement from traditional food through the latter being uprooted from its geography as well as history.

The other aspect of food relates to the retention of local cuisine and maintenance of local taboos about the preservation and storage of food in the face of altered geographies and histories. This often requires a different interpretation of the feudal hierarchy in the distribution of food. Family recipes passed down from generation to generation, adapted to climatic and economic constraints, retaining the local flavour and texture through cooking processes, preserve memory in Frontier cuisines. The choice of foodstuffs considered edible, the authorized mixtures and ways of preparation, the calendar of provisional prohibitions, as Levi-Strauss demonstrated, function through a large number of exclusions and a smaller number of authorizations within a particular circle of compatibility. The old Punjabi social discourse repeats more clearly on the point of food taboos and strictures against violation. Traditional cuisine and food taboos become ways of writing the "narrative of difference inscribed in the rupture between the alimentary time of the 'self', and the alimentary time of the other" (de Certeau 1998: 84).

Finally, an aesthetic of resettlement that helped refugees to inhabit the place allotted to them in the new nation may be reconstructed through oft-repeated fragments in routine conversations.

Paisa te aanda janda rehnda ai, sehat, zindagi, rishte wapas nahin aande

(Money keeps coming and going, health, life and relationship don't come back).

This old Punjabi idiom acquires a particular resonance in the light of the uncertainties of life and fortunes imprinted on the displaced consciousness. Tales of millionaires becoming homeless overnight are not exaggerated. Nor are those of close shaves with death. Under these conditions, normal attachments to wealth, property and land appear to be mistaken priorities. Privileging life, health and relationships over material gains forms a distinctive feature of displaced existence. Yet this ethic coexists with one that is almost contradictory.

Paisa hoye te kuch wi ho sakda ai

(Anything is possible with money).

Family name, lineage and reputation override considerations of wealth in traditional social caste hierarchies. The invocation of family pride and prestige having become an empty signifier in the Partition survival game, individual skills and wealth have displaced traditional caste and lineage hierarchies.

Khao handao

(Eat and consume).[24]

In a land where frugality is a norm and saving a compulsive habit, this consumerist hedonism might appear incongruous, unless placed against the loss of certainties in Partition. Displaced Punjabis live like there is no tomorrow because of the memory of the past in which there were no tomorrows.

Bas munda mehnti hona chayida hai

(The groom should be hard-working).

A community's relationship networks, values and priorities are often reflected in marital eligibility criteria. The displacement of family or kinship ties, status or astrological predictions by individual merit is best reflected in the preceding fragment. Personal skills, labour and industry begin to be privileged above family name, status and horoscopes in defining the eligibility condition for the male.

Mohalla as home

Although the notion of mohalla is not unique to Punjab, the rules of belonging to the Punjabi mohalla differed from those of the old mohallas of Delhi and Lucknow, and it was the refugee colonies that reproduced the heimlichkeit to counter the disorientation that Paul experienced daily on leaving home.

> I belonged to the whole mohalla and the mohalla belonged to me. It is that feeling that I missed. Even today when I think of it, I believe my roots lie there.
>
> (Paul in Gulzar 2017)

The refugees huddled together in resettlement schemes and colonies to recover the sense of belonging to the whole mohalla and the mohalla belonging to one. The rehabilitation camps and refugee colonies in Lucknow and Delhi offered the friendliness, intimacy and homeliness of Punjabi, even Thalochi, Derawal or Multani, accompanied by the pleasure and security of being within the walls of the home. To this effect, old residents of Lajpat Nagar, in which refugees camped in Purana Qila were allotted plots, continue to identify themselves as Lahorian, Pindiwaal, Multani, Sindhi or Jhangi seven decades after Partition (Bhatia, quoted in Shukla 2017).

Notes

1 Excerpts from my essay "Adarsh Nagar diyaan Gallan: At Home in a Resettlement Colony". *Interpreting Homes: South Asian Literature* (ed) Malashri Lal and Sukrita P. Kumar, (Delhi: Pearson Education) 2006, pp 16–33 have been included in this chapter.

2 State records reveal that the government undertook concerted efforts to rehabilitate different categories of refugees in rural and urban areas in different ways ("The Report on the Working of the Relief and Rehabilitation Committee," 1949; "East Punjab Legislative Assembly Debates" 1948).

3 Palang is a carved wooden bed with a backrest carved with Mughal motifs of animals, birds, natural scenery and geometrical patterns and fitted with mirrors and colourful legs called pawas that usually formed a part of the bride's trousseau. Skilled carpenters from Bhera, Chiniot and Hoshiarpur with their provincial characteristics also made "Peeras" and "Pidhis," decorative boxes and wooden toys with ivory inlay work.

4 "The courtyard in a cold climate is usually the heart of the dwelling spatially, socially, and environmentally. Although, the size of the land, to some extent, is influential, the

average sizes of the courtyards are generally determined according to the latitude. They are narrow enough to maintain a shaded area during the heat of the day in summer, but wide enough to receive solar radiation in winter" (Shokouhian, Soflaee, and Nikkhah 2007).

5 In a song of popular Punjabi singer Babbu Mann, the woman admits that she goes to the terrace on the pretext of taking away the washing [kapde sukke laun bahaane, main kothe te aavaan] (2017).

6 The multifunctional manjaa, where ropes are woven according to a wooden bed frame, used to be a must for Punjabi families during the olden times (Kaur 2011).

7 Moving away from the Western notion of place as landscape, they assert that the "emotional geography of Yanyuwa country is embodied in place, body and mind and chronicles a uniquely Indigenous and Yanyuwa way of knowing the world" (2009: 79).

8 "The history of our shop is rooted in India's Partition, when feeding the refugees was a routine" (Chandu Halwai, ndt).

9 "It's where my family is from. I am from Karachi, I was born here but culturally I am also a Delhi Wallah. There should be better relations with India, they are our neighbors, we have much in common" (Yusuf, owner of Delhi Rabri, quoted in Saifi 2017).

10 "One of these is Thakurdas Omprakash Purchun Vikreta, a general provisions shop 'that's as old as independent India,' according to co-owner Umesh Chugh. 'It has remained the way it was when my uncles and father set it up. My family had a shop with a similar name at Hannu ka Chajja in Multan. So they decided to continue with the same name, same trade and same ethics,' he says" (quoted in Suri 2016).

11 "Between 1955 and 1965, the flats were given on lease to families who arrived in Delhi after Partition. Two separate units, on the ground and first floors, were made on plots of 107 to 120 yards" (Nath 2014). As Partha S. Ghosh points out, narrow strips were arranged, packed like sardines to maximize the number of plots with a frontage allotted to refugees with the front-to-depth ratio as stark as 1:4 (2016: 285).

12 For example, the layout of Kirti Nagar, a colony spread of 150 acres situated in the industrial area on Najafgarh Road had been approved by the Town-Planning Sub-Committee and the Delhi Development Sub Committee and was sponsored by the Ministry of Rehabilitation in cooperation with the Punjab National Bank. Unlike the carefully planned Kirti Nagar in which the plots were to be freehold and there was provision of sites for a school, dispensary, cinema, petrol pump and public building, 45 of Delhi's refugee colonies that were made freehold only in 2014 were hovel-like structures.

13 http://sikhsangat.org/2009/pingalwara-society-recreates-charm-of-forgotten-culture-%E2%80%98trinjhan%E2%80%99/

14 http://44.1911encyclopedia.org/a/al/alambagh.htm, accessed on April 24, 2006.

15 Through their camp living, middle-class Punjabi refugees were made to occupy the spaces traditionally occupied by the peripatetic people of Punjab like the *tumbawallah*s (tent-dwellers) and the *khanabadosh* ("people who might come from anywhere and whose ancestors and descent nobody can tell," Timeann, 1970: 492) that Joseph Berland mentions (2003).

16 Twenty-Six A.B. Adarsh Nagar was formed by merging two allotted quarters. For details of housing allotment in Delhi, see V. N. Datta's "Panjabi Refugees and the Urban Development of Greater Delhi." He reports that "by the end of 1951, 529 one-roomed, 3,398 two-roomed, 257 single-storey, and 166 double-storey three-roomed houses; 11,159 single-roomed tenements; 1,518 shops and stalls; and 593 shop-cum-residences had been completed" (Datta 2002: 270).

17 Unlike the Chowk, Adarsh Nagar is not an ethnic enclave. "*Sade biji kehnde si, 'aithe ten ban ban di lakdi ha'*" (This place has wood from all jungles, my mother would say), Deshi, a former Adarsh Nagar resident, recalls (2005). Rather, refugees who were camped in the railway barracks for eight years constructed a "neighbourhood collectivity" by buying houses in this colony.

18 The service street, as in all old Indian colonies, was meant for the use of scavengers, domestic helpers and other service providers. Being a traditionally Jan Sangh constituency, the promised provision of proper sanitation and sewerage in the colony has not been fulfilled as of 2018 despite the ascent of Jan Sangh's new avatar Bhartiya Janata Party in Uttar Pradesh.

19 The Bollywood lyricist, the late Anand Bakshi, had an Adarsh Nagar connection and moved his family from there to Pali Hill.

20 For generations, women living in Punjab's villages wove the khes as a part of the trousseau they would take to their future homes. Traditionally made of cotton, with bold, harmonic and imaginative colour patterns, the thick ones are used as a floor spread or as coverlets or shawls in winter and thinner ones as a bed covering (Garg 2010).

21 This is unlike villages of Punjab, where, according to Garg, the practice of the women weaving the khes lovingly right from the beginning to the end to be gifted to the daughter as part of her trousseau has survived transformation of the rural space (Garg 2010).

22 In spite of its exaggeration, the joke about the rich old trader and his wife who rotated the single pair of trousers (*salwar*) between themselves when required to leave the house encapsulates the shame and humiliation of a large number of Partition survivors. Rushdie parodies this in Bilquees's attempt to retain her *dupatta* when she is caught in the riot in *Shame* (1983).

23 Mira Nair captures this semiotic in the scene in *Monsoon Wedding* (2001) when the father of the bride finally musters the courage to appeal to his paedophile family friend to leave. The removal of the *pagdi* is a significant gesture.

24 Datta cites a couplet to summarize the same ideology:

> Khada peeta lahay da
> Bakee ahmad sabey da
> What we can eat and drink is ours/
> What is left may go to Ahmad Shah (the invader).

(Datta 2002: 282)

9   Moving on

As opposed to Holocaust survivors, whose torturous memories have been meticulously preserved and disseminated in diaries, photographs, letters and museums, the reluctance of Partition survivors to share their stories even with their descendants has remained a matter of speculation. As Dhooleka S. Raj observed, the narratives of refugee families revealed that the different ways in which refugee families remember Partition "reconfigures the interplay of memory, forgetting and ignorance" (2000: 30). Raj argues that "forgetting in one generation turns into a family ignorance which develops an overtly political register as the nation collectively remembers" (2000: 30). However, Raj's sophisticated engagement with intergenerational transmission of Partition memory does not engage the survivors' need to forget. Speculations about the first generation's silence range from repression of traumatic memories (Das 1990; Butalia 1998) to desire to protect their progeny from pain and suffering (Raj 2000) or simply the need to get on with the business of living. The affective economy of Partition has been explored in depth in the analysis of Partition fiction (Bhalla 1999; Kamra 2008; Yusin 2008), testimonies (Das 1990; Menon 2013; Butalia 1998) and anthologies (Tomsky 2008) that trace the melancholia and undertone of mourning that undergirds these narratives. Symptoms of melancholia ranging from amnesia to complete breakdown in the behaviour of traumatized survivors of Partition have been immortalized in fiction, film and other creative genres. Finally, the return of repressed memories of traumatic violence has been traced in forms of deviant behaviour. However, informed explanations of survivors' reluctance to perform the work of mourning have yet to emerge in the literature on Partition.

Fictional and testimonial narratives of Partition have focused on tracing "the melancholic economy," "the traumatic legacy," "the wounded psyche" and "scarred memories" of the tragic violence of Partition. But those who literally bore the scars of Partition on their bodies or psyches chose to remain silent and refused to transmit their saga of suffering even to their descendants. Historians, psychologists, sociologists and literary scholars have endlessly debated the inexplicable causes for the repression of traumatic memories and provided psychological, historical and sociological explanations for forgetting, repression or cathartic recall of the horrific memories of violence (Das 1990; Butalia 1998; Menon and Bhasin 1998; Bhalla 1999; Tai and Kudaisya 2000; Kamra 2002; Didur 2007;

Yusin and Bahri 2008). Responses of Partition survivors, however, range from impregnable silence to perfunctory dismissal or a desire to put the trauma behind them. "What is the use of remembering that bad phase?" says Bajaj, now living in a middle-class suburb where the refugee camp once stood (quoted in Safi 2017). Bajaj's desire to let go of the past and live in the present is typical of that of the majority of Partition survivors.[1] This chapter aims to isolate instances of disjuncture between the melancholia and trauma aestheticized by scholars documenting or analyzing fictional and testimonial narratives of survivors and the silence, forgetting and summary dismissal of the traumatic experience by survivors in sharing it with their descendants. It argues that their struggle to get on with the business of living deprived them of the luxury of mourning and postponed the work of mourning.

Egon F. Kunz's kinetic model of the refugee in flight is applicable to refugees of Partition (1973), particularly to Hindus and Sikhs of a certain class, in their conforming to his push model through their not being poor people or people who had failed within their homeland but successful, prominent, well-integrated, educated individuals, who were pushed out of place. Out of the Partition refugees in flight, a smaller number belonged to his first kinetic type, the "anticipatory refugee" who senses the danger early and makes appropriate and timely arrangements and the majority to the second type, the "acute refugees" who are forced to leave at a moment's notice by fear through an overwhelming push like a war, government policy or political crisis (1973: 131–132). The refugee's relief at arriving safely in the place of asylum and the initial shock is summed up in Bajaj's statement: "We are alive and that is more important" (quoted in Safi 2017).[2] Stephen Keller's view that the trauma of flight produces residual psychological states in the refugee that will affect behaviour for years to come is even more pertinent in understanding the reaction to threat of those who were late in fleeing and suffered the worst hardships and loss (1975). The three residual characteristics that Keller observed in Punjabi refugees – guilt, invulnerability and aggressiveness – are particularly illuminating in comprehending the deferment of the task of mourning by the refugees of Partition. According to Barry N. Stein, the general pattern of refugee adjustment over time can be examined in four stages: 1) the initial arrival period of the first few months; 2) the first and second years; 3) after four to five years; and 4) a decade or more (2018).

Life in the camps

The initial arrival period of the first few months often consists of living in the camps, an aspect of refugee experience that has not received adequate attention. Irrespective of the differences in the material conditions of the camps, the most important features of camp identified by H. B. M. Murphy, "segregation from the host population, the need to share facilities, a lack of privacy, plus overcrowding and a limited, restricted area" defined the camps in which refugees of Partition were initially accommodated (1955). While life in the camps has largely been associated with a sense of dependency and being controlled (Mamdani 1973), camp, as a space for emerging political, ethnic identities and agency, has also been noted (Chatterji 2002). Although survivors mention the lack of basic amenities, cramped spaces and lack of privacy in their initial few months in the camps, they also remember them as a place of community and conviviality.

Instead of reviving memories of the privation, suffering and squalor of refugee camps, refugees recall them as spaces of conviviality in which the spatial crunch, combined with shared memories of loss, suffering and abjection, fostered a culture of openness and the community living of the mohalla that several survivors continue to express a yearning for decades after their migration to more affluent neighbourhoods. Meshi, a resident of an upscale gated colony in East Delhi, recalled, with a faraway look, the *doli*[3] ceremony of her 15-year-old sister when the entire community of railway employees housed by the Indian Railways in the military barracks in Lucknow turned up to bid the child bride farewell. "She was the daughter of the entire community. No eye remained dry as she left the barkaan [barracks]" (Meshi 2006).

Unlike the survivors still compelled to live in deplorable conditions in the last of the camps, survivors who made a successful transition from the camp to the refugee colony and to more affluent neighbourhoods abstain from dwelling on the details of the privations they underwent immediately on arrival or in the first year. A cinematic representation of 'the flying Sikh' Milkha Singh's sister's emotional reaction at being united with her teenaged brother in the Purana Qila camp in *Bhag Milkha Bhag* (2016) is emblematic of the initial relief and joy expressed by survivors on being reunited with their loved ones. The excessive demonstration of affection in Milkha's screen sister caressing and showering kisses on her lost baby brother is naturalized within the visual excess of the melodramatic genre of the Hindi commercial film.[4] But memories of similar melodramatic expressions of relief and joy on finding not only separated kin but also friends or neighbours are shared by survivors. "My mother's friend hugged my mother so hard that her glass bangles broke," recalled the then seven-year-old Deshi (2005). "My uncle would take me to the station every day in the hope that my parents will be on the train. And then one day, they arrived by the train," recalled another who was packed off in a truck with her uncle until they arrived in a camp (Prakash Kaur 2017).

Relief at fleeing violence in a place that offered safety explains their making light of the inhuman conditions of the hastily erected relief camp that inadvertently slip in at the insistent probing of the ethnographer. Following the account of the circumstances that led to the exodus, the closure "And then we arrived in . . . by train/truck/on foot" is offered to signify their own successful escape punctuated by regret for those who were not able to make it. After narrating the tragic tale of the brutal massacre of her grandfather, pregnant mother and sister by their Muslim neighbours, a witness concluded, "The military came and brought us to a camp" (Veeranwali 2006).

However, mention of any single detail is crucial to gauging the specific trauma faced by immigrants on arrival. While memory blotted details of the carnage she witnessed to protect her, she recalled two apparently trivial but telling details of their three-month ordeal in the camp. "I would squirt milk in the new-born's mouth with cotton wool. I couldn't change the dressing on the fractured skull of my four-year-old brother. I would wash the bandage and dry it before reusing it" (Veeranwali 2006), she whispered softly with a frightened gaze. Another survivor recalled swaddling his newborn in his wife's chunni after boarding the train and finding him dead on arrival (Papneja 2017). Memories of being thirsty or drinking water from rivers or nullahs flowing with blood, being provided black gram and jaggery or flattened rice and jaggery on the journey (Chugh 2017) and, finally, the taste of hot food on arrival in the camp (Papneja 2017) recalled for the ethnographer provide a telling comment on the suffering undergone by survivors.[5]

> "They were alert throughout and ordered us to move if they suspected any disturbance. We used to get raw food, grains in the refugee camp. Most of the time, we ate chana daal cooked in boiling water and added salt and red chili powder to it. We walked for days without knowing where we were headed to. We had left properties worth lakhs, valuables and vehicles and most importantly, our ancestral town where we spent our childhood," she shares.
>
> (Kanta Arora quoted in Arora 2015)

Statements like "I slept outside the shop or I sold my wares on the footpath" must be viewed as metonymic signifiers of the extent of the destitution (Midha, Jairamdas 2017).[6] "I would walk barefoot and my feet would burn until I saved enough to buy a hawai chappal. Now my grandchildren buy sneakers for INR 5000 without thinking twice," Madan Arora summed up his shoestring leap from camp to luxury homes in a single searing memory (2011). "We used to carry sacks of sand, salt or other things" (Midha, Balakram 2017). Memories of being compelled to perform hard labour inevitably return in recall of the initial months. "Once we found a shelter, we began working as labourers" (Harbans Singh 2017). "We lived in the camp until Birlas allotted us plots of land" (Nagpal 2017).[7] Mirroring clichéd representations of the passage of cinematic time, memories compress the anguished and battered memories of heart-wrenching poverty in a metonymic or metaphoric image.

Murphy and his colleagues found that it is during the camp experience that the enormity of what has happened finally strikes the refugee (1955).

> My mother and my siblings went back on the train and as we approached Amritsar, it gradually dawned upon us that we were now refugees.
>
> (Malhotra, quoted in Sahni and Mehta 2011)

However, the struggle for survival in the initial few months leads to a postponement of the work of mourning and remorse and realization of what has been lost.

> Starting a life from scratch was even harder than the move itself and we had to grab whatever odd job came our way. We had no choice. My brother and I first worked at a railway platform and on our first day of work we made 16

rupees ($0.31), a significant sum in those days. That night my mother cel-
ebrated the fact her sons'[sic] earned their first salary!

(Malhotra, quoted in Sahni and Mehta 2011)

Once they had secured a means of earning a livelihood, the reality of having
plunged from a "high occupational and social status at home," from "professional
to menial, from elite to an impoverished minority" (Weiermair 1971; Rogg 1974)
percolated down their consciousness.

When we were still struggling, we often remembered our time in Pakistan, where we lived like princes. While in Pakistan we had vast agricultural
lands, in Delhi we were the paupers of the city, struggling to make ends meet.
We wished Partition never happened, and our minds often wandered to the
other side of the border.

(Malhotra, quoted in Sahni and Mehta 2011)

Since the refugee camp or colony functioned as a signifier of destitution, squalor
and impoverishment in the national imagery, the newcomers' inhabitation of the
stigmatized space automatically demoted them to the degraded position of the
recipient of the munificence of their benefactors. However, newcomers tended
to herd together in the camps for security, state relief and benefits, community
through networks of kinship or grief that ironically facilitated the preservation
of pre-displacement hierarchies. Deshi recalled that they did not feel stigmatized
during their years in the military barracks, as they hardly ever interacted with anyone outside the military barracks and that all the refugees housed in the barracks
held her parents in high regard because they were acquainted with the family's
former status and wealth (2005). Since the families socialized among themselves,
they were oblivious of their perception by the host community, particularly those
belonging to upper castes and classes. Besides, the singlemindedness with which
families and individuals dedicated themselves to restoring themselves to their former status or pursuing new goals deprived them the luxury of indulging in self-
defeating mourning.

The disjuncture between the impossibility of forgetting the loss of loved ones or
places confirmed by admission of deep longing for lost family members, friends
and homes seven decades after the incident and the stoical acceptance of loss in
the years following Partition is explicable when placed within the more press-
ing contingency of ensuring the life and safety of those remaining. In contrast to
Partition fiction that provides an illuminating insight into the tortured sensibilities of individuals affected by Partition's violence, survivors, until coaxed by oral
historians into sharing their traumatized pasts, focused their energies on the business of living and restoring their former status with a dogged tenacity. The stereotype of the stoic Punjabi, who dismissed his losses and fall in fortune with the
characteristic *koi gal nahin* [it doesn't matter], was grounded both in the Punjabi
ethnocultural attribute of *sher da puttar* [lion cub] and in the Sikh ethnoreligious
ethic of *chardi kala* [positive attitude; ascending energy]. Enjoined by religion "to

maintain a mental state of eternal optimism and joy, Sikhs are ideally expected to be in this positive state of mind as a sign of their contentment with the will of God (bhana), even during the times of adversity" (Jhutti-Johal 2012: 240). But the ethic appeared to have been shared by Hindus. The conceptualization of giving in to despair as not only a sign of weakness but against the principles of religion probably enabled humans who had witnessed the worst forms of atrocities to go on with the business of living instead of surrendering to brooding, despair and anguish, emotions that colour the narratives of refugees from Bengal.

Descriptions of life in the camps in contemporary newspapers and reminiscences of prominent individuals and social workers sharply diverge from the recall of camp or barrack life by their residents. In contrast to the inhuman conditions of camps that journalistic and elite accounts isolate to foreground the dehumanization of the refugee,[8] former residents recall their induction into subhuman living conditions in accentuating their invulnerability and to affirm their adaptability, flexibility and resourcefulness. The success of Satnam Sethi, Missisippi's leading entrepreneur, who was 10 years old when he and his family of 10 lived as refugees in a 10' x 12' tent for six years after the 1947 Partition of India, has been ascribed to his being no stranger to risk taking (Farris 2017).

The visual representation of the camp or barracks as a bare shelter provided to refugees with minimal essential services that did not conform to middle-class notions of hygiene, comfort, privacy and community was reconfigured by the newcomers as a dwelling that instilled the virtues of sharing, resilience, risk-taking, adventure and community in the residents. It must be kept in mind that although refugees are forced to share the lack of minimal amenities that is the experience of the rural and urban poor, the middle-class background of several who were forced to live in camps for short or extended periods compelled an adjustment to a severely reduced living standard.

> After a brief stay in Amritsar, our father joined us and we made our way to New Delhi, which we heard had better arrangements for refugees. Once in Delhi, we settled in the refugee camp at Kingsway Camp. It resembled army barracks and the toilets were shared. It took us a while to adjust.
>
> (Malhotra, quoted in Sahni and Mehta 2011)

Limited access to drinking water and sanitation through a few common taps, bathrooms and toilets, lack of privacy in barracks divided through wooden Partitions, cooking in the open and resting and sleeping in the open on winter afternoons and summer nights did not deter residents from their single-minded pursuit of making their lives anew.[9] Men walked or cycled to work, children to school even as women cleaned, washed, cooked, pickled vegetables, sewed and embroidered in their spare time.

> Then I joined an institute in Safdarjung, which was six miles from our camp. I was required to get there early in the morning. I walked the entire distance

on foot until my mother put together some money to get me a bicycle. That is a memory that will always be etched in my mind. I had a lot of temporary jobs, I worked as a salesman and for a while I loaded and unloaded government books at a railway station. But there were days when we had no work at all and we lived off rationed goods provided by the government.

(Malhotra, in Sahni and Mehta 2011)

The drudgery of work and difficult chores, lack of amenities, standing in the queue for water, using the common bathroom and toilet and lack of privacy were partially mitigated by the spirit of adventure, camaraderie, communal living and increased transparency induced by open living. Considering that it took some residents nearly a decade to make a transition from camp to refugee colony, life cycle events such as marriages, childbirth and deaths, child survivors finishing school and young adults entering college or the work force and entrepreneurial ventures failing or succeeding were not impeded by the lack of basic amenities.

I met my wife in the refugee camp. We became friends and our parents arranged our marriage in 1955. We had little money in those days, but we loved going to India Gate and Chandni Chowk.

(Malhotra, in Sahni and Mehta 2011)

This early life of poverty made him (Satpal Sethi) determined to get an education. Even while working three jobs to support his family, he had an insatiable appetite for learning. After graduating from high school in 1954, he earned bachelor and master's degrees from Punjab University and then set his sights on a PhD in the United States.

(Farris 2017)

Madan M Sehgal shared his memories of living in a small room in Sabzi Mandi, Delhi, and of being forced to become the family's breadwinner at the tender age of 13 due to his traumatized father's turning into a recluse. He narrated his struggles to find employment that ended with his being hired in a shop in Chandni Chowk at a monthly salary of Rs. 80 per month (as told to Sahai, 2017).

Moving to the refugee colony

Confronted with the problem of accommodating the refugee influx from the western border,[10] the Indian state immediately plunged into the herculean task of rehabilitating refugees through legal procedures, rural and urban schemes, town planning, training and employment whose execution and implementation stretched over several years.[11] Although the setting up of the rehabilitation camps on the same sites as the planned refugee colonies was part of the larger urbanization plan of town planners to prevent the impending implosion and de-beautification of existing cities and some colonies were set up as early as 1948,[12] refugees could move into refugee colonies only in the 1950s because of the number of years required for the development of the colonies, the lengthy bureaucratic procedures preceding allotments of plots to displaced persons and construction of functional housing. Despite their being designated as refugee colonies, refugees or displaced persons from Punjab received preferential allotment on payment within a limited time period rather than free housing as alleged by East Bengali refugees. In order to raise a sum of Rs 5000–6000 to be able to purchase a plot in a refugee colony, the allottee should have been gainfully employed in the preceding decade to have been able to save. This confirms Ravinder Kaur's argument that self-rehabilitation was at the core of the state's policies of rehabilitation of refugees of Partition and that they were heavily slanted in favour of middle-class refugees with social and entrepreneurial capital (2009). However, Kaur overlooks the fact that the compensation provided to refugees through preferential allotment amounted to a fraction of the movable and immovable properties and shops and businesses they had left behind and that the functional nature of the housing with very basic amenities was a marginal elevation over camp life. For those who were rendered homeless and had to adjust to the inhuman material conditions of camps and barracks, however, house ownership constituted a symbolic claim to the space of the nation irrespective of the size or discomforts of the dwellings.

Urban planners have noted the primacy accorded to the live-work-leisure triangle in the initial design of the urban form that facilitated the alignment of the public with the private and the self-contained nature of the colonies. They have also remarked on the difference between the colonies located away from and within commutable distance of cities in terms of employment and entrepreneurial opportunities.

> With the first squatter refugee settlement in Basai Darapur, a small daily market street came into being, leading from the camps to a Gurdwara, a Sikh Temple, which was established by the residents themselves. This street became a commonly availed one and the market strengthened this spine. Moti Nagar was constructed almost at one go with this bazaar-street becoming the Moti Nagar Market as the structural backbone of the settlement. The market had shops, workshops and small-scale industries as small enterprises run by the residents in and around the area to support their families.
>
> (Chatterjee 2015: 190)

While the predominance of trading classes in these colonies explains the mushrooming of shophouses, workshops and cottage industries as a logical step towards self-rehabilitation, the composition of the colonies gradually became mixed with many of the children of survivors acquiring education and entering the work force and professionals and employed persons preferring to settle there for the security and community offered by the ethnic community. Oral narratives of survivors confirm that the colonies illustrated the live-work-leisure pattern largely due to the informal economy that sprang up overnight requiring the labour of female members.

However, the comparison of the plan of the refugee colony with the chawls of Mumbai suggested by some fails to take into account the specific contexts from which these structures emerged.[13]

> The typical government agency plan (1947–55) consisted of units built on a site of 60 to 70 square meters. The layout of the newer housing schemes were much tighter than the Lodi colony but the rooms were the same size. The backyard was smaller and the units became part of a row of larger blocks.
>
> The building of housing colonies throughout the Nehru years attempted to keep pace with the migration of people to the cities and into India from Pakistan. The units remained much the same but the front garden usually disappeared to be replaced by communal gardens which are an adaptation of the type in the Rajendra Nagar housing. These gardens consist of a fenced lawn, enclosed by an access road, which is surrounded by the housing blocks
>
> ("Architecture of Delhi")[14]

Critiques of rehabilitation programmes that focus on the dilapidated condition of camps in which refugees were provided shelter often overlook the fact that the functional structures of refugee colonies were similar to or marginally superior to the army barracks in which camps were located. The plots in many of these colonies, including Lajpat Nagar, were 15 x 60 feet, resembling army barracks, and had asbestos roofs (Sharma 2018).[15] The inner courtyards in which the refugee entrepreneurs set up their workshops were unpaved, and the bathroom and toilet had tin roofs. In several colonies, the absence of modern sewerage systems and sanitation made the stench from the open drains and pit toilets unbearable. Grateful for having secured a space that fulfilled basic human requirements of privacy, family and security, the owners of these bare, utilitarian homes upgraded them in various stages over the years with the augmentation in their incomes (Gera Roy 2006).

The myth of the state's munificence in rehabilitating the refugees from the western border must be reviewed in light of the bare-bones, no-frills structure of the housing, the poor finish and the price of the plots that was often on par with open market prices. Alternatively, housing was allotted in compensation for property owned by an individual or family in the pre-displacement home.[16] "Silently and without self-pity, they sought to rebuild their lives in India" (Nanda 2018). Although their social, cultural and educational capital facilitated their finding employment or starting businesses, the stoicism with which middle-class refugees accepted menial work or rough working conditions that were not commensurate with their former wealth or status contributed to their reclamation of their former positions.

The sense of community produced in refugee colonies and its role in governing transactions between refugees needs to be examined in detail. In contrast to the instrumentally articulated community of the state, Nancy's ontological understanding of community as an unavoidable co-existence is useful in understanding the politics of community produced within refugee colonies that overturned and subverted instrumentalized communities in the service of governmentality (Bulley 2014). These communities demonstrate complex patterns of community formation, ranging from clustering around primordialist belongings to new hybrid ways of belonging based on the principle of shared suffering and co-existence. The rhetoric of community cited by the state to relocate refugees from particular ethnolinguistic regions in transit camps and ethnicity-based colonies, such as Kohat, Derawal, Multani and so on, concealed the governmentality and tactics of security and community through which the state directed, managed and regulated particular populations (Foucault 2007: 91). In contrast to ethnicity-based colonies, mixed ethnic group colonies emerged through members of professional, entrepreneurial, sectarian groups opting to purchase plots in the same colony. The state's attempt to contain refugees through an ethno-regional distribution of refugees across camps and refugee colonies was appropriated by refugees to consolidate ethnospatial or ethnolinguistic identities through encouraging membership in associations and societies that aided their negotiation with state authorities.[17]

Liisa Malkki, in her study of Hutu refugees from Burundi, shows how experiences of dispossession and violence are remembered and turned into narratives of agency and empowerment (1991). Partition scholars have remarked on the trope of sacrifice invoked by Partition refugees for the nation's attainment of freedom in staking their claims to rehabilitation and citizenship by the newly formed Indian state. However, the negotiating tactic adopted by refugees to negotiate for rights and privileges is anchored in a mytho-narrative mobilized and consolidated among refugees through frequent reiteration. The justification of their sacrifice of homeland, family, life and comforts in the name of defending the Hindu or Sikh faith against Islamic threat, a trope that connects divergent survivor narratives, is framed within the mythico-historical narrative of Hindus' and Sikhs' heroic response to Islamic oppression over the centuries. This countermyth of Punjabi heroic sacrifice to defend the Hindu and the Sikh faiths against the Islamic onslaught runs parallel to and subverts the nationalist ideological agenda of driving out the British invader. The slippage between Hindu and secular nationalism is evident in the mythico-narrative of the struggle, martyrdom and sacrifice that Punjabi and Bengali survivors claim to have made for the achievement of Independence. Urvashi Butalia asserts that the narrative of martyrdom, commemorated in gurdwaras, played a big role in enabling men who had killed their own women in assuaging the guilt of being complicit in honour killings.

A number of refugee colonies named after pre-displacement cities, regions and ethnolinguistic groups were allotted to migrants from those colonies against claims of property owned there. A legal dispute about a disputed property in Derawal Nagar mentions that the inhabitants of the Dera Ismail Khan formed a society under the name D. I. Khan House Building Cooperative Society in 1952 at Delhi. A receipt of membership in the society in the name of Pritam Lal dated January 18, 1955, and a membership certificate dated December 25, 1955, were produced by his heirs to dismiss the claim of the plaintiff, who was unable to produce documentary evidence to prove that his father, Jait Ram, who had migrated in 1947, was a member of the society (Kumar 2010). According to Shilpi Gulati,

20 Derawal biraderi once existed in Delhi, out of which only one is currently functional (2013). Similarly, the "Bannuwal biradri" in Faridabad is a well-knit community strongly attached to their roots and traditions (Shukla 2017). Mianwali colony in Gurgaon was established through the initiative of refugees from Mianwali district in Punjab consisting predominantly of advocates who constituted a committee led by Chaudhary Ghansham Das in 1965 and purchased land at a throwaway price. The members pooled their savings to get facilities like water supply, sewage connection, electricity, roads and parks (TNN 2011).

In contrast to colonies allotted or formed by refugees from particular regions, even mixed colonies such as Lajpat Nagar, whose original settlers make up most of the population of the colony, demonstrate a strong place identification. Lajpat Nagar was established as a low-rise high-density residential colony by the Ministry of Rehabilitation in 1951 to house a population of 45,000 on approximately 750 acres of land. With the improvement in their standards of living, the allottees added a kitchen, bathroom and toilet to the ground floor. Despite the possibility of fabrication of details, a property dispute between the heirs, Des Raj and Hans Raj, of a certain Kanshi Ram, provides a clue to the antecedents of the allottees of plots in Amar Colony, Lajpat Nagar. The family moved from a tent in a refugee camp in Purana Quilla to Barrack, Block No. 12, Quarter No.12/16, Purana Quilla, which was allotted as per the members of the family. It also states that Plot no E 213, Amar Colony, was allotted in the name of the head of the family in lieu of Quarter No.12/16 for Rs. 1350/- and not purchased through Registered Lease Deed dated March 3, 1960, as claimed by Hans Raj. Des Raj claimed that he, as a 10-year-old, started a vegetable stall along with his father near Kunti Mandir at Purana Quilla, where he worked for six to seven years. Subsequently, they were allotted a shop at Purana Quilla in lieu of that vegetable stall. Des Raj claims that Plot No. C 17, Amar Colony Market, was allotted in lieu of the shop no 22 in the name of Kanshi Ram and Desh Raj for Rs.1552/- (Arora 2014).

Moving out

With their emergence from the secluded, restricted, ghettoized space of the camp to the open spaces of the new land in search of education, employment or work, the newcomers confront "the loss of their culture, their identity, their habits. Every action that used to be habitual or routine will require careful examination and consideration" (Eitinger 1960).[18] The stigmatization of the culture, language, food and lifestyles of the newcomer by host communities propels their gradual assimilation into host culture. Inquiries about the erosion of pre-displacement language, habits and rituals among Punjabi refugees, particularly in communities that settled outside Punjab, invariably elicit the same reply, "We were ridiculed," or "They made fun of us" (Bhatija 2013).[19] A marked discrepancy visible between Sikh and Hindu refugees with respect to linguistic and cultural retention foregrounds the ideological work of Sikh religious and political forces in the transmission of Punjabi language and culture over several generations (Aujla 2015).[20] Unlike Hindus, whose consent to the Hindu nationalist programme of promoting Hindi language and Devanagari script deprived them of Punjabi literary heritage transmitted through the shared shahmukhi script, religious injunctions related to reciting verses from the Guru Granth Sahib ensured Sikhs' literacy in Gurmukhi and Punjabi literary texts that were transcribed in Gurmukhi. Additionally, the appropriation of Punjabiyat in Sikh nationalists' political agendas, particularly their couching of Sikh separatist identity as a linguistic demand, ensured the retention of Punjabi ethnolinguistic and ethnocultural identity among Sikh refugees irrespective of places of resettlement for three generations. Hindu Punjabi refugees, trapped between their ideological allegiance to Hindi and the Hindu nation and assimilation into the Indian nation, along with pragmatic material contingencies, relinquished attachment to pre-displacement cultural identities in the public space. The movement out of the refugee colonies in which the presence of the older generation and a significant community ensured the retention of ethnic cultures, to mixed open housing accelerated linguistic and cultural erosion particularly among third- and fourth-generation refugees.

Unbecoming refugees

In examining refugees' subversion of the governmentality of the refugee camps, Dan Bulley mentions several tactics through which refugees evade the state's technologies of control to gain agency (2014). One of the tactics he mentions is called the Card Game in which refugees relocating to other places leave behind their ration cards with others to supplement their rations or exchange them with Kenyan citizens for Kenyan identity cards. Despite their strong objections to being labelled refugees, Partition refugees' pragmatic manipulation of their refugee status to claim relief, educational benefits, government postings, rehabilitation and compensation demonstrates that the state's machinery of knowledge and control might produce unforeseen effects.

The gap between newcomers' protests at being designated refugees and a legal procedure named "becoming refugees" demonstrates how the technologies of governmentality operating through an elaborate bureaucratic machinery activated to regulate, manage and control the movements of population through statistical data and official records were resisted and subverted by new arrivals by claiming privileges through "becoming refugees" that gave a lie to the myth of the passive, infantilized, hapless refugee that cut across all classes.

The impossibility of insisting on the production of official or written documentation in view of the acuteness of their movement introduced a technical flaw in the design of the system compelling officials and administrators to rely on oral, verbal testimony in the verification of claims. As Kaur has rightly pointed out, refugees were able to mobilize social and educational networks to authenticate their claims for compensation of land and housing as well as entry into educational institutions and jobs (2009). But narratives of survivors reveal more complex tactics of obtaining relief that did not necessarily depend on educational, social or entrepreneurial capital but on resourcefulness in capitalizing on the weakness in the system that did not recognize class boundaries. Survivors' descendants recall families with no or negligible capital in pre-displacement homes extracting disproportionate compensation from unsuspecting or unscrupulous officials and lower-level staff on the basis of false testimony provided by their kinsmen or friends to verify their claims. The inability of the pakora shop owner unfairly cheated of compensation in lieu of the shop owned in the pre-displacement home in Kaur's essay may rightly be viewed as his lack of social or financial capital (2009). But a street sharpness that refugees acquired irrespective of their class background was needed in the decade when the state began to settle claims. Ilyas Chattha's new work on prominent builders' nexus in Pakistan effectively demonstrates the rampant corruption built into the relief and compensation process that continues to be exploited by families with political connections (2012).

In order to claim relief or rehabilitation provided by the state, the newcomers were required to undergo a legal process that has been interpreted in common parlance as "becoming refugees." Although the stigmatization of the refugee explained the newcomers' initial reluctance, the process of becoming a refugee entailed registering as a refugee and receiving a refugee card before being able to claim any benefits. While the bureaucratic procedure of collecting statistics on the number, origin, destination, profession, education level and caste of new arrivals has been revealed to be an exercise of governmentality, newcomers' subversion of this machinery to facilitate their self-rehabilitation demonstrates that beneficiaries manipulated the laws in ways that were convenient to them, and their ethics, although legally questionable, followed pragmatic considerations. The sharp division between destitute refugees who were solely dependent on state relief and others who turned to their friends or family for support noted by Partition scholars appears to have been crossed in the lived experience of Partition refugees who were required to draw equally on state and kinship networks to seek self-rehabilitation. Refugees who might have been averse to living in camps or applying for free rations would have accepted forms of benefits such as occupying evacuee property, seeking compensation for lost property, educational relaxations and preferential government postings as just entitlement for losses incurred.

Narratives of survivors display the emergence of a pragmatic and flexible ethics that served as coping mechanisms for the losses incurred. Manik Ram was a railway employee posted in Quetta who opted for a posting in Lucknow, a city he had visited on an official tour in the past.[21] But the process of bringing his transfer orders for which he had to travel back to Quetta on August 14, 1947, at the risk of his life took more than three months.[22] Although he was not entitled to accommodation in the army barracks adjacent to the railway station as a salaried government servant, he, along with other railway employees, took advantage of the subsidized accommodation for the ease of commuting as well as for putting away savings for buying his own house in a refugee colony within the span of a decade, which was no mean task for a 36-year-old with six young children. The story of the school admission of one of his daughters offers a more amusing aside to the narrative. Like that of all schoolchildren, since Deshi's schooling was interrupted by their displacement from Quetta to Lucknow with a three-month transit in Patiala, she was entitled to promotion to the next grade without having completed her annual exams. However, Deshi, who turned seven in January 1947, had already been admitted in Grade III in her previous school. Manik Ram, however, demanded that she be admitted into Grade IV in accordance with the rules issued by the Government of India against the advice of the class teacher, who felt that the child was too young to be admitted into Grade IV. To the delight of Manik Ram and chagrin of Deshi, the class teacher's inadvertent mistake of entering VI instead of IV had the seven-year-old Deshi attending Grade VI with 10-year-old classmates (Deshi 2005). Entrepreneur Dhani Ram, who lost his empire overnight and was forced to accept the support of his 26-year-old gazetted officer son, was technically not destitute. But he moved into an evacuee property in Sabzi Mandi, Delhi, with his two younger sons and four unmarried daughters to begin life anew,[23] which was formally allotted to him subsequently as a compensation for the three residential properties he had owned in Lyallpur. He subsequently received compensation for commercial property in lieu of his shops and godowns in Lyallpur in the Okhla industrial estate on a payment of Rs. 1,00,000 in 1972 (Ram Prakash 2005).[24]

Scholars have pointed out that the policy of self-rehabilitation that was at the core of the state's rehabilitation programme favoured educated, middle-class refugees who had the social and educational capital to manoeuvre legal provisions to their advantage as opposed to the uneducated, lower-class, lower-caste refugees in genuine need of rehabilitation (Kaur 2009). To this effect, middle-class and upper-class refugees cited their diminished lifestyle and social status to make an appeal for rehabilitation exceeding bare subsistence. For families who had lived in palatial houses or havelis before Partition, accommodation in a two-room evacuee property signified hardships they were unaccustomed to. The daughter of the engineer who constructed the heterotopic space of Model Town Lahore, accommodated in an evacuee property on the notorious G. B. Road in Delhi, where they shared a wall with the salon of a courtesan, recalls her family's days in the transit accommodation with some amusement in her autobiography (Hoon 2013). In the same vein, she proceeds to share her being able to complete her aborted master's degree exam following the state's provision of compensation to students whose education was disrupted because of Partition. Students like her were entitled to appear in the exam if they could provide evidence of having served in refugee rehabilitation efforts for at least three months, which she was able to do without much difficulty.

A property dispute between the heirs of a certain Professor Parman Singh on two of his properties, one allotted to him in Nizamuddin in 1950 and the other purchased by him in 2012 in B 22, East of Kailash with rent received from the Nizamuddin house, illustrates educated refugees' acquisition of compensation through rehabilitation schemes encouraging self-rehabilitation mentioned by Kaur (Kumar 2010). Although the facts provided by contending parties to support their case for claims to the property are contested, certain details are verifiable through the documents produced before the judge. These exhibits substantiate the claim that Professor Parman Singh, who found employment as a lecturer on his arrival from Rawalpindi in 1947, used his status as a displaced person to apply for a house in Nizammuddin in 1950, which was allotted to those who could furnish proof of displacement and gainful employment, for a sum of Rs 5946/-, which he was able to pay through his own earnings. Subsequently, the said Prof. Parman Singh was paid Rs. 4000/- as compensation for a house he owned in Rawalpindi. It is interesting to note that the claim and counterclaim is made by the heirs on the basis of whether or not the house in Nizamuddin was an HUF property. This is done through summoning evidence related to the family's properties in their ancestral village or the city of Rawalpindi and the financial capital of Parman Singh on arrival in Delhi in which the oral testimonies of elderly family friends and relatives provide a crucial role. Parman Singh's availing of rehabilitation and compensation he was entitled to despite his being gainfully employed confirms displaced persons' manoeuvring of state policies to restore themselves to their former status.

Stranger citizen

Scholarship on Partition has distinguished Partition displaced persons from refugees by asserting that refugees of Partition were not stateless persons but automatically citizens of the newly formed state. However, the refugees' grievances when negotiating with the state were grounded in their acute consciousness of the differentiated citizenship of the new nation. In privileging the legislative and formal aspects of citizenship, the cultural underpinnings of citizenship invariably get overlooked. Nick Stevenson has shown that culture and citizenship, which are viewed as having nothing in common, are intimately related (2003). He argues that although citizenship is marked with "abstract legal definitions as to who is to be included and excluded from the political community" in institutional terms, "ideas of symbolic challenge and exclusion remain central and defining within society" (2003: 24). Although Hindus and Sikhs crossing across the western border were legally defined as political citizens of the newly formed nation, they continued to be excluded from the cultural space of the nation as strangers. Punjabi and Sindhi refugees may be viewed as stranger citizens whose possession of legal and political citizenship does not guarantee cultural citizenship of the nation and inclusion in the social and cultural space of the majoritarian community of the nation. The transformation of the stranger into citizen became contingent on the stranger citizen's de-ethnicization through the relinquishing of pre-displacement cultural markers and adoption of the host culture. The journey from stranger to citizen required the toning down of strangeness through borrowing the host's language, costume, etiquette and lifestyle. The price for inclusion in the cultural space of the nation was to distance oneself from the pre-displacement culture inferioritized as rustic and uncouth by hosts and acquisition of those markers of distinction that ensure social and cultural citizenship of the nation.

The Hindu Punjabi experienced a schizophrenic split in identifying with the Indian nation through his allegiance to the Hindu nation, which demanded disidentification with Punjabi identity, appropriated in the construction of Sikh religious identity. The privileging of the Hindu ethnoreligious over Punjabi ethnolinguistic identity demands a closure of overlapping, flexible, polysemous religious boundaries of Punjab and fluid religious practices to the adoption of a closed, unified, fixed, *sanatani* [orthodox] Hindu identification with the pantheon of Hindu gods who were overshadowed by the mixed saints of Punjabi villages. In arguing that sanskritization in Punjab, unlike in other Indian states, has failed among Dalits because of the difference in Punjab's caste structure, Ronki Ram mentions the difference of the Ad Dharm movement from "the cultural assimilation (sanskritization) drive of the Arya Samaji genre" (2012: 681). Unlike other parts of India in which sanskritization was the strategy followed by lower castes for upward social mobility, the sanskritization drive of the Arya Samaj was largely directed at assimilating Hindus, whose practices demonstrated religious as well as cultural fluidity, in mainstream Hinduism. The return to Vedic rituals enjoined on Arya Samajis that displaced sanatan dharam's [orthodox religion] idolatry had a particular appeal among upper-caste Hindu Punjabis as an effective weapon for rebutting the Islamic and Sikh critique of orthodox Hindu anthropomorphism. In other words, the sanskritization of Hindu Punjabis had already begun with a significant number of upper- and middle-class Hindus lending their support to the Arya Samaj movement that swept Punjab at the end of the 19th century. The process of sanskritization was initiated through educational institutions as evident in the agenda of the DAV schools outlined by Shri Ram Sharma in 1885:

> The primary object will, therefore be to weld together the educated and uneducated masses by encouraging study of the national language and vernaculars; to spread a knowledge of moral and spiritual truths by insisting on the study of classical Sanskrit; to assist the formation of sound and energetic habits by a regulated mode of living, to encourage sound acquaintance with English literature and to afford a stimulus to the material progress of the country by spreading a knowledge of the physical and applied sciences.
>
> (Sharma 1941, quoted in Jones 1976: 72)

The DAV (Dayanand Anglo Vedic) school movement was underpinned by Arya Samaj ideologies as well as nationalist goals and went a long way in strengthening Hindu ideologies through its founding objectives of encouraging the learning of Hindi literature and Sanskrit languages, Vedic texts and practices such as *havan* and *sandhya* inducted into the curriculum from lower primary school. The DAV school movement had a large following among middle-class Hindu Punjabis, particularly Khatri and Arora trading and agriculturalist castes for the upward mobility it promised,

> English language for adjustment, Hindi for communication with the masses, Sanskrit and the works of Dayanand for moral uplift and science for material progress. – Arya offered answers to the most acute dilemmas of occupational mobility and cultural adjustment.
>
> (Jones 1976: 72)

Mandatory reading of Vedic scriptures along with chanting of Sanskrit verses in the performance of *havan* [fire sacrifice] in DAV produced a generation of middle-class Hindu Punjabis literate in Sanskrit and Hindi inducted into the programme of national integration. This project of de-ethnicization of Punjabi identity initiated by the Arya Samaj through educational and religious institutions was completed with the migration of Hindu Punjabis of the same class to urban centres in Punjab, Delhi and other parts of North India. Equally driven by the political agendas of Hindu nationalist parties to resist the Sikh separatist movement by eliciting the support of Hindu Punjabis and social aspirations to upward mobility through assimilation in the mainstream Hindu/Hindi culture, Hindu Punjabis distanced themselves from overt allegiances to Punjabi and Punjabiat in the public space even though Punjabi culture in a modified form remained firmly entrenched in the space of the home.

Notes

1 "It's been 70 years since Independence. And now we wish to forget everything about Pakistan. It's better to leave the past behind and look forward. They've taken over our homes and looted our wealth. They've tried to molest our brothers and sisters and have given us no respect. They've converted our gurdwaras into mosques. So we never want to look back or recall. You will hear this answer from whomever you ask. No one wants to go back there" (Makkad 2017). Harish Chandra Midha stated that for 10 to 15 years they could not even think of "going back" even to collect their valuables that had been kept safely for them by their grandfather's Muslim sarpanch [Village Chief] friend because they were "all busy settling down and managing their lives and hardship" (2017).
2 This was corroborated by the majority of survivors interviewed for the Indian Council of Social Science Research Major Project "After Partition: Post-Memories of the Afterlife of Partition 1947" (2017–18) awarded to Anjali Gera Roy.
3 *Doli* is the farewell given to the bride leaving her parental home for the home of the bridegroom by members of her family and close friends. It is usually accompanied by singing of particular genres of songs.
4 "Have you seen the movie 'Gadar'? It's exactly the same story. There is no change in it" (Midha, Balakram 2017).
5 "Our military had brought along sprouted black gram. That's what we used to eat. No place to bathe, no drinking water, the issue with water was such that since it had rained ponds were full of water – with mosquitoes. No place to go to the toilet . . ." (Chugh 2017).
6 Several of the prosperous textile merchants interviewed in Ranchi confessed to having started their business on the pavements. A survivor whose family traded in textiles even before Partition stated that they started "hawking our wares on the pavement" in the begnning (Midha, Jairamdas 2017), while another, hailing from a family of sugar and jaggery merchants "set up a footpath shop near the post office (Makkad 2017)" and another from a landowning background "got into a few random jobs like selling ice-creams or kulfi" (Arora 2017), which paid barely a rupee. "I have sold clothes, tea leaves while roaming around in villages as a hawker, worked in hotels, lent bunker beds to tourists during fairs and made small earnings from it, sold boiled sweet potatoes [breaks into tears]" (Juneja 2017).
7 Clemens Six, in *Secularism, Decolonisation, and the Cold War in South and Southeast Asia*, mentions the relief camps set up by Rashtriya Seva Sangh (RSS) and how the

RSS workers would bring refugees arriving by trains in Purani Dilli to camps in Subzi Mandi (2018).

8 A report in the *Hindustan Times* comments on the lack of privacy in Kingsway Camp, where hundreds of men, women and children were seen bathing in a tank clad in scanty clothing (1947: 8).

9 "The colony [Rajinder Nagar] at that time didn't have individual water connection" (Ghosh et al. 2010).

10 According to Prerana Chatterjee, "of the 47.5 lakhs of people who migrated to India, 495,391 came to Delhi itself" (2015: 187). Datta states that "out of the total urban population of Delhi at that time (1,437,134), about 32.7 percent constituted of refugees" (Datta 2002).

11 Guha shows that the new government proposed 36 Rehabilitation Colonies for refugees named after Indian leaders, such as Rajendra Nagar (after Rajendra Prasad), Lajpat Nagar (after Lala Lajpat Rai), Moti Nagar (after Motilal Nehru) and so on as "Emergency Projects" (Guha 2008). "Moti Nagar was one of the first to be formed 1948–50 with the support of the Delhi Improvement Trust, to accommodate the people living as temporary squatters at Jhandewalan, Shadipur and Basai Darapur" (Chatterjee 2015: 189).

12 "The Pakistan refugees who initially spent a few years in camps like in the Old Fort were allotted plots on 99 year-lease and relocated from camps to 46 refugee colonies developed across the city. Lajpat Nagar, Tilak Nagar, Malviya Nagar, Mukherjee Nagar" (Chhabra 2016).

13 Only the Sion Koliwada Refugee Camp in Mumbai conformed to this pattern. In the 1950s, the state government started constructing chawl-like four-storey buildings in the camp, offering flats to refugee families for sale. Twenty-five buildings were erected on the land, and 1,200 families bought flats in them for Rs 5,830 each. The rate was based on the compensation payable to refugees under the Displaced Persons (Compensation and Rehabilitation) Act, 1954 (Johari 2018).

14 http://delhi-architecture.weebly.com/housing-sector.html

15 The original allottees of Lajpat Nagar were the refugees who were staying at Purana Qila camps after migrating to Delhi from Pakistan. Amar Colony, or Lajpat Nagar IV, consists of 24 blocks in Lajpat Nagar IV. Each of the plots was either 100 or 125 sq. yards. "As per original lease deed issued by L&DO, each of these blocks has 64 flats (32 on ground floor and the remaining 32 on first floor) purely meant for residential purposes. Their standard size was 203.5 square feet. But a majority of people have opened shop in these flats illegally and encroached 15–20 ft public land in the backyard as well as the front side" (Sharma 2018).

16 As Ravinder Kaur rightly points out, the state's programme of self-rehabilitation was heavily biased in favour of educated middle-class refugees who possessed documents or social and commercial networks who could testify to their claims (2009). However, Kaur does not mention the wide gap between the immoveable and moveable assets lost and the compensation provided; refugees whose conscience prevented them from making inflated claims were provided approximately one-third of what they owned as compensation.

17 Some of these associations, such as the Homeless Provinces Refugee Association, that made an appeal for increasing the ration for the refugees and improving its quality, overhauling the management of the camps and making arrangements for sanitation and privacy had been active even in the camps (*Hindustan Times*, April 18, 1948; 10).

18 "The government tried," she says, "with refugee cards and rehabilitation attempts, but the common people were not very welcoming" (Sengupta, Partition 1947 Archive).

19 "When Sindhis migrated in Maharashtra, they had to acculturate in a different social order. The popular belief was that the Sindhi migrants are unclean, unhygienic and 'papad-khau' (people who eat papads – a popular Sindhi savoury). The nasal tone of

the language became a target of mockery for Sindhi children in their schools. Also the fact that Sindhis originally come from Sindh, Pakistan, prevented them from expressing any affiliation to the "enemy" nation: "So are you Pakistanis if you don't have a region in India?" (Bhatija 2013). According to Harish Bhagchandani, managing trustee of Sindhu Sewa Samaj, a leading trust in Ahmedabad, "The Sindhis migrated from Sindh in Pakistan. They found shelter in different parts of India. Wherever they settled, they adopted the local language, culture and festivals as their own. They wanted to achieve financial progress, and they knew that wouldn't be possible through Sindhi language. As a result, today Sindhi literature, language and script all face the danger of becoming extinct" (quoted in Vora 2016).

20 Aujla points out that Punjabis of Delhi couldn't get justice for the Punjabi language for several reasons (2015).

21 Hindu and Sikh government servants affected by Partition were given the option to opt for a posting in any part of India with the expectation that Muslim servants would opt for Pakistan. Manik Ram had opted for Lucknow, as the exodus of Muslim railway employees to Pakistan was expected to absorb cross-border migrants. The process was formalized through such optees deemed to be on a month's paid leave from August 14, 1947, and on other kinds of leave for the following months (Rai 1965).

22 He continued to serve in the railways for those three months under police protection provided to railway employees and miraculously escaped massacres at both Quetta and Mianwali Railway Stations, having boarded the train minutes before. He recalled hiding in trenches along with his neighbour, an army officer, and firing to escape a Muslim mob on the final journey from his house to the station (Deshi 2018).

23 This must have been after May 8, 1954, when the Minister for Rehabilitation announced, in the Council of States, the government's decision "to acquire the rights and title of 'evacuee owners' in their properties, and to use these properties for giving compensation to displaced persons" ("Editorial" 1954: 539).

24 Since each claimant was entitled to 20 percent of his claim from the evacuee property, the evacuee property was subsequently allotted to Dhani Ram as compensation for claims to three houses he had owned in Lyallpur. Although the Government of India implemented several acts for the rehabilitation of refugees from the West, including the Delhi Land Requisition and Acquisition Act, 1948; The Administration of Evacuee Property Act, 1950; The Claims Act, 1950; and the Compensation and Rehabilitation of the Displaced Persons Act, 1954, they were abused by both officers at the implementation level and by the refugees themselves.

10 Partitioned subjects

Deshi did not believe in purchasing expensive items of furniture because her husband, a senior civil servant, was frequently transferred to different parts of India and furniture, booked on long-distance transportation services, would invariably arrive in a damaged condition. Deshi would pack all their essential belongings in king-sized tin trunks that could be booked along on their train journeys and set up home again with functional, throwaway wooden, plastic or rattan items. She reiterated the refrain, "Who knows how long we are going be here?" when offered durable, aesthetically designed home furniture she had always yearned for when the family finally settled down in the Indian capital (2005). When asked about when her family had purchased their apartment in Mumbai, Gyan Kaur recalled anxieties produced by homelessness when the family had migrated from Rawalpindi in 1947. "I told my husband, even birds have nests. We should have a house of our own" (1982). The tension between forced recognition of the transience, temporariness, impermanence of home and yearning for rootedness offers an opening into the exploration of the ambivalent effects of the violence and displacement of Partition on the production of a particular form of sensibility and subject that may be termed the Partitioned subject.

Although displacement is widely acknowledged as a universal condition of the 20th century, the discursive construction of displacement and refugee is still in a nascent stage. Liisa Malkki's pioneering work on refugees and displacement offers an appropriate starting point for the exploration of the meaning of refugeeness, refugee subjectivity, displacement and emplacement (1991). While admitting the existence of refugees in the past, Malkki situates the emergence of the refugee as a universal phenomenon to World War II that transmogrified into a Third-World problem with decolonizing movements and nation formation. Refugeeness refers to "a way of understanding the particular subjective experience in relation to existing refugee policies" (Lacroix 2004: 163). Malkki critiques the discursive construction of the refugee as a single, essential, universalizing condition as well as the romanticization of rooted communities and homeland identities. She is equally critical of the anchoring of refugee identity in a territorial pre-displacement homeland in the literature on refugees and displacement and of the assumption that displacement essentially entails a loss of a rooted identity while at the same time pointing out the gaps in the idea of a stable, homogenized homeland identity. Malkki makes a distinction between exile, which she defines as a pre-20th-century individual condition attached to the realm of aestheticization, and refugeeness which is a mass 20th-century phenomenon tethered to the realm of politics and development. She also asserts that being a refugee was not necessarily a negative or stigmatizing identity, but rather it could come to stand for "a sign of the ultimate temporariness of exile and of the refusal to become naturalized" (Malkki 1992: 35). Malkki's examination of the refugee as an epistemic object of discursive domains, as the passive recipient of humanitarian aid and a problem in the discourse of development leads her to attempt to explore the multiple ways in which refugeeness or refuge subjectivity is formed, consolidated and mobilized. "Permanent temporariness" or forced nomadism perfectly defines the displaced/refugee subjectivity formed in relation to the transience, mobility and contingency that marked life in the camps in which Partition survivors were secluded. However, Agamben's conceptualization of the camp as exception, through juridical production of bare life by sovereign power, which has dominated the theorization of camp subjectivities fails to elucidate the excluded included subjectivities of refugee citizens displaced by Partition who could not be included through political exclusion (1998). Similarly, the discursive construction of the refugee as a precarious victim and passive object of humanitarian aid and a problem in being subjected to sovereign power is refuted by the resilient, industrious, resourceful, autonomous, entrepreneurial subjects produced through forced displacement.

Refugeeness and refugee subjectivities

Malkki, in "The Rooting of Peoples and the Territorialization of National Identity Among Scholars and Refugees," reexamines widely held commonplace assumptions linking people to place and nation to territory to call attention to the theoretical implication of "such deeply territorializing concepts of identity for those categories of people classified as 'displaced' and 'uprooted'" (1992: 25). She demonstrates that the relationship between people and place is conceptualized in naturalized and botanical terms that permeate language and social practice leading to a peculiar form of sedentarism and focuses on the figure of the refugee to critique the sedentarist metaphysic. She shows that the normalization of sedentarism in the national order of things and deep sedentarism in our thinking leads to the pathologization of the refugee. Arguing that groups of refugees illuminate the complexity of the ways in which people construct, remember, and lay claim to particular places as "homelands" or "nations," she proposes "a sociology of displacement," a new "nomadology" (1992: 38). Unlike *udbastu* [uprooted], the Bengali term for refugee, *jarhon puttna* [pull out from the roots], its colloquial Punjabi equivalent, has not entered literary or academic jargon even though the rhyming phrase *lutte putte* [looted and uprooted] was naturalized in the survivors' vocabulary to describe the Partition experience. Although Partition survivors' narratives exhibit a strong place attachment and nostalgia for roots that affirms their inherent sedentarism, the shared experience of being uprooted and of witnessing the precariousness of life and property led to their questioning of sedentarist assumptions through a form of anti-sedentarism that eludes the category of post-modern nomadism. This book argues that the event of Partition constructed a peculiar Partitioned subjectivity in which the sedentarist relation between people and homeland, roots and nation, was ruptured. This anti-sedentarism, it argues, illustrates Said's exilic subjectivities rather than Bradiotti's nomadic subjectivities or migrant subjectivities (2011).

The powerful sedentarism that newcomers from across the border in the West and the East shared with their hosts and the pathologization and criminalization of the refugee as an uprooted person accounts for their need to situate themselves in the lost homeland, ancestral home or lineage. This corroborates Malkki's observation that loss of homeland should be linked with the loss of cultural identity or that "homelessness" entails a precondition of a home and that the "notion of displacement implies emplacement, 'a proper place' of belonging" (Malkki 2002: 353). As she has pointed out, the identity of refugees or the displaced in the camps is complex, diverse and variegated and cannot be subsumed within a generalized refugee stereotype. The query about origins and the counter-query in Punjabi, *pichche se* [originally from], that set Urvashi Butalia on the Partition trail or the notion of the des [village, nation] that serves as an icebreaker in conversations among Bengali speakers gesture to the continuity of the sedentary metaphysics and rootedness among Partition survivors. In contrast to *jarhan*, the Punjabi word for roots, which is closer to the biological metaphor of the tree and intersects with the meaning of roots as land that Malkki deconstructs in examining the meanings of being rooted and uprooted, the Bengali bastu [foundation], as the space where the *kuladebata* or the family deity is housed, confirms Malkki's assertion that "the link between people and place is viewed as deeply metaphysical" (Malkki 1992: 27).

The anti-sedentarist orientation necessitated by forced migration cannot be confused with anti-sedentarist positions that emerged with the formulation of a migrant aesthetic, migrant sensibility or diasporic subjectivities in post-colonial theory formulated from the privileged position of the post-colonial creative writer (Rushdie 1982) or intellectual (Bhabha 1994), of settler discourses on migrant subjectivities (Carter 1996), or of the nomadic subjectivities (Bradiotti 2011) in the new mobility narratives emerging in globalization (Chambers 1994; Scheller 2014). It resonates with the exilic subjectivity described by Edward Said when he wrote in *Reflections on Exile* that "our age . . . is indeed the age of the refugee, the displaced person, mass immigration" (2000: 1974). Malkki's distinction between exile as the privileged position of the elite individual and refugee as a mass political concept confounds the construction of the Partition refugee or displaced person. Although the forced migration of close to 15 million people was a mass exodus, the sense of loss and nostalgia underpinning the narratives of the displaced is akin to the aesthetic condition of exile expressed in a language of longing and desire. Similarly, the difference between refugee, displaced person and stateless person is crucial since those displaced by Partition were technically not stateless persons but citizens.[1]

The anti-sedentarism of the Partitioned subject is forced by the recognition of the precariousness of life, livelihood and lifestyles through the survivors' occupation of the precarious subject position of the refugee. In a broader sense, the notion of trust that has been invoked to understand the conflicting experience of refugees is significant here. As Pradip Bose puts it, the disjunction between familiar ways of being in the world and "a new reality that not only subverts that way-of-being but also forces one to see the world differently" causes an erosion of trust (2010). Yet the loss of stability, meaning and place that sedentarism treats as normal released the Partitioned subject from the sedentarist bias in which subjectivity is defined in relation to ancestral land, family status and kinship networks. The loss of immoveable land and property, dynastic wealth and privileges and professional position through which subjectivity was traditionally defined made survivors sharply aware of the breakdown of pre-displacement verities and adopt an anti-sedentarist position that permitted the imagining of home and homeland delinked from territoriality.

Despite embodying the paradigmatic condition of postmodern homelessness, the Partitioned subject does not dwell-in-travel but in dual homes, the real home constructed by memory and the new home that is akin to being in exile. Unlike the Bengali compound *udbastu* or *bastuhara*, approximating the English *uprooted*, that facilitates the conceptualization of the experience of displaced Bengalis, the deployment of the Urdu *khanabadosh* or the colloquial *jidda agga pichcha nahin* [one who has no front or back] enables Punjabis to articulate the condition of forced nomadism or vagrancy. Forced nomadism, combined with the desire for rooted identity, among those displaced by Partition produced multiple, complex subjectivities that elude the discursive construction of anti-sedentarist migrant, diasporic, nomadic subjectivities that are used to define refugees. The desire of the displaced subject for home and location of the homeland elsewhere several generations after displacement in conjunction with allegiance to the secular nation as a citizen engenders a form of exilic subjectivity that is not the aestheticized intellectual or artistic angst of the exiled artist or intellectual but the shared condition of a collective formation.

Butalia's autorickshaw driver's use of the colloquial *pichche se* [originally from] to locate his origins and the phrase *jidda agga pichcha nahin* encapsulate the attachment to rooted identity among Partitioned subjects seven decades after displacement, which is vicariously shared by their descendants through frequent reminders of origins, notwithstanding their assimilation in the wider national and local regional cultures. In the absence of a conscious reminder of origins and retention of identification with specific regional languages and cultures, the location of home in the past rather than in resettled homes by descendants of displaced persons even after four generations confirms the retention of cultural identity in refugee camps. The refugee of Partition bristles at her objectification as homo sacer through her reiteration of former home, status and social networks because of the stigmatization of a person without agga pichcha, whose antecedents are not known, as an object of suspicion in traditional Punjabi society.

Sharanarthi to purusharthi

The category of refugee was constructed in Partition discourse on the basis of key assumptions about the displaced subject traumatized by violence and inscribed with the feminine – docile and controllable, which were reproduced in law and policy, to produce knowable subjects who could be controlled. The state's construction of refugee as a docile subjectivity enshrined in the meaning of the term *shararanarthi* was resisted by new arrivals through their adamant refusal to identify with it and their construction of a new subject position in conjunction with the Hindu philosophical construct of *purushartha* that was translated as *purusharthi*. The reversal of the standardized and represented category of the sharanarthi or refugee as helpless and dependent disseminated through media, policy and legal formations in public discourse through refugees' emancipating themselves from the subjugated position of dependence and control, however, occurred through their engaging in work that needed compromises with conventional gendered, class and caste norms regulating work and behaviour.

In her book, *In Freedom's Shade*, Anis Kidwai mentions the introduction of an unpronounceable new word, *sharanarthi*, one who seeks refuge, into the idiom of Delhi (2004). She also refers to Punjabi newspapers' objection to the use of the word by Punjabi migrants, who did not view themselves as recipients of charity but as *purusharthis*, meaning "one who labours" (2004: 64). The dichotomy between the statist construction of the refugee as sharanarthi and the newcomers' self-ascription as purusharthi corroborates new perspectives on the meaning of refugee that critique and complicate the Agambenian conceptualization of refugee as bare life and of refugeeness as regulated by sovereign power (1998). As these studies show, multi-layered, divergent and complex refugee subjectivities formed in camps interrogate the conventional representation of refugee subjectivities as subjugated, feminized or infantilized.[2]

The trope of purusharthi that undergirds Partition narratives foregrounds the resistance to the inscription of refugees inscribed in statist and public narratives as vulnerable, helpless, emasculated victims of humanitarian relief. The ambivalence exhibited by new arrivals towards the legal process of "becoming refugees" that facilitated the granting of humanitarian relief; making claims to compensation for moveable and immoveable property left behind; preferential admission into educational institutions and recruitment in government jobs; granting of entrepreneurial loans; and the stigmatizing overtones of the term *refugee* complicates the discursive construction of refugees. Cross-border arrivals' reluctant acceptance of relief and compensation was based on their perceived entitlement to rehabilitation measures as compensation by the state for the sacrifices they had made for the greater common good or as a form of vartan bhanji assistance from their affluent, interiorized, settled kinsmen in a literal translation of the trope of the national family invoked by the state. The collapse of the refugee with the recipient of *dāna* in the national and political imaginary that objectified them as traumatized, homeless destitutes deserving of compassion was interpreted by them as the reneging of the implicit pact of ensuring dispensation of relief and rehabilitation by the sovereign state and its non-displaced citizens as a just political rather than a religious charitable obligation or favour. When offered charitable or humanitarian relief by religious or state institutions, new arrivals declined it after being forced to accept it on immediate arrival and demanded instead either employment or other forms of support to begin entrepreneurial ventures. In view of the delays in the state's provision of the same, they turned to their own resources, kinship or place networks to establish themselves. This process of beginning life anew with minimal initial support provided them the confidence to disown the ascription of refugee and resignify themselves as the ones who rose to their feet through their own labour.

Literature on refugees, asylum seekers and migrants has focused on masculinity as a site of conflict that requires negotiation with competing discourses and public narratives of the meaning of being a refugee. Refugee subjectivity has been inscribed with traditionally feminine characteristics with the male "genuine refugee" portrayed as an emasculated, pathetic, helpless, dependent victim deserving of humanitarian protection based on his representation as a "sentimentalized, composite figure – at once feminine and maternal, childlike and innocent" (Malkki 1996).[3] Scholars have investigated the impact of being placed in particular bureaucratic categories, such as refugees, asylum seekers and migrants, on the conceptions of masculinity in these groups and their positioning of themselves as "men" through their engagement with vulnerability, victimhood and agency in the construction of their self narratives. Survivors from hypermasculinist, patriarchal Punjabi and Sindhi societies, confronted with an acute crisis in masculinity, replied to statist and public gendered conceptions of the category of refugees as feminized or infantilized refugees through embracing and valorizing an aesthetic of hard work that included manual labour. The masculine ethic of labour, *mehnatan keetian* [we laboured], a recurring trope in survivor narratives that connects the rags-to-riches narratives of survivors from Punjab and Sindh, enables survivors' repudiation of the discursive construction of the hapless, pathetic, emasculated victim of violence and their self-construction as agents scripting their lives through drawing on their own efforts.[4] The pride with which survivors who were unaccustomed to physical labour, recount their opting for hard labour rather than begging or accepting charity is underpinned with an assertion of a robust masculinity that replies to the emasculation of the refugee through being imbued with feminine characteristics, particularly helplessness, passivity and docility. Affluent entrepreneurs and professionals recall with unmistakable pride the days when they loaded and unloaded goods, carried baskets as construction workers, drove horse carts or hawked fabric. Their deep-seated patriarchal attitudes prevented them from permitting their womenfolk from engaging in domestic work in the homes of others unlike destitute widowed or single women who were forced to enter the work force immediately after Partition after being provided training by the state in nursing, tailoring, embroidery, pickle-making and basket-weaving (Bhardwaj 2004). The powerful visual image of a tall, well-built Punjabi male performing manual labour or peddling wares on the streets of Indian towns and cities overwrites the stereotyped representation of the refugee as starved, naked humanity.

The appropriation of the proverbial wisdom of the warrior or self-dependent communities in the repudiation of emasculation through their discursive construction of the refugee is epitomized in the invocation of the hypermasculinist Punjabi epithet *sher da puttar* [lion cub] to mobilize a rhetoric of courage, bravery and willingness to take on challenges among survivor communities confronted with unemployment, impoverishment and destitution to give a lie to the myth of the effete, devastated refugee. Refugeeness has been examined in relation to the refugee's performativity in authenticating claims of asylum or privilege through becoming a refugee or in acquiring agency through subverting stereotyped depictions. The performativity of the valorized warrior in the construction of the figure of "the refugee warrior" of Partition is disjunctive with the militarized refugee warrior who resorts to violence to achieve his ends in contemporary discourses. The performativity of the refugee warrior who remains cheerful in the face of adversity effectively masked counter-images of inadvertent glimpses of grown men breaking down in private or while sharing confidences with ethnographers and prevented traumatized males from descending into negativity or clinical depression. The valorization of the aggressive subjectivity of the warrior in the epithet, whose historical origins lie in the summoning of aggression in deflecting Punjab's multiple invasions, is, however, appropriated in the construction of a new form of refugee subjectivity through the refugee's subversion of docile subjectivity, which may be called aggressive subjectivity. Although refugees did not resort to physical violence to respond to insults, the codes of culture of honour underpinning Punjabi patriarchal structures regulated the verbal and behavioural aggressiveness that has since become naturalized as the hallmark of Punjabi subjectivity (Nisbett and Cohen 1996).[5]

This hegemonic masculinity traditionally constituted in relation to the warrior ethic in Punjab and Sind was simultaneously required to undergo a radical shift when collectively affirmed in the face of a refugee regime that sought to create new subjectivities through changing the notion of the division of labour in which the division between "men's work" and "women's work" seriously impacted men's sense of masculinity. Migration studies have focused on the availability of low-skilled work particularly in the domestic domain designated as "women's work" to refugees, asylum seekers and migrants due to the deskilling of professional qualifications or loss of entrepreneurial capital and the reversal of gendered roles through female migrants' forced assumption of the role of providers (Malkin 2004).[6] Partition literature has been attentive to the redefinition of "women's work" and transformation in gendered subjectivities through female members', particularly young single and widowed women's, assumption of traditionally defined male subject positions and has viewed it as both oppressive and emancipating (Midha 2017).[7] Although migration did not oblige men "to adopt several practices that are usually associated with the construction of femininity, such as being tied to the house . . . and domestic chores" (Malkin 2004: 79), men were compelled to make occupational choices labelled feminine. The refugee arrival in cities like Delhi, Mumbai and Lucknow has been associated with the erosion of traditional cuisines with the introduction of Punjabi restaurant and street food visually imprinted on the local imaginary by men rolling food carts, carrying food accompanying tandoori rotis. In view of the stigmatization of the male who performed "women's work" in traditional Punjabi and Sindhi societies, the economic contingencies that compelled displaced males to hawk street food or manufacture pickles or engage in other "women's work" was framed within the definition of hegemonic masculinity that prohibited men to permit their women to engage in waged labour in public spaces. Male survivors' engagement in work traditionally labelled feminine in conjunction with hegemonic masculinity confirms the fluid nature of masculinity through their reshaping of masculinity that was fluid and adapted to the changing demands of their altered positions.

Docile and aggressive subjectivities

Literature on refugees has focussed on subjectification or "a technology of government that works through the construction of certain forms of refugee subjectivities" (Olivius 2014: 43) in which the "refugee" is constructed as a subject position that refugees and asylum seekers are required to adopt in order to "fit in" with the policies providing them assistance and support. Peter Nyers (2006), Nevzat Soguk (1999) and William Walters (2008) have issued a caveat against viewing refugee subjectivities as preordained identity constructions inscribed with helplessness. Viewing refugees as voiceless, passive, subordinate, victimized subjects strips refugee subjects of any political agency, thus reiterating stereotyped concepts of "migrants as passive and helpless beings" (Walters 2008: 188). The oscillation between hospitality and hostility in the reception of new arrivals may be framed within the dissonance between the sovereign state's subjectification of cross-border migration through the technologies of care and control and the migrant's refusal to be subjectified as a docile subject. The refusal of the new arrival to identify with the standardized docile subjectivity of the refugee through which the sovereign state engendered a new constitution of the refugee as an unreliable, aggressive, unethical subject threatening the existing national order reinscribes the refugee as an agent. The attempt of the refugee at self-reliance, independence and resilience that subverted the standardized depiction of the docile subject was inscribed as a form of aggressive subjectivity antithetical to national character. This discursive construction emerged through a new process of subjectification in response to the Punjabi refugee's recalcitrance in subjecting himself to the technologies of containment through which the sovereign power sought to know and control the bodies of the new arrivals.

Since this aggressive subjectivity of the refugee permeated the national imaginary, its historical origins must be systematically located to comprehend its being mapped on particular groups of refugees. Although certain forms of aggressive speech and behaviour have been traditionally employed in the construction of warrior communities, particularly those from Punjab, another form of aggressive subjectivity that was the product of refugeeness was articulated to the traditional stereotype of Punjabi aggressiveness. This is the new aggressiveness that Stephen Keller has described as the third stage of three residual characteristics – guilt, invulnerability and aggressiveness – that he noted among those who were late to flee violence. Without articulating it to the legendary aggressiveness of warrior communities, Kellner views aggressiveness as a fallout of the other two states: a displacement of the guilt onto others and a willingness to take risks because one is invulnerable. The experience of having faced the worst, as Kellner pointed out, produced a sense of invulnerability and the ability to take risks. In the case of Punjab, this new aggressiveness results in an increased willingness to innovate, to take risks, to make the effort to build a new life.

> The refugees are more willing to do new things or do old things in new ways. They are more geographically mobile, more occupationally mobile, and more likely to adapt innovations sooner than non-refugees.
>
> (Keller 1975: 271)

> Perhaps, when your roots are pulled out, resettlement and unfamiliar terrain fail to intimidate.
>
> (Khattar 2013)

The predisposition to political and economic risk taking that refugees developed through the process of invulnerability that Kibreab Gaim views as an asset and driver of economic growth (2004) was construed and represented as an amoral, aggressive subjectivity by the risk-averse majority in rural and urban India. Keller (1975) and Awasthi (2005), who are of the view that competition between refugees and non-refugees legitimized and institutionalized synergy, attributed synergy, the socially shared view of competition as intrinsically healthy, to the economic success of Punjabi refugees. However, it also intensified the hostility of non-refugees and the construction of aggressive subjectivities that threatened the genteel, moral fabric of society (Awasthi 2005: 455).

Aggressive subjectivity may also be defined as the subject position carved by the refugee through disidentification with compassionate or controlling refugee-ness and self-identification as a right-bearing citizen of the Indian state. Ravinder Kaur's unveiling of distinctive citizenship is pertinent in the transformation of the new arrival from refugee to citizen. Kaur argues that self-rehabilitation, "the ability to become a productive citizen of the new nation state without state intervention" was the defining principle of the official resettlement policy and that "the onus of performing a successful transition – from refugee to citizen – lay on the resourcefulness of the refugees rather than the state" (2009: 429).

The experience of the displaced refugee bereft of material and cultural belongings similarly made the corporeal body – labouring, entrepreneurial, professional – pivotal to Partitioned subjectivity. Rather than ancestral wealth, property or lineage, individual competencies for survival came to be valorized as essential to self-definition.

Notes

1 As Simpson (1938) has put it, "Not all stateless people are refugees, nor are all refugees technically stateless. . . . Statelessness is not the essential quality of a refugee,

though many refugees are in fact stateless people." Displaced person has come to be used widely as a synonym for refugee; in a legal sense, the two terms are not interchangeable, though they overlap in substantial ways (1938). In 1969, the Organization of African Unity (OAU) Convention Governing Specific Aspects of Refugee Problems in Africa provided an expansion of the individual-centred 1951 definition of the refugee that stresses an individual's "well-founded fear of persecution" (116: 23).

2 Malkki shows that "standardizing discursive and representational forms (or perhaps more precisely, tendencies) have made their way into journalism and all of the media that report on refugees" (Malkki 1996: 386).

3 Durieux and Adam maintain that refugees "who remain 'in place' are both feminized and depoliticized through the purported benevolence of humanitarian aid and through the suspension of refugees' basic human rights" (Durieux and Adam 2004). In their examination of refugees from the Global South encamped in refugee centres, Jennifer Hyndman and Giles argue that the "the material conditions and depictions of such refugees as immobile and passive contributes to a feminization of asylum in such spaces" (Hyndman and Giles 2011: 361).

4 Speaking of the ethic of labour through which embodied Jat subjectivity is produced, Radhika Chopra explains that "crafting identity through manual work is of immense significance to his sense of self worth, a way of marking out his location within the cultural context of village life. Work is seen to simultaneously craft the body and a sense of self. . . . The Jat status is embodied and seen to be embodied, and differences carried literally and metaphorically on and through the body" (Chopra 2004: 44). Although Chopra's essay engages with Jat subjectivity specifically, since Jat's labouring body has been traditionally valorized in Punjab, the aesthetic of embodiment and labour is incorporated by other Punjabi castes other than Brahmins in their self-constitution.

5 "A culture of honor is a culture in which a person (usually a man) feels obliged to protect his or her reputation by answering insults, affronts, and threats, oftentimes through the use of violence. Cultures of honor have been independently invented many times across the world" ("Culture of Honor").

6 Malkin asserts that "in many cases, migration obliges men to adopt several practices that are usually associated with the construction of femininity, such as being tied to the house . . . and domestic chores" (Malkin 2004: 79).

7 Harish Chandra Midha recalled that women in their families also worked because "they were 7 to 8 members in each family." He reminisced that as his father tried to cultivate barren land allotted to the family in Haryana, his mother took up tailoring jobs in Ranchi to supplement the family income and that, as a child, he would tag along with her when she went to others' houses and gave them their clothes. He stated that they had "kept the stitching machine," which his mother used to work on (Midha, Harish Chandra 2017).

Bibliography

Agamben, Giorgio. 1998. *Homo Sacer: Sovereign Power and Bare Life*. Stanford, CA: Stanford University Press.

Aguilar-San Juan, Karin. 2013. "Staying Vietnamese: Community and Place in Boston and Orange County." In *The Urban Sociology Reader*, edited by Jan Lin and Christopher Mele. London: Routledge.

Ahmed, Imaduddin. 2007. "Contrasting Memories of Pre and Post-Partition Lahore: Rehana Bano Bokhari". *The Friday Times*. April 7. Accessed December 10, 2018. https://imadahmed.com/2007/04/07/i-remember-rehana-bano-bokhari/.

Ahmed, Ishtiaq. 2002. "The 1947 Partition of India: A Paradigm for Pathological Politics in India and Pakistan." *Asian Ethnicity* 3 (1): 9–28.

———. 2006. "The Lahore Effect." *Seminar*, No 567, November. Delhi: IIC.

———. 2011. *The Punjab Bloodied, Partitioned and Cleansed: Unravelling the 1947 Tragedy through Secret British Reports and First Person Accounts*. New Delhi: Rupa Publications.

———. 2012. "The Lahore Film Industry." In *Magic of Bollywood: At Home and Abroad*, edited by Anjali Gera Roy. New Delhi: Sage.

Alavi, Hamza A. 1972. "Kinship in West Punjab Villages." *Contributions to Indian Sociology* 6 (1): 1–27.

Alexander, Horace. 1951. *New Citizens of India*. Oxford: Oxford University Press.

Ali, Imran. 1989. *The Punjab under Imperialism: 1885–1947*. New Delhi: Oxford University Press.

Ali, Sehba. 2015. "Friends from the Other Side: Hardships Faced in Unison." *The Lucknow Observer* 2 (17), August 5.

Alimuddin, Salim, Arif Hasan, and Asiya Sadiq. 1920. "The Work of the Anjuman Samaji Behbood and the Larger Faisalabad Context, Pakistan." IIED Working Paper 7 on Poverty Reduction in Urban Areas. Accessed December 10, 2018. www.ucl.ac.uk/dpu-projects/drivers_urb_change/urb_infrastructure/pdf_public_private_services/W_IIED_Hasan_Community_Anjuman.pdf.

Alonso, Ana Maria. 1988. "The Effect of Truth: Re-Presentations of the Past and the Imagining of Community." *Journal of Historical Sociology* 1 (1): 33–57.

"Amnesty International Report: The State of the World's Human Rights." 2006. London: Amnesty International Publications.

Anderson, Ben. 2009. "Affective Atmospheres." *Emotion, Space and Society* 2 (2): 77–81.

"Annales." *Encyclopaedia Britannica*. Accessed November 15, 2017.

"Architecture of Delhi." Accessed December 10, 2018. http://delhi-architecture.weebly.com/background.html.

Arora, Kanta. Arora, Bhanvi. 2015. "I-Day Special: Survivors of 1947 Partition Wish Lines had not Divided Two Nations." In *DNA India*, edited by Swati Bhasin. August 13. Accessed December 10, 2018. http://54.254.97.154/locality/chandni-chowk/i-day-special-survivors-1947-Partition-wish-lines-had-not-divided-two-nations-66964.

Arora, Naveen. 2014. "Suit No. 76/14 Des Raj vs. Hans Raj on 7 April." *Delhi District Court*. Accessed December 10, 2018. Accessed April 4, 2006. https://indiankanoon.org/doc/189610272/articles/art.php?id=49.

Asad, Hashim. 2017. "Memories of Partition: One Man's Return to Pakistan. Seventy Years on a Now 92-Year-Old Man Returns to the Home He Fled During the 'Poison' of Partition." Accessed December 10, 2018. www.iosminaret.org/vol-12/issue8/A_Legacy_of_Division.php/.

Aujla, Harjap Singh. 2015. "Punjabis of Delhi Could Not Get Justice for Punjabi Language." *Punjab News Express*, June 15. Accessed December 10, 2018. http://punjab newsexpress.com/punjab/news/punjabi-s-of-delhi-couldn-t-get-justice-for-punjabi-lan guage-41059.aspx.

Awasthi, U.K. 2005. "Displacement and Social Change: The Success Stories of Punjabi Refugees in India." In *South Asia Today,* edited by Gopal Singh and Ramesh Chauhan, 451–65. Delhi: Anamika Distributors.

Azad, Maulana Abul Kalam. 1959. *India Wins Freedom: An Autobiographical Narrative.* Bombay: Orient Longmans.

Babur, Zahīr ud-Dīn Muhammad. 1922. *The Babur-nama in English (Memoirs of Babur)*, Vol. 1. Edited by Annette Susannah Beveridge. London: Luzac and Co.

Bachelard, Gaston. 1994. *The Poetics of Space*. Translated from the French by Maria Jolas, with a new foreword by John R. Stilgoe. Boston, MA: Beacon Press.

Bagchi, Jasodhara and Subhoranjan Dasgupta, Eds. 2003. *The Trauma and the Triumph: Gender and Partition in Eastern India*. Kolkata: Stree.

Bakhtin, Mikhail. 1981. "Form of Time and Chronotope in the Novel." In *The Dialogic Imagination: Four Essays*, edited by Michael Holquist, 84–258. Austin: University of Texas Press.

Balouch, Akhtar. 2014. "In Karachi, Memories of Bombay, Meri Jaan." *Scroll*. December 26. Accessed December 10, 2018. https://scroll.in/article/697018/in-karachi-memories-of-bombay-meri-jaan.

Bansal, Bobby Singh. 2012. "The Dwindling Sikhs of Kabul: A Forgotten Community." *NRI.Net*. London, February 18. Accessed December 10, 2018. http://nriinternet.com/NRI_Columnists/A_D/B/Bobby_Bansal/2012/Dwindling_Sikhs.htm.

Barthes, Roland. 1981. "The Discourse of History." (trans.) Stephen Bann *Comparative Criticism* 3: 7–20.

Bartlett, F. C. 1964 [1932]. *Remembering: A Study in Experimental and Social Psychology*. Cambridge: Cambridge University Press.

Basu Raychaudhury, Anasua. 2004. "Nostalgia of 'Desh', Memories of Partition." *Economic and Political Weekly* XXXIX (52): 5653–60.

Bates, Crispin. 2011. "The Hidden Story of Partition and Its Legacies". *BBC*. Accessed December 10, 2018. http://www.bbc.co.uk/history/british/modern/partition1947_01.shtml.

Bauman, Zygmunt. 1995. "Making and Unmaking of Strangers." *Thesis Eleven* 43 (1): 1–16.

Bedi, Rajinder Singh. 2006 [1976]. "Lajwanti." Trans. Khushwant Singh. In *Writings on India's Partition*, edited by Ramesh Mathur and Mahendra Kulasrestha, 126–35. Calcutta: Simant Publications.

Berland, Joseph C. 2003. "Servicing the Ordinary Folk: Peripatetic Peoples and their Niche in South Asia." In *Nomadism in South Asia*, edited by Aparna Rao and Michael J. Casimir. New Delhi: Oxford University Press.

Berlant, Lauren. 1997. *The Queen of America Goes to Washington City: Essays on Sex and Citizenship*. Durham, NC: Duke University Press.

Bhabha, Homi K. 1994. *The Location of Culture*. London: Routledge.

Bhalla, Alok. 1999. "Memory, History and Fictional Representations of the Partition." *Economic and Political Weekly* 34 (4): 3119–28.

Bhalla, Guneeta Singh. 2014. "The Blood & Tears of 1947." *Darpan*, March 15. Accessed December 10, 2018. www.darpanmagazine.com/magazine/feature/the-blood-tears-of-1947/.

Bhardwaj, Anjali. 2004. "Partition of India and Women's Experiences: A Study of Women as Sustainers of their Families in Post-Partition Delhi." *Social Scientist* 32 (5/6): 69–88.

Bhatija, Tulika. 2013. "Sindhi – The Language of Refugees." *The Alternative*, September 16. Accessed December 10, 2018. www.thealternative.in/society/tulika-bathija-sindhi-the-survival-of-the-language-of-refugees/.

Bloch, Maurice. 1992. "Internal and External Memory: Different Ways of Being in History." *Suoman Anthropology* 1: 3–15.

———. 1996. "Memory." In *Encyclopaedia of Social and Cultural Anthropology*, edited by A. Bernard and J. Spencer. New York: Routledge.

Blunt, Alison. 2003. "Collective Memory and Productive Nostalgia: Anglo-Indian Home-making at McCluskieganj." *Environment and Planning D: Society and Space* 21 (6): 717–38.

Bokhari, Rehana Bano. 2007. "Contrasting Memories of Pre and Post-Partition Lahore." *Friday Times*. Accessed December 10, 2018. https://imadahmed.wordpress.com/2007/04/07/i-remember-rehana-bano-bokhari/.

Bonnett, Alastair. 2015. *The Geography of Nostalgia: Global and Local Perspectives on Modernity and Loss*. London: Routledge.

Bonnett, Alastair and Alexander Catherine. 2013. "Mobile Nostalgias: Connecting Visions of the Urban Past, Present and Future Amongst Ex-Residents". *Transactions of the Institute of British Geographers* 38 (3): 391–402.

Bose, Pradip. 2010. "Refugee, Memory and the State: A Review of Research in Refugees Studies." *Refugee Watch*, December, 36: 1–30.

Bourdieu, Pierre. 1984. *Distinction: A Social Critique of the Judgement of Taste*. Translated by R. Nee. Cambridge, MA: Harvard University Press.

———. 1986. "The Forms of Capital." In *Handbook of Theory and Research for the Sociology of Education*, edited by John G. Richardson, 241–58. New York: Greenwood Press.

———. 1990. *Distinction. A Social Critique of the Judgement of Taste*. Translated by Richard Nice. Cambridge, MA: Harvard University Press.

———. 1991 [1982]. *Language and Symbolic Power*. Translated G. Raymond & M. Adamson. Cambridge, MA: Polity Press.

——— and L. J. D. Wacquant. 2002. *An Invitation to Reflexive Sociology*. Chicago: University of Chicago Press.

Boym, Svetlana. 2001. *The Future of Nostalgia*. New York: Basic Books.

Bradiotti, Rosi. 2011. *Nomadic Subjects: Embodiment and Sexual Difference in Contemporary Feminist Theory*, 2nd ed. New York: Columbia University Press.

Brass, Paul. 1974. *Language, Religion, and Politics in North India*. Cambridge, MA: Cambridge University Press.

————. 2003. "The Partition of India and Retributive Genocide in the Punjab, 1946–47: Means, Methods, and Purposes." *Journal of Genocide Research* 5 (1): 71–101.

Brothman, Brien. 2001. "The Past that Archives Keep: Memory, History, and the Reservation of Archival Records." *Archivaria* [S.L.] January: 48–80.

Brun, Cathrine. 2001. "Reterritorializing the Relationship between People and Place in Refugee Studies." *Geografiska Annaler. Series B, Human Geography* 83 (1): 15–25.

Bulley, Dan. 2014. "Inside the Tent: Community and Government in Refugee Camps." *Security Dialogue* 45 (1): 63–80.

Burke, Peter, Ed. 1989. *Historical Writing*. Cambridge, MA: Polity Press.

Butalia, Urvashi. 1998. *The Other Side of Silence*. New Delhi: Viking.

Campbell Johnson, Alan. 1951. *Mission with Mountbatten*. Bombay: Jaico Publishing House.

Carter, Paul. 1996. *The Lie of the Land*. London: Faber and Faber.

Caruth, Cathy. 2016. *Unclaimed Experience: Trauma, Narrative and History*. Baltimore: Johns Hopkins University Press.

Chakrabarty, Dipesh. 1995. "Remembered Villages: Representations of Hindu-Bengali Memories in the Aftermath of the Partition." *South Asia: Journal of South Asian Studies* 18 (sup001): 109–29.

Chambers, Ian. 1994. *Migrancy, Culture, Identity*. London: Routledge.

Chandu, Halwai. "About Punjabi Chandu Halwai." *Delight Foods*. Accessed December 10, 2018. www.delightfoods.com/pch.

Chatterjee, Partha. 2010. *Empire and Nation: Selected Essays*. New York: Columbia University Press.

Chatterjee, Prerana. 2015. "Managing Urban Transformations of Refugee Settlements in West Delhi from Camps to Nagars: The Story of Moti Nagar and Kirti Nagar." *Creative Space* (CS) 2 (2): 183–208, January. Accessed December 12, 2018. http://dspace.chitkara.edu.in/jspui/bitstream/1/531/1/22011_CS_Prerana%20Chatterjee.pdf.

Chatterji, Joya. 1995. *Bengal Divided: Hindu Communalism and Partition 1932–1947*. Cambridge, MA: Cambridge University Press.

————. 2001. "Right or Charity? The Debate over Relief and Rehabilitation in West Bengal, 1947–50." In *The Partitions of Memory: The Afterlife of the Division of India*, edited by Suvir Kaul, 74–110. Indiana: Indiana University Press.

————. 2002. *Bengal Divided: Hindu Communalism and Partition, 1932–1947*. Cambridge, MA: Cambridge University Press.

Chattha, Ilyas. 2011. *Partition and Locality: Violence, Migration, and Development in Gujranwala and Sialkot 1947–1961*. Karachi: Oxford University Press.

————. 2012. "Competitions for Resources: Partition's Evacuee Property and the Sustenance of Corruption in Pakistan." *Modern Asian Studies* 46 (5): 1182–211.

————. 2013. "Partisan Reporting: Press Coverage of the 1947 Partition Violence in the Punjab." *South Asia: Journal of South Asian Studies* 36 (4): 608–25.

Chhabra, Rahul. 2016. "Plot Conversion from Leasehold to Freehold Torments Pak Refugee Families." *Deccan Herald*. New Delhi, July 18. Accessed December 10, 2018. www.deccanherald.com/content/558633/plot-conversion-leasehold-freehold-torments.html.

Chopra, P. R. 2012. "Suit for Partition Cs(Os) 374/1993. Shri Gajinder Pal Singh Vs Shri Mahtab Singh and Ors. High Court of Delhi at New Delhi July 09." *Delhi High Court*. Accessed December 10, 2018. https://delhidistrictcourts.nic.in/July12/Gajinder%20Pal%20Singh%20Vs.%20Mahtab%20Singh.pdf.

Chopra, Radhika. 2004. "Encountering Masculinity: An Ethnographer's Dilemma." In *South Asian Masculinities: Context of Change, Sites of Continuity*, edited by Radhika Chopra, Caroline Osella, and Fillipo Osella, 36–59. New Delhi: Women Unlimited.

Chopra, Satish. 2017. "Situationer: Lahore in Aug '47, As Etched on My Mind." *Dawn,* August 13. Accessed December 10, 2018. www.dawn.com/news/1351334.

Choudhry, Khaliqquzaman. 1961. *Pathway to Pakistan.* Lahore: Longmans.

Cohen, William and Ryan A. Johnson. 2005. *Filth: Dirt, Disgust, and Modern Life.* Minneapolis: University of Minnesota Press.

Conley, Tom. 2000. "Introduction. Other Cities: Cultural Politics, Part 2." In *The de Certeau Reader,* edited by Graham Ward. Malden, MA: Wiley-Blackwell.

Connerton, Paul. 1989. *How Societies Remember.* Cambridge, MA: Cambridge University Press.

"Culture of Honour". *Psychology Research.* Accessed December 10, 2018. https://psychology.iresearchnet.com/social-psychology/cultural-psychology/culture-of-honor/.

Dalrymple, William. 2006. "In the Kingdom of Avadh." Accessed December 10, 2018. www.travelintelligence.net/php/.

———. 2012. *The Age of Kali: Travels and Encounters in India.* New Delhi: Harper Collins.

———. 2015. "The Great Divide: The Violent Legacy of Indian Partition." *New Yorker,* June 29. Accessed December 10, 2018. www.newyorker.com/magazine/2015/06/29/the-great-divide-books-dalrymple.

Darling, Jonathan. 2009. "Becoming Bare Life: Asylum, Hospitality, and the Politics of Encampment." *Environment and Planning D: Society and Space* 227: 649–65.

Darling, Malcolm Lyall. 1948. *At Freedom's Door.* Da-Rus-Salam: Oxford University Press.

Das, Gurcharan. 2010. "Scenes from a Punjabi Childhood." In *From Remembered Childhood,* edited by Malavika Karlekar and Rudrangshu Mukherjee. Delhi: Oxford University Press. Accessed December 10, 2018. http://gurcharandas.org/punjabi-childhood.

Das, Veena. 1990. *Mirrors of Violence: Communities, Riots, and Survivors in South Asia.* New Delhi: Oxford University Press.

———. 1990. "Our Work to Cry: Your Work to Listen'." In *Mirrors of Violence: Communities, Riots and Survivors in South Asia,* edited by Veena Das, 345–99. New Delhi: Oxford University Press.

———.1995. *Critical Events: An Anthropological Perspective on Contemporary India.* Delhi: Oxford University Press.

———. 2000. "The Act of Witnessing: Violence, Poisonous Knowledge, and Subjectivity." In *Violence and Subjectivity,* edited by Veena Das, A. Kleinman, M. Ramphele, and P. Reynolds. New Delhi: Oxford University Press.

———. 2007. *Life and Words: Violence and the Descent into the Ordinary.* Los Angles: University of California Press.

Datta, Nonica. 2008. "Transcending Religious Identities: Amrita Pritam and Partition." In *Partitioned Lives: Narratives of Home, Displacement and Resettlement,* edited by Anjali Gera Roy and Nandi Bhatia. New Delhi: Pearson Longman.

———. 2009. *Violence, Martyrdom and Partition: A Daughter's Testimony.* New Delhi: Oxford University Press.

———. 2017. "Reframing Partition: Memory, Testimony, History." *Südasien-Chronik – South Asia Chronicle,* July: 61–93.

Datta, Vishwa Nath. 2002. "Panjabi Refugees and the Urban Development of Greater Delhi." In *Inventing Boundaries: Gender, Politics and the Partition of India,* edited by Mushirul Hasan. New Delhi: Oxford University Press.

Davidson, Joyce, Liz Bondi, and Mick Smith, Eds. 2005. *Emotional Geographies.* Hampshire, UK and Burlington: Ashgate.

Davis, Fred. 1979. *Yearning for Yesterday: A Sociology of Nostalgia.* New York: Free Press.

Davud, Seyyed Ali Al-i and Amir Hushang Nazerian. "Abū al-Qāsim Kāshānī." 2008. *Ency-clopaedia Islamica*. Editors-in-Chief: Wilferd Madelung and, Farhad Daftary. Accessed December 22, 2018. http://dx.doi.org/10.1163/1875-9831_isla_COM_0125.

De, Sharmistha and Anjali Gera Roy. 2014. "Fluid Borders and Continuous Displacement: Partition Stories from Talbagicha Kharagpur". In *Globalisation: Australian-Asian Perspectives*, edited by Cynthia Vanden Driesen and T. Vijay Kumar. Delhi: Atlantic.

de Certeau, Michel, Luce Girard, and Pierre Mayol. 1998. *The Practice of Everyday Life*. Berkeley, CA: University of Minnesota Press.

Deleuze, Giles. 1998. *Essays Critical and Clinical*. Translated Daniel W. Smith and Michael A. Greco. New York: Verso.

Deo, Shashi Bhushan. 2018. *Capital Cuisine. The Hindu*, July 29. Accessed December 10, 2018. www.thehindu.com/opinion/open-page/capital-cuisine/article24541837.ece.

Derrida, Jacques. 2000. "Of Hospitality." In *Anne Dufourmantelle Invites Jacques Derrida to Respond*. Stanford, CA: Stanford University Press.

Devi, Jyotimoyee. 2005 [1995]. "Epaar Ganga, Opar Ganga." Translated from the Original Bengali by Enakshi Chatterjee. New Delhi: Women Unlimited.

Dey, Sushil Kumar. 1945. *Bangla Prabad*. Calcutta: Sahitya Samsad, Bengali Diary.

Didur, Jill. 2007. *Unsettling Partition: Literature, Gender, Memory*. Toronto: University of Toronto Press.

Dixon, Robert. 1995. *Writing the Colonial Adventure. Race, Gender and Nation in Anglo-Australian Popular Fiction*. Cambridge, MA: Cambridge University Press.

Douglas, Harper. "Testimony." *Online Etymology Dictionary*. Accessed December 10, 2018. www.etymonline.com/word/testimony.

Douglas, Mary. 1966. *Purity and Danger: An Analyis of Concepts of Pollution and Taboo*. New York: Fredick A Praeger.

Downs, Roger M. and David Stea. 1977. *Maps in Minds: Reflections on Cognitive Mapping*. New York: Harper & Row.

Dudley, Sandra. 2010. *Materializing Exile: Materialize Culture and Embodied Experience Among Karenni Refugees in Thailand*. New York: Berghahn Books.

Dulong, Renaud. 2002. "La Dimension Monumentaire du Témoignage Historique." *Sociétés & Représentations* 13 (1): 179–97.

Durieux, Jean-François and Jane McAdam. 2004. "Non-Refoulement through Time: The Refugee Convention in Mass Influx Emergencies." *International Journal of Refugee Law* 16 (1): 4–24.

Dutt Nirupama. 2009. "Diamonds that Were Not Forever." *South Asian Ensemble* 1 (1), Autumn. Accessed December 10, 2018. http://apnaorg.com/prose-content/english-arti cles/page-58/article-6/index.html.

"East Punjab Legislative Assembly Debates, 8 March, 1948." 1949. Shimla: East Punjab Government, East, Punjab.

Editorial. 1954. "Evacuee Property." *The Economic Weekly: A Journal of Current Economic and Political Affairs* VI (20). Accessed December 10, 2018. www.epw.in/system/ files/pdf/1954_6/20/evacuee_property.pdf?0=ip_login_no_cache%3D568cff184816b4c ec3b935772bbce9ee.

Edlund, Lars-Erik. 2018. "Some Reflections on Mental Maps." *Journal of Cultural Geography* 35 (2): 274–85.

Edney, Matthew. 1997. *Mapping an Empire: The Geographical Construction of British India, 1765–1843*. Chicago: University of Chicago Press.

Eglar, Zekiye Suleyman. 1960. *Vartan Bhanji: Institutionalized Reciprocity in a Changing Punjabi Village*. New York: Columbia University Press.

Eitinger, Leo. 1960. "The Symptomatology of Mental Disease among Refugees in Norway." *Journal of Mental Science* 106: 947–66.

Engels, Frederic. 1858. "The Siege and Storming of Lucknow." *New York Daily Tribune*, January 30. Transcribed by Tony Brown. Accessed December 10, 2018. www.marxists.org/archive/marx/works/1858/01/30.htm.

Farris, Debbie. 2017. "From Poverty to Prosperity: Refugee, Professor and Entrepreneur." *Impact: Transformational Experiences in the College of Science*, October 20. Accessed December 10, 2018. http://Impact.Oregonstate.Edu/2017/10/Poverty-Prosperity-Refugee-Professor-Entrepreneur/.

Felman, Shoshana and Dori Laub. 1991. "In an Era of Testimony: Claude Lanzmann's Shoah." *Yale French Studies, Literature and the Ethical Question* 79: 39–81.

———. 1992. *Testimony: Crises of Witnessing in Literature, Psychoanalysis, and History.* New York and London: Routledge.

Foucault Michel. 2007. *Security, Territory, Population: Lectures at Collège de France 1977–1978*, translated by G Burchell. London: Palgrave Macmillan.

French, Patrick. 1997. *Liberty or Death: India's Journey to Independence and Division.* New York: Harper Collins.

Freud, Sigmund. 1919. "The Uncanny." Translated by Alix Strachey. *Imago*, Bd. V. reprinted in Sammlung, Fünfte Folge.1–21. Accessed December 10, 2018. https://web.mit.edu/allanmc/www/freud1.pdf

Fritzsche, Peter. 2001. "Specters of History: On Nostalgia, Exile, and Modernity." *The American Historical Review* 106 (5): 1587–618.

Frye, Northrop. 1957. *Anatomy of Criticism.* Princeton, NJ: Princeton University Press.

Funkenstein, Amos. 1986. *Theology and the Scientific Imagination: From the Middle Ages to the Seventeenth Century.* Princeton, NJ: Princeton University Press.

Galtung, John. 1969. "Violence, Peace, and Peace Research." *Journal of Peace Research* 6 (3): 167–91.

———. 1990. "Cultural Violence." *Journal of Peace Research* 27 (3): 291–305, August 1.

Garg, Poornima. 2010. "The Khes of Punjab." *Gatha: A Tale of Crafts*, February 12. Accessed December 10, 2018. http://gaatha.com/the-khes-of-punjab/.

Gaventa, Jonathan. 2003. *Power after Lukes: An Overview of Theories of Power since Lukes and their Application to Development.* Brighton: Participation Group, Institute of Development Studies.

Gera Roy, Anjali. 2004. "Not Speaking a Language that is Mine." *Translation Today*, October. 1(2): 26–43.

———. 2006. "Adarsh Nagar diyaan Gallan: At Home in a Resettlement Colony." In *Interpreting Homes: South Asian Literature*, edited by Malashri Lal and Sukrita P. Kumar, 16–33. New Delhi: Pearson Longman.

Gera Roy, Anjali and Nandi Bhatia. 2008. *Partitioned Lives: Narratives of Home, Displacement and Resettlement.* New Delhi: Pearson Longman.

Gera, Sparsh. 2017. "What was It Like to Migrate from Pakistan to India during Partition?" *Quora*, March 10. Accessed December 10, 2018. www.quora.com/What-was-it-like-to-migrate-from-Pakistan-to-India-during-Partition.

Ghosh, Ambika, Richi Verma, Ruhi Bhasin, Neha Pushkarna, Neha Pushkarna, Neha Lalchandani, Megha Suri Singh and Ambika Pandit. 2010. "Delhi, A City of Refugee Enterprise." *The Times of India*, January 24. Accessed December 10, 2018. https://timesofindia.indiatimes.com/india/Delhi-a-city-of-refugee-enterprise/articleshow/5493706.cms.

Ghosh, Amrita. 2016. "Refugees as Homo Sacers: Partition and the National Imaginary in The Hungry Tide." In *Revisiting India's Partition: New Essays on Memory, Culture, and Politics*, edited by Amritjit Singh, Nalini Iyer, and Rahul K. Gairola. Lanham: Lexington Books.

Ghosh, Partha S. 2016. *Migrants, Refugees and the Stateless in South Asia*. Thousand Oaks, CA: Sage.

Ghosh, Subhasri. 2013. "Representation of Forced Migrants: A Case Study of The East Bengali Migrants to West Bengal." *Conserveries Mémorielles* [En ligne], #13 | Mis en Ligne le 10 Mars. Accessed December 10, 2018. http://journals.openedition.org/cm/1490.

Giard, Luce, Ed. 2000. *The Certeau Reader*. Oxford: Wiley-Blackwell.

Gilley, Jessey. 2010. "Geographical Imagination." In *Encyclopaedia of Geography*, edited by Barney Warf, 1222–26. Thousand Oaks, CA: Sage.

Gilmartin, David. 1988. *Empire and Islam: Punjab and the Making of Pakistan*. Los Angeles: University of California Press.

———. 1994. "Biraderi and Bureaucracy: The Politics of Muslim Kinship Solidarity in 20th century Punjab." *International Journal of Punjab Studies* 1 (1): 1–29, January-June 1.

———. 2004. "Migration and Modernity: The State, the Punjabi Village, and the Settling of the Canal Colonies." In *People on the Move: Punjabi Colonial, and Post-Colonial Migration*, edited by Ian Talbot and Shinder Thandi, 3–20. Karachi: Oxford University Press.

———. 2015. "The Historiography of India's Partition: Between Civilization and Modernity." *The Journal of Asian Studies* 74: 23–41.

Ginsberg, Robert. 1999. "Meditations on Homelessness and Being at Home: In the Form of a Dialogue." In *The Ethics of Homelessness: Philosophical Perspectives*, edited by John G. Abbarno. Amsterdam: Rodopi.

Ginzburg, Carlo. 1992a. *The Cheese and the Worms: The Cosmos of a Sixteenth-Century Miller*. Translated by John and Anne C. Tedeschi. Baltimore: Johns Hopkins University Press.

———. 1992b. "Just One Witness." In *Probing the Limits of Representation: Nazism and the "Final Solution"*, edited by Saul Friedländer. Cambridge, MA: Harvard University Press.

_____. 1993. "Microhistory: Two or Three Things That I Know about It." (translated) John Tedeschi and Anne C. Tedeschi. *Critical Inquiry*, Autumn. 20 (1): 10–35.

Gonzalez, Luis Pueblo Envilo. 1968. *Microhistoria de San Jose de Gracia*. Guanajuato, Mexico: El Colegio de México.

Götz, Norbert and Janne Holmén. 2018. "Introduction to the Theme Issue: Mental Maps: Geographical and Historical Perspectives." *Journal of Cultural Geography* 35 (2): 157–61.

Gould, Peter and Rodney R. White. 1974. *Mental Maps*. Harmondsworth: Penguin Books.

Graham, Elspeth. 1976. "What is a Mental Map?" *Area* 9: 259–62.

———. 1982. "Maps, Metaphors and Muddles." *The Professional Geographer* 34 (3): 251–60.

Gregory, Derek. 1994. *Geographical Imaginations*. Cambridge, MA and Oxford: Wiley-Blackwell.

Grene, Marjorie. 1968. *Approaches to a Philosophical Biology*, Vol. 465 of Basic books. New York: Basic Books.

Griffith, Ralph Thomas Hotchkin. 1889. *The Hymns of the Rigveda*. Benaras: E.J. Lazarus Collection.

Guha, Ramchandra. 2008. *India After Gandhi: The History of the World's Largest Democracy*. London, New Delhi: Picador, Picador India.

Gulati, Shilpi. 2013. " 'Dere Tun Dilli' (From Dera to Delhi): Exploring Identity Formation of Refugees from Dera Ismail Khan Living in Delhi." *Subversions: A Journal of Emerging Research in Media and Cultural Studies* 1 (1). Accessed December 10, 2018. http://subversions.tiss.edu/vol1-issue1/shilpi/#_ftnref9.

Gupta, Dipankar. 1996. *The Context of Ethnicity: Sikh Identity in a Comparative Perspective*. New Delhi: Oxford University Press.

Gupta, Narayani. 1981. *Delhi Between Two Empires 1803–1931: Society, Government and Urban Growth*. New Delhi: Oxford University Press.

Hadjiyanni, Tasoulla. 2009. "The Aesthetics of Displacement – Hmong, Somali, and Mexican Home-Making Practices in Minnesota." *International Journal of Consumer Studies – Special issue on Consumer Issues in Housing* 33: 541–49.

Haider, Qurratulain. 1999. *Chandni Begum*. New Delhi: Bharatiya Gyanpeeth.

Halbwachs, Maurice. 1950. *The Collective Memory*. Translated Francis J. Ditter Jr. and Vida Yazdi Ditter. New York: Harper & Row.

———. 1951. *On Collective Memory*. Edited and Translated, and with an Introduction by Lewis A. Cose. Chicago: University of Chicago Press.

Hamid, A. 2006. "Lahore Lahore Aye: It was Always Tea-time in Lahore." *Daily Times: Sunday*, April 23. Accessed December 10, 2018. http://apnaorg.com/columns/ahameed/column-5.html.

Harley, Brian. 1989. "Deconstructing the Map." *Cartographica* 26 (2): 1–20, Summer.

Harrell-Bond, Barbara, Eftihia Voutira, and Mark Leopold. 1992. "Counting the Refugees: Gifts, Givers, Patrons and Clients." *Journal of Refugee Studies* 5 (3–4): 205–25.

Hasan, Khalid. 2003. "Memories of Pre-1947 Lahore." *Daily Times*. Friday, January 3. Accessed December 10, 2018. http://apnaorg.com/prose-content/english-articles/page-118/article-5/index.html.

Hasan, Mushirul. 2002. "Partition Narratives Source." *Social Scientist* 30 (7): 24–53.

Hashmi, Sohail. "The Role of Partition in Making Delhi What It is Today." *The Wire*, August 15, 2017. Accessed December 10, 2018. https://thewire.in/history/partition-new-delhi

Hayden, Dolores. 1997. *The Power of Place: Urban Landscapes as Public History*. Cambridge, MA and London: MIT Press.

Hirsch, Marianne. 2008. "The Generation of Postmemory." *Poetics Today* 1 (29): 103–28.

———. 2012. *The Generation of Postmemory: Writing and Visual Culture After the Holocaust*. New York: Columbia University Press.

Hoon, Visharda. 2013. *From Lahore to Chennai*. Chennai: Centre for Action Research on Environment Science and Society.

Hosain, Attia. 1961. *Sunlight on a Broken Column*. London: Chatto and Windus.

Hutton, Patrick H. 1993. *History as an Art of Memory*. Hanover, NH: University Press of New England, For the University of Vermont.

Huyssen, Andreas. 2000. "Present Pasts: Media, Politics, Amnesia." *Public Culture* 12 (1): 21–38.

Hyndman, Jennifer and Wenona Giles. 2011. "Waiting for What? The Feminization of Asylum in Protracted Situations." *Gender, Place & Culture* 18 (03): 361–79.

Iggers, Georg G. 1997. *Historiography in the Twentieth Century: From Scientific Objectivity to the Postmodern Challenge*. Hanover, NH: Wesleyan University Press.

"Imaginary." *Wikipedia*. https://en.wikipedia.org/wiki/Imaginary_(sociology).

Inder Singh, Anita. 1987. *The Origins of the Partition of India, 1936–1947*. London: Oxford University Press.

Jackman, Mary R. 2002. "Violence in Social Life." *Annual Review of Sociology* 28: 387–415.

Jackson, Michael. 1995. *At Home with the Word*. Durham, NC: Duke University Press.

Jalal, Ayesha. 1994. *The Sole Spokesman: Jinnah, The Muslim League, and the Demand for Pakistan*. Cambridge, MA and Cambridgeshire and New York: Cambridge University Press.

Jentsch, Ernst. 1997. "On the Psychology of the Uncanny (1906)." *Angelaki* 2 (1): 7–16.

Jhutti-Johal, Jagbir. 2012. "Sikhism and Mental Illness: Negotiating Competing Cultures". In *Religion and the Body: Modern Science and the Construction of Religious Meaning*, edited by Rebecca Sachs Norris and David Cave. Leiden: Brill.

Johari, Aarefa. 2018. "Facing Eviction, Residents of a Mumbai Partition-Era Colony Fear They will become Homeless Again." *The Scroll*, August 01. Accessed December 10, 2018. https://scroll.in/article/887276/facing-eviction-residents-of-mumbais-Partition-era-colony-fear-they-will-become-refugees-again.

Jones, Kenneth W. 1976. *Arya Dharm: Hindu Consciousness in 19th-century Punjab*. Oakland: University of California Press.

Joyner, Charles W. 1999. *Shared Traditions: Southern History and Folk Culture*. Chicago: University of Illinois Press.

Kabir, Ananya Jahanara. 2013. *Partition's Post-amnesias: 1947, 1971 and Modern South Asia*. New Delhi: Women Unlimited.

———. 2014. "Affect, Body, Place: Trauma Theory in the World." In *The Future of Trauma Theory: Contemporary Literary and Cultural Criticism*, edited by Gert Buelens, Samuel Durrant, and Robert Eaglestone. London: Routledge.

Kakar, Sudhir. 1996. *The Colors of Violence: Cultural Identities, Religion and Conflict*. Chicago: University of Chicago Press.

Kalhana. "Itihasa." *Wikipedia*. Accessed November 15, 2017. https://simple.wikipedia.org/wiki/Itihasa.

Kalra, Satish. 2015. "Hand Drawn Map of Bhakkar Before 1947 on the Basis of the Mental Map of His Grandfather Chela Ram." *History of Bhakkar*. Accessed December 10, 2018. www.facebook.com/bhakkar12/.

Kammen, Michael. 1995. "Frames of Remembrance: The Dynamics of Collective Memory." *History and Theory* 34 (3): 245–61.

Kamra, Sukeshi. 2002. *Bearing Witness: Partition, Independence, End of the Raj*. Calgary: University of Calgary Press.

———. 2008. "Partition and Post-Partition Acts of Fiction: Narrating Painful Histories." In *Partitioned Lives: Narratives of Home, Displacement and Resettlement*, edited by Anjali Gera Roy and Nandi Bhatia. New Delhi: Pearson Longman.

Kapuria, Radha. 2015. "Rethinking Musical Pasts: The Harballabh Festival of Punjab, c. 1875–1950." *Social Scientist* 43 (5/6) (May – June): 77–91.

———. 2017. "Music and Its Many Memories: Complicating 1947 for the Punjab." In *Partition and the Practice of Memory*, edited by Anne Murphy and Churnjeet Mahn. Basingstoke: Palgrave McMillan.

Kaur, Manjit. 2011. "Very Few Still Making Punjabi Furniture." *The Star*, November 25. Accessed December 12, 2018. www.thestar.com.my/news/community/2011/11/25/very-few-still-making-punjabi-furniture/#SzEwdsTfR6sFkgDT.99.

Kaur, Ravinder. 2007. *Since 1947: Partition Narratives among Punjabi Migrants of Delhi*. New Delhi: Oxford University Press.

———. 2008. "Invisible Delhi". *Outlook India*. January 24. Accessed December 10, 2018. https://www.outlookindia.com/website/story/invisible-delhi/236564.———. 2008. "Narrative Absence: An 'Untouchable' Account of Partition Migration." *Contributions to Indian Sociology* 42 (2): 281–306. Accessed December 10, 2018. https://doi.org/10.1177/006996670804200204.

_____2009. "Distinctive Citizenship: Refugees, Subjects and Postcolonial State in India's Partition." *Cultural and Social History* 6 (4): 429–446.

Kearney, Amanda. 2009. "Homeland Emotion: An Emotional Geography of Heritage and Homeland." *International Journal of Heritage Studies* 15 (2–3): 209–22.

———— and John J. Bradley. 2009. "'Too Strong to Ever Not Be There': Place Names and Emotional Geographies." *Social & Cultural Geography* 10 (1): 77–94.

Kearns, Robin A. and Lawrence D. Berg. 2002. "Proclaiming Place: Towards a Geography of Place Name Pronunciation." *Social & Cultural Geography* 3 (3): 283–302.

Keller, Stephen. 1975. *Uprooting and Social Change: The Role of Refugees in Development*. New Delhi: Manohar Book Service.

Khan, Samra M. 2009. "Analysis of Environmental Sustainability and Architectural Design in the Allah Buksh Sethi Haveli of Mohalla Sethain, Peshawar." *Master's Thesis, Allama Iqbal Open University, Islamabad* 80: 141–43. Accessed December 12, 2018. http:// westminsterresearch.wmin.ac.uk/18329/1/Khan_Samra_thesis.pdf.

Khan, Yasmin. 2007. *The Great Partition: The Making of India and Pakistan*. New Haven: Yale University Press.

Khattar, Jagdish (with Suveen Sinha). 2013. *Driven: Memoirs of a Civil Servant Turned Entrepreneur*. Delhi: Penguin Books India.

Khosla, Gopal Das. 1949. *Stern Reckoning: A Survey of the Events Leading Up to and Following the Partition of India*. New Delhi: Bhawnani.

Kibreab, Gaim. 2004. "Pulling the Wool over the Eyes of the Strangers: Refugee Deceit and Trickery in Institutionalized Settings." *Journal of Refugee Studies* 17 (1): 1–26, 1 March.

Kidwai, Anis. 2004. *In the Shadow of Freedom*. Translated by Ayesha Kidwai. New Delhi: Zubaan.

————. 2011. *In Freedom's Shade*. Translated by Ayesha Kidwai. New Delhi: Penguin.

Kristeva, Julia. 1982. *Powers of Horror: An Essay on Abjection*. Translated by Leon S. Roudiez. New York: Columbia University Press.

————. 1991. *Strangers to Ourselves*. New York: Columbia University Press.

Kudaisya, Gyanesh. 1995. "The Demographic Upheaval of Partition: Refugees and Agricultural Resettlement in India, 1947–67." *South Asia: Journal of South Asian Studies* 18 (sup001): 73–94.

————. 1998. "Divided Landscapes, Fragmented Identities: East Bengal Refugees and their Rehabilitation in India, 1947–79." In *Freedom, Trauma, Continuities: Northern India and Independence (Studies on Contemporary South Asia series)*, edited by D. A. Low and Howard Brasted. New Delhi: Sage.

Kumar, Akanksha. 2011. "Post-Partition Refugees from NWFP in Delhi: An Ignored and Underplayed History of Dalit Refugees." *Proceedings of the Indian History Congress* 72: 1344–53. Accessed December 10, 2018. www.jstor.org/stable/44145745.

Kumar, Rajinder. 2010. "Suit No.381/06." *Delhi District Court*, February 26. In the Court of Sh. Rajinder Kumar vs Dera Ismail Khan House Building Cooperative Society, Derawal Nagar. Accessed December 10, 2018. https://indiankanoon.org/doc/177808090/.

Kunz, Egon. 1973. "The Refugee in Flight: Kinetic Models and Forms of Displacement." *The International Migration Review* 7 (2): 125–46.

LaCapra, Dominick. 1994. *Representing the Holocaust: History, Theory, Trauma*. Ithaca: Cornell University Press.

Lacroix, Marie. 2004. "Canadian Refugee Policy and the Social Construction of the Refugee Claimant Subjectivity: Understanding Refugeeness." *Journal of Refugee Studies* 17 (2): 147–66, June 1.

Lahiri, Jhumpa. 1999. *Interpreter of Maladies: Stories of Bengal, Boston and Beyond*. New Delhi: Harper Collins India.

Le Goff, Jacques. 1992. *History and Memory*. Translated by Steven Rendall and Elizabeth Claman. (European Perspectives.). New York: Columbia University Press.

Lee, Kerwin Klein. 2000. "On the Emergence of Memory in Historical Discourse." *Representations, No. 69, Special Issue: Grounds for Remembering* (Winter): 127–50.

Lefebvre, Alain. 2014. *Kinship, Honour and Money in Rural Pakistan*. London: Routledge.

Lefebvre, Henri. 1991. *The Production of Space*. Translated by Donald Nicholson and Smith. Oxford: Wiley-Blackwell.

Levi, Giovanni. 2001. "On Microhistory." In *New Perspectives on Historical Writing*, edited by Peter Burke, 97–119. Cambridge, MA: Polity Press.

Levi-Strauss, Claude. 1966. *La Pensee sauvage* (Paris, 1962). Translated by George Weidenfield & Nicolson, Ltd, *The Savage Mind*. Chicago: University of Chicago Press.

———. 1968. *L'Origine des Manieres de Table. Part II, Chapter 2*. Paris: Plon.

———. 1969. *The Elementary Structures of Kinship*. Boston: Beacon Press.

Leys, Ruth. 2011. "The Turn to Affect: A Critique." *Critical Inquiry* 37 (3): 434–72.

Louch, A. R. 1969. "History as Narrative." *History and Theory* 8 (1): 54–70.

Lowenthal, David. 1985. *The Past is a Foreign Country*. Cambridge, MA and New York: Cambridge University Press.

Luther, Narendra. 2017. "Lahore, His Camelot." *The Hindu*, June 15. Accessed December 10, 2018. www.thehindu.com/todays-paper/tp-features/tp-metroplus/lahore-his-camelot/article19052367.ece.

Luthra, P. N. 1971. "Problem of Refugees from East Bengal." *Economic and Political Weekly* 6 (50): 2467–72. Accessed December 10, 2018. www.jstor.org/stable/4382855.

Lynch, Kevin. 1960. *Image of the City*. Cambridge, MA: MIT Press.

Malhotra, Anchal. 2017. *Remnants of a Separation. A History of the Partition through Material Memory*. New Delhi: Harper Collins.

Malhotra, Balraj Bahri. Diksha Sahni and Nikita Mehta. 2011. "Delhi's Refugees: The Story of Bahrisons Bookshop." *Hindustan Times*, December 12. Accessed December 10, 2018. https://blogs.wsj.com/indiarealtime/2011/12/12/delhis-refugees-the-story-of-bahrisons-bookshop/.

Malhotra, Vijay Kumar. 2013. "When Humanity Died a Thousand Deaths." *The Pioneer*, August. Accessed November 15, 2017. www.dailypioneer.com/columnists/big-stor/when-humanity-died-a-thousand-deaths.html.

Malinowski, Bronislaw. 1920. "Kula; The Circulating Exchange of Valuables in the Archipelagoes of Eastern New Guinea." *Man* 20.

Malkin, Victoria. 2004. "'We Go to Get Ahead': Gender and Status in Two Mexican Migrant Communities." *Latin American Perspectives* 31 (5): 75–99.

Malkki, Liisa. 1991. *Purity and Exile: Violence, Memory and National Cosmology among Hutu Refugees in Tanzania*. Chicago: University of Chicago Press.

———. 1992. "National Geographic: The Rooting of Peoples and the Territorialization of National Identity Among Scholars and Refugees." *Cultural Anthropology* 7 (1): 24–44, February.

_____. 1995. "Refugees and Exile: From 'Refugee Studies' to the National Order of Things." *Annual Review of Anthropology* 24: 495–523.

———. 1996. "Speechless Emissaries: Refugees, Humanitarianism, and Dehistoricization." *Cultural Anthropology* 11: 377–404.

_____. 2002. "News from Nowhere: Mass Displacement and Globalized 'problems of Organization'." *Ethnography* 3 (3): 351–60.

Mallett, Shelley. 2004. "Understanding Home: A Critical Review of the Literature." *The Sociological Review* 52 (1): 62–89.

Mamdani, Mahmood. 1973. *From Citizen to Refugee: Uganda Asians Come to Britain.* London: Frances Pinter (Publishers) Ltd.

Mandelbaum, Maurice. 2001. "A Note on History as Narrative." In *The History and Narrative Reader Responsibility,* edited by Geoffrey Roberts. London: Routledge.

Mann, Babbu. 2017. "Baarish ke Bahane." *Baarish ke Bahane.* Mumbai: Zee Music Company.

Mansergh, Nicholas. 1983. *The Transfer of Power 1942-7: The Mountbatten Viceroyalty, Princes, Partition, and Independence,* 8 July–15 August 1947. London: H.M. Stationery Office.

Manto, Sa'adat Hasan. 1994. ""Khol Do". (trans.), Alok Bhalla, as "Open It"." In *Stories about the Partition of India,* Vol. II, edited by Alok Bhalla. New Delhi: Harper Collins.

———. 1994. ""Siyah Hashiye". (trans.), Alok Bhalla, as "Blank Margins"." In *Stories about the Partition of India,* Vol. I, edited by Alok Bhalla. New Delhi: Harper Collins.

———. 1994. ""Thanda Ghosht". (trans.), Alok Bhalla, as "Cold Meat"." In *Stories about the Partition India,* Vol. I, edited by Alok Bhalla, 91–97. New Delhi: Harper Collins.

———. 1994. ""Toba Tek Singh" (Urdu). (trans.), Tahira Naqvi." In *Stories about the Partition of India,* Vol. III, edited by Alok Bhalla. New Delhi: Harper Collins.

Massumi, Brian. 1995. "The Autonomy of Affect." *Cultural Critique, No. 31, The Politics of Systems and Environments, Part II* (Autumn): 83–109.

Matsuda, Matt K. 1996. *The Memory of the Modern.* New York: Oxford University Press.

Mauss, Marcel. 1950. *The Gift: Forms and Functions of Exchange in Archaic Societies.* with an Introduction by E. E. Evans-Pritchard, Essai sur le Don in Sociologie et Anthropologie Published by Presses Universitaires de France Paris.

———. 1997. *Resisting Regimes: Myth, Memory and the Shaping of a Muslim Identity.* New York: Oxford University Press.

Mayaram, Shail. 2004. *Against History, Against State: Counterperspectives from the Margins.* New York: Columbia University Press.

Meagher, Michelle. 2003. "Jenny Saville and a Feminist Aesthetics of Disgust." *Hypatia* 18 (4): 23–41.

Mehta, Siloo. 2010. "Memories of the North." *The Hindu,* August 14. Accessed December 10, 2018. www.thehindu.com/features/friday-review/history-and-culture/Memories-of-the-North/article16131957.ece.

Mehta, Ved. 2007. "How I Became A Pseudo – Secularist." *The Outlook,* November 19. Accessed December 10, 2018. www.outlookindia.com/magazine/story/how-i-became-a-pseudo-secularist/236027.

Menon, Jisha. 2013. *Performance of Nationalism: India, Pakistan and the Memory of Partition.* Cambridge, MA: Cambridge University Press.

Menon, Ritu. 2003. "Birth of Social Security Commitments: What Happened in the West." In *Refugee and the State: Practices of Asylum and Care in India,* edited Ranabir Samaddar. New Delhi: Sage.

Menon, Ritu and Kamla Bhasin. 1998. *Borders and Boundaries: How Women Experienced the Partition of India.* Brunswick, N J: Rutgers University Press.

Menon, V. P. 1961. *The Story of the Integration of the Indian States.* Bombay: Orient Longmans.

Middleton, David. 2002. "Succession and Change in the Socio-Cultural Use of Memory: Building-In the Past in Communicative Action." *Culture & Psychology* 8 (1): 79–95.

Miraj, Muhammad Hassan. 2013. "Lyallpur – A City on the Hill." *Dawn*, April 29. Accessed December 10, 2018. www.dawn.com/news/1025756.

Moon, Penderel. 1961. *Divide and Quit: An Eye-Witness Account of the Partition of India*. London: Chatto & Windus.

Mooney, Nicola. 2008. "Of Love, Martyrdom and (in)-Subordination: Sikh Experiences of Partition in the Films Shaheed-e-Mohabbat and Gadar: Ek Prem Katha." In *Partitioned Lives: Narratives of Home, Displacement and Resettlement*, edited by Anjali Gera Roy and Nandi Bhatia, 26–49. New Delhi: Pearson Longman.

Moore, Robin. 1974. *The Crisis of Indian Unity, 1917–1940*. Oxford: Clarendon Press.

Mukherjee-Leonard, Debali. 2008. "The Diminished Man: Partition and 'Transcendental Homelessness'." In *Partitioned Lives: Narratives of Home, Displacement and Resettlement*, edited by Anjali Gera Roy and Nandi Bhatia, 50–64. New Delhi: Pearson Longman.

Müller, Max. 1879. "Brihadaranyaka Upanishad." *The Upanishads, Part 2* (SBE15). Accessed December 10, 2018. sacred-texts.com.

Murphy, H. B. M., Ed. 1955. *Flight and Resettlement*. New York: Columbia University Press.

Myers, Garth. 1996. "Naming and Placing the Other: Power and the Urban Landscape in Zanzibar." *Tijdschrift voor Economische en Sociale Geografie* 87 (3): 237–46.

Nayak, Siddhi. 2017. "Unbox Happiness." *Outlook India*, April 8. Accessed December 12, 2018. www.outlookbusiness.com/enterprise/regional-brand/unbox-happiness-3507.

Naithani, Priyanka. 2011. "Karachi Sweet Mart: Adding a 'Namkeen Mithaas' to Pune Since 1948." *DNA*, September 25. Accessed December 12, 2018. www.dnaindia.com/mumbai/report-karachi-sweet-mart-adding-a-namkeen-mithaas-to-pune-since-1948-1591328.

Nanda, Reena. 2018. *From Quetta to Delhi: A Partition Story*. New Delhi: Bloomsbury.

Nandy, Ashis. 1995. "History's Forgotten Doubles." *History & Theory* 34 (2): 44–66.

Naqvi, Tahir Hasnain. 2012. "Migration, Sacrifice and the Crisis of Muslim Nationalism." *Journal of Refugee Studies* 25 (3): 474–90.

Nath, Damini. 2014. "Partition Refugee Colonies Can Finally Get Building Plans Cleared." *The Hindu*. Accessed December 10, 2018. www.thehindu.com/news/cities/Delhi/Partition-refugee-colonies-can-finally-get-building-plans-cleared/article6198948.ece.

Navarro, Zander. 2006. "In Search of a Cultural Interpretation of Power: The Contribution of Pierre Bourdieu". *IDS Bulletin* 37(6): 11–22.

Nehru, Jawaharlal. 1972. *Selected Works of Jawaharlal Nehru (SWJN), Vol. 4: A Project of the Jawaharlal Nehru Project Fund*. Hyderabad: Orient Longman.

Neville, Pran. 2003. "Memories of Pre-1947 Lahore." Khalid Hasan. *Daily Times,* Friday, January 3. Accessed December 10, 2018. http://apnaorg.com/prose-content/english-articles/page-118/article-5/index.html.

Ngai, Sianne. 2005. *Ugly Feelings*. Cambridge, MA: Harvard University Press.

Nisbett, R. E. and D. Cohen. 1996. *Culture of Honor: The Psychology of Violence in the South*. Boulder, CO: Westview Press.

Nixon, Deborah and Devleena Ghosh. 2008. "Fires in the Kangra: A British Soldier's Story of Partition." In *Partitioned Lives: Narratives of Home, Displacement and Resettlement*, edited by Anjali Gera Roy and Nandi Bhatia. New Delhi: Pearson Longman.

Noorani, A. G. 2012. "Horrors of Partition." *Frontline* 29 (4) February 25-March 09. Accessed December 10, 2018. https://frontline.thehindu.com/static/html/fl2904/stories/20120309290407300.htm.

Nora, Pierre. 1989. "Between Memory and History: Les Lieux De Mémoire." *Representations* 26: 7–24.

————, Ed. 1996. *Realms of Memory: Rethinking the French Past (Vol. I: Conflicts and Divisions)*. New York: Columbia University Press.

Novick, Peter. 1988. *That Noble Dream: The "Objectivity Question" and the American Historical Profession*. New York: Cambridge University Press.

Nussbaum, Martha. 2004. *Hiding from Humanity: Disgust, Shame, and the Law*. Princeton, NJ: Princeton University Press.

Nyers, Peter. 2006. "Taking Rights, Mediating Wrongs: Disagreements over the Political Agency of Non-Status Refugees." In *The Politics of Protection: Sites of Insecurity and Political Agency*, edited by Jef Huysmans, Andrew Dobson, and Raia Prokhovnik, 48–67. London: Routledge.

Oberoi, Harjot. 1993. *The Construction of Religious Boundaries: Culture, Identity, and Diversity in the Sikh Tradition*. New York: Oxford University Press.

Oberoi, Naintara Maya. 2015. "What Does it Mean to be a Punjabi." In *Excerpt from Chillies and Porridge: Writing Food*, edited by Mita Kapur. New Delhi: Harper Collins.

Olick, Jeffrey K. 2007. *The Politics of Regret: On Collective Memory and Historical Responsibility*. New York: Routledge.

———— and Joyce Robbins. 1998. "Social Memory Studies: From "Collective Memory" to the Historical Sociology of Mnemonic Practices." *Annual Review of Sociology* 24: 105–40.

————, Vered Vinitzky-Seroussi, and Daniel Levy, Eds. 2011. *The Collective Memory Reader*. New York: Oxford University Press.

Olivius, Elisabeth. 2014. "(Un)Governable Subjects: The Limits of Refugee Participation in the Promotion of Gender Equality in Humanitarian Aid." *Journal of Refugee Studies* 27 (1): 42–61, 1 March.

"Oral History Association." Accessed December 10, 2018. www.oralhistory.org/about/do-oral-history/.

Page, David. 1998. *Prelude to Partition: The Indian Muslims and the Imperial System of Control, 1920–32*. New Delhi: Oxford University Press.

Pandey, Gyanendra. 1992. "In Defense of the Fragment: Writing about Hindu-Muslim Riots in India Today." *Representations* 37: 27–55, Winter.

————. 1997. "Partition and Independence in Delhi: 1947–48." *Economic and Political Weekly* 32 (36): 2261–72, September 6–12.

————. 2001. *Remembering Partition: Violence, Nationalism and History in India*. Cambridge: Cambridge University Press.

Papastergiadis, Nikos. 2006. "The Invasion Complex: The Abject Other and Spaces of Violence." *Geografiska Annaler. Series B, Human Geography* 88 (4): 429–42.

"Papers and Correspondence with A.P Jain", (M/o Rehabilitation) Relating to The Rehabilitation Scheme and Grant of Compensation to Displaced Persons from West Pakistan (1952–53)." S. No. 64 N. Gopalaswamy Ayyangar Papers, NMML.

Parry, Jonathan. 1986. "The Gift, the Indian Gift and the 'Indian Gift'." *Man. New Series* 21 (3): 453–73, September.

Paul, Joginder. 2017. In "A Dialogue: Gulzar and Joginder Paul on Partition and their Fiction." Gulzar. Footprints on Zero Line: Writings on the Partition. Translated by Rakshanda Jalil. Delhi: Harper Perennial.

————, Sunil Trivedi, and Sukrita Paul Kumar. 2007. "From Sleepwalkers." *Manoa* 19 (1): 144–47. Accessed December 10, 2018. https://muse.jhu.edu/.

Philips, Cyril Henry. 1962. *The Evolution of India and Pakistan (1858–1947)*. London: Oxford University Press.

———— and Mary D. Wainwright. 1970. *The Partition of India: Policies and Perspectives, 1935–1947*. London: Allen & Unwind.

Pickering, Michael and Emily Keightley. 2006. "The Modalities of Nostalgia." *Current Sociology* 54 (6): 919–41.

———. 2015. *Photography, Music and Memory: Pieces of the Past in Everyday Life (Palgrave Macmillan Memory Studies)*. Basingstoke: Palgrave Macmillan.

Pile, Steve. 2010. "*Emotions and Affect* in Recent Human Geography." *Transactions of the Institute of British Geographers* 35 (1): 5–20.

Plato. 360 B.C. *Phaedrus*. Translated by Benjamin Jowett. Accessed November 15, 2017. http://classics.mit.edu/Plato/phaedrus.html.

Pocock, D. C. D. 1972. "City of the Mind: A Review of Mental Maps of Urban Areas." *Scottish Geographical Magazine* 88: 2.

Portelli, Alessandro. 1991. *The Death of Luigi Trastulli and Other Stories: Form and Meaning in Oral History*. Albany, NY: SUNY Press.

———. 2005. "A Dialogical Relationship: An Approach to Oral History." In *Expressions Annual*, edited by Manish Jain. Accessed December 10, 2018. www.swaraj.org/shikshantar/expressions_toc.htm.

———. 2009. "What Makes Oral History Different." In *Oral History, Oral Culture, and Italian Americans. Italian and Italian American Studies*, edited by L. D. Giudice. New York: Palgrave Macmillan.

———. 2014. "On the Uses of Memory: As Monument, as Reflex, as Disturbance." *Economic and Political Weekly* 49 (30): 43–47, 26 July.

Porteous, Douglas J. 1985. "Smellscape." *Progress in Physical Geography: Earth and Environment* 9 (3): 356–78.

———. 1990. *Landscapes of the Mind: Worlds of Sense of Metaphor*. Toronto: University of Toronto Press.

Pritam, Amrita. 2003 [1950]. *Pinjar*. New Delhi: Hind Pocket Books.

Punwani, Jyoti. 2009. "Sweet Karachi." *Indian Express*, January 31. Accessed December 12, 2018. https://indianexpress.com/article/opinion/columns/sweet-karachi/.

Rai, Satya M. 1965. *Partition of the Punjab: A Study of its Effects on the Politics and Administration of the Punjab: 1947–56*. New Delhi: Asia Publishing House.

———. 1986. *Punjab Since Partition*. New Delhi: Durga Publications.

Raj, Dhooleka S. 2000. "Ignorance, Forgetting, and Family Nostalgia: Partition, the Nation State, and Refugees in Delhi." *Social Analysis* 44 (2): 30–35.

Ram, Ronki. 2012. "Beyond Conversion and Sanskritisation: Articulating an Alternative Dalit Agenda in East Punjab." *Modern Asian Studies* 46 (3): 639–702.

Randhawa, Mohan Singh. 1954. *Out of the Ashes: An Account of Rehabilitation of Refugees from West. Punjab in Rural Areas of East Punjab*. Bombay: New Jack Printing.

Ray, Manas. 2008. "Growing Up Refugee: On Memory and Locality." In *Partitioned Lives: Narratives of Home, Displacement and Resettlement*, edited by Anjali Gera Roy and Nandi Bhatia. New Delhi: Pearson Longman.

Rebeiro, Sydney. 2013. "India in the 1940s: The Way We Were." *Hindustan Times*, compiled by Aasheesh Sharma, Saudamini Jain, Shreya Sethuraman, Rachel Lopez, and Amrah Ashraf. August 10. Accessed December 10, 2018. www.hindustantimes.com/brunch/india-in-the-1940s-the-way-we-were/story-6YvIKdsJU1haXzYJbOJEML.html.

"Rehabilitation of Displaced Persons." "Chapter 38. First Five Year Plan." *Five Year Plans*. Planning Commission. Government of India. Accessed December 10, 2018. http://planningcommission.nic.in/plans/planrel/fiveyr/1st/1planch38.html.

"Report of the Progress of Education in the Punjab." 1950. Shimla.

"Report on the Working of the Relief and Rehabilitation Committee, Patiala, From 6th April, 1947 to 25th February, 1948." 1949. Shimla: The Publicity Department, Government of Punjab.

Ricoeur, Paul. 2006. *Memory, History, Forgetting*. Translated by Kathleen Blamey and David Pellauer. Chicago: University of Chicago Press.

Riffaterre, Michael. 1984. "Intertextual Representation: On Mimesis as Interpretive Discourse." *Critical Inquiry* 11 (1): 141–62.

Rodoway, Paul. 1994. *Sensuous Geographies: Body, Sense, and Place*. London: Routledge.

Rogg, Eleanor Meyer. 1974. *The Assimilation of Cuban Exiles: The Role of Community and Class*. New York: Aberdeen.

Rohatgi, Vijay. "Memories of Chandni Chowk and India's First Independence Day." *Dadinani.com*. Accessed December 10, 2018. www.dadinani.com/images/pdf/rohatgi/chandnichowk.pdf.

Rothman, Lily. 2017. "How India Celebrated Its First Independence Day 70 Years Ago." *Time*, August. Accessed December 10, 2018. http://time.com/4891743/india-independence-1947/.

Roy, Anjali. 2000. "Microstoria: Indian Nationalism's "Little Stories" in Amitav Ghosh's The Shadow Lines." *Journal of Commonwealth Literature* 35 (3): 35–49.

Roy, Haimanti. 2012. *Partitioned Lives: Migrants, Refugees, Citizens in India and Pakistan, 1947–65*. New Delhi: Oxford University Press.

Royle, Nicholas. 2003. *The Uncanny*. Manchester: Manchester University Press.

Rushdie, Salman. 1982. *Midnight's Children*. London: Pan Books.

———. 1983. *Shame*. London: Picador.

———. 1991. "Imaginary Homelands." *From Imaginary Homelands: Essays and Criticism 1981–1991*. London: Granta.

Rybczynski, Witold. 1986. *Home: A Short History of an Idea*. Markham, Ontario: Viking Penguin Books.

Safi, Michael. 2017. "India's Partition: 'People in Their Final Years are Desperate to Open Up." *The Observer, India*. August. Accessed December 10, 2018. www.theguardian.com/world/2017/aug/05/india-Partition-people-in-final-years-desperate-open-up.

Said, Edward W. 1994. *Representations of the Intellectual*. New York: Pantheon Books.

———. 2000. "Invention, Memory, and Place." *Critical Inquiry* 26 (2): 175–92.

———. 2001. *Reflections on Exile and other Literary and Cultural Essays*. New Delhi: Penguin Books.

———. 2005 [1978]. *Orientalism*. London and New York: Penguin Books.

Saifi, Sofia. 2017. "A Taste of India in the Heart of Pakistan." *CNN*, August 10. Accessed December 10, 2018. https://edition.cnn.com/2017/08/08/world/taste-of-delhi-in-karachi/index.html.

Sangari, Kumkum. 2011. "Viraha: A Trajectory in the Nehruvian Era." In *Poetics and Politics of Sufism and Bhakti in South Asia: Love, Loss and Liberation First*, edited by Kavita Panjabi, 256–87. Hyderabad: Orient Blackswan.

Sangat Singh. 2016. "Lyallpur is in their Hearts – Part 1." *India of the Past: Preserving Memories of India and Indians*, June 7. Accessed December 10, 2018. www.indiaofthepast.org/contribute-memories/read-contributions/life-back-then/524-lyallpur-is-in-their-hearts-part-1.

Sarkar, Bhaskar. 2009. *Mourning the Nation: Indian Cinema in the Wake of Partition*. Durham, NC: Duke University Press.

Sarre, Phillip. 1972. "Perception". *In Channels of Synthesis: Perception and Diffusion*, edited by Phillip Saree and Geoffrey Edge. Bletchley: The Open University Press.

Scheller, Mimi. 2014. "The New Mobilities Paradigm for a Live Sociology." *Current Sociology* 62 (6): 789–811.

Scheper-Hughes, Nancy and Philippe Bourgois, Eds. 2004. "Introduction." In *Violence in War and Peace: An Anthology*. Oxford: Wiley-Blackwell.

Schwartz, Barry. 1996. "Memory as a Cultural System: Abraham Lincoln in World War II." *American Sociological Review* 61 (5): 908–27.

Sealy, Allan. 1988. *The Trotternama*. New York: Alford A. Knopf.

Sehgal, Madan Mohan. 2017. *In Search of Justice: Memoirs of an NRI Who was made to Pay the Price for Being an Entrepreneur in India (As Narrated to Geeta Sahai)*. Delhi: Educreation Publishing.

Sengupta, Debjani. 2015. *The Partition of Bengal: Fragile Borders and New Identities*. New Delhi: Cambridge University Press.

Seth, Pran. 2010. *Lahore to Delhi: Rising from the Ashes*. Bangalore: Punya Publishing Private Limited. Accessed December 10, 2018. www.pranseth.com/Home/Chapter-2.

Sethi, Jatinder Pal. 2012. "My Memories of Lyallpur." *India of the Past*. Accessed December 10, 2018. www.indiaofthepast.org/contribute-memories/read-contributions/life-back-then/310-my-memories-of-lyallpur.

Sharma, Sunil. 2000. *Persian Poetry at the Indian Frontier: Mas'ūd Sa'd Salmān of Lahore*. New Delhi: Permanent Black.

———. 2004. "The City of Beauties in the Indo-Persian Poetic Landscape." *Comparative Studies of South Asia, Africa and the Middle East* 24 (2): 73–81.

Sharma, Vibha. 2018. "12,000 Properties in Delhi's Key Refugee Colonies May Face Sealing." *Hindustan Times*, New Delhi, March 21. Accessed December 10, 2018. www.hindustantimes.com/delhi-news/12-000-properties-in-delhi-s-key-refugee-colonies-may-face-sealing/story-h1am3WIOzy8sYpO8SjbteL.html.

Sheikh, Majid. 2014. "Harking Back: Sharing Memories of A 'Paradise' Lost Forever." *Dawn*, August 24. Accessed December 10, 2018. www.dawn.com/news/1127334.

Shokouhian, M. F. Soflaee and F. Nikkhah. 2007. "Environmental Effects of Courtyards in Sustainable Architecture of Iran (Cold Regions)." Accessed December 10, 2018. www.inive.org/members_area/medias/pdf/inive/palencaivc2007/volume2/palencaivc2007_v2_075.pdf.

Shouse, Eric. 2005. "Feeling, Emotion, Affect". *M/C Journal* 8 (6): 1–5. Accessed December 10, 2018. http://journal.media-culture.org.au/0512/03-shouse.php.

Shroff, Shunali Khullar. 2017. "Jinney Lahore nahi Vekhiya . . ." March 2. *Conde Naste Traveller*. Accessed December 10, 2018. www.cntraveller.in/story/jinney-lahore-nahi-vekhiya/.

Shukla, Vivek. 2017. "Ramlila Keeps the Urdu Tradition Alive." *The Tribune*, September 23. Accessed December 10, 2018. www.tribuneindia.com/news/comment/ramlila-keeps-the-urdu-tradition-alive/471301.html.

Simmel, Georg. 1971. "The Stranger." In *On Individuality and Social Forms*, edited by Donald N. Levine, 143–50. Chicago: University of Chicago Press.

Simpson, J. 1938. "The Refugee Problem." *International Affairs (Royal Institute of International Affairs 1931–1939)* 17 (5): 607–28.

Singh, Gurmukh and Mukhtiar Singh Gill. 1994. *Punjabi-English Dictionary*. Edited by S. S. Joshi and Mukhtiar Singh Gill. Patiala: Punjabi University Publication Bureau.

Singh, Amardeep. 2016. *Lost Heritage: The Sikh Legacy in Pakistan*. Himalayan Books.

Singh, Harbhajan. 2006. In Srivastava, Ashutosh. "Punjab Rhymes with Nawab." *Hindustan Times*, October 13. Accessed December 10, 2018. www.hindustantimes.com/india/punjab-rhymes-with-nawab/story-OKbS7UycGZzkDbiPMCp39J.html.

Singh, Harmeet Shah. 2017. "Why It's Worth Remembering Partition this Independence Day?" *Daily O*, August 8. Accessed December 10, 2018. www.dailyo.in/politics/Partition-independence-day-august-15-pakistan/story/1/18826.html.

Singh, Mehar. 2004. "The Changing Rural House Type of Punjab: An Expression of Socio-Economic and Cultural Change." In *Cultural Geography Form and Process (Essays in Honour of Prof A. B. Mukerji)*, edited by Neelam Grover and Kashi Nath Singh, 75–96. New Delhi: Concept Publishing Co.

Sinha-Kerkhoff, Kathinka. 2004. "From 'Displaced Person' to being 'a Local': Cross Border Refugees and Invisible Refugees in Ranchi." In *State, Society and Displaced People in South Asia*, edited by Imtiaz Ahmed, Abhijit Dasgupta, and Kathinka Sinha-Kerkhoff, 149–68. Dhaka: University Press Limited.

Six, Clemens. 2018. *Secularism, Decolonisation, and the Cold War in South and Southeast Asia*. London: Routledge.

Smith, Michael P. 1994. "Can You Imagine? Transnational Migration and the Globalization of Grassroots Politics." *Social Text* (39): 15–33.

———. 2016. Explorations in Urban Theory. New Brunswick: Transaction Publishers.

Soguk, Nevzat. 1999. *States and Strangers. Refugees and Displacements of Statecraft*. Minneapolis: University of Minnesota Press.

Somerville, Peter. 1992. "Homelessness and the Meaning of Home: Rooflessness or Rootlessness?" *International Journal of Urban and Regional Research* 16 (4): 529–39.

Sorokin, Pitirim A. 1964. *The Basic Trends of Our Times*. New Haven, CT: College and University Press Services.

Srivastava, Anupam. 2006. "Punjab Rhymes with Nawab." *Hindustan Times*, October 13. Accessed December 10, 2018. www.hindustantimes.com/india/punjab-rhymes-with-nawab/story-OKbS7UycGZzkDbiPMCp39J.html.

Stancati, Margherita and Ehsanullah Amiri. 2015. "Facing Intolerance, Many Sikhs and Hindus Leave Afghanistan." *The Wall Street Journal*, January 12. Accessed December 10, 2018. www.wsj.com/articles/facing-intolerance-many-sikhs-and-hindus-leave-afghanistan-1421124144.

Stein, Barry N. 1981. "The Refugee Experience: Defining the Parameters of a Field of Study." *The International Migration Review* 15 (1/2): 320–30, Refugees Today (Spring – Summer).

Stevenson, Nick. 2003. *Cultural Citizenship: Cosmopolitan Questions*. Maidenhead and Berkshire: Open University Press.

Stewart, Kathleen. 1988. "Nostalgia – A Polemic." *Cultural Anthropology* 3 (3): 227–41.

Stewart, Susan. 1984. *On Longing: Narratives of the Miniature, the Gigantic, the Souvenir, the Collection*. Baltimore, MD: John Hopkins University Press.

Stoller, Paul. 1995. *Spirit Possession, Power and the Harka in West Africa*. New York: Routledge.

———. 1997. *Sensuous Scholarship*. Philadelphia: University of Pennsylvania Press.

Suleiman, Susan. 2002. "The 1.5 Generation: Thinking about Child Survivors and the Holocaust." *American Imago* 59 (3).

Sullivan, Robert E. 2016. *Geography Speaks: Performative Aspects of Geography*. Aldershot: Ashgate.

Suri, Brinda. 2016. "Multan Lives in Delhi." *The Hindu: Business Line*, September 30. Accessed December 10, 2018. www.thehindubusinessline.com/blink/takeaway/multan-lives-in-delhi/article21703593.ece1.

Tai, Yong Tan and Gyanesh Kudaisya. 2004. *The Aftermath of Partition in South Asia*. London: Routledge.

Talbot, Ian. 1995. "Literature and the Human Drama of the 1947 Partition." *South Asia: Journal of South Asian Studies* 18 (sup001): 37–56.

————. 1996. *Freedom's Cry: The Popular Dimension in the Pakistan Movement and Partition Experience in North-West India.* Karachi: Oxford University Press.

————. 2006. *Divided Cities: Partition and Its Aftermath in Lahore and Amritsar 1947–1957.* Karachi: Oxford University Press.

————. 2007. "The Punjab under Colonialism: Order and Transformation in British India." *Journal of Punjab Studies* 14 (1): 3–10.

————. 2011. "Punjabi Refugees' Rehabilitation and the Indian State: Discourses, Denials and Dissonances." *Modern Asian Studies* 45 (1): 109–30, (From Subjects to Citizens: Society and the Everyday State in India and Pakistan, 1947–1970). January.

Terdiman, Richard. 1993. *Present Past: Modernity and the Memory Crisis.* Ithaca and London: Cornell University Press.

Thapliyal, Mansi. 2017. "The Friendship that Survived the Division of a Nation." *BBC,* August 4. Accessed December 10, 2018. www.bbc.com/news/world-asia-india-40749476.

Thompson, Willie. 2004. *Postmodernism and History.* Basingstoke: Palgrave Macmillan.

Thrift, Nigel. 2004. "Intensities of Feeling: Towards A Spatial Politics of Affect." *Geografiska Annaler: Series B, Human Geography* 86 (1): 57–78.

————. 2007. *Non-representational Theory: Space, Politics, Affect.* London and New York: Routledge.

TNN. 2004. "Major Fire at Mohan Market". *Times of India.* April 10. Accessed December 10, 2018. https://timesofindia.indiatimes.com/city/lucknow/Major-fire-at-Mohan-Market/articleshow/609235.cms

————. 2011. "Mianwali Colony: Rooted in History, Embracing the Future." *Times of India,* January 23. Accessed December 10, 2018. https://timesofindia.indiatimes.com/city/gurgaon/Mianwali-Colony-Rooted-in-history-embracing-the-future/articleshow/7343425.cms?utm_source=contentofinterest&utm_medium=text&utm_campaign=cppst.

TNS. 2009. "Pingalwara Society Recreates Charm of Forgotten Culture 'Trinjhan'". SSN News. Sikhsangat.Org. Accessed December 10, 2018. http://sikhsangat.org/2009/pingalwara-society-recreates-charm-of-forgotten-culture-%E2%80%98trinjhan%E2%80%99/

Tolman, Edward C. 1948. "Cognitive Maps in Rats and Men." *The Psychological Review* 55 (4): 189–208.

Tomsky, Terri. 2008. "Fifty Years On: Melancholic (Re)collections and Women's Voices from the Partition of India." *Life Writing* 5 (1): 61–78.

Tonkin, Elizabeth. 1991. *Narrating Our Pasts: The Social Construction of Oral History.* Cambridge, MA: Cambridge University Press.

Tuan, Yi-Fu. 1974. *Topophilia.* Englewood Cliffs, NJ: Prentice-Hall.

————. 1977. *Space and Place: The Perspective of Experience.* Minneapolis: University of Minnesota Press.

————. 1979. *Space and Place: The Perspective of Experience.* Minneapolis: University of Minnesota Press.

Tuker, Francis. 1950. *While Memory Serves.* London: Cassell Publications.

Turner, Bryan S. 1987. "A Note on Nostalgia." *Theory, Culture and Society* 4 (1): 147–56.

Tyler, Imogen. 2013. *Revolting Subjects: Social Abjection and Resistance in Neoliberal Britain.* London and New York: Zed Books.

Underwood, Benton J. 1969. "Attributes of Memory." *Psychological Review* 76 (6): 559–73.

Upton, Dell, Ed. 1986. *America's Architectural Roots: Ethnic Groups that Built America.* Washington, DC: Preservation Press.

Van Der Horst, Hilje and Jantine Messing. 2006. " 'It's Not Dutch to Close the Curtains': Visual Struggles on the Threshold Between Public and Private in a Multi-Ethnic Dutch Neighborhood." *Home Cultures* 3 (1): 21–37.

Veyne, Paul. 1984. *Writing History: Essay on Epistemology*. Translated By Mina Moore-Rinvolucri. Manchester: Manchester University Press.

Virdee, Pippa. 2008. "Partition in Transition: Comparative Analysis of Migration in Ludhiana and Lyallpur." In *Partitioned Lives: Narratives of Home, Displacement and Resettlement*, edited by Anjali Gera Roy and Nandi Bhatia. New Delhi: Pearson Longman.

———. 2018. *From the Ashes of 1947: Reimagining Punjab*. Cambridge, MA: Cambridge University Press.

Vohra, Paromita. 2016. "Lahore: In Search of 150, Anarkali." *Livemint*, April 23. Accessed December 10, 2018. www.livemint.com/Leisure/51FGNwLSrG77uprf7TH1aI/Lahore-In-search-of-150-Anarkali.html.

Vora, Rustam. 2016. "Tongue-tied in Sindhi." *The Hindu Business Line*, April 01. Accessed December 10, 2018. www.thehindubusinessline.com/blink/know/tonguetied-in-sindhi/article8418394.ece.

Vygotsky, Lev S. 1929. "The Problem of the Cultural Development of the Child." *Journal of Genetic Psychology* 36: 415–34.

WSJ Staff. 2011. "Picture Focus: Delhi, a City of Refugees". *The Wall Street Journal*, December 9. Accessed December 10, 2018, https://blogs.wsj.com/indiarealtime/2011/12/09/picture-focus-delhi-a-city-of-refugees/.

Wakil, Parvez A. 1970. "Explorations into the Kin-Networks of the Punjabi Society: A Preliminary Statement." *Journal of Marriage and Family* 32 (4): 700–07, Decade Review. Part 1 November.

Walters, William. 2008. "Acts of Demonstration: Mapping the Territory of (Non-)Citizenship." In *Acts of Citizenship*, edited by Engin G. Isin and Greg M. Neilson, 182–206. London: Zed Books.

Weiermair, K. 1971. "Economic Adjustment of Refugees in Canada: A Case Study." *International Migration* 9: 1–2, 5–35.

Werbner, Richard. 1998. *Memory and the Postcolony: African Anthropology and the Critique of Power*. London: Zed Books.

Whately, Richard. 1846. *Elements of Rhetoric: Substance of the Article in the Encyclopedia Metropolitana*. Oxford: W Baxter Published for John Murray London & J Parker Oxford.

White, Hayden. 1973. "Interpretation in History." *New Literary History* 4 (2): 281–314, On Interpretation: II (Winter).

———. 1966. "The Burden of History." *History and Theory* 5 (2): 111–34.

———. 1980. "The Value of Narrativity in the Representation of Reality." *Critical Inquiry* 7 (1): 5–27, On Narrative (Autumn, 1980).

———. 1984. "The Question of Narrative in Contemporary Historical Theory." *History and Theory* 23 (1): 1–33, February.

———. 1989. "The Rhetoric of Interpretation." In *The Rhetoric of Interpretation and the Interpretation of Rhetoric*, edited by Paul Hernadi, 1–22. Durham, NC: Duke University Press.

———. 1990. *The Content of the Form: Narrative Discourse and Historical Representation*. Baltimore and London: Johns Hopkins University Press.

———. 2014 [1973]. *Metahistory: The Historical Imagination in Nineteenth-Century Europe*. Baltimore: John Hopkins University Press.

Wilson, Elizabeth. 1997. "Looking Backward, Nostalgia and the City." In *Imagining Cities: Scripts, Signs, Memory*, edited by Sallie Westwood and John Williams. London and New York: Routledge.

Wright, Jr. Theodore P. 1974. "Hindu-Muslim Stereotypes in South Asia." *Journal of Asian and Middle Eastern Muslims* 3 (1): 1860–923.

————. 1974. "Indian Muslim Refugees in the Politics of Pakistan." *Journal of Commonwealth and Comparative Politics* 12 (2): 21–34.

Yates, Frances A. 1966. *The Art of Memory*. Chicago: University of Chicago Press.

Yusin, Jennifer and Deepika Bahri. 2008. "Writing Partition: Trauma and Testimony in Bapsi Sidhwa's Cracking India." In *Partitioned Lives: Narratives of Home, Displacement and Resettlement*, edited by Anjali Gera Roy and Nandi Bhatia. New Delhi: Pearson Longman.

Zachariah, Benjamin. 2001. "Rewriting Imperial Mythologies: The Strange Case of Penderel Moon." *South Asia: Journal of South Asian Studies* 24 (2): 53–72.

Zavaleta, Sarab Kaur. 2017. "Face of Partition, India 1947 The Mass Migration." *Sikh Foundation International*, September 10. Accessed December 10, 2018. www.sikhfoundation.org/people-events/face-of-Partition-india-1947-the-mass-migration/.

Zinkin, Taya. 1957. "Focus on the Bengali Refugees." *The Economic Weekly Annual*, January: 89–90. Accessed December 10, 2018. www.epw.in/system/files/pdf/1957_9/3-4-5/focus_on_the_bengali_refugees.pdf.

Films

Ali, Muzaffar (dir). 1986. *Anjuman*.

Ali, Shaad (dir). 2005. *Bunty aur Babli*.

Mehra, Rakeysh Omprakash. 2013. *Bhaag Milkha Bhaag*.

Nair, Mira (dir). 2001. *Monsoon Wedding*.

Interviews

Arora, Madan Lal. 2011. Age 78. Interviewed by Anjali Gera Roy. January 20. Lucknow.

Arora, Meherchand. 2017. Age 84. Interviewed by Oral History Intern Ankita Halder in Ranchi on August 12. "After Partition: Post-memories of Afterlife of Partition 1947", Indian Council of Social Science Research Major Project (2017–2018) awarded to Anjali Gera Roy.

Baldev Singh. 2017. Age 88. Interviewed by Oral History Intern Ankita Halder in Ranchi on August 12. "After Partition: Post-memories of Afterlife of Partition 1947", Indian Council of Social Science Research Major Project (2017–2018) awarded to Anjali Gera Roy.

Begum, Arch Fatimanissa. 2017. Age 78. Interviewed by Oral History Intern Bashir Ahmed in Thaskan Grong, Kargil Ladakh on July 7. "After Partition: Post-memories of Afterlife of Partition 1947", Indian Council of Social Science Research Major Project (2017–2018) awarded to Anjali Gera Roy.

Bishen Lal. 2017. Age 63. Interviewed by Oral History Intern Satyendra Raj in Lucknow on July 16. "After Partition: Post-memories of Afterlife of Partition 1947", Indian Council of Social Science Research Major Project (2017–2018) awarded to Anjali Gera Roy.

Chakraborty, Samir Kumar. 2017. Age 82. Interviewed by Oral History Intern Sumedha Bose in Kolkata on June 9. "After Partition: Post-memories of Afterlife of Partition 1947", Indian Council of Social Science Research Major Project (2017–2018) awarded to Anjali Gera Roy.

Chakravorty, Noni Gopal. 2017. Age 87. Interviewed by Oral History Intern Sumedha Bose in Kolkata on June 10. "After Partition: Post-memories of Afterlife of Partition

1947", Indian Council of Social Science Research Major Project (2017–2018) awarded to Anjali Gera Roy.

Chawla, Mohan. 2015. Interviewed by Oral History Intern Zenia Nanra in Jamshedpur on May 15.

Chowdhury, Nand Kishore. 2017. Age 82. Interviewed by Oral History Intern Ekata Biswas in Ranchi on December 19. "After Partition: Post-memories of Afterlife of Partition 1947", Indian Council of Social Science Research Major Project (2017–2018) awarded to Anjali Gera Roy.

Chugh, Kishenlal. 2017. Age 79. Interviewed by Oral History Intern Satyendra Raj in Lucknow on July 14. "After Partition: Post-memories of Afterlife of Partition 1947", Indian Council of Social Science Research Major Project (2017–2018) awarded to Anjali Gera Roy.

Deshi. 2005. Interviewed by Anjali Gera Roy. Bangalore. December 31.

———. 2012. Interviewed by Anjali Gera Roy. Bangalore. April 4.

———. 2018. Interviewed by Anjali Gera Roy. Bangalore. December 18.

Girdhar, Rishi Kesh. 2017. Age 87. Interviewed by Oral History Intern Ankita Halder in Ranchi on August 12. "After Partition: Post-memories of Afterlife of Partition 1947", Indian Council of Social Science Research Major Project (2017–2018) awarded to Anjali Gera Roy.

Gyan Kaur. 1982. Age 55. Interviewed by Deshi. Mumbai. August 14.

Harbans Singh. 2017. Aged 85. Interviewed by Oral History Intern Ankita Halder in Ranchi on August 12. "After Partition: Post-memories of Afterlife of Partition 1947", Indian Council of Social Science Research Major Project (2017–2018) awarded to Anjali Gera Roy.

Juneja, Ghanshyam Das. 2017. Age 75. Interviewed by Oral History Intern Ankita Halder in Ranchi on August 2. "After Partition: Post-memories of Afterlife of Partition 1947", Indian Council of Social Science Research Major Project (2017–2018) awarded to Anjali Gera Roy.

Kathuria, Sona. 2006. Interviewed by Anjali Gera Roy. March 18. Kalka.

Khanna, Satya Pal. 2015. Interviewed by Zain Ali. *The Partition 1947 Archive*.

Lennon, Olive. Age 92. 2017. Interviewed by Anjali Gera Roy in Kharagpur on August 18. "After Partition: Post-memories of Afterlife of Partition 1947", Indian Council of Social Science Research Major Project (2017-2018) awarded to Anjali Gera Roy.

Majumder, Jogesh Chandra. Age 82. 2017. Interviewed by Oral History Intern Kajri Raymahasay in Kolkata on June 10. "After Partition: Post-memories of Afterlife of Partition 1947", Indian Council of Social Science Research Major Project (2017–2018) awarded to Anjali Gera Roy.

Makkad, Govardhandas. 2017. Age 81. Interviewed by Oral History Intern Ekata Biswas in Ranchi on December 9. "After Partition: Post-memories of Afterlife of Partition 1947", Indian Council of Social Science Research Major Project (2017–2018) awarded to Anjali Gera Roy.

Manchanda, Shanti. 2011. Age 81. Interviewed by Anjali Gera Roy. Lucknow. January 20.

Mangal Singh. 2011. Age 78. Interviewed by Anjali Gera Roy. Lucknow. December 20.

Manorama. 2017. Age 80. Written Transcript sent to Oral History Intern Ayushi Aastha in Kolkata on December 20.

Mela Ram. 2013, December. Age 91. Anjali Gera Roy in Kashipur. January 20.

Meshi. 2006. Interviewed by Anjali Gera Roy. Kharagpur. July 21.

Midha, Balakram. 2017. Age 91. Interviewed by Oral History Intern Ekata Biswas in Ranchi on December 8. "After Partition: Post-memories of Afterlife of Partition 1947", Indian Council of Social Science Research Major Project (2017–2018) awarded to Anjali Gera.

Midha, Harish Chandra. 2017. Age 75. Interviewed by Oral History Intern Ankita Halder in Ranchi on December 28. "After Partition: Post-memories of Afterlife of Partition 1947", Indian Council of Social Science Research Major Project (2017–2018) awarded to Anjali Gera Roy.

Midha, Jairamdas. 2017. Age 84. Interviewed by Oral History Intern Ekata Biswas in Ranchi on December 9. "After Partition: Post-memories of Afterlife of Partition 1947", Indian Council of Social Science Research Major Project (2017–2018) awarded to Anjali Gera Roy.

Mohan, Brij. 2017. Age 87. Interviewed by Oral History Intern Ankita Halder in Ranchi on December 29. "After Partition: Post-memories of Afterlife of Partition 1947", Indian Council of Social Science Research Major Project (2017–2018) awarded to Anjali Gera Roy.

Mukherjee, Sova. 2017. Age 86. Interviewed by Oral History Intern Kajri Raymahasay in Kolkata on June 12. "After Partition: Post-memories of Afterlife of Partition 1947", Indian Council of Social Science Research Major Project (2017–2018) awarded to Anjali Gera Roy.

Nagpal, Lal Singh. 2017. Age 97. Interviewed by Oral History Intern Nayantara Gautam. Pai, Karnal in August. "After Partition: Post-memories of Afterlife of Partition 1947", Indian Council of Social Science Research Major Project (2017–2018) awarded to Anjali Gera Roy.

Nagpal, Radha Krishna. 2017. Age 85. Interviewed by Oral History Intern Ankita Halder in Ranchi on August 12. "After Partition: Post-memories of Afterlife of Partition 1947", Indian Council of Social Science Research Major Project (2017–2018) awarded to Anjali Gera Roy.

Papneja, Hari Chand. 2017. Age 94. Interviewed by Oral History Intern Ankita Halder in Ranchi on August 12. "After Partition: Post-memories of Afterlife of Partition 1947", Indian Council of Social Science Research Major Project (2017–2018) awarded to Anjali Gera Roy.

Paul, Mira. 2017. Age 77. Interviewed by Oral History Intern Sumedha Bose in Kolkata on June 11. "After Partition: Post-memories of Afterlife of Partition 1947", Indian Council of Social Science Research Major Project (2017–2018) awarded to Anjali Gera Roy.

Prakash Kaur. 2017. Age 78. Interviewed by Oral History Intern Ekata Biswas in Kharagpur.

Prakash, Ram. 2005. Age 73. Personal Diary Entry. January 15.

———. 2012. Age 79. Anjali Gera Roy. Bangalore. April 3.

Pujandi. 1993. Age 80. Quoted from Memory by Deshi. Lucknow.

Raj, Prakash. 2011. Age 79. Interviewed by Anjali Gera Roy. Lucknow. December 11.

Rajpal. 2006. Age 67. Interviewed by Anjali Gera Roy. Delhi. February 7.

Roy, Haripada. 2017. Age 88. Interviewed by Oral History Intern Sumedha Bose in Kolkata on June 10. "After Partition: Post-memories of Afterlife of Partition 1947", Indian Council of Social Science Research Major Project (2017–2018) awarded to Anjali Gera Roy.

Sengupta, Krishna. Partition 1947 Archive.

Sharma, Avadhesh. 2017. Interviewed by Ayushi Aastha in Patna. August 1. "After Partition: Post-memories of Afterlife of Partition 1947", Indian Council of Social Science Research Major Project (2017–2018) awarded to Anjali Gera Roy.

Sidana, Datta Ram. 2017. Age 91. Interviewed by Oral History Intern Ankita Halder in Ranchi on August 12. "After Partition: Post-memories of Afterlife of Partition 1947", Indian Council of Social Science Research Major Project (2017–2018) awarded to Anjali Gera Roy.

Tabassum, Akhon Mohammad Shafi. 2017. Interviewed by Oral History Intern Bashir Ahmed on July 7 in Thaskan Grong, Kargil Ladakh. "After Partition: Post-memories of Afterlife of Partition 1947", Indian Council of Social Science Research Major Project (2017–2018) awarded to Anjali Gera Roy.

Veeranwali. 2006. Age 70. Interviewed by Anjali Gera Roy. Kalka. March 23.

Vohra, Brij Mohan. 2017. Age 78. Interviewed by Oral History Intern Satyendra Raj in Lucknow on July 10. "After Partition: Post-memories of Afterlife of Partition 1947", Indian Council of Social Science Research Major Project (2017–2018) awarded to Anjali Gera Roy.

Wafa, Basheer Ahmed. 2017. Interviewed by Oral History Intern Bashir Ahmed in Balti Bazaar on July 4. "After Partition: Post-memories of Afterlife of Partition 1947", Indian Council of Social Science Research Major Project (2016–2017) awarded to Anjali Gera Roy.

Archives

"History of Bhakkar." Accessed December 10, 2018. www.facebook.com/bhakkar12/.

India of the Past. December 10, 2018. www.indiaofthepast.org/contribute-memories/read-contributions/life-back-then/524-lyallpur-is-in-their-hearts-part-1.

"Indian Memory Project." Accessed December 10, 2018. www.indianmemoryproject.com/.

"The 1947 Partition Archive." Accessed December 10, 2018. https://in.1947Partition archive.org/.

Index